Introducing Manchester Airport

We think Manchester Airport is one of the best airports in the world and we are proud to serve an equally world renowned city. People seem to agree with us too. During 2006, readers of eight individual travel trade magazines and judges for the British Travel Awards voted Manchester, Best UK Airport.

This is because we are constantly striving to give our customers as smooth and enjoyable experience as possible. That's why we offer a wide choice of shops, bars and restaurants, plus technology such as Wireless Internet access.

But that's only part of it. We like to welcome people into the city with a smile. And wave them off with one too. Everyone who works at the airport goes out of their way to make the passengers journeys as easy as possible.

Whether you travel through our airport for business or pleasure, we're determined you'll be relaxed and ready for your destination.

Manchester is a city with so much to do and see. We're part of that city and we're proud to represent it. We're particularly proud that we bring so many people here every year and give them the opportunity to explore our great city.

Rowena Burns, Group Commercial Director
The Manchester Airports Group

Manchester Airport

www.manchesterairport.co.uk

> Manchester is the place where people do things... 'Don't talk about what you are going to do – do it'. That is the Manchester habit. And through the manifestation of this quality, the word Manchester has become a synonym for energy and freedom and the right to do and to think without shackles.

Judge Parry, 1912

MANCHESTER

The complete guide

2007

Graffiti: Edward Jung

CREDITS

Editor and principal writer
Jonathan Schofield

City Life
1 Scott Place, Manchester
M3 3RN *www.citylife.co.uk*

Contributors
Marissa Burgess, Wayne Clews, Paul Handler, Sue Little, Nicola Mostyn, Steve Timms, Lucy Tomlinson

Photography
Getti images, PA photographs, the Manchester Evening News photographers plus the editor and the designer

Illustrator
Alex Evans

Cover picture
Clockwise from the top: Manchester Cathedral detail on Peveril of the Peak pub, City of Manchester stadium, Town Hall detail, the Manchester Wheel

Design and graphics
Beckie Best

Advertising sales
For advertising queries **0161 279 4361**

Distribution
Tim Woosey **0161 211 2633**
First published 1996. This edition 2007

Acknowledgements:
Thank you to the Lowry, Manchester Art Gallery, Manchester Town Hall, the National Gallery, Steve Jones (Wicked Publications), the Local Studies Department at Central Library, Chetham's Library and the Whitworth Art Gallery. Extra special thanks, gratitude, love and so on to the many people - staff, freelancers, placements, family and friends - who have worked on the guidebooks over the last seven years. No city in the UK has been better served. It's been a ball.

The Big Wheel

Manchester's Big Wheel returns to Exchange Square, **6B**, in late Spring 2007 and stays until Christmas. Prices have yet to be confirmed. A spin in the enclosed gondolas on the 59m (195ft) high wheel is worth it for the dramatic views of the city and the surroundings. On a good day, the Welsh hills, 60 miles (100km) away, to the south west can be seen. You also get an intimate view of people in Selfridges bar from about 4 metres away as you glide past the store window. Each gondola comes with a commentary which can be activated if you want the highlights of the view to be pointed out. In 2008 a larger wheel is arriving of 79m (260ft). This will stay permanently, but probably on a different site.

M EN media CityLife

Architects impression of Media City, Salford Quays as it may look in 2010 ›

CONTENTS

THE CONTEXT

THE GUIDE

THE GUIDE

PRACTICAL INFORMATION

Manchester in quotes

Throughout the ages visitors have been intrigued or bemused by the city and its population. They have never found it a comfortable place. It is an edgy, bolshy, radical city with ideas of its own. This aspect of Manchester and the Mancunian character is explored in greater detail on page 34.

'I still have to gaze upon the Cathedral... or for that matter, upon Marx and Engel's old rendezvous in Chetham's. But I have sailed in a narrow boat, heard one of the world's great orchestras playing Stravinsky and drunk the cheapest ale in Britain. Can a man ask for more?' **Jim McGilchrist, *The Scotsman*,1998**

'By no stretch of the imagination is Manchester a picturesque city. It is however, emphatically if unconventionally beautiful. In common with all things beautiful... it is fundamentally flawed. It has a compulsion to preen and show off. It is narcissistic, contrary and wayward, and yet you cannot help but love it. It is both admirable and maddening.' **Chris Lethbridge, *Change and Contradiction*, 1994**

'Look again at those buildings... as examples of frozen energy they fill you full of amazement. Some Mancunians must have been giants. What dreams did these people have? And do they still have them?'
Charles Jennings (referring to former textile warehouses), *Up North*, 1995

'There is an energy about Manchester that seems lacking in other cities, and if you see what the pigeons can do to a statue in Albert Square, the birds, have it too.'
Manchester comedian Les Dawson

In those days [pre-World War II] for a Mancunian to visit [London] was an exercise in condescension. London was a day behind Manchester in the arts, in commercial cunning, in economic philosophy... Manchester was generous and London was not.'
Anthony Burgess's autobiography, *Little Wilson, Big God*, 1987

'Manchester...the only place in England which escapes our characteristic vice of snobbery.'

'The cotton trade combines with the climate to make the inhabitants of Manchester a kindly people.'

'Manchester is the only English city which can look London in the face, not merely as a regional capital, but as a rival of how men should live in a community.'
Historian, journalist and AJP Taylor, various publications in the mid twentieth century

'If Engels had lived not in Manchester but in Birmingham, his conception of 'class' and his theories of the role of class in history might have been very different. In this case Marx might have been not a communist but a currency reformer. The fact that Manchester was taken to be the symbol of the age in the 1840s, was of central political importance in modern world history.'
Asa Briggs, *Victorian Cities*, 1961

'[Mancunians] make an affectation of candour and trade a little on their county's reputation for uncouthness.'
Harod Brighouse, *Hobson's Choice*, 1917

'I would like to live in Manchester. The transition between Manchester and Death would be unnoticeable.'
A disapproving Mark Twain in the C19

'The Age of Ruins is past. Have you seen Manchester? Manchester is as great a human exploit as Athens.'
Benjamin Disraeli, *Coningsby*, 1844

'When entering for the first time a town like Manchester, a stranger, overwhelmed by the new and interesting spectacle presented to him, scarcely dares look this giant full in the face.' **JG Kohl, Ireland, *Scotland and England*, 1844**

'It is here that the human spirit becomes perfect, and at the same time brutalised, that civilisation produces its marvels and that civilised man returns to the savage.'
Count Alexis de Tocqueville, *Memoir on Pauperism*, 1840

'This town is very industrious, driving an extraordinary trade. The women are generally very handsome, by which they have acquired the name of Lancashire Witches.'
James Ray, 1746

INTRODUCTION

M*anchester, the Complete Guide,* has changed to a new format. It's smaller in size but longer in length. Handier to use: but with all the authority of a guidebook from people who know the city and region inside out. The book still captures Manchester's culture, heritage, food and drink, sport, entertainment and architecture. And again we give clues to rewarding excursions out of the city across the North West of England and North Wales. This year we've added an expanded section on key moments from the city's history including the slavery abolitionists, the free trade movement and much else.

The guide underlines how easy it is to enjoy Manchester. The recent growth in attractions, and the immense amount of day-to-day activities in which people can participate or spectate, makes the city an increasingly popular destination. And for good reason because Manchester is big enough and small enough. The centre is comfortable to walk over (and walking is the best way to see it) and the attractions and venues pull in the biggest touring stars and exhibitions. Meanwhile the city is surrounded by splendid and easily accessible countryside.

We know you'll enjoy Manchester. It's a great city and best of all, not yet too clogged with tourists. You can make the place your own: we trust this book will help you.

Jonathan Schofield – Editor

How to use

The first part of this book up to page 50 looks at the history of Manchester, it's attitude, it's architecture and so forth. The second part, The Guide, from page 51, explores the places and activities people can visit and do. Throughout the guide there are feature panels examining particular events, locations and personalities in greater depth. We've tried to keep things as simple as possible. Map references in the city centre follow the entries, for example Manchester Town Hall **6E**. To save space, we've usually written the eighteenth century C18, and nineteenth century C19 and so on. Distances come in miles first and then in kilometres, 5 miles (8km). This is because British road signs still give the distance in miles. However heights are given with metres first and feet second, 30m (100ft). Any overseas visitors are now probably confused. All we can do is apologise and agree that this is an odd country. Finally, details may change rapidly, so to avoid disappointment phone ahead.

Inside track

For weekly listings and events pick up a copy of the Manchester Evening News on Friday with it's *City Life* section containing listings and reviews for cinema, music, clubs, theatre, sport, comedy, food and drink and much more. You might also consider buying our sister guidebook, this ***City Life, Food and Drink, Manchester*** (£5). This is the most authoritative guide to cuisine in the region.

Manchester achievement

Manchester was the world's first industrial city. In the last years of the C18 and the first years of the C19, the city provided a model of the emerging industrial society for the world. This city led the world, for better or worse, into the modern age.

Politics, religion & society

The Anti-Corn Law League – The was the first modern political movement. It employed full-time administrators, teams of public speakers, mail shots, lobbying and the latest technology: the new telegraph. Its methods were the model for later political lobbying groups.

Vegetarianism – The movement began in 1809 in Salford Bible Christian Church, inspired by the sermons of the local preacher named, of all things, the Rev. William Cowherd. A vegetarian cookbook was published here by Martha Brotherton from 1812 and her husband, Joseph, was the first vegetarian MP.

Votes for women – Emmeline Pankhurst founded the Women's Social and Political Union in 1903. This body eventually went millitant and was nick-named the Suffragettes. Earlier in 1867, the National Society for Women's Suffrage was founded in Manchester by Lydia Becker.

TUC – The first general meeting of the Trades Union Congress was held in 1868 in the Mechanics' Institute, Princess Street.

Shakers – Ann Lee, founder of the Shaker religion, was born in Manchester in 1736. She emigrated to America in 1786, taking her visions with her.

Science & industry

Atomic theory, meteorology, colour blindness – John Dalton is a scientific colossus of Manchester. His atomic theory (1803), with its pioneering work on the constitution of elements, was the precursor of all modern chemistry, whilst his lectures on meteorology turned the study of weather into a science. He was the first to describe colour blindness.

First Law of Thermodynamics – Law of physics concerning the mechanical equivalence of heat discovered by James Prescott Joule (1819-89): commemorated by the unit of energy the 'joule'.

Precision engineering – Sir Joseph Whitworth (1803-87) was the father of precision engineering. His work finding true planes allowed him to gain accuracies in tool making up to 0.000001 inch. He was the

AV Roe and his early 'plane

INTRODUCTION

first to develop a standard screw thread and the first to design a mechanical street cleaner.

Cast iron beam – The introduction of cast iron beams strong enough to span large distances was the work of Eaton Hodgkinson and Sir William Fairbairn for bridge building, in particular the Britannia Tubular Bridge across the Menai Straits. They also began the large-scale use of plated wrought iron. Fairbairn (1789-1874), an engineering giant, was responsible for advances in boiler making and the invention of the riveting machine.

Steam hammer – Invented in 1840 by James Nasmyth at his Patricroft.

Industrial estate – The first purpose-built industrial estate was Trafford Park in 1896.

Earth density – Monton born John Henry Poynting established the mean density of the earth in 1891. The Poynting Robertson Effect helps explain the effect of radiation from the sun.

Splitting the atom – Ernest Rutherford, working at Manchester University, discovered how to spilt to the atom in 1919. His assistant was Hans Geiger of the Geiger Counter fame.

Computers – The first computer with a stored programme and a memory, nicknamed 'The Baby', was developed at Manchester University in1948 by Professors Tom Kilburn and Fred Williams.

Obstetrics – Doctor Charles White pioneered new practices in obstetrics, including the use of fresh water and fresh air for women after giving birth.

Medical ethics – Dr Thomas Percival, in the late C18, founded the science of medical ethics.

Transport

Modern canal – In Britain, this was the Bridgewater Canal in 1761: (as depicted above in this painting by Ford Madox Brown) a totally artificial waterway independent of natural rivers.

Railway – The world's first true railway began operating from a purpose-built station on Liverpool Road in1830. Stockton and Darlington had the first line but it was the success of the Liverpool and Manchester Railway that launched the railway revolution.

Submarine – The first mechanically powered submarine was launched in 1880 to the designs of Hulme curate, the Rev. George Garrett. He also invented an armour-plated mortarboard for academics under attack.

Swing aqueduct – The first and only swing aqueduct in the world is at Barton, west of the city. Built in 1893, it carries the Bridgewater Canal over the Ship Canal together with 800 tons of water.

British plane and aviator – Local man, AV Roe, designed and flew the first totally

British aeroplane in 1908. Roe pioneered the enclosed cockpit and single joystick. In 1928, one of his Avro Avians, made in Manchester, became the first plane to complete a solo flight to Australia.

Trans-Alantic flight – Former Manchester Central High School students, JW Alcock and AW Brown, were the first to fly the Atlantic Ocean non-stop in 1919.

First municipal airport – Manchester established the municipal airport in 1929.

Trams – Trams were reintroduced on to UK streets in 1992 with the Metrolink service.

Arts

Professional, permanent orchestra – This was the Hallé Orchestra, set up in 1858 by German Charles Hallé who was later knighted for his work.

Repertory theatre – Ann Horniman began British repertory theatre in 1908 at the Gaiety, Peter Street.

Art Treasures Exhibition – Following the success of London's Great Exhibition with science and industry, Manchester, in 1857, began a trend for international art exhibitions.

Top of the Pops – The now defunct TV show was first broadcast from Rusholme in 1964, headlined by The Rolling Stones and The Hollies.

Roget's Thesaurus – Whilst first secretary of Manchester's Portico Library, Peter Mark Roget began his helpmate for wordsmiths: the *Thesaurus of English Words and Phrases.*

Sport

The Football League – The world's first professional football league was set up in 1888 in the Royal Hotel, Piccadilly.

European Cup, treble – Manchester United were the first English football team to win the European Cup in 1968. In 1999, they became the first team to win the Holy Trinity – European Cup, FA Cup and League Championship – in one season.

Crowds – The only time that the crowd at a English club match has exceeded 84,000 was

An early Rolls-Royce in Manchester

at Maine Road in 1934, when Manchester City played Stoke City in the FA Cup 6th round. The actual attendance was 84,569 and City won.

Civic achievement

Gas supply – Manchester Corporation Gas, the first in the country, was set up in 1818 at a cost of £40,000.

Municipal parks – Philips Parks, Queens Park and Peel Park opened in 1846 to become the first municipal parks.

Water – Manchester led the way in providing the citizens of the new big cities with a supply of pure, fresh water when it opened its Longdendale Reservoirs in 1851.

Municipal libraries – Salford Borough Library opened in 1850, followed in 1852 by Manchester's, which operated the first Children's Library from 1862.

Free public library – Perhaps the nation's first free, public library opened as Chetham's Library, off Long Millgate, in 1653.

Miscellaneous

First casuality of English Civil War – This was Richard Perceval, linen weaver, shot on Market Street, 1642.

Bullfighter – Frank Evans from Salford was Britain's first matador and has fought many times in Spain.

Marks & Spencer – Despite a market stall in Leeds, the first Marks & Spencer store opened in Manchester in 1894.

Rolls-Royce – In 1904, Frederick Royce met Charles Rolls at the Midland Hotel where they set up the famous company.

UFO landing pad – In the new Hulme Park, there is to be a UFO airport located on ley lines. Manchester likes to think ahead.

Greater Manchester people

Not all these people were born in the boroughs of Manchester, Salford, Bolton, Bury, Oldham, Rochdale, Stockport, Tameside, Trafford and Wigan but they have deep connections with one or more of them.

Arts & literature

Harrison Ainsworth – writer. **Mrs Linnaeus Banks** – author of *The Manchester Man*. **Nicholas Blincoe** – contemporary novelist. **Robert Bolt** – playwright of *A Man for All Seasons* and the screenplays of *Lawrence of Arabia* and *Dr Zhivago*. **Harold Brighouse** – playwright of *Hobson's Choice*. **Anthony Burgess** – author of over 30 novels. **Frances Hodgson Burnett** – children's writer of *The Secret Garden* and *Little Lord Fauntleroy*. **Sir Neville Cardus** – cricket and music critic. **John Cooper Clarke** – punk poet. **David Constantine** – poet. **Richmal Crompton** – novelist famous for the *Just William* stories. **Shelagh Delaney** – playwright of *A Taste of Honey*. **Roger Fenton** – first war photographer from Rochdale with Crimean War images. **Thomas De Quincy** – writer of *The Confessions of an English Opium Eater*. **Sir Terry Farrell** – architect. Norman Foster – architect. **Elizabeth Gaskell** – author whose books include *North and South, Wives and Daughters, Mary Barton*. **George Gissing** – author or *New Grub Street*. **Walter Greenwood** – author of *Love on the Dole*. **Debbie Horsfield** – scriptwriter. **Howard Jacobson** – contemporary novelist. **Louise Jopling** – artist, first woman to be elected a member of the Royal Society of British Artists. **Mike Leigh** – screenwriter and director. **LS Lowry** – artist. **Val McDermid** – contemporary crime novelist. **Maisie Mosco** – best-selling novelist. **Harold Riley** – artist. **Jack Rosenthal** – scriptwriter husband of Maureen Lipman. **Evelyn Rose** – cookery writer. **Peter Saville** – graphic designer. **Lemn Sissay** – poet. **Dodie Smith** – author of *101 Dalmatians*. **Annie Swynnerton** – artist, first woman to be elected an Associate of the Royal Academy. **Adolphe Valette** – artist. **Tim Willetts** – novelist. **Edgar Wood** – architect.

Comedy

Caroline Aherne. Steve Coogan. Les Dawson. Mike Harding. Will Hay. Jimmy Jewel. Peter Kay. Bernard Manning. Frank Randle. Eric Sykes. John Thomson. Victoria Wood. Mike Yarwood.

Entertainment

Alan Badel – character actor famous for *This Sporting Life*. **Danny Boyle** – film director of *Trainspotting, The Beach, 28 Days Later*. **Brenda De Banzie** – actress. **Violet Carson** – the ferocious Ena Sharples in *Coronation Street*. **Harry Corbett** – remembered for his role as the father in *Steptoe and Son*. **Ayub Khan Din** – actor and writer of *East is East*. **Robert Donat** – classic Oscar winner from the great film age with *The Thirty-Nine Steps* and *Goodbye Mr Chips*. **Christopher Eccleston** – actor. **Frank Finlay** – actor, *Bouquet of Barbed Wire, Candide*. **Albert Finney** – actor, *Saturday Night Sunday Morning, Billy Liar, Tom Jones*. **Anna Friel** – talented actress. **Dame Wendy Hillier** – screen and stage actress, *Love on the Dole, Pygmallion* and *Sons and Lovers*. **Bernard Hill** – actor.

From left to right: Victoria Wood, Ayub Khan Din, Shelagh Delaney, Ben Kingsley

Ben Kingsley – actor, most famous for his role in *Gandhi*. **Joan Littlewood** – theatre director and actor. **Sir Ian McKellen** – actor, including role of Gandalf in *The Lord of the Rings*. **Ian McShane** – actor famous for his role as *Lovejoy*. **John Mahoney** – father, Martin Crane, of *Frasier*. **Dominic Monaghan** – Merry in *The Lord of the Rings*. **Vivien Merchant** – actor. **Pat Phoenix** – actor. Robert Powell – TV and movie actor. **Beryl Reid** – actress. **Richard and Judy** – celebrity TV couple. **John Thaw** – actor famous for his role as *Inspector Morse*. **David Threlfall** – actor. **Joanne Whalley** – Hollywood actor. **Colin Welland** – scriptwriter of *Kes* and *Chariots of Fire*, journalist.

Media

Joan Bakewell – broadcaster. **Bob the Builder** – Altrincham based construction super-hero. **Judith Chalmers** – TV presenter. **Alistair Cooke** – radio icon through *Letter from America*. **Dangermouse** – Chorlton based animal superhero. **Stuart Hall** – TV personality and sports commentator and presenter. **Harold Evans** – journalist and editor of *The Times* and *Sunday Times*. **Anna Ford** – first female British newsreader. **Paul Morley** – journalist and pop entrepreneur. **Brian Redhead** – adopted Mancunian, editor and broadcaster. **CP Scott** – legendary *Guardian* editor. **Kenneth Wolstenholme** – "they think it's all over" commentator. **Simon Kelner** – *Independent* editor and the man who cut the broadsheet down to size.

Music

808 State. 10CC. Badly Drawn Boy. Michael Ball – composer of many successful pieces for brass bands and also orchestral and choral works. **Sir John Barbirolli** – conductor of the Hallé. **The Bee Gees** – brought up in Manchester. **Elkie Brooks. Buzzcocks. Happy Mondays. Inspiral Carpets. Joy Division. Sir Peter Maxwell-Davies** – composer. **Siann Edwards** – the first woman to conduct the Royal Opera Company. **Georgie Fame** – singer. **Gracie Fields** – Rochdale born singer and actress. **Wayne Fontana and the Mindbenders. George Formby** – singer and comedian. **Freddie and the Dreamers. Martin Fry** – singer with ABC. **David Gray** – singer-songwriter. **Sir Charles Hallé** – creator of the Hallé Orchestra. **Herman's Hermits. The Hollies. Mick Hucknall and Simply Red. Davy Jones** – lead singer of The Monkees. **Sid Lawrence** – brought the big band sound back to Britain. **LEwan MacColl. New Order. Oasis. The Smiths. The Stone Roses. Peter Skellern. Mark E Smith** – cult pop star with The Fall. **Lisa Stansfield. Jackie Valentine** – went to the top in the '50s with 'Christmas Alphabet'. **The Verve. Sir William Walton** – classical composer. **Shayne Ward** – X Factor winner 2005. **Russell Watson** – multi-million pound opera singing phenomenon. **Anthony H Wilson** – launched Manchester's Factory Records as well as In the City festival with **Yvette Livesey**, former Miss England. DJs include **Paul Burnett, Wes Butters, Sarah Cox, Gary Davies, David Hamilton, Dave Haslam, Andy and Liz Kershaw** – siblings, DJs and TV presenters, **Dave Lee Travis, Mike Pickering, Mark Radcliffe, Sasha, Jimmy Savile**.

Politics & religion

Sir James Anderton – controversial former Chief Constable of Greater Manchester. **Samuel Bamford** – radical politician. **John Bradshaw** – judge at trial of Charles I. **John Bright** – free trade Liberal MP. **Barbara**

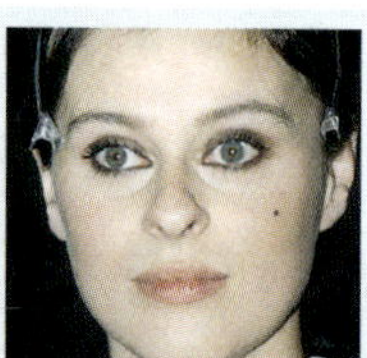

From left to right: Sir Ian McKellen, Lisa Stansfield, Shayne Ward, Joanne Whalley

Castle – Labour cabinet minister, MP and MEP. **Richard Cobden** – MP, free trader and radical. **Brenda Dean** – union leader. **Charles Ewart** – hero of Waterloo. **David Lloyd George** – Prime Minister born in Manchester. **Edward Hyde** – Earl of Clarendon and friend of Charles II. **William 'Lord Haw Haw' Joyce** – Nazi propagandist and traitor. **Cardinal Thomas Langley** – medieval churchman. **Ann Lee** – founder of the Shaker movement. **Pankhurst family** – campaigners for the female vote. **Sir Robert Peel** – Prime Minister and founder of the Police Force. **Harry Pollitt** – lifetime communist who got a Soviet ship named after him. **Chaim Weizmann** – Israel's first president lived in Manchester for many years.

Science & industry

Alcock and Brown – aviators. **Richard Arkwright** – inventor of the water frame. **George Bradshaw** – compiler of first railway timetable. **Sir James Chadwick** – discovered the neutron in 1932. **Roy Chadwick** – designed the wartime Lancaster bomber. **Richard Christie** – founder of Christie Hospital. **William Crabtree** – astronomer. **Samuel Crompton** – inventor of the spinning mule. **John Dalton** – scientist. **Sir William Fairbairn** – engineer. **Benjamin Dancer** – inventor of microphotography. **Hans Geiger** – well known for his Geiger counter. **William Henry** – Henry's Law chemist. **James Prescott Joule** – physicist, Joule's Law and the unit of energy. **John Kay** – inventor of the flying shuttle. **Tom Kilburn** – co-inventor in 1948 of the world's first electronically stored memory computer at Manchester University. **Lord Leverhulme** – founder of the multi-national soap maker Unilever. **Bernard Lovell** – inspiration behind Jodrell Bank. **James Nasymth** – engineer inventor of the steam hammer. **Sir Alliot Verdon Roe** – aeroplanes pioneer and founder of AVRO. **Frederick Royce** – founder partner of Rolls-Royce. **Ernest Rutherford** – winner of the Nobel Prize for Chemistry in 1908. **Francis Sturgeon** – discoverer of the electro-magnet. **Alan Turing** – aided the development of the digital computer and helped break the German Enigma code. **Sir Joseph Whitworth** – engineer and developer of the first standard screw gauge.

Sport

Michael Atherton – former England and Lancashire cricket captain. **Peter Barnes** – City, United and England footballer. **Colin Bell** – City and England footballer. **Jackie Brown** – boxer. **Joe Brown** – rock climber. **Sir Matt Busby** – legendary Scottish manager of Manchester United. **Roger Byrne** – the captain of United when he died in the Munich disaster of 1958. **Darren Campbell** – athelete. **Bobby Charlton** – one of the greatest footballers of all time. **Joe Corrigan** – MCFC and England goalkeeper. **Johnny Cusick** – boxer. **Giant Haystacks** – wrestler. **Geoff Hurst** – West Ham and England World Cup winner. **Brian Kidd** – player for both City and United. **Bert Trautmann** – German prisoner of war turned Manchester City goalkeeper. **Nat Lofthouse** – Bolton and England footballer. **Billy Meredith** – MCFC and MUFC footballer. **Diane Modahl** – athlete. **David Platt** – former England football captain. **Fred Perry** – last British male champion at Wimbledon in the 1930s. **Brian Statham** – cricket craftsman for both England and Lancashire. Current United players: **Ryan Giggs, Paul Scholes, Gary Neville and Wes Brown.**

INTRODUCTION

From left to right: William Crabtree, Ryan Giggs, Diane Modahl, Richard Arkright

Chronology of the city

79 Manchester, 'Mamucium', founded by the Romans.
410 Romans leave Manchester.
920 Manchester mentioned in the *Anglo-Saxon Chronicle* when Edward the Elder occupies the town.
1282 Market charter granted to Manchester.
1322 A fulling mill reported, indicating a textile industry already in place.
1375 According to tradition, a group of Flemish weavers set up in the town.
1421 St Mary's Church becomes Collegiate – one with a college of priests and elevated status.
1515 Manchester Grammar School is founded by Hugh Oldham, Bishop of Exeter.
1605 Outbreak of plague in Manchester. And again in 1645.
1642 Civil War: Parliamentarian Manchester repels the Royalists.
1712 St Ann's Church is consecrated.
1729 First Cotton Exchange, later the Royal Exchange, is built.
1745 Bonnie Prince Charlie passes through Manchester.
1751 John Wesley, founder of Methodism, preaches in Manchester.
1752 Manchester Infirmary, (later Manchester Royal Infirmary) founded.
1761 Opening of the Bridgewater Canal.
1772 Manchester's first bank opens.
1783 First steam mill in the city.
1787 The first British anti-slavery petition organised in Manchester.
1804 Rochdale Canal opens – first trans-Pennine canal link.
1806 Portico Library, Mosley Street, opens.
1809 New Exchange opens on Market Street.
1817 Manchester Gas Works built on Water Street.
1819 Peterloo Massacre.
1820 Manchester Chamber of Commerce founded. Manchester Guardian founded.
1823 Royal Manchester Institution formed – now Manchester Art Gallery.
1826 Manchester branch of the Bank of England opened.
1830 Liverpool and Manchester Railway opened.
1832 Reform Act gives Manchester two members of Parliament and a third for Salford.
1838 Anti-Corn Law League is founded by Manchester industrialists. The town gains an elected Council.
1842-44 Friedrich Engels settles in Manchester and writes *The Condition of the English Working Class*.
1846 John Owens leaves money to found Owens College, now Manchester University.
1847 Collegiate Church becomes Manchester Cathedral.
1853 Manchester formally declared a city.
1857 Art Treasures Exhibition comes to Old Trafford.
1858 First Hallé concerts held.
1862 Famine in Lancashire and Manchester due to interruption of raw cotton supply during the American Civil War.
1867 Fenian murder of Sergeant Brett on Hyde Road. Three Irishmen, 'the Manchester martyrs' hanged.
1877 New (present) Town Hall in Albert Square opens.
1894 Manchester Ship Canal opens. Thirlmere Aqueduct provides Manchester with clean Lake District water.
1938 Ringway Airport, now Manchester International Airport, opens.
1940 Christmas Blitz.
1948 World's first electronic stored programme computer developed in Manchester.
1952 Smokeless zones introduced.
1956 Granada Television established.
1958 Munich air disaster kills 23 including 9 of Manchester United's 'Busby Babes'.
1960 First episode of *Coronation Street* is aired.
1962 *The Manchester Guardian* decamps to London.
1962 Co-operative Insurance Society building opens – then the tallest office block in Europe.
1968 Royal Exchange ceases trading.
1974 Greater Manchester Council created with Manchester as official centre of 2.5m people - dissolved 1984.
1976 Royal Exchange Theatre opens.
1977 The Arndale Centre opens – Europe's biggest city centre shopping mall.
1982 Haçienda nightclub opens (closed 1996).
1986 G-Mex Centre opens for conferences and conventions.
1992 Metrolink opens – trams return to the streets.
1996 IRA bomb wrecks city centre. The Bridgewater Hall opens.
1998 The Trafford Centre opens six miles west of city, threatening traditional centres.
1999 Manchester United win the first treble in club football.
2000 Manchester International Convention Centre opens. The Lowry (arts complex) opens.
2002 The Commonwealth Games comes to Manchester. Imperial War Museum North opens.
2003 The European Cup Final is held at Old Trafford.
2006 Labour Party Conference held in Manchester. The BBC decide to partially relocate here.
2007 Manchester is chosen as the site for Britain's first Las Vegas-style 'super-casino'.

A quiet beginning

It all started with the Romans. No record has been found of buildings related to the Setantii branch of the local Brigantes tribe, so it must have been the cohorts of the 20th Valeria Victrix legion, under General Agricola, who identified Manchester's potential in 79AD. In particular they recognised the strategic value of the rounded bluff over the confluence of the Rivers Irwell and Medlock and named it Mamucium or 'breast shaped hill'.

The Romans stayed for over three centuries. Their fort was garrisoned, at its peak, by an 800-strong mixed force of infantry and cavalry. This was an auxiliary regiment, not native Romans, but recruits or conscripts from the other provinces. Primarily the place was military in character but as often happened outside Roman forts, a civilian settlement grew that accommodated the unofficial wives of the soldiers and attracted artisans and craftsmen, who set up furnaces and workshops. During excavations, a Christian 'magic square' dating from 185AD was found. This coded inscription spells the word 'Paternoster', the opening words of the Lord's Prayer in Latin. It's the oldest evidence of Christianity in the country. A copy can be seen at the Cathedral Vistors Centre – see Prinicipal Buildings.

The Romans chose their site well. Seven roads met at the fort, more than at any other site in the North. Future movements of people and resources would, for convenience sake, move along these routes and come directly through Manchester. Many of the main routes into the city still follow Roman lines.

The Romans abandoned Britain in 410AD. The Saxons moved in and the town in later years underwent a sex change. The 'Mam' of Mamucium became 'Man' whilst the Latin word 'castrum' meaning fort was twisted into the 'chester' element of the name.

The Saxons also signed their names right across the region. Greater Manchester is full of tons, hams, fords and hulmes. There is also one physical remnant of the Saxon period. Straggling through the south of the city, Fallowfield and Levenshulme, is the old boundary division of Nico Ditch. But the key development of the time was the movement of the settlement a mile down the Roman road to the area of, what is now, the Cathedral. The rocky outcrop here, where the Rivers Irwell and Irk joined was, in the often lawless Dark Ages, easier to defend. It is here that the first church was built. The Angel-stone preserved in the Cathedral may be fragment from this time.

But the Dark Ages really were the Dark Ages in Manchester and after the Romans departed, recorded history in effect ceased

'The Romans Building a Fort at Mancenion AD60' by Ford Madox Brown Both the date and name were wrong

for 600 years. Manchester, like all Lancashire, suffered from its location. At that time, the county was an inhospitable place of marsh and bog, isolated between the sea and the wild hills of the Pennines. When the *Domesday Book* was compiled, after the Norman Conquest in 1066, Lancashire and Manchester warranted less than two pages out of 1700, and that as an appendix to Cheshire. The town grew slowly but steadily and in 1227, the annual fair was confirmed by royal grant. Shortly after it became a borough whose burgesses paid a rent rather than being obligated in the feudal way to give service to the local lords, the Grelley family – an important freedom that allowed them to carry on their own business without undue interference. By this stage of the Middle Ages, the economy of the town was already tending towards weaving and the production of textiles. As early as 1375, tradition states there was a colony of Flemish weavers in Manchester.

The Parish Church was enlarged to a Collegiate Church in 1421 – one with its own college of priests. In 1515 a grammar school was founded, which later became Manchester Grammar School. The prodigious traveller Leland described Manchester soon after as 'the best builded, quikkest and most populous tounne of al Lancastreshire'. In the time of Elizabeth I, wool and linen production was important, the latter produced from locally grown and imported flax from Ireland. Around 1600, the import of cotton from Smyrna, now Izmir, in Turkey and Cyprus began. Forty-two years later, Manchester touched on the national scene in the English Civil War and unlike most of Lancashire, supported Parliament against the King – see panel, below.

In the 18th century, the pace of development began to accelerate. In 1710 Celia Fiennes described Manchester as a "thriving place". In 1729, the first Exchange for the pursuit of the town's textile business

HISTORY

^ **Civil War mural in the Town Hall by Ford Madox Brown**

English Civil War

During the Civil War, Manchester was one of very few towns in Lancashire to support Parliament against King Charles I. Indeed it bears the dubious distinction of claiming the first casualty of the war. In a skirmish on Market Street in 1642, linen weaver Richard Percival was shot dead. In September of the same year, Lord Strange, in command of 3-4,000 Royalists, attacked the town along Deansgate and across Salford Bridge. When Strange demanded that the town give up its store of gunpowder and weapons, he received the reply that he would get "nothing, not even a rusty dagger". The defenders were led by Robert Bradshaw and William Radcliffe under advice from Colonel Rosworm, a German mercenary. At the battle's height, two barns caught fire, the smoke of which caused confusion. As the smoke cleared, it became clear that the assault had failed. Strange lifted the siege on 1 October. As a consequence of the victory, Parliament gave the town its first MP. The new representative was one of the local Parliamentarian gentry: Sir Charles Worsley from Platt Hall in Fallowfield. When a vengeful monarchy was restored in 1660, Manchester's support for Parliament was remembered and it lost its MP. It didn't get one back until 1832.

was opened. In the 30 years between 1720 and 1750, the town's population doubled from 10,000 to 20,000.

War again gave Manchester a bit part on the national stage, when Bonnie Prince Charlie, the young Stuart pretender to the throne, arrived in 1745. He recruited 250 volunteers from Manchester to join his campaign against the Hanoverian dynasty that had supplanted his own. The venture was doomed from the start. After inevitable defeat, the officers of his Manchester Regiment were executed and the heads of two of their number, Deacon and Syddall, impaled on the roof of the Manchester Exchange.

Such moments were almost incidental: the industrial cataclysm was coming. Cotton had now established its local dominance. Technological advances accelerated the process: Kay invented the Flying Shuttle in 1733, then between 1760 and 1790 Hargreaves invented the Spinning Jenny, Arkwright the Water Frame, and Crompton the Spinning Mule. They were all Lancashire men. Meanwhile good turnpike roads were improving communications between the capital and the other burgeoning centres of industry. Cheap coal arrived in Manchester with the construction of the Bridgewater Canal in 1759 and the first steam mill fired up in the city in 1783. Manchester's first bank had already opened in 1771.

In Lancashire, Cheshire and Yorkshire at the beginning of the 19th century, there were 89 steam engines in factories, 32 of them inside Manchester mills. Location, coal, steam, innovation and experience were placing the town at the centre of a new world. All this attracted attention, some of it unwanted. In 1785, a German named Baden was tried at Lancaster, and fined £500, for having visited Manchester and enticing cotton operatives to return to Germany with him.

Notoriety – the 19th century

Where the actual touch paper of industrialisation was lit has been the subject of much debate, but its first urban product was Manchester. The growth of the city, in terms of those times, was astonishing. By 1801 the population had climbed to 90,000 and by 1861 it was 355,000. As usual this was a misleading figure. If the wider urban area outside Manchester's narrow boundaries was taken into account, the city was half a million in population, packed into an area not much larger than today's city centre. By 1901, there were more than two million people in the area of present day Greater Manchester.

The whole place was a bustling melting pot of people and businesses: for instance in 1849, along just 300 metres of Oxford Road, there were 70 types of occupation from the nation's biggest locomotive works to watchmakers, surgeons and tea dealers. In 1844, Benjamin Disraeli had called Manchester 'the most wonderful city of modern times'. The wonder lay in the way the city had changed economically and socially and had become the model for the new capitalism and its positive and negative effects. Manchester had crashed into international consciousness – it was, in historian Asa Briggs words, 'the shock city of the age'.

The growth in the wealth, fame and prestige corresponded to a similar growth in pride and confidence. As the century progressed, art galleries and museums were founded, new libraries opened, parks were laid, and theatres were established. The Collegiate Church was raised to Cathedral status in 1847. Soon after, in 1851, Manchester gained a new university: only the fifth in Britain. In 1853, Manchester gained the overdue Royal Charter that gave it formal city status. The new city played host to several important exhibitions, notably the Art Treasures Exhibition of 1857 – the first international exhibition of its kind (see pages 114-115).

Cotton (see pages 22-23) might have made

Manchester famous but it certainly wasn't the only employer. Iron founding, boiler making, heavy and precision engineering became key players in the local economy at the same time. Similarly, Manchester came second only to London in the number and variety of its banks and insurance houses, which also employed large numbers of people. The city also became the centre for regional retailing. One of the first major stores was the Bazaar, which opened in 1839, concentrating on drapery and furniture. This is still going strong across the road from the old location, albeit with the name changed to House of Fraser.

The grandeur and the wealth of this epoch can best be gauged in the streets of the city, where the Victorian architecture tells its own story. The dignified rows of Renaissance-inspired warehouses gave a street scene that was compared to Rome. Indeed, the typical warehouse became known as the Manchester Palazzo. The Town Hall, completed in 1877 to the designs of Alfred Waterhouse, illustrates the extraordinary vigour of the age. At its opening, politician John Bright declared, "[We are] standing in a district more wonderful in some respects then can be traced out on a map in any other Kingdom of the world. The population is extraordinary in its number, extraordinary for its interests and industries, for the amount of its wealth, for the amount of its wages, and for the power which it exercises on other nations".

Often this energy was harnessed to political ends. Throughout the century, the city was at

HISTORY

The Liverpool and Manchester Railway

When the Prime Minister, the Duke of Wellington, opened the Liverpool to Manchester Railway in 1830, he ushered in a transport revolution. Despite the earlier line at Stockton and Darlington, it was this system that proved rail travel had a future as it quickly made money. With an emphasis on passenger travel, it also made travel more democratic - for the first time poor people could journey regularly for a reasonable price. The station still stands at the Museum of Science and Industry. It all got off to an inauspicious start with an angry crowd at Manchester protesting about the price of food and about the lack of representation. There was tragedy too when William Huskisson MP was run down and killed by a train. Less seriously, people wondered if horses would be made redundant and if hens close to the line would be too frightened by the noise to lay eggs. The railways made travel easier but also the separation of the classes more pronounced as the commuter towns of south Manchester such as Wilmslow, Alderley Edge, Sale and Cheadle Hulme spread over farm fields. This led to a debate about those who owed their wealth to the city abandoning it. "If God made the country and Man made the town... the Devil made the suburbs," thundered Charles Rowley in 1899.

George Bradshaw

As the railways became more complex, Mancunian George Bradshaw (1801-1853) came up with a national railway map and then the famous *Railway Companion* in 1839. This was the first national timetable: 'seldom has the gigantic intellect of man been employed upon a work of greater utility' wrote one commentator. This, and subsequent guides, were unpopular with railway companies who found themselves tied to running services on time. In 1844, *Bradshaws Continental Guide* appeared. A byword in his own time, Bradshaw has a part to play in the metronomic nature of modern life, the schedules and due dates.

the forefront of radical political thought. The most infamous act of Manchester's political life was the Peterloo Massacre in 1819 (see panel on pg 36). In the years after Peterloo, the Anti-Corn Law League was formed and was centred in Manchester. This began as a protest about the Corn Laws which guaranteed corn prices for British landowners and, thus, in years of bad harvests forced the price of bread beyond the means of the poor. At the same time the imposition of duty on forieign corn entering the country to maintain aristocratic incomes meant that those countries responded in kind with tax on textile products and so on. The theories behind the Anti-Corn Law League led to the formation of the so-called Manchester School (see page 38-39).

Manchester inherited a reputation for liberalism and radicalism from such events that has existed to the present day. *The Manchester Guardian,* now simply *The Guardian,* embodied these principles when it first went to print in 1821. Also, mass Western vegetarianism began in Salford in 1809, the co-operative movement began in Rochdale in 1844 and the Trades Union Congress first met in the city in 1868. The Lancashire (later National) Public Schools Association was formed in the city in 1849 advocating 'secular instruction only; leaving to parents and guardians the inculcation of doctrinal religion.' If the governement had adopted this then many of the problems and debating points of the early C21 in education in England may have been avoided.

A year earlier, the Reform Bill of 1867 enfranchised most of the male population but excluded females. In response, Mancunian Lydia Becker formed the National Society for Woman's Suffrage to fight, through constitutional means, for the vote. Later the Manchester family of the Pankhursts would turn the movement radical.

In 1832, the Reform Act had, at last, given Manchester two MPs but it wasn't until 1838 that the town gained a modern administration. This blossomed to such an extent that by the end of the century Manchester was an expansionist city state running education, parks, water, gas, the police and much else. The Council even provided a large part of the money to build the Ship Canal.

In science and engineering too, Manchester

(continued on page 26)

John Edward Taylor

John Edward Taylor (1791-1844) moved to Manchester as a young man and became a journalist on the *Manchester Gazette*. At the Peterloo Massacre, Taylor found that the only national reporter present had been arrested: he began interviewing eyewitnesses and his report appeared in *The Times* two days later. The launch of his own newspaper came about in an unlikely fashion. Tried for libel in Lancaster in 1819, Taylor justified rather than denied what he had published. The jury was divided 11 to 1, but the dissenter stood firm and persuaded the other jurors to change their minds. This success convinced Mancunians to support Taylor's own paper, *The Manchester Guardian*. The prospectus promised it would enforce the principles of civil and religious liberty. Taylor remained the editor until his death. The newspaper, now simply *The Guardian*, fled to London in the 1960s.

Elizabeth Gaskell

The greatest C19 novelist working in Manchester documented the changes taking place in the city. Gaskell (1810-65) lived for many years on Plymouth Grove and her novels such as *Mary Barton, North and South* and *Ruth* looked at the new industrial age from both a working and middle class viewpoint, although many of the latter thought her picture of them was unjust. Mrs Gaskell was married to the Rev. William Gaskell of Cross Street Unitarian Chapel, a notable figure himself. She took up writing on her husband's suggestion to take her mind from the grief of losing an infant son. She is also famous for her novels *Cranford* and *Wives and Daughters*, set in the pretty southern Manchester town of Knutsford (described in the Regional Sightseeing section).

HISTORY

Cottonopolis

Why did Manchester become the cotton capital?

A part truth is that it has a wet, humid climate ideal for spinning yarn. More importantly, southeast Lancashire's fast-flowing streams provided power for the mills and gave soft water for the washing and bleaching of cotton. Nearby there was a coalfield to fire steam engines, salt supplies for developing chemicals and easy access to the west coast for importing the raw material and exporting the finished product. Crucially Lancashire's industrial organisation was fluid. Manchester was unhampered by guilds and trade restrictions. Entrepreneurs were encouraged.

Beginnings

Traditionally textiles arrived with an influx of Flemish weavers in 1363. By the reign of Elizabeth I, wool and linen production was important, followed by manufacture of fustians, a mix of linen and cotton. But it was the manufacture of pure cottons in the mid C18 that really made Manchester. The process was run on the 'domestic system': merchants 'putting out' raw cotton to spinners, weavers etc who worked from home. Technological advance gradually swept this method away and the factory system took over. Kay invented the Fly Shuttle in 1733, and between 1760 and 1790 Hargreaves invented the Spinning Jenny, Arkwright the Water Frame, and Crompton the Spinning Mule. Meanwhile good turnpike roads were improving communications, cheap coal arrived with the Bridgewater Canal in 1761 and the first steam mill fired up in 1783. 1,000 tonnes of cotton were imported by 1751, rising to 45,000 tonnes by 1816.

Heyday

By 1841 imports of raw cotton had risen to 205,000 tonnes and would peak in 1914 at almost a billion tonnes. The character of the city changed. The cotton mills employed less as the century wore on – by 1840 only 18% of the workforce was in cotton manufacture. Manchester became the commercial centre of the industry. The dominant building was the stately warehouse for the display of finished goods or the ornate bank and office providing loans for the production of cotton. Above all, it was the town of the Royal Exchange (page 70). Production became concentrated in the outer towns, spinning in nearby Bolton, Oldham and Stockport, weaving in towns to the north such as Preston, Burnley and Blackburn. The trade in cotton amounted to 50% of British exports in the 1830s, and stood at 80% of global cotton piece goods in the 1880s.

Decline

Reliance on a distant raw material made the trade vulnerable. The American Civil War showed this, when the supply from the Confederate States was blockaded by the Union North. Sourcing raw cotton from India and Egypt and the growth of trade with the British Empire maintained the industry until after WWI. But business declined as production rose in countries close to the raw material and with cheaper labour or with more up-to-date methods. To shore up the industry, there was a rise in tariffs for cotton imports plus schemes to reduce excess production. It was too late – a reluctance to develop new business practices and to invest in new machines, for example moving from spinning mules to ring spinners, cost the trade dear.

HISTORY

1. Weaver's cottage This a typical moorland weaver's cottage from the hills around Manchester. Located at Bleak Hey Nook in Saddleworth, it is a 'domestic system' building from the late C18, with distinctive second floor windows maximising light for the intricate labour of weaving or spinning. This system of working from home gave way to the more debasing but efficient factory system in the early C19. For handloom weavers, this was a decline from self-employment into wretchedness – small wonder that they played a part at the Peterloo Massacre. In many similar properties, owners profiteered on overcrowding by dividing the house between various families.

2. The Manchester Palazzo By the 1840s the Renaissance style of Italy was being adopted by cotton merchants. The simple yet grand design gave plenty of light but didn't waste undue space on decoration. The sale-rooms with cotton samples were on the upper floors, the first floor provided the counting house and the administration, whilst the lower basement contained the steam engines and boilers. Cotton goods left from the iron gate-way on the rear or side. This picture shows one of the elegant Princess Street buildings by Clegg and Knowles, 1869. As CR Reilly (1924) described: '[The] warehouses represent the essentials of [Manchester's] trade, the very reason for her existence. They are too near to her heart, for any light treatment. Hence their simplicity, strength, and sincerity, and consequently their real beauty.'

3. Packing warehouses A late C19, early C20 development was the huge packing warehouse. Instead of sole occupancy, these were split between several companies. Here 'finished cloth went to a packing warehouse for quality control, making into a piece, labelling and baling for shipment and storage before it was ready for export' (Nick Dixon, 1997). Typically terracotta or Portland stone, packing warehouses are monumental. St James' House, pictured, has a Baroque façade of Portland stone. It was built in 1912 for the Calico Printers' Association and contains over 1,000 rooms. Round the back there is a functional grid of concrete and glass. Oxford Road, Great Bridgewater Street and Whitworth Street are dominated by these edifices.

4. The mills Between Jersey Street and Redhill Street, half a mile from Piccadilly Gardens alongside Rochdale Canal, you'll find 'dark satanic mills'. The mills are currently being transformed into offices and apartments. The oldest is of 1798, and the last from 1912. French writer Alexis de Toqueville commented in the 1830s about the largest here, McConnel and Kennedy (illustrated previous page): '1,500 workers labouring 69 hours a week… three quarters of the workers in [the] factory are women and children'. To visitors, the scale of the new industrial process was something far beyond their range of experience. 'Here are buildings seven to eight storeys, as high and as big as the Royal Palace in Berlin,' said the German architect Schinkel in 1825.

Manchester 1889

This extraordinary bird's eye view illustrated by H Brewer (printed in The Graphic Magazine) shows the city in its full industrial splendour. Magnificent and towering buildings grace the city. In the foreground is the Cathedral. To the right and above lies the Town Hall with the Royal Exchange in between, all described in this book. Manchester was a city proud of its position in the world and proud of the distance it had come since the problems of Peterloo in 1819 - see page 36. As politician John Bright said in 1877, 'The population is extraordinary in its number, extraordinary for its interests and industries, for the amount of its wealth, for the amount of its wages, and for the power which it exercises on other nations'. But a price had been paid for this position. The river, in the foreground, for instance, is described by a contemporary, as an open sewer. 'Whole wagon-loads of poisons from dye-houses and bleach-yards [are] thrown into it; steam boilers discharge their steaming contents, and drains and sewers their fetid impurities…' Crowded around the central area lie the insanitary rookeries of the poor.

was prominent in many areas. This was a period when engineers and scientists such as John Dalton, JP Joule, William Fairbairn, Eaton Hodgkinson, Joseph Whitworth and James Nasmyth were internationally famous.

There was a price for all the dynamism. Visitors were amazed by the contradictions between the wealth in the centre and the suburbs where the rich lived and the poor areas where the factories and the dwellings of the workers lay side by side. The French political philosopher, de Tocqueville remarked, 'Everything in the exterior appearance attests the individual powers of Man: nothing the directing powers of society'. The most famous commentator was Friedrich Engels with his 1844 book *The Condition of the Working Classes in England* (see panel pg 37).

Generally, though, the forces at work in this industrial maelstrom were misunderstood or ignored. The drive for increased production and profit ensured that the city grew randomly with little regulation. As a consequence, the poor were largely at the mercy of their masters and any economic vagaries. People frequently led dreadful lives, overworked from an early age and living in insanitary and cramped conditions. The lack of regulation meant that pollution destroyed the quality of the air, the water and the earth. The unpredictable nature of the cotton industry, with its periods of boom and bust, simply exacerbated the problem.

The worst time of deprivation occurred during the American Civil War in the 1860s when working days in factories fell from six to two or less. This was caused by the severing of the supply of raw cotton, as the Northern blockade of the Southern States became effective. People in the cotton areas of South East Lancashire found themselves penniless and starving. It took a national campaign of relief and the end of the war to ease the destitution.

Conditions were slow to improve. Real national regulation of industry came in 1833 with the first partially effective Factory Act, and there were local initiatives with the private development of factories and hospitals. But generally, Manchester's unregulated expansion provided a grim model for future urban development.

Life could be so hard that some have wondered why people moved here at all. Money was the key. For many Manchester provided an opportunity to become rich, for others it offered the prospect of a more or less regular wage. 'From this filthy sewer, pure gold flows,' de Tocqueville said. More lived in the sewer than got the gold, but the potential was more attractive than an unpredictable rural life or a small town hierarchy.

It was the opportunities here that made the city a magnet for national and international immigration. In *Manchester: the Victorian Age*, Gary Messinger summed this up. 'Manchester was an extraordinarily open town... which became a kind of Eldorado. From the farms, villages and towns of neighbouring areas, successive waves of English labourers migrated towards it. From across the sea came the poor of Ireland. From the north came Scotsmen fleeing the harsh life of the Highlands and the slums of Edinburgh and Glasgow. And from the Continent more settlers arrived; some fleeing religious persecution, others fleeing civil strife, such as the Greeks during the revolution of 1821 and Italians during the wars leading up to national unification in the 1840s. Others, particularly the large number of Germans from Hanseatic cities were attracted by the chance of high monetary returns. In the northern part of the city, east European Jews arrived to join their Spanish and Portuguese brethren, Italians set up their own community in Ancoats.'

Two other events need to be mentioned in the context of the C19, both involving transport. The first, of world significance, was the Liverpool to Manchester railway of 1830, the first successful goods and passenger railway. The second transport landmark, towards the end of the century, was the construction of the Manchester Ship Canal, connecting the city directly to world markets. Both the railway and canal were important beyond just the needs of transport. The development of the railway provided the city with an alternative to its dependency on cotton, in the form of engineering. The Ship Canal reinforced the movement away from cotton and was to lead to the growth of Trafford Park industrial estate, at one time the largest concentration of industry in Europe.

Retrenchment – the 20th century

The new century proved a false dawn. The previous century had been predominantly Britain's century and the city had taken full advantage. Manchester in the eyes of the world meant cotton, and in cotton its position seemed unassailable. But by the end of World War II it was obvious that the glory days of the trade had been left behind – international forces over which Manchester had no control were at play.

There was sadness in this. Manchester was built by industry, particularly the cotton and manufacturing industries. As these declined, and then largely disappeared, the city struggled to come to terms with the new reality. As one of the great manufacturing cities, Manchester had had a clear place in the world: as a leading centre of production there was honour and influence that can never be recovered.

There were still notable advances. In the early years of the century Ernest Rutherford, working at the University, began an examination into the nature of the atom which would lead to its first splitting, in 1919. In 1904, Rolls met Royce in the Midland Hotel to form the company of the same name, and in 1911 Ford opened its first European plant at Trafford Park. In aviation, AV Roe made the first British sustained flight in 1908. Eleven years later, two Manchester men, Alcock and Brown, were the first to fly the Atlantic. In 1948, the first stored computer programme was run at the University.

Another step forward took place when Manchester Airport got off the ground in the 1930s: an invaluable asset to the city ever since. At the same time, Manchester Corporation embarked on massive housing programmes. The most famous of these at Wythenshawe.

Both World Wars affected the city, the first through the loss of valuable youth, the second more directly through the Blitz - see panel below.

Another tragedy was the Munich Disaster of 1958. On the night of February 6, a plane carrying Manchester United's skilful young team, nicknamed the 'Busby Babes', crashed on take-off in Munich following a European Cup tie. Twenty three people died, including nine of the team

This event displayed the power and emotion of sport, and of popular culture in general. Indeed, throughout the years of economic decline and into the recent renaissance, Manchester's contribution to music, broadcasting and sport has been huge (this is explained more fully in later chapters). The sporting achievement culminated in 2002 with the city hosting the XVII Commonwealth Games. This set a benchmark for future games.

Manchester Blitz

During the Second World War, Manchester suffered severe bombing. The worst nights of the Blitz were on 22 and 23 December 1940, when over 700 people were killed and 2,500 injured. Over 100,000 homes in the area were damaged, as well as the Cathedral, the Royal Exchange and the Free Trade Hall. At one point, the fire, fanned by the wind, was so fierce that buildings were demolished to stop its spread.

Renaissance Manchester today

Today the city is no longer pigeonholed by a single industry or business. Manchester has a similar mixed economy, with an increasing emphasis on services, as most major Western centres.

One of the largest growth areas has been in education. The city, in terms of its university provision, has doubled then tripled in size and now holds more than 84,000 full and part-time students. The recent merger with UMIST has made the University of Manchester comfortably the largest in the UK, with 36,000 students in a single institution. Under the Vice-Chancellor Alan Gilbert, the university has a clear target of becoming one of the best unversities on the planet. Initiatives such as attracting acclaimed novelist Martin Amis into his first teaching post shows the ambition. One department that is already a world-leader is the School of Computer Science, with its research into reliable systems and much else.

The last five decades have also witnessed large-scale immigration. Manchester is now the host city to peoples from every continent, with significant Asian, Black and East European communities alongside centuries old Irish and Jewish communities. These have become an integral part of the modern city, with success stories such as athletes Diane Modahl, Darren Campbell, restauranteurs Harry and Gerry Yeung, clothing manufacturer Shami Ahmed and the recent Lord Mayor, Councillor Afzal Khan. Each community celebrates its identity within Britain in festivals and processions that take place over the year. If there is a cloud on the horizon of community relations – it takes the form of the British National Party (BNP) and a lack of integration amongst some ethnic groups. After riots in the North Western towns of Burnley and Oldham in 2002, the BNP won council seats in Burnley and Oldham (although it failed to follow up those successes in subsequent local elections). Thus whilst the party remains insignificant in terms of membership and real electorial impact, it has cleverly exploited the failure of the established parties to address problems, real and perceived, amongst poor, white communities. Meanwhile extremism on one side has led to extremism on the other, especially within a minority of Pakistani and Bangladeshi youth.

There are other grim aspects of city life. The wealth in central Manchester and in the south of the city masks the desperate conditions of the poor in the north and east. The worst statistics come via the National Health Service, with the inner areas of Manchester at the bottom or near the bottom of most indicator charts, from heart disease to obesity. There are a number of projects in place such as New East Manchester, which are ambitious in scope and provide real hope but there is still a long way to go in the most severly blighted areas.

Crime is an issue too. Of most concern perhaps are the armed gangs running the drug trade across the region. Murders in Manchester, but also Birmingham, Nottingham and in particular, London, have emphasised the need to address these problems nationally.

A huge demographic problem remains too. Whilst the Greater Manchester population figure has remained stable and that in the travel to work areas to the south dramatically increased, the population in the inner areas of Manchester and Salford has halved and is predominantly poor – despite an influx of wealthy city centre residents. This is down to the flight to the suburbs that has occurred throughout the UK but also down to the short-sighted export of thousands from the city to the surrounding towns in the '50s and '60s in the name of slum clearance. The result is that the administrative area of Manchester finds itself trapped in its old boundaries facing the task of maintaining an international profile and standards without the financial support of the large and wealthy population that lives just over the boundary.

At the same time there has been a gross reduction in local authority power over the last 50 years. Responsibility over services such as education, the administration of utilities plus the construction and management of huge numbers of council owned houses have all been, at various times, eroded or removed.

One of the worst periods for this loss of authority occurred during Margaret Thatcher's government in the '80s. The wholesale restructuring of the British economy, and the effective dismantling of heavy manufacturing by the government, hit the North particularly hard. Mass unemployment savaged areas such as Greater Manchester. Socialist city councils, in attempting to fight back, went militant. This in turn discredited them with the government and resulted in a loss of council power and the creation of centralised and undemocratic quangos – which are beginning to proliferate once more.

It was up to Manchester to find its own way out of the sorry mess. Under the leadership of Graham Stringer, at one time a militant left-winger himself, the city ditched the blanket application of municipal socialism and took a more pragmatic approach. As the '80s gave way to the '90s Manchester started to restore itself by developing a climate of free enterprise and job creation whilst retaining its commitment to public services. Most importantly it began to work with the private sector in planning, raising monies and delivering large-scale change. This remarkable u-turn resulted in Manchester now being considered, internationally, as a model city for public private partnership. The change of mood away from post-industrial depression was also stimulated by the abortive bids for the Olympics in the '90s and the successful delivery of the Commonwealth Games in 2002.

Then came the massive June 1996 IRA bomb – the largest ever exploded in anger in mainland Britain. But instead of dampening the upbeat mood, the bomb reinforced it.

A walk across the city centre today reveals a city more open and accessible and enlivened with new buildings and squares, yet with easy access to countryside and outer districts. The central area has become residentially popular, reversing a hundred years of English suburban sensibility: office and shop rents have risen, thousands of people have moved in, with one sheer glass apartment block selling duplexes at £2m. Unemployment in Manchester area is the lowest it has been for decades – at around 3%.

1996 bomb

The IRA placed 80,000 lives at risk on a busy Saturday morning in the city centre by detonating a 3500lb (1700kg) bomb. But in a remarkable operation, the emergency services, given 45 minutes warning, cleared the streets and nobody was killed. The bomb was inside a van and positioned next to the postbox pictured here. This survived the blast, and is the only thing that carries any memorial to this event. The damage estimates from the explosion, which ripped out the prime retail area of the city, amounted to £700m, with 670 businesses having to relocate. The city response was lively and positive and the atrocity was turned into an opportunity. Within a few weeks and months, a Lord Mayor's fund had raised money to help those affected and a decision had been taken to rebuild the city centre better than before.

The Super-casino and how it may look

Significantly the profile of the city has risen internationally. One company reported: 'Manchester has been at the cutting edge of innovation over the last years. It is a model for a city with a great past… combining traditional and revolutionary architecture… giving its citizens a fine and stimulating environment for work and leisure.' According to 2006 figures the Manchester city region generates £47 billion per year which is equal to the output of Liverpool, Leeds and Sheffield combined.

Meanwhile, Manchester's twins Salford and Trafford have conceived and delivered the Lowry and the Imperial War Museum North. In 2007 the city also has the biggest regional airport in the UK with more than 22m users, the busiest concert venue in the world, the MEN Arena, and, of course, the most profitable sporting club anywhere with Manchester United. Hilton Tower, which will be completed in 2007, will provide some of the highest living space in Europe inside a 47-storey glass tower rising to 171m (561ft). At least two more towers, one even taller than Beetham, are planned.

For many commentators, one of the most unexpected consequences of this turn-around is that Manchester has become a UK tourist destination with some of the highest visitor numbers in the country – 94m visitors in 2005 across Greater Manchester, contributing more than £3.92 billion to the local economy.

Meanwhile the BBC have confirmed a major decentralisation in the coming years. Key departments such as Sport, Radio 5 Live and the children's arm of the Corporation will move north to a 'media city' on some 200 acres of land at the Quays in Salford. This looks set to be an exciting development which will deliver not only a new hub for the economic activity of Manchester and the north, but also some extraordinary architecture for tourists to enjoy.

More surprising was the early 2007 decision to give Manchester the first 'super-casino' in the UK. Covering a huge site next to the City of Manchester Stadium, the 5,000 sqm complex will have up to 1,250 unlimited jackpot gaming machines, as well as a multi-purpose arena, a swimming pool, an urban sports venue, restaurants, bars, a nightclub and a hotel. The bookies favourites had been London and Blackpool, and city

Manchester over the seas

As Manchester was the first industrial city, it was only natural that when industry grew in other countries, their industrial areas were compared with the city: thus Melbourne was known as the Manchester of Australia, Osaka the Manchester of Japan and so on. The city name also became synonymous with textiles – in Sweden, corduroy is called 'Manchester fabric', whilst the linen departments of Australian stores go by the city name. Other communities, especially in North America and the other former Empire countries, are called Manchester directly via emigration from the parent city. The most inexplicable namesake amongst the 50 plus Manchesters is that on the Rio Manuripi, a tributary of the Amazon in Bolivia.

council chiefs were so unprepared that no official celebration had been planned. But this success again underlines how savvy the city and its business community have become in perparing and winning bids which will benefit the economy and the amenity of the whole Manchester region.

Certainly it's been satisfying for Mancunophiles to observe how the parochial attitudes of the previous decades of industrial decline have been thrown aside in favour of thinking big. Manchester has again begun to conceive on a grand scale: it is living up to the expansionist liberal tradition that made it one of the global players.

Jim McClellan, writing in *Esquire* magazine in the late '90s, perceptively anticipated the changes. 'Manchester's size makes the social processes more visible. You can see how things are developing. Where they might end up is another matter. Perhaps it'll be the first place to show us whether our new cities work.' McClellan was, in effect, repackaging sentiments that Benjamin Disraeli was articulating in the 1840s (see page 19) – but Mancunians knew exactly what he meant. To be ground-breaking, to be a step ahead, is the city's birthright. As McClellan also said, 'Manchester, as Mancs love to tell you, has been ahead of the game.'

There has been no treaty signed, no key battle fought, no art movement announced, yet Manchester led the world into a new age in the 19th century. As the city moves forward with confidence, it is as well to remember this – and all the attendant problems and prizes that brought.

Manchester politics

Manchester's administration is run on the cabinet model with the highest authority resting in the Council Leader, at present Sir Richard Leese. The leader can only be drawn from an elected councillor. But a great deal of authority and influence resides with the Chief Executive, an unelected official, currently Sir Howard Bernstein. The Lord Mayor's office is honorary and wields no effective power. At the time of printing there were 96 councillors, 61 of which are Labour, 34 Liberal Democrat and 1 Green. There are no Conservative representatives. Indeed Manchester has been a Labour stronghold – virtually a one-party state – for more than two decades. However voter disillusionment with the national Labour Party, and a perception amongst the poorer residents that the Council was concentrating too much resource on the city centre, allowed the Liberal Democrats to dramatically increase its share of councillors in the first five years of the C21. By 2006, this reaction to Labour seemed to have worked itself out. In the May local elections Labour regained four wards, as the Liberals focused on very parochial issues and a bitter war of words. The lesson here might be that the citizens of Manchester are just as afraid of a return to the small-minded days of the seventies and eighties as the politicians.

Manchester and Salford

Manchester stretches 12 miles from Heaton Park in the north to Manchester Airport in the south. It is never much more than four miles wide. The quoted population of around 450,000 is a nonsense. The city should be viewed in the same way as the city of London: a significant part of the whole. Manchester proper, the continuously built-up area within the central area of the conurbation, would then give a population figure of around a million.

Salford (216,119) is Manchester's Siamese twin. Despite the city having a fierce identity of its own, the centre is really Manchester city centre. But Salford has the Catholic Cathedral for the region and its own University, as well as most of the Quays. This is the Mancunian equivalent of London Docklands, but with better cultural attractions in the Lowry and the Imperial War Museum North. But this latter officially lies in Trafford Metropolitan Borough within Old Trafford and close to Lancashire Cricket Club and Manchester United. Confused?

Greater Manchester

Made up of ten boroughs, the other nine components of Greater Manchester crowd round the city like iron filings around a magnet. Manchester as the clearing house of cotton and as the natural centre was the reason for their early growth and wealth. Yet all the towns of the conurbation have a fierce independence. To them the city can be an alien place, in thought and speech. Indeed the harder, quicker, more ethnically influenced Manchester accent is far removed from the slower, deeper accents on either side.

North of the city lie the three West Pennine boroughs of Bolton (261,035), Bury (180,612) and Rochdale (205,233). Both Bolton and Rochdale have Town Halls that would grace major cities, whilst Rochdale's is set in the finest civic space in the north of England. All

have football clubs, with Bolton Wanderers in the Premier League. Two of the finest regional markets are at Bolton and Bury, whilst the latter town also hosts the embarkation point for the East Lancs Railway – the tourist line that runs up the Irwell Valley to Rawtenstall and beyond. Rochdale is the home of the co-operative movement and has a museum dedicated to it. There is fine moorland countryside.

The two eastern boroughs are Oldham (217,393) and Tameside (213,045), both with newish attractions in Gallery Oldham and Setantii respectively. The eastern districts of both, but particularly those of the Saddleworth area, contain beautiful stone-built villages, country pubs and miles of moors.

South lie Stockport (284,544) and Trafford (210,135). Stockport has an entertainingly up and down town centre with an iconic railway viaduct striding through. There are also the two historic houses at Lyme Park and Bramall Hall. Trafford has its own must-see house at Dunham Massey. The northern end of the borough, in reality very much part of Manchester, contains the shiny retail palace of the Trafford Centre, a marble shopping mall with a daft dome and atrocious sculpture but 10,000 free car parking spaces. The adjacent Trafford Park is still the largest industrial estate in the United Kingdom, employing 55,000 people. Here too lie Manchester United, Lancashire Cricket Club and the Imperial War Museum North. The whole arc from Disley and Bramhall in Stockport, through to Hale and Altrincham via Wilmslow and Alderley Edge, is wealthy South Manchester – the so-called 'stockbroker belt of the North'.

To the west lies Salford and Wigan (301,417). Immortalised by George Orwell's 1937 *Road to Wigan Pier*, Wigan has a handsome centre and parish church, an excellent country house in Haigh Hall and produces its own whisky, Red Rose Whisky.

"What Manchester does today, London does tomorrow"

Manchester attitude

In a country famous for its class system, Manchester has always stood out. The historian AJP Taylor called it 'the only place in England which escapes our characteristic vice of snobbery'. Since the Industrial Revolution, the position you've worked towards rather than the status with which you were born has always been of first importance in Manchester.

Another characteristic is braggadocio. Whilst the neighbour city of Liverpool has a reputation of whining, Manchester has a reputation for strutting. Indeed it has a winsome way of believing it's the best in Britain, no matter the evidence. 'What Manchester does today, London does tomorrow' was the C19 and early C20 mantra. Recently this has been characterised as 'Manchester attitude' – there's even a section devoted to this perceived spirit in Manchester Art Gallery. It's typical that Manchester United, for instance, has a metropolitan assumption of success (although this isn't popular with Manchester City supporters). This type of arrogance is usually the stick with which the rest of the country likes to beat London.

Certainly Manchester has long been known as a brash, edgy, radical, multiethnic, competitive and humorous city. Peter Saville, the Mancunian guru of modern design and a man who has worked with the likes of New Order, Suede and Dior, attempted to articulate the 'attitude' in January 2004 talking about his time at the city's Factory Records. "There's a wilful elitism about Manchester which is very condensed, compared to other cities, one which elsewhere becomes diversified and weakened. There's something historically, geographically, socially about the climate, the people, that prepares you for something. We didn't think we were the best – we knew we were."

It's perhaps this attitude that has resulted in so much radical thought. Support for Parliament in the English Civil War, the first anti-slavery petition, the Peterloo Massacre, the vegetarian movement, the Guardian newspaper, the novels of Elizabeth Gaskell, the Anti-Corn Law League and the Free Traders, the Lancashire Public Schools Association, the Cooperative Movement, the Trades Union Congress, the Votes for Women campaign and the Suffragettes, the formation of the Independent Labour Party, the first football trade union, the Mass Trespass of 1932, United's entry into Europe, Clause 28 protests in the eighties by the Gay and Lesbian community and so on.

Some track record. Being radical is something which Manchester seems to enjoy very much.

"We didn't think we were the best — we knew we were"

Manchester and the abolition of slavery

Manchester played a lead role in the abolition of the slave trade, the bicentennary of which is being celebrated in 2007.

At first glance this might appear strange. The town made money through slavery. Manchester as a textile and cotton town, supplied the Liverpool traders with cloth and fabric used in procuring slaves in Africa. And of course there would have been investors in the town who supported slavery.

But much of Manchester was thinking differently. This least aristocratic of British towns was by the 1780s beginning to flex its industrial muscles. At the same time it was learning to think for itself. Led by middle class citizens, often with a non-conformist edge, it was at odds with the established forms of British government.

Thus when the slavery abolitionist Thomas Clarkson rode from Liverpool to Manchester in 1787 he was given a very different reception from the one he'd received in the port city. There an attempt had been made on Clarkson's life. In Manchester he was warmly welcomed and urged to speak in the Collegiate Church, now the Cathedral.

On 28 October 1787, to a packed house, including a significant number of black people, he delivered a powerful indictment of the slave trade. He highlighted the conditions in which Africans were traded. If the British wished to show 'a proper abhorrence of this detestable trade' they must embrace

> **“a proper abhorrence of this detestable trade”**

the cause of abolition he stated. Thus a movement was born.

After the speech the Manchester abolition committee printed resolutions in the local and national press and called for the towns and cities of Britain to join them in petitioning parliament. The resulting Manchester petition in 1788 contained the names of a quarter of Manchester's entire population - around 11,000 signatures. More than 100 other petitions followed it from around the country.

▲ BBC news reader Moira Stuart visiting Manchester Art Gallery to view the *Black Victorians* exhibition in 2005/06. Here she's viewing, a portrait of **Ira Aldridge as Othello**, 1826, by James Northcote. The painting, bought in the C19, was purchased to emphasise Manchester's role in the anti-slavery movement.

The popular abolitionist movement in Britain, born from that petition, and co-ordinated through campaigners such as William Wilberforce, together with slave revolts in North America and the Caribbean, created the conditions for the abolition of the slave trade in 1807.

Yet Manchester wasn't finished. After that success the fight continued. The city played a lively role up to 1833, when not only the trade but the keeping of slaves was banned in the British Empire. Nor did it end there. In 1854, for example, Manchester hosted an Anti-Slavery Conference focusing on the North American slave trade, with speakers including US black activist William Wells Brown.

The climax was a public meeting at the Free Trade Hall in 1862 which attracted people from all walks of life and pledged support to President Lincoln and his emancipation of slaves during the American Civil War. The correspondence between the president and the city is marked by a statue and a square (see page 56).

ATTITUDE

The Peterloo Massacre

The massacre took place on 16 August 1819. The curious name arose through the location of the event at St Peter's Field and because participants on both sides had fought at the Battle of Waterloo in 1815. The site now lies under the Convention Quarter of the city centre. The meeting was part of a larger movement campaigning for a national extension of the vote to all adults at a time of deepening poverty. To have little direct influence on the government was a cause of growing anger. Thousands of handloom weavers, in particular, were caught in a downward spiral of wages and a rise in the price of bread. Representation was a matter of life and death.

Words typical of the mood were incorporated in the declaration to be sent to London by the protesters: 'Governments, not immediately derived from and strictly accountable to the People, are usurpations and ought to be resisted and destroyed'. The leader of the meeting, Henry Hunt, asked people to come 'armed with no other weapon but that of a self approving conscience; determined not to be irritated or excited'. It was the town's magistrates that became agitated.

Shortly before 1pm, they decided to arrest Hunt. Failing to do so, they called for the troops. Unfortunately it was the volunteer Manchester and Salford Yeomanry who reacted first. Moving into a mass of around 60,000 people, the Yeomanry became separated from each other, panicked and started to lash out with their sabres. Finally the regular soldiers, the 15th Hussars, arrived and within 15 minutes the field was clear. Eleven people died on the day and a further four later; 600 were injured. One man survived when a sabre cut lodged in the cheese he'd stored under his hat.

There had been similar acts of repression before and there would be afterwards, but Peterloo was different because journalists were present to record it for a national audience. Whilst the immediate reaction was further repression, the long-term influence was one of disenchantment with the existing electoral system. The indignation of many in the nation at British soldiers killing British people faded but never disappeared. A first significant step to the reform of Parliament in 1832 had been taken.

Friedrich Engels

One of the most important C19 political thinkers, Friedrich Engels, lived for almost 22 years in Manchester between 1842 and 1870. He came as an agent for a textile company in which his father had a partnership. Although he loathed the job, it allowed him to examine how Manchester had developed. Touring the city with common-law wife Mary Burns, a working-class girl with access to the roughest areas, he compiled material for his famous work *The Condition of the Working Class in England*. This influenced all subsequent thought on industrialisation, in particular the work of Engels' close friend Karl Marx. The following is an extract from the book regarding Little Ireland off Oxford Road: 'The cottages are old, dirty, and of the smallest sort, the streets uneven, fallen into ruts and in part without drains or pavements; masses of refuse, offal and sickening filth lie among standing pools in all directions; the atmosphere is poisoned by effluvia.'

Engels was not just a social reformer in a sober suit – in character he was warm and approachable. He loved sport and frequented the fox hunt in Cheshire. More than anything else, his character shines through in the list of confessions Eleanor Marx extracted from him at his Manchester residence in 1869. The following are a few of them: 'Your favourite virtue: jollity. Your idea of misery: to go to the dentist. The vice you excuse most: excess of any kind. The vice you detest most: cant. Your favourite hero: none. Your favourite heroine: too many to name one. Your favourite maxim: not to have any. Your favourite motto: take it easy.'

ATTITUDE

Pan-Africanism

In October 1945, the fifth Pan-African Congress met in Manchester at Chorlton on Medlock town hall, now part of the Metropolitan University. The site is marked by a plaque on the building. The previous meetings, beginning in 1900, had been dominated by Black American activists, but in Manchester the African and West Indian delegates would set the agenda. Thus the chair of meeting was George Padmore, the veteran West Indian journalist and campaigner. Many famous names attended such as Jomo Kenyatta (pictured later in life) and Kwame Nkrumah.

Galvanised by the helplessness of many of the colonial powers when threatened by Hitler, plus the rise of the USA and the Soviet Union, but perhaps most of all by the role played by Africans and Caribbeans during the war, the time felt right to strike for independence.

One of the resolutions affirmed, 'the right of all colonial peoples to control their own destiny'. It was scarcely covered in the press at the time and a report to the British government claimed that nothing of importance was being discussed and that the Congress would lead nowhere.

The writer of the report was wrong. As Jomo Kenyatta said, this was 'a landmark in the struggle for unity and freedom.'

In Manchester in 1945, in the gloom of ration-hit post war Britain, the Fifth Pan-African Congress proved to be the first coordinated step to independence in Africa and the West Indies.

THE MANCHESTER SCHOOL

The myth we live by

IN the house where the editor of this guide grew up there was a niche and in the niche was the bust of a politician: John Bright MP, free trader and one of the fathers of the Manchester School. The bust, still there, dates back to the nineteenth century, when a belief in progress and the steady improvement of mankind, morally and materially, was part of the Victorian credo.

Politics was clearly the principal method by which this improvement would be delivered – especially in a country that had historically stopped short of revolution. Thus local figures with a national and international profile were celebrated with alabaster busts and other bric-a-brac produced for general sale. The nature of celebrity having changed, in the early C21, a bust of footballer Wayne Rooney on a mantelpiece seems more likely than that of Tony Blair.

Not that Blair will leave a legacy to rival John Bright's. After all it was Bright and his ally Richard Cobden who in the 1840s were the architects of the Manchester School, a line of thought which still influences the way we live.

The definition of the Manchester School goes like this. Take away government interference in the economy, let business and trade look after itself and free enterprise will flourish. Thus by encouraging entrepreneurship and rewarding hard work everyone will benefit. Regulate the economy and society will become mired, clogged by a lack of enterprise and limited ambitions. Bright himself said, 'all legislative interference with the labour market [is] unjustifiable in principle and mischievious in [its] results.' The nick-name, Manchester School, incidentally, comes via a political opponent, Benjamin Disreali.

For Manchester businessmen the delivery method would be free trade, where states removed all tariff barriers to the flow of goods and services between nations. The impetus behind the idea came from Britain's Corn Laws, which, by taxing imported corn, impeded business, kept the necessities of life for the poor

Tory PM Disreali (left) disapproves as Bright flirts with Britannia

(in this case bread) expensive and along with other tariffs caused strife between nations which in turn got in the way of wealth creation for all society from top to bottom.

The Manchester School is thus entwined with liberalism (not to be confused with the very different Liberal Democrat Party in Britain today). Another name comes dressed up in French, *laissez-faire*, whilst the ugliest is Manchesterism.

The influence of the philosophy was important through much of the mid and late nineteenth century as free trade was increasingly adopted by nations. It withered in the twentieth as governments again raised tariff barriers and nationalism re-established itself. But the idea still had legs. Christened neo-liberalism, the Manchester School sprung up in the 1980s with Margaret Thatcher and Ronald Reagan. The underlying morality of the original idea had been lost though, and its symbol became the movie *Wall Street*.

Then the Berlin Wall fell and the political economist Francis Fukuyama wrote *The End of History* (1992) which declared that Western liberalism had won the final battle in the war of world doctrines. The future was bright, the future was private enterprise, trade between nations would replace conflict. The Manchester School had come a long way. Fukuyama's simplistic idea was flawed of course but the truth is that many developing nations have, with varying degrees of success, adopted the liberal ideal. The free trade movement, twisted into globalisation, has cast its net wide.

It's not surprising then that for the left the Manchester School has always been suspect. It represents the harsh, inequitable side of a cold careless economy: a system where the rich get richer and social justice is scorned as an impediment to personal gain. This is the Manchester School as articulated by Gordon Gekko in *Wall Street*: 'Greed is Good.' In Germany, Manchestertum, as it is called, is a term of open abuse.

Bright and Cobden would have been astonished by this turn of events. But they might have half expected it. Manchester, as a city and a concept, carries potency. Opposite

"Manchester, as a city and a concept, carries potency. Opposite orthodoxies have always found common ground in condemning the city"

orthodoxies have always found common ground in condemning the city and way it developed.

For the left the city was created purely by capitalism and therefore its philosophy and ambitions must be wrong. For conservatives and aristocrats the city threatened the established relationship between the propertied and the poor, whilst free trade threatened the concept of the nation state. As John Bright said in Manchester in 1849 after the last vestige of the Corn Laws had ceased to exist, 'As a people we have found that we have some power. We have discovered that we were not born with saddles on our backs, and that country gentlemen were not born with spurs.' No wonder the Establishment was worried.

Detmar Doering, keen on redressing the balance, wrote in 2004, 'Even today, popular conceptions of 'Manchesterism' are shaped by the view projected by this unholy alliance [between left and right]. It has managed to convince people that nationalism and an authoritarian state are more human than cosmopolitanism and liberty.' Yet, 'the Manchester Liberals created a far freer internal market in Europe than the Eurocrats in Brussels have achieved today.' Similarly although the neo-liberals of the 1980s approved of a dose of Manchesterism, for them it was all about the pursuit of wealth as an end in itself.

So this is the strangeness of the Manchester School: its popular notoriety, as with so much political theory, bears only a passing resemblance to how its founders thought. Free trade unencumbered by governmental meddling might have been an aspect of the Manchester School but it went much deeper than that.

For instance, both Bright (who was a Quaker) and Cobden were anti-war and anti-imperialist, opposing the Crimean War in 1854. In their version of the doctrine, free trade would ensure world peace, no less. Inevitably this would result in higher living standards for everybody with the ultimate goal of ending conflicts between individuals, groups and nations. In this way and with these freedoms the human spirit would be raised up. Cobden speaking in Manchester in 1846 said, 'I believe that the motive for large and mighty empires, for gigantic armies and great navies, for those materials that are used for the destruction of life, and the destruction of the rewards of labour, will die away.' Much later John Bright, in 1877 when the application of free trade as a policy had made itself felt, said, 'The workman of England is no longer a human machine. He is a man into whom, by these changes has been infused a new life, and to whom is given a new and wholesome responsibility.' Although Bright's brushing aside in his own mills of factory legislation aimed at improving conditions - this was clear governmental interference - laid him open to criticism.

But the myth of the Manchester School, the leftist and the rightist one, has overcome the reality. And like the myth of ceaseless rain in Manchester it shows no sign of losing its force.

Yet a more accurate reading of the Manchester School reveals why people across Britain would buy alabaster busts of key campaigners such as John Bright and put them in places of honour. These were heroes, great men, leading the country and the world with integrity towards a brighter, more equitable future.

Architecture

This architectural history deals principally with the area inside the Greater Manchester boundaries and only with surviving buildings. Many of the buildings are more fully described elsewhere, so check the index.

Feast or famine. Or rather famine then feast. Isolated behind the Pennine hills from the main north-south communication routes, Manchester and Lancashire took a long time to jump on the roller-coaster of architectural fashion. Aside from some bits and pieces of Roman and Prehistoric ruins, and traces of Romanesque buildings, such as a repositioned arch in Middleton parish church, there's little to show until well after the Norman Conquest.

It's with the Perpendicular style of English Gothic architecture – that national passion for the vertical line - in the 1300s and 1400s that things start to happen. This can be traced in numbers of churches but most importantly in **Manchester Cathedral** which also provides some of the best late-medieval woodwork in the country. Ashton Parish Church, **St Michael**, to the east has a sequence of stained glass based on the life of St Helens from the same period which is also nationally important.

Given that churches were often altered perhaps the most evocative buildings from this period are the manor houses, places such as **Ordsall Hall** and **Bramall Hall** with their timber frames. Other fine examples survive at **Smithills** and **Baguley**. All are very impressive. Several rare timber churches remain in the region such as **St Lawrence** in Denton.

Secular stone buildings start to appear at this time such as **Chetham's** (first half of the 1400s) in the city centre. Brick, which will become a dominant building material, makes a grand entry on to the scene with **Hough End Hall** (1596) in Chorlton. As prosperity in the region rose sturdy stone houses appear on the fringes of Pennines, such as **Hey House** (1616), Holcombe and **Clegg Hall** (approx 1618), Milnrow.

Thus far in the built history of Greater Manchester all the work away from the churches had been unburdened by a style (in otherwords a particular regime of building such as Gothic or Classical). Hough End in its plan and Clegg Hall with cute Classically inspired columns in the porch (see picture below) show this is starting to change. Previously, secular buildings were places built to fit the local climate in practical ways that also lent prestige to the owners. In all of these buildings it's hard to discern the ego of an architect, in fact we almost never know the architect's name – architects were at the time craftsmen, not part of a precious profession. The result is that these are almost organic structures which in terms of atmosphere and charm have never been beaten.

By the 1700s that had changed. Classical architecture arrived in Manchester with **St Ann's Church** (1709-1712) by John Barker complete with Corinthian columns and pilasters. Of course not all the sweetness disappeared with the advent of the new style. **Foxdenton Hall**, in Chadderton (1710-30) is a sole survivor of a Yeoman house of the period and is lovely. **Platt Hall** (1763-4) by Timothy Lightoler is less lovely but gives us a taste of the Palladian style (elegant Classical buildings inspired by Andrea Palladio and very fashionable at this time). **Alkrington Hall** in Middleton is a grander version of the same. This last work was by

Clegg Hall as it looked in the early C19th

St Augustine by GF Bodley

James Leoni who also rebuilt the far more impressive **Lyme Park** with its gorgeous courtyard.

Another gem is **Heaton Hall** (1772-8) by James Wyatt with masterful interiors by a variety of craftsmen. Disgracefully allowed to decline by the city council this is on its way back, paradoxically with the help of the city council, to something resembling its original state. Georgian terraces have rarely survived although **St John Street** in the city centre is a decent example. There are more examples of one-off Georgian town houses such as **Cobden House** (1770) on Quay Street, a very large residence with good surviving interiors – now barristers' chambers. Other traces survive around Lever Street and other Greater Manchester towns. A whole network of C18 dwellings, streets and a church, remain at **Fairfield** in Droylesden, east of the city. These were built by the Moravian community as a place set apart but are now swamped by urban sprawl.

Numbers of pre-industrial houses with domestic workshops illuminated by long rows of windows on the top floor also hint at a disappeared past. These are the earliest surviving buildings of the humble to survive. The Pennine hills around Greater Manchester make an especially happy hunting ground for such buildings particularly the villages of Saddleworth (see page 23 for picture).

The C19 has now been reached. Churches in the early part of the century were being built once more as Gothic, but only as a species of Gothic dreamed up in the architects' heads without the principles developed in medieval buildings. Because of this these can be great fun, such as Charles Barry's **All Saints** (1826), Stand, with its tall, Gothic-horror porch. A crucial building nationally is the much messed about **St Wilfred RC** (1842) in Hulme by AWN Pugin. This was one of the first 'archeological' churches, harking back to the principles of the Middle Ages. After it everything with churches had to be done correctly according to the dictates of Early English, Decorated and Perpendicular architecture from the first half of the millennium.

A selection of the best C19 churches include **St Mark**, Worsley (1846, GG Scott), **St Mary**, Hulme (now apartments, 1858, Crowther), the **Holy Name**, University (1871, Hansom) and **St Augustine**, Pendlebury, (1874, Bodley). This last building was considered by architectural critic, Nikolaus Pevsner, to be 'one of the English churches of all time'. Two curiosities are Edmund Sharpe's church, **Holy Trinity**, Rusholme, (1845) built entirely out of terracotta, and J Medland Taylor's **St Edmund** (1873) in Rochdale which is as much a temple to Freemasonry as the Almighty. But then again most things by the latter architect are a curiosity such as his **St Annes** (1882), Denton described as Arts and Crafts Gothic and worth a long detour to visit.

Thomas Harrison was one of the first to bring the Greek Revival to the city with the **Portico Library** (1806) whilst Charles Barry added the grandest of these building, with what is now, **Manchester Art Gallery**. The most individual take on this style was Charles Cockerell's **Bank of England** (1845), now offices, on King Street. But we have to return to Barry for one of the most inspirational buildings in the city's history. This was the **Athenaeum** (1837), based on Italian Renaissance palaces. With its dignified, grand appearance it was adopted

From top, Victoria Square, a Hulme Crescent (demolished) and New Islington

ARCHITECTURE

Housing

One of the civic battles which has raged in Manchester over the past hundred or so years concerns the provision of good housing.

The first big municipal slum clearance and housing project was Victoria Square by architects Spalding and Cross in 1897. This takes the form of an impressive five storey tenement with central courtyard. But it was the big council house building programmes between the World Wars that, across the country, changed the urban landscape. Loosely based on the Garden City ideal pioneered in England before the end of the C19 huge estates of semi-detached houses sprawled out in every direction as the central rookeries and slums were thinned or emptied. One of the largest schemes anywhere - was Wythenshawe on land acquired by Manchester from Cheshire.

Architectural fashion had shifted by the 1950s but the necessity for new housing was as pressing as ever. With ideas misapplied from the International Modern movement in architecture, and through untested theories dreamt up by middle class designers, municipal housing in the UK plunged into catastrophe. Manchester, in particular, paid for its enthusiasm for the new ideas. The result was that concrete hells such as Hulme Crescents, Fort Ardwick and others blighted the city. Critic Nikolaus Pevsner writing in 1969 had asked whether these would 'be the slums of fifty years hence.' They were slums within ten years. Perhaps even worse was the social engineering involved whereby poorer central populations were shifted to council estates many miles from the city without consultation. Isolated in inward looking communities with less and less access to jobs as the regional economy declined these inevitably became sink estates.

Today many of the worst of the sixties and seventies disasters have been cleared. Hulme, a little to south of the city centre, has become, of sorts, a model

Re-development for the UK, with the re-invention of traditional streets, gardens and so forth. One community here though, Homes for Change, has tried to maintain the ideal of high-density that failed so completely in the sixties, with flats and maisonettes around a central lawn and courtyard plus a theatre, work spaces and café. But generally planners over the last ten years, as the economy improved once more, have been more circumspect and cautious than they were in the 1960s.

This might be about to change. Manchester-based developer Urban Splash has begun a project of mixed social and private housing, including a health centre and other facilities, which will test the limits of urban living in the UK once more. Called New Islington, the first element is the most gimmicky and designed by FAT of London. This looks like a funky dead-end and it's to be hoped that subsequent work will be stronger. The same developer's innovative reinvention of the traditional red-brick terrace in the Langworthy area of Salford, renamed Chimney Pot Park, seems much more likely to provide a long-term solution.

by cotton barons as the style of choice for their warehouses. Manchester now gained a streetscape specific to itself filled with buildings inspired by Italy, and nicknamed 'Manchester Palazzos'.

Edward Walters was a fine palazzo architect, but his best weren't warehouses. His masterpiece was the **Free Trade Hall** (1856), the main façade of which survives, in the Radisson Edwardian Hotel, whilst the **Manchester and Salford Bank** (1860), now the Royal Bank of Scotland, on Mosley Street isn't far behind in brilliance. Earlier JT Gregan in St Ann's Square had built the most exquisite palazzo of them all, **Heywood's Bank** (1846), a triumph of Manchester architecture, with its attached manager's house – the first in beautifully cut stone, the second in no-nonsense brick.

The palazzo, as with all art and architectural ideas soon lost its purity and became a shape to hang off a variety of designs: an excuse for showmanship. This led to remarkable structures such as Travis and Magnall's **Watts Warehouse** (1858), now the Britannia Hotel. This was the greatest of the textile warehouses occupied by a single company and a cocktail of architectural styles including Italian, French, Elizabethan and even Egyptian motifs.

By the 1850s Manchester had changed completely from the place it had been in 1800. It had left its pre-industrial small town status far behind. The city could not now be confused with anywhere else, in effect it was a city state, confident of its place in the world and in control of its own destiny.

This is reflected in the architecture whether in the warehouses or in the banks. It was also reflected in the architectural practices. Manchester starts to get dynasties of designers. The most prominent was that begun by Alfred Waterhouse and continued by his sons (although Waterhouse later decamped to London). In 1859, at the age of 29, the Liverpool born, Manchester trained architect, won the commission to build the **Assize Courts** in the city. This essay in modern Gothic was a total success.

It was followed by **Manchester Town Hall** (1877), described as 'a classic of its age', and the **Victoria University** (1887), now the University of Manchester, plus numerous other buildings.

◂ For many people Manchester means terrace houses of red brick marshalled into military rows. It's certainly true that working class housing for more than a hundred years conformed to this stereotype. Legend states that they are usually worthy only of demolition. This is not the case, if renovated carefully, terraces can provide excellent housing. For many purchasers they are again proving attractive.

Waterhouse's contemporary was Thomas Worthington who began a practice which still survives in the city. His contribution straddles both buildings and monuments in a variety of Gothic styles such as the **Albert Memorial** (1862) and the **Memorial Hall** (1866), both Albert Square, and the **City Police and Sessions Court** (1875), Minshull Street, now Crown Courts.

The middle years of the C19 have been called the Battle of the Styles in Britain, an often passionate debate between those who favoured Gothic and those who favoured Classical, and its various offshoots. In Manchester, unlike, for instance, in Liverpool, Gothic boxed the ears of Classical. No doubt the new money industrialists and businessmen found it warmer and more charming than the colder aestheticpurities of the other style. Edward Salomans, Manchester's most prominent Jewish architect, must have felt the same, or at least his clients did. His best building the **Reform Club** (1871) is in splendid Venetian Gothic. The style still cast a shadow over the end of the century when Basil Champneys designed the last great flowering of Gothic in the UK with **John Rylands Library** (1900), a *tour-de-force* in red sandstone.

Manchester Ship Canal opened in 1894

and with a general upturn in business a building boom hit the city The steel framed building arrived at the same time. The buildings in the late 1890s until the outbreak of WWI in 1914, and for a decade after 1918, are the the most bombastic in the city. This was the Imperial Age, the triumph of Pax Britannica, where the sun never set on the Empire and never set on Manchester's cotton and manufacturing interests either.

A man who seized the opportunities presented by the good times was Harry S Fairhurst - another dynasty maker. His early buildings such as **Lancaster House** and **India House** (both 1906) Whitworth Street, and **Bridgewater House** (1912), Whitworth Street, are fine examples of the new larger warehouses needed in the city. They also reflect the new fashion for a crazy, supercharged version of Renaissance meets Baroque architecture. After the First World War, Fairhurst shaped the city with more essays in gargantuan Classical structures

Ship Canal House, 1927, by Harry S Fairhurst, perhaps the most prolific and versatile of Manchester's architects ➤

Sir Owen Williams' black glass **Daily Express Building** from 1939 more than holds its own amidst the modern apartments ▼

such as **Ship Canal House** (1927) on King Street. His **Lee House** (1931) is very different, eight storeys of Art Deco colliding with the International Modern.

A contemporary was Charles Heathcote who mingled dainty detail with powerhouse punch. Notable buildings of his include **Parrs Bank** (1902), York Street, the **Eagle Star Building** (1911), Cross Street, **Lloyd's Bank** (1915), King Street, and the earlier **107 Piccadilly** textile warehouse (1899). Notable for its sheer scale is Clegg, Fryer and Penman's **St James' Building** (1913), Oxford Road, in colossal Baroque.

Many of the earlier buildings in this period, such as **Lancaster House** and also Charles Trubshaw's **Midland Hotel** (1903) and the **Refuge Assurance Building** by Alfred and Paul Waterhouse from 1891, are faced in terracotta and faience. This was a popular material at the time because large decorative patterns could be manufactured quickly and smoke and soot didn't adhere so readily.

Working outside the city centre – perhaps they simply failed to get commissions - was the practice of Edgar Wood and JH Sellars. This remarkable pair, first separately and then together, moved from Arts and Crafts, through a proto-Expressionism to the International Modern in their buildings. Edgar Wood's, **First Church of Christ Scientist** (1903), Daisy Bank Road in Victoria Park, is both original and startling. Other buildings survive particularly in the suburb town of Middleton. Similarly original is the eccentric but delightful Mediterranean inspired work of Richard Harding Watt, a Mancunian glove manufacturer turned amateur architect, in Knutsford, south of the city.

Before the International Modern movement with its clipped functional aesthetic swept the older styles aside after WWII, Edwin Lutyens designed the **Midland Bank** (1929), King Street, now HSBC, in another grand take on Classical. Meanwhile the city council provided **Central Library** (1934) and the **Town Hall Extension** (1938), both by Vincent Harris. The first is a circular Classical building, the second a rewarding oddity with high gables and sheer facades.

Tallest wins

The first building to push higher than 30m (100ft) in Manchester was the Collegiate Church (now the Cathedral) sometime after 1421. This ruled the roost for almost 400 years. Then industry came crashing in and mill chimneys started to dominate the landscape. Manchester was the first city where industry asserted itself physically over churches and palaces. Mill chimneys rose to over 60m (200ft) in the city, although these were dwarfed by the 100m (328ft) monsters in outlying cotton areas, such as the giant in Rhodes, near Middleton (demolished 1982). The Town Hall wrested the Manchester skyline away from industry and passed it to local government with a tower rising over 87m (288ft) in 1877. It wasn't until almost a hundred years later, that commerce in turn trumped administration. In 1962 the Cooperative Insurance Society decided to give the city profile a flash of corporate Americana with their tower of 118m (387ft). Now forty years on Hilton Tower rules the roost at 171m (561ft).

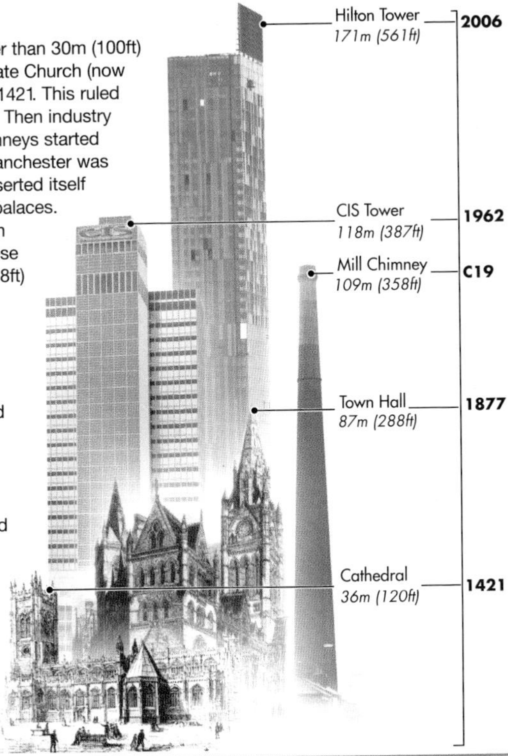

But the movements sweeping across architecture outside Britain were now making themselves felt in Manchester. JW Beaumont's **Kendals Department Store** (1939) on Deansgate and Sir Owen Williams' Daily Express Building (1939), now offices, on Great Ancoats Street, provided examples of how the world was moving on. **The Daily Express Building,** sleek and sophisticated in a coat of black glass, might have been amongst the earliest of Manchester Modernist buildings but it has never been bettered.

The Manchester Plan of 1945 envisaged massive changes across the post World War II bomb damaged city to meet with the new world situation. But Britain's decline from power and a recession in manufacturing meant that much was never realised. Still if the changes that did happen were piecemeal they were often major. The best commercial buildings were GS Hay and Gordon Tait's, Co-operative Movement complex on Miller Street, including **New Century House** and the soaring 25 storey CIS Tower (both1962). The best academic work was by Gibbon of Cruickshank and Seward off Sackville Street with buildings such as the **Renolds Building** (1962). Other interesting work includes LC Howitt's, **Hollings College**, Wilmslow Road, Fallowfield (1960), nicknamed the 'Toast-rack' because of its appearance. More controversial was Covell, Matthews and Partners', **Piccadilly Buildings** (1965), a vast redevelopment on bomb damaged land which was a Brutalist essay in concrete. This dominates one of the most public parts of the city and has weathered badly and been treated worse in the years following construction. Just about

Factory Music did things differently. When the company decided to open a club in 1982 it wanted to move away from the mirror balls, the flock and the fading glam of the '70s. So they appointed Ben Kelly. He gave the Factory club, the **Haçienda** (top), a utilitarian and industrial aesthetic that fitted the building and the moment perfectly. Later he did the same with Factory bar, **Dry** (bottom). The hard-edged, almost brutal good looks of both designs were much copied around the world ➤

everybody wants it gone apart from a few stubborn architects defending their profession. Instead it's being repackaged in a dreary grey - the worst of solutions.

In the 1980s Manchester played a brief cameo role as a leader in club and bar design with the **Hacienda** (1982, demolished) and **Dry Bar** (1989). Both came from the pen of Ben Kelly and both delivered a pared down, hard industrial aesthetic that was aped round the globe.

Recent architectural work includes much by local design practices. Indeed with firms such as Ian Simpson Architects and Mills Beaumont Leavey Channon the dynasties have returned. The latter practice have been responsible over the last fifteen years for buildings such as **Siemens Building**, Princess Parkway, West Didsbury, **Homes for Change**, Chichester Road, Hulme and the **Manchester Metropolitan University Library**, Aytoun Street.

Civil engineering

Manchester and region have been at the forefront of civil engineering in the UK since the Industrial Revolution. The Bridgewater Canal (1759-65), supervised by James Brindley and John Gilbert pioneered new techniques in canal building whilst the Rochdale Canal (opened 1804) was the first trans-Pennine waterway. The Liverpool and Manchester Railway (opened 1830) and overseen by George Stephenson was just as epoch-making as the Bridgewater Canal. Perhaps the biggest breakthrough was the least noticeable to the general public. Eaton Hodgkinson, working with William Fairburn, in Manchester in the 1820s, produced an H profile cast iron beam lighter and more efficient than any previously developed. This was the basis for all subsequent cast-iron building design. Notable surviving works from industry include Ancoats Mills and the great textile warehouses of Manchester, many of which used progressive constructional methods particularly in fire-proofing. The C19 viaducts around the city are of interest too.

Manchester Ship Canal, completed in 1894, as a single project, remains the largest civil engineering undertaking in the nation's history. Barton Swing Aqueduct (pictured), which carries the Bridgewater Canal over the Ship Canal by Edward Leader Williams, is a remarkable engineering solution trapping and then swivelling 880 tons of water over the Ship Canal. A couple of years later the Thirlmere aqueduct reached Manchester from the Lake District bringing fresh water. In the 1930s Haweswater was dammed and added to Manchester's mains supply.

Recent notable civil engineering projects, often with a clear aesthetic ideal, have included several bridges such as Hulme Arch, Trinity Bridge and, the Lowry footbridge.

The last ten years have seen the rise of football stadia as defining structures. The best in terms of looks is Manchester City's, City of Manchester stadium by Arup Associates originally built for the Commonwealth Games. The most impressive in terms of bulk, but an architectural hotpotch, is Manchester United's Old Trafford Stadium with a capacity of 76,000.

ARCHITECTURE

Ian Simpson Architects meanwhile have almost single-handedly reshaped the skyline gaining several of the key commissions after the IRA bomb of 1996. Indeed the practice helped develop the masterplan for the redevelopment of the city centre after that event. Simpson buildings include refurbishments of **Manchester Museum** and the **Museum of Science and Industry**, plus new build such as **Urbis**, Corporation Street, and the apartments at **No1 Deansgate** and **Hilton Tower** (called by most locals Beetham Tower after the developers). Indeed the change from manufacturing giant to middle ranking, mixed economy European city is most keenly expressed in the fact that the most expensive and biggest Hilton Tower is occupied by the architect Ian Simpson. Football players have bought other apartments. The cottontots who built the 'palazzos' and made Manchester a metropolis are long extinct.

Other notable local practices who have completed good work include: Stephenson Bell with the **Eastgate** refurbishment, Castlefield, and the **International Convention Centre**, Windmill Street; OMI with **Martinscroft Housing**, Boundary Lane, Hulme, **Fourth Church of Christ Scientist**, Peter Street, **Dukes 92**, Castle Street; Hodder Associates with **Centenary Building**, Salford University and **Cross Street footbridge**. A young, practice Walker Simpson, have produced a splendid structure with **North City Library and Sixth Form Centre** in Harpurhey, north Manchester featuring an eye-catching wall

Imperial War Museum North

Civil Justice Centre

of photovoltaic panels to help cut carbon emissions. Meanwhile Maurice Shapero has stirred up emotions in the suburb of Whalley Range with an extraordinary extension to **Palmiro** restaurant.

Significant non-local designers include: Nicholas Thompson of RHWL with **The Bridgewater Hall**; Michael Hopkins Associates with **Manchester Art Gallery** extension and refurbishment; Michael Wilford with **The Lowry** at the Quays; Santiago Calatrava with **Trinity Bridge**, off St Mary's Parsonage; Daniel Libeskind with the **Imperial War Museum North** at the Quays and Tadao Ando with his **Piccadilly Gardens Pavilion**.

This last structure is derided by most as a waste of time, other work such as the refurbishment of **Manchester Art Gallery** have been praised for a combination of subtlety and strength.

A recent building which combines flash looks with a degree of restraint is the excellent, 81m (266ft) tall, **Civil Justice Centre** by Australian practice Denton Corker Marshall. With protruding glass elements floating one over the other, it gives the west of the city centre an exciting new silhouette. The building will contain 47 courts and, as with North City Library, also features pioneering environmental features.

Whether this type of building or show-boating architecture such as **Ando's Pavilion**, Libeskind's **Imperial War Museum North** or Wilford's **Lowry**, will stand the test of time remains to be seen. Perhaps it will be the local practices, as so often done in the past, that will be remembered longest in the city and in the end contribute most to the evolving Manchester city scene.

Hilton Tower

Hilton Tower is a splendid slice of slender simplicity (most Mancunians call it Beetham Tower after the property developers who built it, but Hilton Tower is the proper title). The building cost £150 million and is 171m and 47 storeys tall. It's best viewed from the side where the astonishing size zero profile is revealed. In terms of height to depth it is one of the thinnest towers in the world. The first 23 three floors make up the Hilton Hotel and the rest are apartments. The building's architect, Ian Simpson, lives in the penthouse duplex which features an internal garden containing twenty-one 4m high olive, lemon and oak trees. The public areas in the hotel are notable for a pared down luxury reminiscent of the classic Modern Movement hotels of the fifties and sixties. Imagine a hotel bar where you'd expect to see Sean Connery as James Bond circa '64 sampling a 'shaken not stirred'.

THE GUIDE

Cloud 23

Manchester unlocked

If you want to get straight to the meat of the matter this section might help. It provides a quick reference to the top sites, scenery and sport in Greater Manchester (or a couple of miles over the border). These are placed alphabetically not in order of merit. The pages numbers indicate where you can look up the full entries.

Significant buildings

Manchester Town Hall *66*
A Victorian Gothic triumph of civic pride with spectacular decorations and some famous murals

Manchester Cathedral 78
Atmospheric church with superb late medieval woodwork and modern stained glass

Chetham's Library and School 74
Almost 600 years old, and a remarkable and charming survival. Unique in the UK

John Rylands Library *76*
Manchester's Taj Mahal with a world beating collection of books in jaw-dropping building

Rochdale Town Hall *70*
Another example of civic pride in stunning Gothic architecture

Styal Mill *136*
A reconstructed mill in splendid grounds which takes visitors back to the industrial age

Manchester Town Hall Extension

Museums and Galleries

Bolton Museum and Art Gallery *130*
The best of the town museums, good on natural history and much else

Imperial War Museum North *89*
Attention seeking building with a thought provoking exhibition (pictured above and below are images from the Second World War exhibition)

The Lowry *105*
Spectacular architecture and varying programme of exhibits

Manchester Art Gallery *109*
Lovely buildings and excellent collections of British art particularly Pre-Raphaelites

Manchester Museum *92*
A higgledy piggledy Victorian gem, recently modernised with good natural history and Egyptology sections

Museum of Science and Industry *94* The biggest such museum in the country underlines just how important

this city has been

Manchester United Museum *233*
Love 'em or loathe 'em but the tour and museum are good

Whitworth Art Gallery *112*
Fine collections of textiles, watercolours, prints and engravings plus great café

Houses and gardens

Bramall Hall *121*
Medieval and mysterious, half-timbered and handsome, in large grounds

Dunham Massey *122*
Bold and brick with good interiors and excellent garden and grounds

Heaton Hall *123*
Cool, uncluttered C18 hall set amidst vast grounds filled with interesting features

Lyme Park *124*
The most dramatic house in the region, set high on the hills with great interiors (pictured above)

Tatton Park *126*
Decent house with superb gardens and grounds including the oldest Japanese-designed garden in the West (pictured below)

Live entertainment

The Academy *207*
Bands of various shapes, sizes and ages

Apollo *207*
Better known versions of the above (usually)

Bridgewater Hall *72*
The Hallé conducted by Mark Elder might just be the best orchestra in Britain

Frog and Bucket *225*
Barrels of laughs in a local comedy club

Late Room *207*
Rock and rock re-runs in an intimate and popular space

Matt and Phreds *213*
Jazz every night until late

MEN Arena *207*
Come on down for the world's major acts such as The Killers and Kylie

Night and Day *191*
Grungy, down at earth, guitar music heaven, where Manchester bands are born

Palace theatre/ Opera House *224*
Old-fashioned theatres staging touring musicals and pantomime

Royal Exchange Theatre *223*
Great space and good for premieres of new plays and the classics

Food

Akbars *180*
Great service and great Indian food

Barburrito *186*
Snack heaven, easy going and cheap Mexican food

Café Jem'n'I *180*
In the suburb of Didsbury but modern British worth the journey

Lounge Ten *179*
An absolute and resolute original, dirty, lush and with live entertainment

The Market *182*
Cosy restaurant with classy modern British food

Piccolino *184*
Almost unreasonably popular and sassy Italian

Room *179*
Spectacular dining room with top class cuisine

Sam's Chop House *184*
The best for classic British cuisine

Harvey Nichols

River Restaurant, The Lowry Hotel *179*
See and be seen place with an excellent chef

Suburb *187*
Not food as such but the best for coffee in town

Barburrito

Top ten attractions outside Manchester (within 60 miles (100km)

Alton Towers *168*
The biggest theme park with rides to match in the UK

Blackpool Golden Mile *168*
A model of the tacky British seaside resort but still splendid in the sunshine

Chatsworth House *170*
A northern palace filled with artworks, spectacular interiors and equally amazing gardens and grounds

Blackpool

Chester Walls *166*
A rewarding walk along two miles and 2000 years of history

Chester Zoo *168*
The biggest, most professional and best such attraction in the region (Komodo Dragon pictured above)

Conwy Castle *158*
One of the great castles of Europe

Liverpool Waterfront *160*
Great architecture meets a dramatic location plus top-notch museums

Liverpool Walker Art Gallery *161*
Internationally important collection of art from the Renaissance onwards

National Football Museum *170*
For the football fanatic and those with a passing interest in the game

Alderley Edge

Landscapes within 60 miles (100 km)

Alderley Edge *145*
Wooded sandstone ridge south of the city with spooky wizard myth and great walks

Blackstone Edge *149*
Tough-boned millstone grit landscape with views and permanent gales that has history as well as beauty

Dovedale *154*
A sometimes gentle, sometimes dramatic limestone landscape great for walks and relaxation

Formby sands *159*
Huge sand dunes, pine woods (and fabulous Anthony Gormley sculptures *Another Place* at nearby Crosby)

The Snake Pass/ Alport Castle *154*
Left from the dramatic pass in the Peak District and you find a wild and unpopulated landscape including the largest landslip in the country

Trough of Bowland *157*
Take the valley of the River Hodder for beautiful walks and drives, in the exact centre of the United Kingdom

Marble Arch

If these don't inspire at least in Manchester you should:

- Drink a pint of ale in the Marble Arch
- Visit the Hallé Orchestra
- Take in a gig at Night and Day
- Root round Affleck's Palace
- Be fey with a Pre-Raphaelite artwork in the Art Gallery
- Watch a football match (not necessarily United or City)
- Dream to the Cathedral choir
- Have a laugh at a comedy club
- Visit Cloud 23 for the view
- Take a Town Hall tour
- Dine at Sam's Chop House
- Go curry mad in Rusholme
- Dance all night at Mr Scuff's 'Keep it Unreal'
- Take a walk through the streets

Active Manchester

(spectate and participate)

- Manchester United or City
- Lancashire Cricket Club
- Salford Reds
- Sale Sharks
- Belle Vue Dogs
- National Cycling Centre
- Heaton Park golf course
- Manchester Climbing Centre
- Sport City (tennis or squash)

The city centre and central walks

The city centre is an easy and rewarding place to walk around. The distance from end to end, Castlefield to Piccadilly Station and from Victoria Station to Oxford Road Station, is scarcely more than a mile (1.8km) and there is interest to be had everywhere.

The key to any visit is to look above the ground floor, where you'll frequently be rewarded with fanciful sculpture and elaborate details.

You'll also notice that few buildings survive from before the time of the Industrial Revolution. The Manchester that visitors see is, almost totally, a city of the C19 and C20. If you detect a degree of flashiness, especially with the Victorian and Edwardian buildings, that is because they so often acted as bricks and mortar advertisements for their proprietors. Thus we have an anthology of styles. Not only are neighbouring buildings different from each other, but often the same building completes startling architectural acrobatics. The effect can be overdone but the result is usually entertaining with wild patterns, a crazy riot of window decoration, and grinning gargoyles and sculptures. Note too the very good work from the last few decades, much by distinguished local designers.

You may be forgiven for wanting a bit of space as you wander. Sorry, Manchester is the city of the restricted perspective. As the world's first industrial city, the city grew where capital demanded. It was the proto-Tiger economy city and, as such, had no time or desire to plan great boulevards or central parks. Only now is open space being seriously considered.

Guided tours with Blue Badge Guides

There are many tours that start from the Visitor Information Centre in St Peter's Square. These take place chiefly on weekends, and provide an informed and entertaining way to learn about the city. There is a charge for each walk, £5 adults, £4 kids and concessions A programme is available at the Information Centre and also at libraries.

Part 1

Start at the door of the Visitor Information Centre, St Peter's Square, and follow the arcade alongside the Town Hall Extension. See pages 70 and 64 for this and its neighbour the Central Library. Across Peter Street is the brown and red terracotta mass of the **Midland Hotel**. This was built in 1903 by Charles Trubshaw for the Midland Railway Company. The building mixes stylistic motifs with wild abandon but is still one of the city's most eye-catching structures. In 1904 Charles Rolls met local manufacturer Frederick Royce in the hotel. Together they created the Rolls-Royce Motor Company. Previously this was the site of the Gentlemen's Concert Hall where Liszt, Paganini and Chopin played. Still on the site, but round the corner, there was the People's Concert Hall, where the audience occasionally became so unruly that a wire net had to be hung over the stage to protect the performers.

Follow Lower Mosley Street to the left of the hotel alongside the tramlines. Cross over and make for the Bridgewater Hall (page 72). If you continue down Lower Mosley Street, you arrive at one of Manchester's finest period pubs, the Britons Protection. Cross back over the tramlines after visiting the Bridgewater Hall and pass by the front of **Manchester Central**. This forms the conference and convention centre of the city with the modern building next door.

The main exhibition space was formerly Central Station and is an impressive piece of refurbished C19 railway engineering. The designer was Sir John Fowler with Sacre, Johnson and Johnstone, and it opened in 1880. It was built principally for the Midland Railway Company, and has the widest unsupported iron arch in Britain after St Pancras in London. The magnificent brick arcades that elevated the station to track level are said to have used 34 million bricks, but also destroyed 225 houses and displaced over 1,000 people to provide space for the station and its approaches. In 1969, it was decided that Manchester had too many railway termini and Central Station was closed. For many years it was one of the city's grandest car parks then, in the mid-1980s, it was converted by EGS, working for the now-defunct Greater Manchester Council, into the Exhibition Centre. The most exciting part of the building is the interior. When it is empty, the visitor stands isolated in 10,000 square metres of uninterrupted space. Next door and linked is the convention centre, a tasteful and elegant design from local architects Stephenson Bell.

Continue down by the side of the Midland Hotel on Mount Street, turning left into Peter Street. The first building on the left is the former YMCA, now **St George's House** – an office block. It was built in 1911, again in terracotta, with Art Nouveau panels and a copy of Donatello's *St George*. It was the first building with a reinforced concrete frame in the city and used to have swimming pool on its top floor. The next building is the former **Theatre Royal**, now a nightclub. Built in 1845 by Irwin and Chester, this also featured water up on high, with a 20,000-gallon tank placed in the roof space as a fire precaution – the previous theatre had burnt down. The grand classical portico shelters one of the very few, if one of the very worst, external statues of Shakespeare in the country. Some of the greatest Victorian and Edwardian actors appeared in the theatre, including Henry Irving, William Macready, Edmund Keen and Jenny Lind. The first production of *La Boheme* in English was performed here in 1897 with composer Puccini in the audience.

On the other side of the road, you might be able to make out a blue plaque on the wall of the newer building. This marks the site of the **Gaiety Theatre**. In the early years of the C20, Annie Horniman ran Britain's first repertory theatre from here. Horniman was a striking lady who dressed in elaborate brocade dresses, wore a monocle and smoked a cigar. Her chief director, Lewis Casson, married celebrated actress Sybil Thorndike.

Next door is the **Free Trade Hall** – now the Radisson Edwardian Hotel. It was the only building in the UK named after a principle, free trade, and stands on the site of the Peterloo Massacre (see page 36). Externally, this is one of the finest buildings in the city. It is also one of Manchester's spiritual centres. The current building was the third hall on the site and was completed in 1856. The design was by Edward Walters and is based on the Renaissance style of northern Italy. The façade is decorated over the arcade with the coats of arms of the Lancashire towns that fought to rid Britain of the restrictive Corn Laws (see pages 21 and 38and 39). Above the windows of the first floor are carved figures by John Thomas representing the Arts, Commerce, Agriculture and the Continents. In the central panel Free Trade herself, spreading her arms to give and receive, bestows her favours upon the nation and Empire. For 150 years the hall hosted speeches, readings, theatre, dancing and was the home of the Hallé Orchestra. Guests included, amongst others, Charles Dickens, David Livingstone, Benjamin Disraeli, David Lloyd George, Winston Churchill, Bob Dylan and the Sex Pistols.

Across the road and down a little is the former Albert Hall, now **Brannigans**. It was built in 1910 as a Methodist meeting hall. When it was built, this building was strictly temperance, but today evenings are alcohol-fuelled. The dramatic change of use probably accounts for the angry ghost that haunts the building.

On the left-hand side, behind **Bar 38**, a new square has been created with a pleasant public performance area. This allows us to see the impressive bulk of the **Great Northern Railway Company's Goods Warehouse**, built in 1898. It was formerly a unique transport interchange. In a tunnel underneath, goods could be shipped in by canal. On other floors there was road access, and through the great southern gates the main rail lines entered. Much of the building is now a top-notch casino, Manchester 235. The Deansgate façade is a luscious length of Victoriana, all dressed up in the so-called 'streaky bacon' style advertising the places

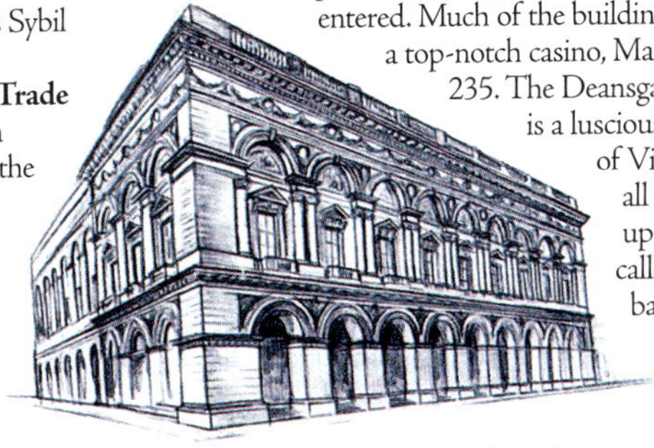

The Free Trade Hall prior to re-development

CITY WALKS

with which the railway company traded.

Cross over Deansgate and proceed down Quay Street to the **Opera House**, built by Mills and Murgatroyd in 1912. Harold Leek came to the Opera House in the European premier of *Oklahoma*, the programme writer got his name wrong, and Harold Leek went away as Howard Keel. Later, in the 1950s, Sean Connery appeared in a production of *South Pacific*. Matt Busby came down from Old Trafford to see if the actor would sign for Manchester United. He refused, so United missed out having James Bond play for them. The Opera House is still one of the key live venues especially for touring West End musicals.

Turn back and return up Quay Street. You skirt by **Sunlight House**, a white Portland stone splash of Art Deco built by the flamboyant Joe Sunlight in 1931. Sunlight was a rags-to-riches entrepreneur, who fled with his family as a 12-year-old refugee from Russia. The family name was anglicised. From small property speculations, Joe rose to be one of the country's greatest property developers. One of his passions was Hollywood and he went to extraordinary lengths to court the stars, becoming friendly with Douglas Fairbanks – hence the name of the swimming pool in the **Living Well Health Club** on the site. His other passion was owning horses and gambling. On one occasion he is said to have lost £30,000 in one day, only to win it back on the next. On the street side there is some delicate Adam-style ironwork with flowers and urns. Maintaining the celebrity link is the pub in the building. **The Old Grapes** is owned by *Coronation Street* star Liz Dawn, who has placed a photographic shrine to herself in one corner of the pub.

Continue up Quay Street, to Deansgate, and turn left. Deansgate follows the path of the original Roman road of more than 1,800 years ago, which means, of course, that it is straight. There are many possible reasons for the curious title of the street. The best story is that it is named after the Danes – the Vikings in other words – who burnt the little Saxon town in the C9. Thus Dean is a corruption of Dane and gate is a corruption of the Scandinavian word 'gata' meaning street.

After a short walk, you arrive at **John Rylands Library** (page 76). Just before the library, cross to the right and walk up the pedestrianised Brazennose Street to **Lincoln Square**. The square houses one of the oldest pubs in the city, the **Rising Sun**, and one of the best restaurants, **Wings**. The statue of Abraham Lincoln commemorates the letter of support Manchester sent Lincoln during the American Civil War. Manchester workers saw the war as a fight to preserve the Union but also to abolish slavery. Memories were fresh of the hideous conditions that had prevailed in the Lancashire factories earlier in the century. For many, the conditions had reduced them to a level comparable with the slaves in the USA. The letter was sent despite the Union blockade cutting off cotton supplies from the southern states and thus causing severe distress, including starvation, in the Manchester region.

Take the first left after the statue and you come to **St Mary's RC Church** (page 82). Retrace your steps to Deansgate and cross to John Rylands Library. Take the street to its right, Wood Street. A little way down is **Wood Street Mission**. This was founded in 1873 by Alfred Alsop to help the poor, particularly children. It has continued its mission ever since and still provides clothing, bedding and recreational activities. The streets off Deansgate were famously tough when Wood Street opened – there were said to be 46 brothels in the vicinity.

Between the Mission and Deansgate is a narrow cobbled alleyway under two bridges. Take this alleyway – it might be a tight fit between the wheelie bins here – following its dog-leg through to Bridge Street. As you exit, on your left is **Rational House**, containing a menswear shop called Richard Creme. It was near this site in 1848 that the first annual meeting of the Vegetarian Society took place – the menu consisted of such tasty courses as rice fritters, vegetables, blancmange, semolina and fruit juices.

Turn left down Bridge Street to the River Irwell. Just before the New Bailey Bridge, which was opened in 1783, is the **People's History Museum**. On the right of the bridge, down the steps, there is a statue to Joseph Brotherton, glowering at the other river bank. He was the first MP for Salford from 1832, but stands on the Manchester side of the river after Salford sold him off in an economy drive in the 1960s. He was also a cotton manufacturer and the first vegetarian MP. His wife Martha wrote one of the earliest vegetarian cookbooks in 1816 with over 1,000 recipes.

Double back and take the street on your first left called St Mary's Parsonage. Immediately after the fine tower block of the Inland Revenue from 1959 there is a path that leads to the spectacular **Trinity Bridge**, from 1996, by the celebrated Spanish engineer Santiago Calatrava, with on the Salford side the five-star **Lowry Hotel**. Stand in the centre of the bridge and you can see to your right a view of the Cathedral. In roughly the same area, Mark Addy was born in a rickety riverside house. Whilst helping out at his father's boat-hiring business, Addy rescued more than 50 people from the toxic soup that masqueraded as a river. After his last rescue of a child in 1889, he said, "to see the joy of his brother and sister when I brought them out, to feel their grip round my legs, and hear them thank me a hundred times, was more to me than all besides". Earlier he had been awarded the Albert Medal by Queen Victoria and had been given 200 guineas by the people of Salford. His death is said to have been hastened by swallowing so much filthy water.

The Argo and Golden Fleece, relief, St Ann's Square

Retrace your steps and turn left until you come to the little oasis of Parsonage Gardens. Turn right along the path by the side of the Gardens' wall. The latter was the graveyard wall of St Mary's Church, which was demolished in the 1890s when the houses gave way to offices. Turn first right down South Gate Street. Directly under the bridge linking the car park with the rear entrance to Kendals department store is the site of the **Ermin and Engels Office** where Frederick Engels, the German socialist and writer, worked. Engels considered the office environment his personal prison, but he was committed to providing his friend Karl Marx with enough subsidy to allow him to continue his studies in the British Library. In 1869, after almost 22 years, Engels celebrated his last day with a champagne dinner.

Continue down South Gate Street to King Street West and turn left to the junction with Deansgate. The building you have walked beside is **House of Fraser**, formerly Kendal, Milne and Faulkner. This was the city's first department store and has occupied more or less the same site since 1836 when it was called simply the Bazaar. The present building dates from 1939.

Cross over Deansgate and walk up pedestrianised King Street. The enjoyable variety of façades reflects the independent nature of the businesses in former times. Towards the top end of the pedestrianised part of King Street is a brick Georgian town house from 1736. In 1776 the house, now a shop, became a bank which in turn became the Manchester and Salford District Bank.

Double back and turn right through St Ann's Passage. The passage opens into the peaceful paved area around **St Ann's Church** (page 82). The square in front of St Ann's Church used to be called Acresfield. From 1227 it was the site of the town's annual fair. This took place over three days every September, largely for the sale of livestock. In those unsophisticated times, the inhabitants would gather on the opening day at the entrance to the field. When the first animal entered, they would pelt it with acorns and beat it with whips. Simple pleasures.

With your back to the church, on the opposite corner right, is the beautiful Rennaissance style Heywood's Bank (now the **Royal Bank of Scotland**) from 1848 by John Gregan, with next to it, down St Ann's Street, the brick and stone manager's house. The tall white Portland stone building in the same block but fronting the square was the offices of shippers, **Manchester Liners**. It carries a fabulous relief of the Argo with the Golden Fleece. In the square there is a statue of the free trader, Richard Cobden, a Boer War Memorial and a weak fountain by Peter Randall Page, 1996, in the shape of a cotton flower bud. Turn left from the War Memorial and walk to the Barton Arcade, built in 1871 by Corbett, Raby and Sawyer. Inside the arcade, light floods in from the airy domes whilst the delicate balconies seem to float over the shops. When the IRA bomb exploded in 1996 (page 29), every pane of glass was shattered.

Make your way back into St Ann's Square to visit the **Royal Exchange** (page 70). Return to St Ann's Square and walk across St Mary's Gate to New Cathedral Street, which runs alongside **Marks & Spencer** and **Selfridges**. The building they share was designed by Building Design Partnership (BDP). On the left of New Cathedral Street is the Shambles West development with more shops, including Harvey Nichols - also by BDP. On the extreme west is the huge glass shape of **No 1 Deansgate** apartments by Ian Simpson Architects.

The site occupied by Shambles West was for many centuries the Market Place – the heart of secular Manchester. Increasingly by-passed in the C19, it was effectively finished off by the Luftwaffe in December 1940. Here the conduit ran with claret on the occasion of Charles II's return from exile in 1660, here Bonnie Prince Charlie halted on his way through and out of England, here Captain Mouncey was killed in a duel with Cornet Hamilton, here the heads of traitors were displayed. More importantly here, away from great events, generations of countless Mancunians traded stories and goods and measured out their lives. For one of most remarkable tenants of the Market Place check the panel about Eizabeth Raffald in the Food and Drink section.

Follow Cathedral Street north to **Exchange Square**. The design of the square by New Yorker Martha Schwartz includes curving paths between heavy walls. On the higher ground to Corporation Street lie benches like the wheels of railway trains – a lame reference to Manchester's past. More interesting are the large but odd windmills slowly spinning on steel columns canted at different angles. If you walk down to the three outflow pipes of the water feature and turn, you may catch a reflection of the sandstone Corn Exchange – now the **Triangle Shopping Centre** – in the windows of Selfridges. Manchester Metropolitan University thought this resembled a huge sandcastle, so they stuck these out-sized beach windmills in front of it.

The water feature is the best part of the new square when it is working. This follows the course of Hanging Ditch, a long disappeared natural water course that emptied over a waterfall or rapids into the River Irwell a short way to the west. This watercourse, together with the Rivers Irwell and Irk, formed a defensible position protected on three sides, inside which Saxon and Medieval Manchester developed.

Proceed down to the pubs of **Sinclair's Oyster Bar** and the **Old Wellington Inn**. Both were moved down the hill from their original site because they were in the path of New Cathedral Street. This wasn't the first time they'd been moved – they were jacked up to fit with a new square in the 1960s. Sinclair's dates from the C18 and has a charmingly complicated interior floor plan full of nooks and crannies. For many years it was John Shaw's pub. His punch was so strong, you could only drink one pint if you were alone or a quart if in company. The city has a tradition that this is the derivation of the expression 'mind your Ps and Qs'. In the C19 it was frequented by Lady Spittlewick, whose pleasure it was to consume at least 40 oysters each day. This habit continued until, in her advanced years, Lady Spittlewick was rushed to the Infirmary where she died. She had choked on a pearl. The Old Wellington is one of the city's oldest buildings, dating from the 1530s, but not the oldest as the boards claim here. The original elements of the timber frame are in the darker wood. A trip to the third floor ceiling space is especially rewarding. John Byrom, poet, wit and inventor of a phonetic system of shorthand, was born in the building.

Turn left in front of The Old Wellington and the Mitre Hotel and walk past the

Cathedral Visitor's Centre (page 79) with its medieval bridge beneath, to Victoria Street. Cross to Victoria Bridge, where Manchester and Salford kiss. The River Irwell swirls below. Note how high and proud the Cathedral sits above the waters – a good place to defend. It was around this point where the 'ford' of Salford lay. The first bridge was probably wooden-built a thousand years ago. This last was finished in 1839 and dedicated to Queen Victoria – note the royal orbs at the centre of each side. It was officially opened 12 years later by the Queen herself. A typesetter at *The Times* was dismissed when he couldn't resist amending the line 'Her Majesty passed over the bridge and duly declared it open'. He changed the 'a' in 'passed' to an 'i'. The bridge was also an important meeting and market place.

Retrace your steps to the Cathedral (page 78) and walk past the rear of the Old Wellington pub to Cathedral Street and turn left. Cross over Fennel Street to Long Millgate. The building rising on the right is **Urbis** (page 100). Note the undulating gardens here with their water features and rare trees by BDP.

Continue on Long Millgate, past **Chetham's School and Library** (page 74), to **Victoria Station**. The long façade of 1904 is impressive enough, but the delight is in the detail. The outside canopy of delicate glass and iron, advertising destinations from Bolton to Belgium, is a joy. So is the interior white tile map of the former rail routes over a vigorous war memorial incorporating St George and St Michael. The panelled booking offices are as sturdy as ever, and the vast interior all the better for the blue and gold mosaic advertising the former services. The domed restaurant, decorated with a riot of fruit and other goodies, is also a treat. Attached to the station is the monolithic **MEN Arena** (1995). The best part, the impressive inner amphitheatre, has seating for 20,000 and plays host to major visiting acts and occasional sporting events.

Between Victoria Station and Chetham's lies the steep slope down to Walkers Croft. This cobbled street lies over a culverted River Irk. Walk up Todd Street to Corporation Street and cross over. The complex of buildings here form part of the co-operative movement: banking, insurance, retailing, undertaking etc, amounting to around £6bn in value. The first successful co-operative was created in Rochdale in 1844, with the headquarters moving here later in the century. Walk in front of the **Co-operative Bank** to the statue of Robert Owen. Owen was a pioneer of co-operation and also an astute businessman. At 20 years of age, he was a manager at one of the city's cotton factories. Later he moved north and built New Lanark Mills, near Glasgow.

If you appreciate the progressive architecture of the sixties follow Corporation Street to Miller Street and then turn right. Here is, first, **New Century House** and then the cloud tickling **Co-operative Insurance Society** tower, both dating from 1962 by Hay and Burnet, Tait and Partners. In terms of quality, the 25-storey CIS tower knocks the rest of the 1960s city skyscrapers into a cocked hat. From viewpoints all around, it hunches over the northern end of the city centre like a eagle over its eyrie. This is appropriate as nature has made a return to the city here in the form of peregrine falcons. Take a trip to the top floor of Ian Simpson Architects 'superb, crystal-like multi-storey car park behind the CIS and watch the birds dive

Old Wellington Inn and Sinclair's Oyster Bar

bombing pigeons from the top of the tower. By the way, the service block is blue because it's been covered in photo-voltaic panels which convert daylight into energy.

Retrace your steps back down Corporation Street, past the **Printworks** leisure complex, through Exchange Square to the red postbox under the splendid twisted bridge by Stephen Hodder. The postbox has been moved slightly since 1996, when it was smack next to the van full of 3,500lb of explosives that devastated the city centre. As the blast crumpled walls and windows for hundreds of metres around, the 100-year-old postbox seems to have occupied some magical eye of the storm. Aside from paint scratches, it stood firm. A few days later a postman picked his way through the rubble, removed the letters and parcels and sent them on their way. If you really want to ensure your post arrives then this is the box for you.

Part 2

Start the walk from the junction of Back Pool Fold and Cross Street. Back Pool Fold is a very atmospheric and narrow alleyway. The name refers to the moat of Radcliffe Hall, which was formerly in this area. The moat was the location for Manchester's ducking stool. This was an open-bottomed chair attached to a pole, which could be levered over blocks into the moat, thus ducking the miscreant in the water. It was used to punish 'lewde women and scoldes': prostitutes and women who tampered with weights and measures in the market place. Many of these entertaining little passages between the major streets are medieval in origin, following old paths along field boundaries.

Walk up the alleyway and then turn right, down Chapel Walks, past Grinch bar to Cross Street. The modern office block on your left contains, on the ground floor, the Unitarian **Cross Street Chapel**. This little place has exercised an enormous influence on the city. At its heyday in the C19 there were probably no more than 2,000 members of the congregation, yet the chapel provided the city with its first five mayors and the region with 12 MPs. One of the ministers was the Rev. William Gaskell, the husband of the novelist Elizabeth Gaskell. Another member of the Congregation was Thomas Potter, who was a principal sponsor of the *Manchester Guardian* when it was established in 1821, price 7d.

Turn left on Cross Street. The charming little pub on your right is **Mr Thomas's Chop House**, rebuilt in the present style in 1901. This little terracotta gem has a wonderful green tiled interior and is a great place for lunch. On your left after **Lloyds Bank** is King Street. The bank occupies the site of the original Manchester Town Hall from 1825 until 1877 when the administration moved to the present building. Previously the site was occupied by the town house of Doctor Charles White (1728-1813). White was instrumental in establishing the first hospital in Manchester, the Infirmary. He was also a noted physician and obstetrician – his advocacy of fresh water and air greatly reduced mortality rates amongst women after they had given birth.

The next building up King Street, on the same side, is a striking black structure in tooled Swedish granite. It dates from 1969 and was formerly the **NatWest Bank** by Casson and Conder. The architects wanted the bank to merge in with all the other smoke-darkened buildings around but their worthy ambition was made nonsense when the other buildings were cleaned. The NatWest has been converted at ground level into up-market shops, a process that underway throughout the length of the street. At one time this was purely the domain of finance and commerce: the splendid introduction into what was known as the 'Half Square Mile' in mimicry of London's 'Square Mile.' Technology, bank mergers and the changing needs of modern finance have left these buildings seeking new uses. Across the road is CR Cockerell's handsome classical building from 1846, formerly the **Bank of England**. This was the first provincial branch of the bank. It is now shops and offices. Attached to its rear is the 82 King Street tower from Holford Associates in 1995.

Further up, on the right, is the massive **Ship Canal House** by Harry Fairhurst from 1929 in Portland stone. The bronze doors are particularly impressive. The problem of Manchester's street pattern denying good views of the city is graphically illustrated here: you have to lean at a spine endangering angle to get any view of the statue of Neptune at its roofline. Attached to Ship Canal House is Collezione Armani in the old Atlas Insurance building. Again the doors are magnificent, capped with a pained-looking Atlas hoisting the world. The top of the street is finished off with two very different buildings. On one side there is the pure white slice of towering efficiency that is Edwin Luytens' Midland Bank from 1929, now **HSBC Bank**. This clever structure reduces telescopically as it climbs to the pavilions on its roof. If the bank is open, go in and have a look at the columns all capped with little bells on the capitals – a Lutyens' trademark. On the other side is the old **Reform Club** building in a style called Venetian Gothic from 1871. This mad piece of High Victoriana has wild turrets on the two front corners, sculptured panels, granite pillars and carvings writhing all over its surface. Its architect was Edward Salomons. It was built as the city headquarters for the Liberal Party. On the first floor is a balcony from which such figures as William Gladstone and Winston Churchill spoke during election campaigns. Behind the balcony is the magnificent dining room of the club with its huge oak ceiling, now Room Restaurant.

King Street terminates with the former bank of the Lancashire and Yorkshire Bank. Take the street to the right, Spring Gardens, down to Fountain Street. Both these locations take their name from the fresh water supply of the early town and city that bubbled up out of the fields here. Cross Fountain Street to Mosley Street. Over the road here is the classical **Portico Library** (page 78). Continue left down Mosley Street past one of the finest C19 buildings in the city from 1860 by Edward Walters. Formerly the Manchester and Salford Bank, this is now the **Royal Bank of Scotland** and is a model of elaborate Classical detailing working in rhythm to produce a lovely Italianate building. Architects Harry S Fairhurst added the sympathetic addition to the south in 1975.

Continue up Mosley Street past Primark to the **Abbey National Bank** on the corner with Market Street. The bank occupies part of the Royal Buildings built on the site of the Royal Hotel where the world's first professional football league was set up in 1888.

Turn right across the tramlines to the Victorian statues on the north side of **Piccadilly Gardens**. Here in a row you'll find Robert Peel (1853), reforming Prime Minister and local man, James Watt (1857), the important steam engineer, and the Duke of Wellington (1856), national hero of Waterloo. Sitting inside a neo-Baroque canopy of white limestone is a terrifying statue of Queen Victoria in full regalia – the stern matriarch of nation and Empire.

The Gardens have been completely redesigned by the internationally renowned team of Tadao Andao. The sunken gardens have gone, replaced by a fountain – beloved of children – and a level green sward. This is finished by the simple curved wall of bare concrete complete with two glass pavilions - aggressive stuff, especially from the bus station side. The jury of opinion, even that of aesthetic opinion, is still out. But far worse is the brick office block on the east side from Allies and Morrison of London. This is the wrong colour, in the wrong place and for such a key site remarkably dull.

The Gardens were previously the less attractively named Daub Holes, where

HSBC formerly Midland Bank

clay was taken to make bricks for the early town. In 1755 the present Gardens area was donated by the then Lord of the Manor, Sir Oswald Mosley, for the building of a new Infirmary. The site was cleared in 1909 when the overcrowded Infirmary decamped south to the present university area.

North of this point up Oldham and Tib Street is the **Northern Quarter** with its many artworks. You might want to make a detour to this colourful area to take in the independent, often creative, businesses and the curry cafés etc. The street scene is in transition here with the decrepit side by side with the rejuvenated. There are numerous artworks in the area to emphasise the creative spirit. Some of the more obvious include the massive *Tib Street Horn* by David Kemp perched on the bay window of an old ruined warehouse at the junction of Tib Street and Church Street. Opposite on Afflecks Palace, large and literal lightbulbs flower in the dark early evenings of winter. Further along, the dreary multi-storey car park has been improved with humourous tiled reliefs by Estelle Hayes, depicting the long gone circus. Up above, the bridge link has been filled with coloured glass by Martin Donlin, referring to the street's past and present. Higher again is the *Neon Light Tower*, an icon for the Northern Quarter from Peter Freeman. The street name tiles come from Tim Rushton and Majolica Works. The blue letters on white are for north and south, while white letters on blue are for east and west streets. Tim Rushton has also produced *Soundbites*, on Oldham Street, near Dry Bar. Metal pavement plaques here contain allusions to the city's pop heritage. A particularly lovely work is Kate Malone's ceramic pineapple – a symbol of welcome and warmth – high atop an old building on Thomas Street

Watts Warehouse, now the Britannia Hotel

To return to the walk, the 1960s skyline on the south west side of Piccadilly Gardens was part of the belated redevelopment of bomb-damaged property from World War II. The buildings, now being refurbished, were called collectively **Piccadilly Plaza** and were designed by Covell, Matthews and Partners and finished in 1965. They are being rebranded and rewrapped as this guide goes to print. They will still be cumbersome and hard to love after the changes.

Cross through the gardens, under the new pavilion, and turn left to Portland Street and then right. You can't miss the **Britannia Hotel** on the west side of the road here. This vast building was formerly the S&J Watts warehouse which, occupying the whole city block, was always the biggest of the city's sole occupancy textile warehouses. It cost £100,000 in 1857/8 and the architects were Travis and Mangnall. Each floor has a different architectural treatment with Egyptian at the base rising through Italian Renaissance, Elizabethan and French Renaissance to four great roof projections lit by rose windows. It's worth going inside to see the magnificent iron cantilever staircase rising from ground to top floor and the moving memorials to employees killed in the World Wars. In its heyday, the warehouse would process the 1,000 large to small orders received each morning by close of business. In 1867, a journalist from *Freelance* magazine expressed his astonishment on encountering the building: 'I am not naturally of a sceptical or suspicious cast of mind. I have eaten sausages and kidney pudding without asking questions but when I was told that this was only a warehouse, I felt that it was necessary to draw the line of credulity somewhere.'

In December 1940, the whole area was hit by incendiary bombs. With the cotton bales blazing at thousands of degrees, many buildings were consumed, whilst others were demolished to prevent the fire spreading.

One of those that had to be sacrificed was the S&J Watts warehouse. The decision was passed to Chief Fireman Wilf Beckett of the company's own brigade. He refused to budge. Incredulous, the authorities cut off the supply of water to Beckett. The little volunteer force then fought the fires with blankets and sheets until the temperatures outside cooled. In 1941 the building received direct hits once more, and again Beckett and his band saved the day. Later that year he was honoured, on behalf of his men, at Buckingham Palace.

Follow Portland Street south until you encounter on the right a delightful row of buildings, which include the **Circus** and **Grey Horse** pubs. All the smaller older buildings here used to be pubs as well. At third floor level, long rows of windows allow increased light into what was a workshop – usually for the intricate task of handloom weaving. The Circus is, inside and out, a remarkable survival of a modest C19 city pub and has probably the smallest bar in the country.

From the Circus, walk to the junction and turn right down Princess Street and then right again down Faulkner Street. Ahead is the **Chinese Arch**. This structure from 1987 is decorated in red and gold dragons and phoenixes: colours and symbols of luck and prosperity. Erected as a token of friendship between the Chinese people and Manchester, it was the first true Imperial Chinese arch in Europe.

Manchester's **Chinatown** dates from 1970s, as the warehouses in the area gradually became redundant the restaurants moved in. This in turn led to a corresponding growth in the services developed to serve them and their customers. This became more pronounced when the area became the focus for the Chinese community in the whole of the north of England, with medicine shops, health centres, financial and legal service providers, shops, supermarkets and Sunday schools. In this way, Manchester's Chinatown has become the Chinese village for the north of England. This role has been enhanced with creation of several old people's homes in the city centre. One of the city's major festivals is Chinese New Year, when thousands of spectators and performers come together to follow the biggest dancing dragon in Europe. Whilst in Chinatown, make sure you pop into some of the supermarkets – and if you fancy a snack, the honey buns from Ho's Bakery on Faulkner Street are legendary.

Return to Princess Street and turn right to St Peter's Square, and the Tourist Information Centre passing **Manchester Art Gallery** (page 109). The little gardens in the square here are called the **Peace Gardens**. In 1980, with the Cold War at its height, the then City Council decided in their wisdom to declare Manchester the world's first 'nuclear-free city'. This meaningless gesture was commemorated here by the gardens and a sculpture. The latter is *Messenger of Peace* by Barbara Pearson, an Earth Mother surrounded by Doves – locals have christened this *Woman Feeding the Pigeons*.

Part 3

Start from the Visitors Information Centre and turn right and then right again through the arcade of the **Town Hall Extension** (page 70). Cross through the Metrolink tram station to your left and into the Memorial Gardens and onto the **Cenotaph**. This last was the work of Sir Edwin Lutyens in 1924. The Portland Stone of the monument has weathered exposing the fossils within. In the memorial Gardens there is a cross incorporating angels holding the keys to heaven. This commemorates the church of St Peter which was demolished in 1907.

The Oxford Street/Peter Street axis has

The Chinese Arch

been a centre for entertainment for the last 150 years and continues to be so today with the Library and Palace Theatres and so on.

Proceed left with your back to the Cenotaph down Oxford Street. A little way down on your right is the façade of **Prince's Buildings**, built in 1903, by I Birkett. This is a fabulous display of buff terracotta with Art Nouveau details, terminating in tall chimneys linked by delicate semi-circular loops. In many of the later warehouses, insurers, worried by the risk of fires specified that flues and chimneys had to be separated and placed on the building edges to lessen the risk and give greater access to the fire services.

Continue over Portland Street and cross to the right hand side of Oxford Street. On the right in the middle of Great Bridgewater Street is an example of how buildings in Manchester get recycled. The underground bar here called the, **The Temple**, is a former gentleman's urinal. You can flush out some good tunes on the excellent jukebox. The modern building with the Chinese restaurant on the north side of Great Bridgewater Street lies on the site of the former Manchester Hippodrome. Wigan entertainer George Formby found early success here. His affection for the venue continued after his death, when a reproduction of the proscenium arch of the Hippodrome was

Palace Hotel, formerly the Refuge Assurance

placed over his grave during his funeral. Formby's brand of bawdy humour was typical of the music halls. Thus from *The Window Cleaner*: 'The blushing bride she looks divine/ the bridegroom he's doing fine/ I'd rather have his job than mine/ when I'm cleaning windows.'

For **St James' Buildings** on the other side of Oxford Street see page 23. On this side is **Churchgate House**, a splendid lump of stripy terracotta, pink brick and chubby attached columns from 1898 by Gibbon Sankey. It was the headquarters and warehouse of Tootal, Broadhurst and Lee and includes a war memorial on the stairwell to the company employees who were killed in the World Wars.

Further down Oxford Street on the left, over the Rochdale Canal, is the **Palace Theatre**. Refaced in 1956 it contains a lovely Victorian auditorium from 1891. Charlie Chaplain has appeared on the stage, as have a whole roster of top-flight stars including Frank Sinatra and Manchester band, the Smiths. Cross over Whitworth Street West and walk up Oxford Road Station Approach between the **Cornerhouse** and the Cornerhouse Cinema. **Oxford Road Station** is one of the best buildings from the second half of the C20 in Manchester. It was designed by Headley and Glendinning and opened in 1960. Some people have enthusiastically compared the roofline to a scaled down Sydney Opera House. The surviving furniture and ceilings, full of sweeping laminated timber, are perfect for a station, creating the impression of movement.

Leaving the station, double back, and follow the viaduct to the right and then down the steep flight of steps to the cobbled street below. Turn left after the Salisbury pub into James Leigh Street. This was a vision of hell in the 1840s. Extending south was an area nicknamed **Little Ireland**. Here by the banks of the open sewer which was the River Medlock, Irish immigrants settled, driven by their poverty to the worst areas of the city. 4,000 people lived in 200 cottages often with livestock. Human and animal waste choked the streets, fresh water was difficult to find and mortality rates through the damp, insanitary conditions were high. Little Ireland was largely swept away by the railway when it pushed through the area in 1849.

Return to Oxford Road. On the other side is the massive bulk of the **Palace Hotel**, formerly the Refuge Assurance building. One of the most colourful descriptions ever given to a Manchester building is that of Professor CR Reilly's early in the C20. According to him it resembled 'a tall young man in flannel trousers escorting two charming but delicate old ladies in lace.'

Cross Oxford Street carefully and take a closer look at the Palace Hotel. Constructed for one of the most prominent insurers, it rose, to the designs of Alfred Waterhouse, his son Paul and Stanley Birkett, between 1891 and 1930. Above the original entrance on the corner of Oxford Street and Whitworth Street is a terracotta castle indicating that customers' money was safe with the company. Just inside the porch on the corner is a splendid display of tilework. The main lounge, formerly the banking hall, is worth visiting for more beautiful tilework and is also a grand place to take refreshment. You might spot around the doorways the initials, RA, of the company baked into the tiles. The closing scene of classic British film noir, *Hell is a City* with Stanley Baker was filmed on the roof of the Refuge in 1959.

Walk down Whitworth Street away from the Cornerhouse. This is a magnificent street, a deep canyon of terracotta. Most of the buildings were constructed in the building boom following the opening of Manchester Ship Canal in 1894. Two of the biggest warehouses on the street are the last two on the right before the junction with Princess Street, **India House** and **Lancaster House**. Both of these terracotta and brick leviathians have been converted to apartments. They were designed by Harry S Fairhurst in 1906. He placed the best example of Art Nouveau work in the city centre between them in the form of a twisted and evil looking lamp. The gate describes a perfect circle when closed.

If the gates are open, walk between them to the fence high over the River Medlock. This has one of the great dark views of the city. The backs of the warehouse spread west along the river banks, the 1849 viaduct strides across the middle foreground, whilst below the muddy waters of the river trickle between broken brick, filthy silt and weeds. Below to the right, under the wall, you stand upon, is the culvert for Shooter's Brook, which became so soiled it was known as Shitter's Brook.

Back on Whitworth Street, the building over the road at the junction with Princess Street is **Dominion House**, a former textile warehouse playfully designed to look like a Scottish Castle. Turn right down Princess Street and then second left along Granby Row. The two warehouses on the right are by Goldsmith. The first is **Orient House** from 1914, its Classical façade anticipating a Hollywood movie set of Imperial Rome. This is a typical example of Manchester 'fur coat no knickers architecture': a fancy façade to attract custom and then tucked round the back a functional, cost-effective, grid of glass and concrete.

Cross over Sackville Street on Granby Row. On the left is the large block of the **University of Manchester**. The oldest part is from 1902 and was the Manchester Technical College built in response to growing competition from Germany and America challenging Britain's industrial ascendancy. On the right is a big timber bottle by Kerry Morrison in the gardens marking the invention of the Manchester soft drink, Vimto, on this site in 1908. This was a herbal drink intended as a temperance refreshment and named after the contemporary phrase vip and vim: thus vim and tonic, Vimto. It's a shame that the anagram is vomit.

Return to Sackville Street and turn right. Cross over Whitworth Street and into Sackville Gardens, and to the statue of Alan Turing. For a fuller description of the area see the Gay and Lesbian section from page 264. Cross over the Rochdale Canal which came through here in 1804 and turn left down Canal Street to the junction with Princess Street and turn right. This presents another strong palazzo warehouse streetscape, see page 23. A short way up on the right is the former **Mechanics Institute** from 1854 by J Gregan. In here the Trades Union Congress came together for the first time in 1868.

Continue up Princess Street, over Portland Street, to St Peter's Square and the start point at the Visitor's Centre.

Key buildings

The main public and religious buildings of the city centre

QUICK-FIX

Style: Victorian Gothic
When: Opened 1877
Architect: Alfred Waterhouse
Why visit: 'A classic of its age', the embodiment of a High Victorian building

The Great Hall >

Manchester Town Hall

Albert Square, City 0161 234 5000 6E
FREE *Mon-Fri 9am-4.30pm (phone ahead for weekend entry)*

Completed in 1877, this Alfred Waterhouse building is also Manchester's greatest monument. For many, it is a candidate for the Victorian building par excellence – the whole age summed up in one: the extravagance, the energy, the self-belief and the achievement. At the opening banquet, MP John Bright described the way the city

Alfred Waterhouse

This architect was the perfect Victorian, both through his principles and in the coincidence of his life span (1830-1905) which almost exactly matched the duration of Queen Victoria's reign (1837-1901). Born in Liverpool, he studied architecture in Manchester under fellow Quaker Richard Lane. After setting up a practice in 1853, his first big success came in 1859 (he was just 29) when he won the competition for the new Assize Courts in Manchester. There was no holding him back after that. In Manchester he built major buildings such as the Town Hall, Strangeways Prison and the main University block, and in London he designed the Natural History Museum. The nation is stamped with Waterhouse buildings. He was President of the Royal Society of British Architects from 1888-91, and was a kindly man, married twice and fathering 12 children.

felt about the new building: 'With regard to this edifice, it is truly a municipal palace. Whether you look at the proportions outside or the internal decorations…there is nothing like it…in any part of Europe.'

The first-time visitor coming into Albert Square from Cross Street or Lloyd Street might well agree. A cliff of ornate Gothic stonework drags the eyes upward to the giant clock tower above – the minute hand is 3m in length and spire 87m above ground level.

On the top of the spire is a golden ball with spikes symbolising a cotton bud about to burst, but also the sun, for wherever the sun shone Manchester had business, the cotton trade for instance was international. The roofline is a wonderland of pinnacles, gables, chimneys and metalwork.

The city is lucky to have the building. In the competition judged on St Valentine's Day 1868, Alfred Waterhouse's design ranked only fourth in terms of appearance, but was superior to the others in its practical use of the awkward triangular site and the best in its handling of light, access and ventilation. The style chosen was Gothic from the C13th – a style called Early English and seen as patriotic. Gothic was also intended to form a link with the medieval trader cities of the Hanseatic League and of the Low Countries, from where legend said that Manchester's textile roots had sprung. Manchester was being fashionable too, adopting the in-vogue Gothic style in conscious contrast with the Classical style favoured by Liverpool.

The celebrations for the opening in September 1877 extended over several days, and included a procession of cavalry and infantry, police force and fire brigades, a banquet, a ball and a gathering of over 40,000 local working men with examples of their crafts. The outpouring of feeling was reinforced by the fact that the city was desperate for a new Town Hall. Manchester by 1877 had become a city state. It controlled the local administration, the gas, the water, the police, the education, the parks and roads, and it was rich. The full construction cost of over £1m was met by the rate-payers.

If the Town Hall looks familiar, it may be because it's the TV and movie body double for the Palace of Westminster (Houses of Parliament) for dramas such as *House of Cards* and *State of Play*.

The Town Hall is still the focus for civic events and remains the political and administrative centre of the city.

Tours take place on many Saturdays from the Visitor Information Centre in the Town Hall Extension, St Peter's Square, at 2pm. You can tour the Town Hall on your own but you will have to sign in at one of the reception desks, where you will be given a security badge and told which rooms can be visited. Watch out for the weddings which may impede tours. The Town Hall, given its memorable architecture, provides a popular backdrop for marriage.

VICTORIAN DREAMING – a tour round the Town Hall

Before entering, take a walk around the building to get a full idea of its size and ingenuity. All four sides are different, each with varied treatments of stonework and statuary. On the corner of Princess Street and Albert Square, statues of key characters (1) from the city's history stare down at passers-by. Waterhouse cleverly placed a statue of General Agricola, the Roman who founded Manchester in 79AD, over the main doorway. The city's introduction into history introducing its main building.

Enter and you find yourself walking directly under the great tower and a ceiling decorated with the Royal Coat of Arms (2). This ceiling is a disguised trapdoor through which the bells of the Town Hall can be raised or lowered. On each side is a statue commemorating two of the city's most important scientists: John Dalton (3), atomic theory, colour blindness and meteorology, and James Prescott Joule, physics. The main entrance chamber lies to the right and is now the Sculpture Hall with works commemorating famous people or events. Take the staircase to the right of the reception desk. As you climb the stairs, notice the stylised constellations above (4).

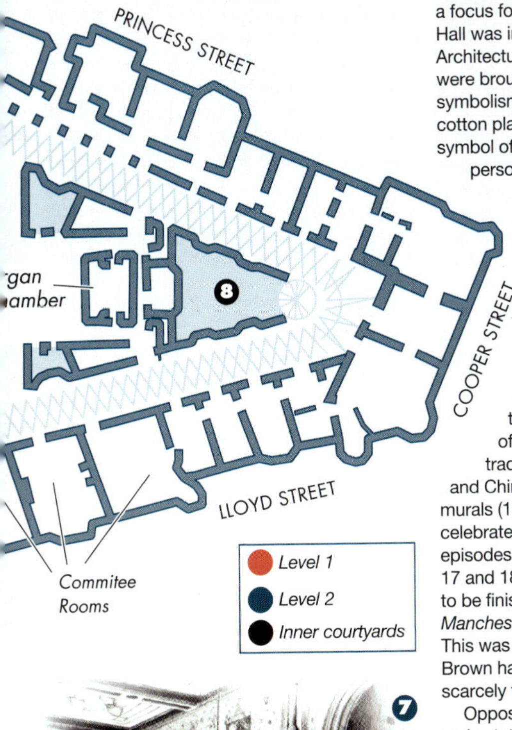

Aside from the practical aspect of providing a focus for the city administration, the Town Hall was intended to be a unified piece of art. Architecture, fine arts, sculpture and music were brought together amidst a mass of symbolism (5). Throughout, the visitor will spot cotton plants, flowers and bees the latter a symbol of the city's industrious hardworking personality. For instance, on the landing at the top of the stairs, there is a simple pattern in mosaic of bees (6) and cotton flowers. Push open the wooden doors to your right here and enter the Great Hall (see illustration, pg 66), which John Ruskin called 'the most truly magnificent Gothic apartment in Europe'. Above, in the panels of the great hammerbeam roof, there are richly gilded coats of arms of the nations with which Manchester traded, including the USA, Russia, India and China. On the walls are the famous 12 murals (1879-1893) by Ford Madox Brown, the celebrated Pre-Raphaelite artist, illustrating episodes in Manchester's history (see pages 17 and 18 for examples of these). The last to be finished was *Bradshaw's Defence of Manchester AD 1642* in the English Civil War. This was painted with the artist's left hand after Brown had suffered a stroke. The viewer can scarcely tell.

Opposite the Great Hall are the elaborate main staterooms. These are saturated with all the decoration and detail the High Victorians adored. They are all worth visiting, but perhaps the two most impressive are at either end. The present Conference Hall (7) was originally the Council Chamber. It contains a vast Gothic chimney piece, the Lord Mayor's chair, an oak screen and galleries for the press and public. The Banqueting Hall has a minstrels' gallery and curtains from the Royal School of Art Needlework, South Kensington.

Pause to look into the inner courtyards (8), and you will gain a vision of Manchester in its industrial glory and grime. The stonework has never been cleaned and is black – coated in soot spewed from numberless chimneys.

KEY BUILDINGS

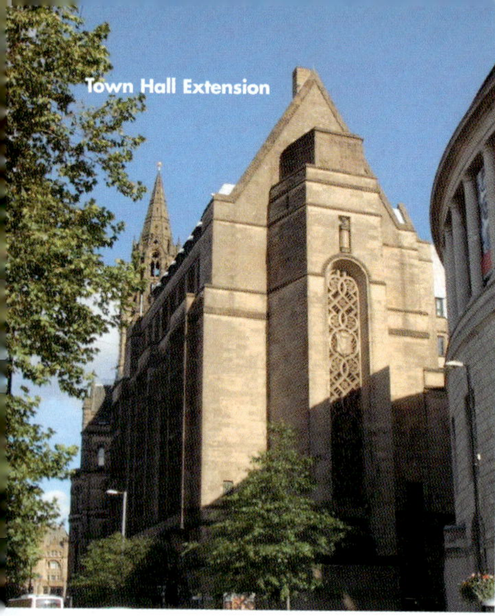

KEY BUILDINGS

Town Hall Extension 5E

Lloyd Street, City 0161 234 5000
(Call ahead for permission to visit)

Linked to the Town Hall by elegant bridges over Lloyd Street is the Town Hall Extension. This was opened in 1938 and was designed by Vincent Harris. It was intended to link the Gothic of the Town Hall with the Classical design of the Central Library, between which the Extension is sandwiched. The building has an unusual shape and odd decorations. It is an exciting structure with sheer sides and immense gabled ends with carved shields and vast crawling designs of roses, thistles and shamrocks - the symbols of Great Britain's component countries except Wales. Inside is the current Council Chamber. The Ante Room for this is the most dramatic Art Deco interior in the city. with studded leather doors like a '30s Hollywood set of the Alhambra.

Albert Memorial 5E

Albert Square, City

This dates from 1867 and was designed by Thomas Worthington. Inside is a statue of Prince Albert by Matthew Noble. Manchester had always liked the German consort of Queen Victoria, after all Albert appreciated the need for industrial progress. The memorial, which predates Gilbert Scott's in London, is swathed in heraldry and sculptured details including Art holding a pen and scroll, Commerce resting upon a ship's prow and other idealised representations of the Prince's interests. Also in the Square, again by Thomas Worthington, is the dramatic Jubilee Fountain from 1897, marking Queen Victoria's 60th year on the throne. This was adapted from an earlier, simpler structure, placed here to mark the opening of a new fresh water supply from Thirlmere in the Lake District in 1891.

Royal Exchange 6C

Entrances on Cross Street & St Ann's Square, City FREE *Mon–Sat 10am until late in evening. Limited entry from St Ann's Square during theatrical performances*

'Who would find eternal treasure, must use no guile in weight or measure' – words around the dome of the trading hall.

This impressive Classical structure contains a shopping centre, arcade and offices. The principal feature, though, lies up the grand staircases on either side. Here, under three huge domes of coloured glass and supported on massive Corinthian columns, lies the biggest room in the north of England, formerly the main trading room of the global cotton industry. For a time at the end of the C19 and the beginning of the C20, the Royal Exchange controlled over 80% of the world trade in finished cloth. It is a symbol of the dramatic rise of cotton in Manchester and its equally dramatic fall.

The first Exchange was built in 1729. As the years passed, the established market days became Tuesdays and Fridays when members would meet to do business and swap news. The Exchange (known as 'Change) was expanded and rebuilt on several occasions and attracted manufacturers, merchants, engineers, shippers, bankers and insurers. Each column was marked on one side with letters and on the other with numbers. Members would occupy a position indicated by the intersection of letters and numbers, like a map reference. Thus the textile machinery company of J&H Schofield Limited would meet at J2. Business would spill out onto the streets and into the neighbouring cafés and pubs. It was an international gathering and dazzling whilst it lasted.

By the late 1920s, the Royal Exchange had a worldwide membership of 11,000. Its position seemed assured, but the clouds were gathering over the cotton industry. During the Second World War, the building was severely damaged by bombs. Rebuilding took 13 years, and the hall size was reduced by almost half. Worse still was the growth of the industry in countries that produced the raw material, frequently with cheaper labour costs. It soon became clear that the Exchange was no longer viable, and when the doors closed on 31 December 1968, 249 years of history closed with them.

The city was faced with the dilemma of what to do with the building. The shops and offices around the shell produced good rents, but the central hall had lost its function. A theatre was proposed and, after a long battle, Laurence Olivier announced "I declare this theatre… open!" on 15 September 1976. It has been a success ever since, acclaimed for its range of productions, its talented actors, and for the excellence and immediacy of its in-the-round auditorium. The design is a bold response to the potentially overwhelming space around it. High-tech and powerful, supported from the pillars on

▲ This picture shows a packed day at the Royal Exchange in the 1920s. During the same period, HV Morton, writing in the *Daily Express*, followed a trader as he moved through the crowd.

'As I look down with a feint Olympic feeling from the Strangers' Gallery I try to follow one little man through his adventures on the floor. I see him moving through the monster, a part of it, yet to me the most important part of it because I am thinking of him as an individual and I watch him stop at various groups, edge his way, say his little bit and move on, watching, searching, trying to make money, and the whole thing so casual, so removed from roll-top desks and all the paraphernalia of the business.

'He stops to make a joke. Someone tells him a joke that makes him laugh just a little bit too much. He is anxious to please. Now he looks grave, and rubs his chin with his little hand and shakes his little head. Did someone try to sell him a pup? Sometimes a man comes to him or rather seems swept up against him in the chaos, and they bring out notebooks and look solemn. They have booked an order. He is, I am sure, having a good day. He is a cheerful little man. I watch him tell the same story time after time in different groups. Often I see him standing politely waiting until a conversation ends before he introduces himself. 'Change is the only place in Manchester where a man will not butt into a conversation, no matter how much he wants to. It is not done. And the little man, just as I am beginning to like him, just as I begin to hope that he is kind to his wife and always takes her home presents, when his pencil has been busy on 'Change, goes and loses himself in the rather grim impersonality of the monster. And the voice of cotton goes on and on and on…'

the sides, it nestles like a lunar module under the great dome. It was the work of Richard Negri with Levitt Bernstein Associates.

The bombs returned with the IRA attack in June 1996. Two years and £30m later, the building reopened after repairs and improvements. The theatre was enlarged to take over 750 people and a studio theatre for 150 was created. The eating and drinking facilities were also extended, and purpose-built space provided for the bookshop and the crafts centre. Meanwhile, the upper reaches of the hall, which had been obscured under decades of dust and dirt, were lightened and revealed. Of particular note are the columns with their golden capitals and the glass panels by Amber Hiscott, representing textiles in a variety of shades. Look out for the former trading board close to the ceiling on the western side of the room.

The exterior dates from during and after the First World War by Bradshaw, Gas and Hope. This is covered with reliefs referring to the city as the capital of world cotton.

For a couple of years in the '80s, an associate director of the theatre was Ian McDiarmid, famous for his role as the evil Emperor in the *Star Wars* movies. Careful if you view the display boards on the south side of the chamber - that's the Dark Side.

Bridgewater Hall 5F

Lower Mosley Street, City 0161 907 9000

www.bridgewater-hall.co.uk FREE

From 10am every day, except Sunday

The Bridgewater Hall looks best when illuminated through its various levels during evening performances. High up in the transparent prow, people move between the bars or stand chatting or leaning on the window rails, staring at you staring at them.

The Hall opened in September 1996 and is the home to the Hallé Orchestra, the Manchester Camerata and, oft-times, the BBC Philharmonic. It was the first free-standing concert hall built in the UK since 1951, and is the work of Nicholas Thompson working for RHWL. Quality materials were used throughout, stratified in geological layers. Taken from the canal arm, red sandstone rises from the water through limestone, metal and glass to a steel crown. A mixture of moods was required, thus after the drama of the great glass prow, you enter a cool, gentle interior. In the main entrance area, the visitor should walk straight to the reception desk then turn and look up. Above rises the most impressive feature of the building - the inclined plane of the auditorium wall soaring back over the viewer. On the surface, Derryk Healey has applied a flowing artwork that is intended to resemble the warp threads on a giant loom.

The auditorium, the sacred centre, is entered through heavy, bronze, temple-like doorways. The design of the room is a cross between the traditional shoe-box style of the older concert halls and the more modern vineyard technique where the seats fall in receding terraces. Up on high are the

tremendous steel knuckles and mesh pattern of the ceiling supports. At the far end is the elegant organ from the Marcusson company in Denmark. The attractive seats are clever – tipped up with the auditorium empty, they reflect the music back to the performers on stage as though they are playing to a full house.

Beneath the auditorium is the spooky undercroft. During tours, you can view the huge springs that support the auditorium. These prevent traffic noise and vibrations from the nearby trams from penetrating into the concert hall. Even the stairs are broken by a couple of centimetres to prevent sound transmitting up them. The silence is total.

The auditorium can only be accessed if rehearsals or performances aren't taking place. Tours take place at various times and cost £5 per head - book ahead through the box office. A visit any time is pleasant, especially to the bar overlooking the canal.

▲ The Bridgewater Hall was part of a scheme for the redevelopment of the whole area, including the creation of a quayside along the route of the old Manchester and Salford Junction Canal. Over the canal, reflected in its waters, is the brick cotton warehouse of Chepstow House, built by Sam Mendel in the 1870s. Mendel claimed he was the fastest shipper of cotton around Cape Horn to India and Australia. A year after completing the warehouse, the Suez Canal opened and Mendel went bust. His possesions were sold at auction by Christie's, the sale of his wine collection alone taking six days. The square in front of the hall is named after Sir John Barbirolli, the acclaimed Hallé conductor of the mid-C20. It contains two sculptures: the marble *Touchstone* (1996) by Kam Yasuda and the bust of *Barbirolli* (2000) by Byron Howard. The conductor's name could be hard to pronounce - locals nicknamed him Bob O'Reilly.

Libraries

Libraries are a Manchester speciality. Chetham's can claim to being the oldest free public library anywhere. The city was also the first to react to the Public Libraries Act of 1850. The first children's section in the country opened ten years later and in 1871, the city was the first to employ female library assistants.

Central Library

Central Library 6E

St Peter's Square, City **0161 234 1900**
www.manchester.gov.uk/libraries FREE
Mon-Thu 10am-8pm; Fri-Sat 10am-5pm

From 1934 by Vincent Harris and the largest municipal library in Britain. The circular design was inspired by the Pantheon in Rome.The entrance hall has a stained-glass window dedicated to William Shakespeare. The main reading room on the first floor is also round, dominated by the baldicchino motif of the clock balanced above the central desk. The acoustics are extravagant – the slightest tap on the desk reverberating around the room. The library is special for another reason: literature shares the building with drama in beautiful symbiosis. In the basement is the 50-year-old Library Theatre. This focuses mainly on contemporary work, and is owned by the city. Manchester writers, such as Anthony Burgess, have spent many long hours in here inspired by the works. Of particular note is the Henry Watson Music Library with its collection of early and original music scores. This includes a score of Vivaldi's *Manchester Violin Sonatas*, signed by the composer - so named after their indentification in the city.

Chetham's Library and School of Music 6A

Long Millgate, City **0161 834 7961**
www.chethams.org.uk FREE *Library: Mon-Fri 9am-12.30pm, 1.30pm-4.30pm*

QUICK-FIX

Style: Gothic
When: first half of 1400s
Architect: unknown
Why visit: it's beautiful, charming and significant

Chetham's Library and School is the oldest complete structure in the city, dating from the first half of the 1400s, when both were erected as a single building to house the clergy from the Collegiate church.

After the Reformation, the premises were variously used and abused. They got a new lease of life when they were purchased through the will of local merchant Humphrey Chetham in 1653. He wished to set up a charity school for 40 poor boys and a free public library for the 'use of scholars and others well-affected'. The library is still run by the successors of the 24 feoffees (trustees) Chetham named in his will.

Only the library has daily public access. The security guard will direct you through the ancient gatehouse and across the courtyard to a doorway in a dark passageway. The buildings not only look ancient but feel ancient. If you arrive on a dark winter's afternoon, beware as you look along the murky corridors. The old warden here 400 years ago was the alchemist and scholar John Dee. It is said he dabbled, like Doctor Faustus, with the Dark Arts. In a nearby room there is a hoof-print burn mark where he is said to have raised the Devil.

You will have to press the bell on the library door to call an attendant. Most of the library fixtures and fittings are original and date from the mid-1600s. The books are contemporary from that date and some are older. They are shielded behind C18 gates and were formerly chained to the shelves. In a peculiar reversal of today's values, the buildings cost the trustees of Chetham's half the the value of the books.

The library still collects new books on local matters, but the original collection is more diverse and includes the Mathew Parris C13 *Flores Historiarum*. One C17 buying mission procured Plato's *Complete Works* that had been owned by the renowned poet and playwright Ben Jonson and signed by him.

Down the side corridor is the main Reading Room. On the wall is the wooden relief showing the coat of arms of the benefactor, Humphrey Chetham. Note how the various elements are balanced on wooden books. On one side is a pelican feeding its young with its own blood, a symbol of charity, and on the other a crowing cock, a symbol of vigilance and education.

Many visitors come to view the square table in the bay window. It was here in the 1840s that Friedrich Engels, who spent 22 years in Manchester, would study with Karl Marx, the man he supported with money and ideas. The library has a record of the books they read. Sat at the table with eyes closed, it is possible to imagine the zealous pair thrashing out their ideas of the new

Chetham's Library

world order whilst the first city of capitalism pulsed all around them.

To the left, as you leave the library, is the former cloister, and a little way down on the right, a doorway that leads into the Fox Courtyard. In the centre is the old well. If you look through one of the holes in the cover, you will see the Fox staring back at you. The wall facing the entrance into the courtyard is part of the magnificent Hall with its sweet inglenook, original screens and coved canopy over a dais.

Most of the other parts of building are part of the prestigious School of Music, which takes children from 8 to 18 years of age. On Wednesdays during term time, there are free concerts and tours. These combine history with a performance from one of the students at the music school. To confirm times and book places, call 0161 834 9646.

John Rylands Library 4D

150 Deansgate, City **0161 306 0555**
www.manchester.ac.uk/library
FREE *Mon-Sat10am-5pm*

QUICK-FIX

Style: Victorian Gothic
When: 1899-1900
Architect: Basil Champneys
Why visit: world beating collection of books in one of the last great Victorian Gothic buildings

If you are going to build a tribute to a loved one and you have a some spare cash, you might as well do it properly. Enriqueta Rylands had the money – millions of pounds – and the memorial she built to her dead husband is Manchester's version of the Taj Mahal. Opened on New Year's Day 1900, it is not only one of the city's most beautiful buildings, but also contains one of the top ten collections of manuscripts and printed material on the planet.

John Rylands was a successful and modest cotton merchant and manufacturer. When he died in 1888 leaving an estate of more than £2.5m, his second wife, Enriqueta, resolved to convert his private theological book collection into a public one. This would continue his work of enlightened philanthropy. Her architect, Basil Champneys, designed a building combining the atmosphere of a monastic library with modern amenities.

The main frontage on Deansgate includes the sumptuous entrance with two octagonal towers placed beneath the larger towers. In the centre is the large east window of the reading room with its mass of window tracery. Inside, the place provides one dramatic space after another. The Reading Room includes stained glass and sculptures illustrating literary, religious and philosophical greats. At one end there is a statue of Enriqueta Rylands and at the other, one of John Rylands. The Reading Room is positioned on the first floor to limit noise from Deansgate.

The collections go back to the third millennium BC, and are written on most kinds of materials used by man including clay, papyrus, linen, parchment, paper, wood, bone,

Naughty words

One of the books at John Rylands is known as the Wicked Bible. Printed in London in 1631, it had a typographical error: the word 'not' was omitted from the seventh commandment. Thus it read 'Thou Shalt Commit Adultery'. Not a suggestion, but an order.

Epic of Gilgamesh a cuneiform tablet more than 4000 years old

bark, bamboo and palm-leaf. The works include the oldest fragment of the New Testament, the oldest printed material from Europe, a first edition of Shakespeare's sonnets, most of the Caxtons ever printed, Guttenberg Bibles and medieval illuminated manuscripts. In the Oriental section alone, there are 20,000 manuscripts in 40 different languages. Similarly the Aramaic section is one of the most acclaimed in Europe.

After a major renovation and the addition of new areas, the library re-opens in spring 2007. The opportunity has been taken to give the building the slate roof planned in the original drawings. Meanwhile visitors will be able to find out more about the building and its history through audioguides or by joining a tour. Themed displays will help visitors to interpret the collections and include interactive exhibits.

▲ One of the treaures at John Rylands Library: a **C15 Flemish Book of Hours**

The Freud Letters

Amongst the collection at John Rylands Library is the correspondence between Sigmund Freud and the Manchester side of his family. Mostly he wrote to Sam Freud, the son of Emanuel Freud, Sigmund's half brother who had emigrated to Manchester in 1861. Emanuel would later die, falling from a train between Manchester and Stockport (the original Freudian slip, perhaps?). Apart from that tragedy the Manchester Freuds led a less eventful life than the Viennese branch. Sam never married, and lived with his two maiden sisters and mother, running a household goods business from Bloom Street in the city centre.

The correspondence housed in the John Rylands is interesting, not only as it paints a picture of the private Freud as a gossipy, if rather cranky man, but also because it is, almost entirely, written in English. Freud was an anglophile and loved his visits to the country and Manchester. He said that his desire was 'to become an Englishman…in spite of the fog, rain, drunkenness and conservatism'. He was an avid reader of the Manchester Guardian too.

Much correspondence deals with the difficulties and shortages in Vienna after World War 1, with Freud asking if 'fat corned beef, cocoa, tea, English cakes' could be sent. There's also a lot of discussion of the family. A niece of his becomes engaged and he remarks upon the bridegroom 'I hope he will prove more normal than his gifted yet half-crazy bride.'

In the letters, the father of psycho-analysis has some prosaic interpretations of his own dreams. In the letter to Sam in, 1928, he writes, 'This night I found myself in the company of you and to be sure I understood the meaning of the dream, it corresponded to my intention to write to you on my 72nd birthday.' Nothing too fruity there then.

Portico Library and Gallery 7D

57 Mosley Street, City 0161 236 6785
www.theportico.org.uk FREE *Mon-Fri 9.30am-4.30pm; Sun (third every month) 1pm-4pm. Entrance from Charlotte Street*

After the mysteries of John Rylands and Chetham's, the Portico is bathed in the afterglow of the Age of Enlightenment.

It was completed in 1806 in the Grecian style to the designs of Thomas Harrison. Built and stocked through private subscription, the Portico remains perhaps the oldest such library in the UK. Early members included John Edward Taylor,

founder of The Manchester Guardian, the scientist John Dalton and William Gaskell, chairman of the library and husband of Elizabeth Gaskell, one of the most famous C19 novelists. The latter often accompanied her friend, Charlotte Brontë, to the library. A more recent member was Eric Cantona, the United and French footballer.

On the outside from Mosley Street there is the elegant Ionic portico that gives the building its name. The ground floor was sold off in the 1920s for use first as a bank and now as a pub. The reading room is a lovely space with a saucer dome and a wind dial by Thwaites of London, who later made the clock for Big Ben. The reading room holds art exhibitions. The first secretary was Peter Mark Roget and it is here where he started to compile his famous *Thesaurus*.

If you want to join the library it's £150 per annum for those who live within five miles of the building and £105 for those who live further afield. Carriage costs in the old days were so frightfully expensive, don't you know.

Central churches

Manchester Cathedral 5B

Victoria Street, City 0161 833 2220
www.manchestercathedral.org
FREE *Daily from 8.30am*

QUICK-FIX

Style: mainly Perpendicular Gothic
When: some earlier elements but from 1420s onwards, including much C19 and C20 work
Why visit: for the tranquil atmosphere and the beautiful fixtures and fittings: espicially the late medieval woodwork

› **The Angel Stone** was discovered embedded in the wall of the Cathedral, dated to around C700 and is evidence of an early Saxon church

The present Cathedral lies on the site of a church that dates back over a millennium but is mostly the product of the last 600 years. It has a very complicated dedication to St Mary the Virgin, St Denys and St George. This dates from 1421 when the parish church was raised in status to that of Collegiate Church - one with greater rights and a college of one warden and eight priests. St Denys is the patron saint of France and is included because, according to one story, the King wanted his claim to the French throne recognised. In 1421 the monarch was Henry V and he'd beaten the French at Agincourt.

The expanded building was to be a chantry college where masses were said to speed the souls of the rich to Paradise. In other words, it would earn good cash and attract patronage as well as being the spiritual fountain for a 60 sq. mile (100

Manchester Cathedral Engraving by Robert Young 1837-1855

sq. km) parish. This is why Manchester Cathedral can now claim to have the widest nave of any cathedral in the UK. The chantry chapels for various families were built against the walls. These have been removed, leaving an uninterrupted space from wall to wall wider than any other: indeed the nave width is two thirds the length of the building. Joseph Crowther, the C19 architect who restored the church, described the nave as 'arch behind arch, pier behind pier... posessing one of those features which so fascinate the visitors to the Arabian Mosques.'

In the early 1500s, the Choir was erected, which with the ceilings, comprise some of the finest late medieval wood carving in the north of England. The style is called Perpendicular, which is unique to England and is notable for its strong vertical lines in windows and piers.

Most of the exterior and much of the interior was faithfully rebuilt in the C19 by Joseph Crowther. The West Front was massively - perhaps too massively - reconstructed for Queen Victoria's Diamond Jubilee in 1897 by architect Basil Champneys. By this time, the Collegiate Church had been formally recognised as Manchester Cathedral (1847).

Throughout the C19, stained-glass windows had been added, which had the effect of darkening the interior. In December 1940, the Cathedral suffered a direct hit during the Manchester Blitz. The windows acted like a safety valve and as they shattered, helped release the pressure of the blast. Partly because of this, the structure and woodwork were miraculously preserved. The post-WWII stained glass from Tony Holloway and Margeret Traherne represents the best of the new decoration in the Cathedral. In 2004 the Healing Window by Linda Walton was added. The Carol Weightman paintings, *The Teachings of Christ*, from 1963 at the Chapter House are worth a look too.

The bomb landed in the Regimental Chapel of the Manchester Regiment. In the Books of Remembrance lining the walls is the name of one of the last casualties of WWI: the poet Wilfred Owen, who is also commemorated by a brass plaque in the Chapel.

The Cathedral has a good programme of concerts. If you are around, try to drop in on the family carol service in December. One of the best free city events is Evensong - Tue, Wed, Thu from 5.30pm, Sat 3pm. The Cathedral choir as part of Manchester's radical tradition, was the first in the country to allow choirgirls as well as boys. See page 35 too for an important episode in the Cathedral's history.

A **Christian word square** found at the Roman fort in Manchester, now on display at the Cathedral Visitor Centre (see page 17 for more details) ›

Cathedral Visitor Centre 5B

Hanging Ditch, City **0161 835 4030** FREE

Tue-Sat 10am-4.30pm; Sun noon-4pm

Designed by the architects Hurd Rolland, the centre tells the story of the Cathedral and its place in the city. Within it is an ancient monument: the substantial remains of the 1421 Hanging Bridge which can be viewed from the pleasant basement refectory. The bridge carried people over the now culvetted watercourse of Hanging Ditch to the Cathedral.

A TOUR ROUND MANCHESTER CATHEDRAL

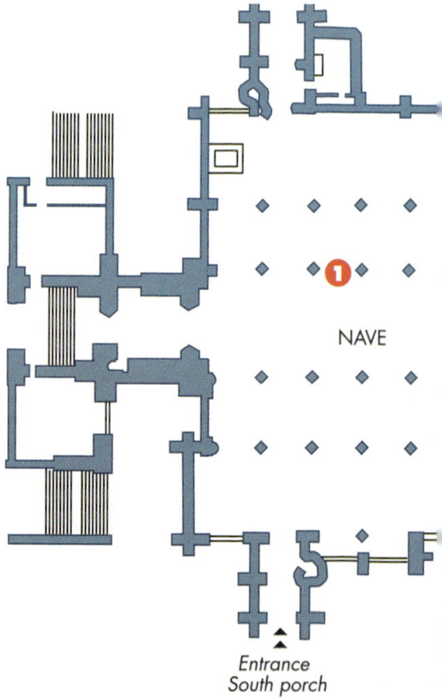

Enter through the south porch, walk to the nave and look up. The beams supporting the ceilings terminate in a consort of angels – a heavenly choir with, amongst others, dulcimer, harp, bagpipes and lute (1). In the C16 it was thought that music was divine as it lifted the soul and we all had guardian angels.

Behind the nave altar lies the choir, carved in the years around 1500. Access is through the lovely screen (6) where you find yourself surrounded by the stalls, or seats, of the choir. These are surmounted by a carved canopies: each a mass of spires and crochets resembling a series of perfect churches, like a late medieval imagining of a new Jerusalem. There is symbolism everywhere – on the benches in front of the choir a lion represents Christ and a dragon represents the Devil.

Under the main seats are the misericords – brackets to help support occupants during long periods of standing. The carvings under these carry an impish sense of humour not often associated with the times. Here you'll find men playing backgammon in a tavern, a woman scolding a man who's broken her cooking pots and rabbits cooking the hunter. All have meanings beside the obvious imagery, thus one shows a sleeping pedlar being robbed by monkeys (2). On one side there is a monkey with a baby and on the other is one with a bottle. This is a urine sample. Doctors said that with a urine sample they could diagnose illness – this satire says you might as well trust your sample or your baby to a monkey and that all doctors want to do is rob you. Also in the choir is the brass of John Huntingdon (3), the first warden of the Collegiate Church who died in 1458. Straight ahead to the east over this brass is the Lady Chapel. This has an arch with

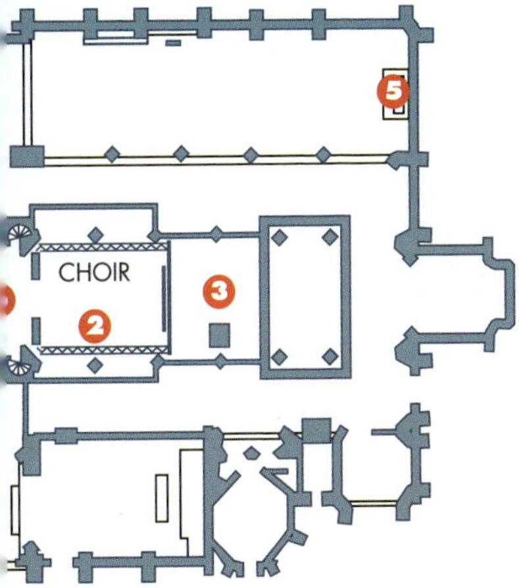

4 *Auxiliary buildings*

a scene of hunting at one end and of beer or wine barrels, formerly called tuns, at the other end. Here we have a rebus, or architectural pun, about the warden's surname.

To the left of the Lady Chapel is the Fire Window (5) by Margaret Traherne, marking where a German bomb fell in 1940. Other modern windows include five by Tony Holloway, on the west wall, to your left from the start of this tour. In order, from the entrance porch, these represent Genesis, St George, St Mary, St Denys and Revelations. The octagonal Chapter House walk to the right from the Lady Chapel is also worth seeking out decorated by Carol Weight's 1963, the Teachings of Christ.

The piers supporting the tower are the oldest part of the building, dating from around 1380. They have at their capitals mysterious faces peering down through the gloom. These are Green Men, pre-Christian symbols of fertility and renewal associated in the Church's mind with the resurrection of Christ. Outside over the auxiliary buildings entrance is an Eric Gill sculpture of the Christ Child with St Mary, St Denys and St George (4).

5

6

KEY BUILDINGS

This poem in the Cathedral is the saddest in the city: Robert Lever's C17 elegy, in the English of the day, to his six dead children – perhaps plague victims.

Here dy'd their Parents hopes and feares,
Once all their Ioy, now all their tearres,
They'r now past hope, past feare, or paine,
It were a sinne to wish them here againe.
Had they liv'd to th'age of Man,
This Inch had growne but to a span.
But now they take the lesser roomes.
Rock't from their cradles to their Toombes,
View but the way from whence wee come,
You'le say He's blest that soon'st at Home.
You see their Age and years of Grace,
I hope that Heaven's their dwelling place.

St Ann's Church

St Ann's Church 5D

St Ann's Square, City 0161 834 0239

FREE *Daily 11.30am-5pm*

St Ann's Church is a handsome, Classical building from 1709, probably designed by John Barker. The interior is as cool as the exterior is elegant, with galleries squatting on chubby Tuscan columns. There is heavy C19 stained glass principally from Frederick Shields. The church is built from the local pinkish red sandstone. The dedication refers to the saint, of course, but perhaps more so to the lady who provided the money, Lady Ann Bland. It was the society church when it was built and pew rents for the best seats were more than £1,000 – an astronomical sum. The poor were left to stand or get a cramped seat in the gallery. Out of the 19 city churches built in the C18, St Ann's is the only survivor. The church tower is the traditional centre of the city. On the left near the tower door is the arrow-like surveyors' mark signifying this. The tombs at the rear include some Manchester dignitries - see the panels there. The church puts on lunchtime events.

St Mary's Roman Catholic Church 5D

Mulberry Street, City 0161 834 3547

FREE *Daily 9am-5.30pm*

The earlier church on this site from 1794 was the first purpose-built Catholic church in England since the Reformation. The present building dates from 1848 by Weightman and Hadfield. This is sign-posted all around the city as The Hidden Gem – christened thus by a visiting bishop. Not all have agreed. The noted architect Pugin, in petulant mood, said the building "shows to what depth of error even good men fall when they go whoring after strange styles". Miaow! The ornate interior has become even more eye-opening with the addition of Norman Adams' *Stations of the Cross* - see below. These are graphic, full of energy and contrast violently with the C19 interior.

St Mary's Church

Castlefield

2F/2G 3F/3G

Castlefield canal basin

Castlefield was declared Britain's first urban heritage park in 1982. It brings together a tough urban industrial landscape of iron, stone and brick surrounding and cut through by canals. There is also the added attraction of the Museum of Science and Industry (see Museums chapter below). A walk around the Castlefield canal basin is recommended, especially in summer and during the festivals held here. The biggest celebration is the extravaganza of contemporary music which is called Dpercussion in August.

The Ox and the White Lion, both Liverpool Road, Dukes 92, Castle Street and Choice and Lava both at Castle Quay, are recommended places for refreshment.

The main places of historical interest in Castlefield include the remains and reconstructed gate, granaries and walls of the Roman Fort of Mamucium (see pg 17), and its attendent vicus (the town that grew outside the fort).

The railway viaducts here chopped up the Roman site. If you take a walk around you'll seee how many of the piers are castellated. The eccentric Victorians destroyed the fort site but showed where it once stood with a series of mini-castles on the viaducts.

Nearby is the Outdoor Arena, which is used many times throughout the year. In 1994, over 20,000 people gathered in the Arena to listen to the verdict of International Olympic Commitee chairman Juan Antonio Samaranch on whether Manchester had got the Olympic Games. Samaranch said Sydney had won. There was a two second pause and then the crowd sang Monty Python's 'Always Look on the Bright Side of Life'.

The principal canal here is the Bridgewater Canal. When this reached Manchester in 1765 from the Duke of Bridgewater's collieries at Worsley seven miles away, it immediately halved the price of coal in the city. The Duke was laughed at for his enterprise and the canal nearly broke him with its cost of over £200,000, yet not long after it was returning profits of £80,000 a year. The Bridgewater was the first modern canal and always the quickest: throughout its journey back to the mines or on to the Mersey estuary there are no locks and it follows the contours of the landscape. Bridgewater Canal engineer James Brindley, used to say that water is like a giant - safest when on its back. On Castle Street, close to the junction with Deansgate, is Grocer's Warehouse. This used to be five storeys high. It has been part reconstructed and reveals Brindley's ingenuity. Under the canal here, the River Medlock flows in a tunnel. The overflow of the canal water into the tunnel below caused the waterwheel inside the Grocer's Warehouse to turn which in turn hauled coal from the canal side to the road above.

The Bridgewater joins the Rochdale Canal in Castlefield. This was the first waterway to cross the Pennine hills and link west and east coasts. An interesting walk leads up the tow path of the Rochdale Canal and traverses the city, through tunnels, a mile (1.6km) to the Piccadilly end of town.

Castlefield is the birth place of Manchester: the place where the Romans built their fort in 79AD. This is a reconstruction of fort gate.

KEY BUILDINGS

Whitworth Art Gallery, 'Flora' by William Morris

Central museums, galleries & heritage

City centre including the University area, Salford Quays and Old Trafford. All the attractions listed below lie within 3 miles (5km) of Manchester Town Hall.

Gallery of Costume

Platt Hall, Wilmslow Road, Rusholme

0161 224 5217 *www.manchestergalleries.org*

FREE *Mon-Fri 10am-4.45pm and last Sat in the month 10am-4.45pm. Ring the doorbell on arrival.*

Useful for those who wish to study costume and fashion, th museum is housed inside a building worthy of note in its own right. In this case, Platt Hall: a fine Palladian house in brick from around 1764. One of the previous owners was the famous Sir Charles Worsley, Manchester's first MP. The best parts of the building are the delicate and refined stairwell, the sweet upstairs corridor and the first-floor dining room with its contemporary Richard Wilson painting. All these spaces are notable for the Roccoco plasterwork. The displays include the brocaded and embroidered clothes of the C17 and C18, the heavy garments of the Victorian and Edwardian periods, 'flapper' and wartime fashions as well as the familiar, distinctive designs of recent decades such as those of Zandra Rhodes, Mary Quant, Vivienne Westwood and many others. *Toilets, shop, school and group, partial disabled access, tours, events.*

Godlee Observatory 9F

Main Building, UMIST, Sackville Street, City

0161 202 2940 *www.manastro.co.uk*

FREE *Thu 7pm-10pm*

The observatory was built in 1902 with a completely timber structure, over an iron skeleton. Access to the telescope chamber is via a wrought iron staircase of three spirals. This beautiful piece of engineering will give the faint-hearted vertigo. Under the white dome of the Observatory, still positioned by rope and wheels, is the original Grubb telescope and refractor. This revolves around its polar axis to follow the movement of the heavens. It is refreshing to see technology that is clear in its functions - a break for anybody whose life is ruled by the hidden mysteries of the microchip. The atmosphere of the Godlee - the name of the benefactor who gave the money - is alive with the enthusiasm of the Manchester Astronomical Society which celebrated its centenary in 2003. *Toilets, school and group visits, guided tours, events.*

Gtr Manchester Police Museum 10C

Newton Street, corner with Faraday Street, City 0161 856 3287

http://www.gmp.police.uk/mainsite/pages/history.htm FREE *Tue 10.30am-3.30pm. Other weekdays by appointment*

Housed in a former police station built in 1879 and in use until 1979, this tells the story of policing in Manchester. The building bulges with memorabilia such as old uniforms, weapons and equipment. Tales of criminal antics and police derring-do enliven the exhibitions. The stars of the show are the grim cells, which could house up to 12 prisoners. This museum is worth a visit because of its sheer oddness and its very knowledgeable and friendly staff. If you want the ultimate in unusual souvenirs, you can use the resources to track whether your ancestors were criminals in the city. *Toilets, shop, school and group visits, partial disabled access.*

Holy Name of Jesus

Oxford Road, University 0161 273 2435

FREE *Access throughout the day*

This church, built in 1871, is a dominant feature on Oxford Road. It was the most important work of Joseph Aloyious Hansom, a gentleman of diverse talents, perhaps better known for his jolly two-wheeled conveyance, the Hansom cab. The building is impressive but sombre. The original design was to have had a 240-foot spire, but Hansom died before completion so Adrian Gilbert Scott finished it off with an octagonal tower with huge windows open to the elements. Round the back are superb flying buttresses. Inside, the feeling of stern power is continued. The nave is incredibly high, supported on the slenderest of columns with light pouring in from the chancel windows. The material used is pale terracotta, highly ornamented and featuring sculptures, an original reredos by the architect and a crucifixion. It is said that Hansom got the inspiration from Amiens Cathedral; it is not recorded how he was inspired to design his two-wheeled conveyance. Most of the internal work would have been designed by his son and business partner Joseph Stanislaus Hansom.

The church figures in the song 'Vicar in a Tutu' by local group The Smiths. The cheeky opening verse runs: 'I was minding my business lifting some lead off the roof of the Holy Name Church. It was worthwhile living a laughable life just to set my eyes on the blistering sight of a vicar in a tutu'. As far as this guidebook knows, none of the clerical staff at the Holy Name have ever worn a tutu, so don't expect too much.

A previous parishioner recounts that back in the '50s, Bing Crosby, looking for a place of worship whilst playing Manchester joined the choir.

The Holy Name Church

Heaven & Hell

By the end of World War One, most of the population of central Manchester had moved away. So former churches were demolished and their churchyards turned into gardens. The best kept and loveliest of these green sanctuaries is St John' Gardens **3E**. The floral effect is enhanced by the proximity of the best surviving and related Georgian terrace in the city. The church of the same name was built in 1769 and demolished in 1932. Its former graveyard holds 22,000 of the dead, now literally employed in pushing up the daisies. Nearer to the retail heart is Parsonage Gardens **4C**. Best caught in spring and early summer sunshine, this handkerchief of land goes back a long way. Given to the church at the Norman Conquest, there was a priest's dwelling here before that – hence the name. The former church, built in 1756, was demolished in 1880. The third site in the city centre is busier. St Peter's Square **6E** was centred on St Peter's Church, demolished 1907. The site of the structure sits next to the Metrolink station on a patch of green behind the Cenotaph. A cross, with St Peter and the keys to Paradise, commemorates this and the dead lie beneath, locked in their crypt tombs. Under the shadow of the CIS Tower, just north of the city centre, lies the most spine-tingling of the gardens. The former church here was that of St Michael. The graveyard was run by the parish. 44,000, at least, lie here, most of these the common dead, the destitute, the workhouse inmates and the diseased. Mass grave pits were dug, in particular, for 'Blue Vomit' (cholera) victims. St Michael's churchyard, despite recent improvement, retains an atmosphere of distress, of poverty, fear and degradation. It has international infamy too, described in *The Condition of the Working Classes in England* by Friedrich Engels – see page 37.

Imperial War Museum North

Trafford Wharf Road, Trafford Park

0161 877 9240 *www.iwm.org.uk*

FREE *Daily 10am-6pm*

QUICK-FIX

Why visit: a stirring building holding fascinating artefacts and hosting quality temporary exhibitions. The theme is deadly serious, literally, and holds the attention and imagination.

As the picture below illustrates this is a show-stopping, jaw-dropping building which reflects the moods of the weather. Designed by acclaimed architect Daniel Libeskind, the museum is based on the concept of a world shattered by war. It concentrates on people's experiences rather than the hardware, although there are over 1,000 objects too. The three 'shards' represent the various theatres of conflict on land, air and sea from 1900. Thus the building, as always with Libeskind, plays an active part in delivering the museum message.

It is not polite architecture though, it is a statement and as such, along with much of the turn of the century CGI style fantasy architecture from the Guggenheim in Bilbao onwards, it is beginning to attract citicism. Architectural fashions change of course, and will again: visitors may love or loathe this bombastic style of building but they are seldom unimpressed.

Entry is under the 55m Air Shard, which carries a platform providing views over the city and canal from 29m. The wind whistles through here, creating an eerie atmosphere that is accentuated by the topsy-turvy lack of verticals – the concrete stairwell is the only vertical, but because of the chaos around, doesn't look perpendicular either. Meanwhile the lift rises at a disconcerting 4° angle. If you have vertigo prepare yourself for the view through the mesh floor back down to *terra firma* below.

The main exhibition space is the Earth Shard, which curves at the same ratio as

MUSEUMS

US Marine Corps Harrier Jump Jet

the surface of the earth. Located in here are 'silos' focusing on particular themes of the C20: Experience of War, Women and War, Impressions of War, Commonwealth and War, Science and War and Legacy of War. Around the wall there is a Timeline – a 3D chronological journey through the war experience with room to expand as the history of bloodshed continues into the C21. There is a facility for locating the graves of lost relatives killed overseas in the world wars.

The most obvious part of any visit are the 360° audio visual experiences called the Big Picture. During these, the Earth Shard darkens and huge projections flash onto the gallery walls accompanied by a soundtrack. There are three subjects: The War at Home, Children and War and Weapons of War. These last up to 20 minutes each and take place on the hour, every hour. Some of the images are difficult to shake from the mind.

The Experience of War silo has a tiny alcove where people tell their stories. A deeply in love Kitty Eckersley learnt of her husband Percy's death in WWI whilst she was seven months pregnant. "He were my life," she says in the local accent before adding, in a breaking voice, "I don't remember the baby being born". It is exhilarating to find a museum intelligently examining something that goes to the core of the human experience. IWMN doesn't glorify war but neither is there condemnation. Visitors are trusted to make up their own minds.

A nearby room holds the dramatic Special Exhibitions Gallery (some exhibitions have an entry fee), cut through on one side by the aluminium wall of the Air Shard. Typical exhibitions might include those of art in the collections of the Imperial War Museum. *Witness 2, Highlights of World War II Art,* started 2007 off with works from Paul Nash and others. The major exhibition for 2007 is *Animals and War,* from 26 May to 6 Jan 2008 which looks at the uses to which animals have been put in times of conflict. There'll also be a photographic recollection of the 'last colonial war', the Falklands conflict of 1982, and a display of artworks from Palestinian and Israeli children.

There are events and workshops – many for families and children. Children, for instance, may get to hold everyday goods and decommissioned military hardware. The shop has a selection of models, books and clothes. The Water Shard holds the restaurant facilities.

To conclude, the Imperial War Museum North is a moving visitor attraction that treads the compromise between traditional and technologically driven museums. It presents a coherent and affecting picture of war and its effects. *Toilets, baby changing, food and drink, shop, school and group visits, disabled access, events.*

Manchester Universities

Manchester and academia have the closest of links. The city plays host to around 84,000 full and part time students in various institutions including:

Manchester Metropolitan University (All Saints Building, Oxford Road, University. 0161 247 2000), **The Royal Northern College of Music** (Oxford Road, University. 0161 275 2077), **Salford University** (The Crescent, Salford. 0161 295 5000), the **University of Manchester** (Oxford Road, University. 0161 275 2930).

The University was set up in 1851 under the will of John Owens, a local entrepreneur. It was the fifth university to be created in Britain. Formally reorganised in 1870, it moved to the present location shortly after. In 2004 the University merged with the University of Manchester, Institute of Science and Technology which traces its history back to 1824 and the creation of the Mechanics Institute in the city. The combined university is now the largest in the UK with 35,000 students, providing research and teaching in over 50 disciplines.

From a visitor's point of view, the principle places of interest are found in the older buildings. The main Gothic block of the University on Oxford Road was built piecemeal between 1870 and 1902 with the grandest parts the ensemble around tower, main gate and Whitworth Hall. The architect was Alfred Waterhouse (also Manchester Town Hall - see page 66), succeeded by his son Paul. The Whitworth Hall is impressive with vaulted spaces, grand staircases, fine stonework and a hammerbeam roof. Much of this older work has been sensitively refurbished by Ian Simpson Architects.

The University of Manchester Institute of Science and Technology, now integrated into the University, also has an interesting site. The first half of the main building on Granby Row is the oldest from 1895-1902 by Spalding and Cross and was originally Manchester Technical School. This was built partly in response to growing worries that foreign competition was beginning to hit local competitiveness. There are enjoyable classical sculptured heads around the building designed to encourage the students to study. On top is the Godlee Observatory (see page 86).

The gardens adjacent to Granby Row are entertaining. Nobly standing here is a large bottle more than four metres high, carved from wood. This is by Kerry Morrison and paid for by the Vimto company to celebrate the first mixing of their popular temperance refreshment of the same name in 1908 by John Noel Nicholls. Further along is 'Technology Arch' by Axel Wolkenhaur from 1989. This length of artfully twisted steel rope reflects the technological skills of the university. Underneath the nearby railway arch is the far more fun Archimedes in his bath at the moment of shouting "Eureka!" This is the work of Thompson Dagnall from 1990. On the other side of the railway viaduct is the smart '60s extension to UMIST over a pleasant lawn.

For overseas students, the International Society of the University is a good place to meet and socialise. The society hosts events and trips almost every weekend for its 3,000 members. For more information, phone 0161 275 4959, visit the link on www.manchester.ac.uk or email int.soc@man.ac.uk

The University of Manchester

Manchester City and Manchester United Museums

- See Sports section.

Manchester Jewish Museum

Cheetham Hill Road, Cheetham Hill 0161 834 9879 *www.manchesterjewishmuseum.com* ***Adults £3.95, children and concessions £2.95, family £9*** *Mon-Thu 10.30am-4pm; Sun 11am-5pm. Closed Jewish holidays*

Located almost a mile outside the central core of the city, this museum tells the story of Manchester Jewry and the people associated with it whilst also putting on special events and exhibitions. The building was built as the Spanish and Portuguese Synagogue in the Moorish style in 1874 by the Manchester Jewish architect Edward Salomans. The tours around the building for non-Jewish visitors are interesting for the insight they give into the religion. Notable members of the local Jewish community have included Chaim Weizmann, first President of Israel and resident in Manchester for many years, and the writers Jack Rosenthal, Howard Jacobson and Maise Mosco. Just down the road, the first Marks & Spencer store opened in the 1890s. A broader picture of the development of the community can be gained by joining the regular heritage walks.

Toilets, shop, group, school visits, tours, events.

Museum of Transport

Boyle Street, Cheetham Hill 0161 205 2122 *www.gmts.co.uk* ***Adults £4, children & concs £2, family £10*** *Wed, Sat-Sun and public holidays 10am-5pm (4pm winter)*

A wonderfully quirky, volunteer-run museum, packed with as many vintage buses as possible inside, appropriately, a former bus depot. The collection ranges in age from 20 to 100 years and includes fire engines and lorries. The vehicles are beautifully and lovingly maintained and restored in workshops on the premises. Indeed the museum has the biggest collection of restored vintage buses and coaches in the UK – over 80. It's great for children and adults who like to sit behind huge steering wheels and pretend they're the driver on the number 19 and the volunteers are

Museum of Transport

enthusiastic and friendly. The café looks like an authentic recreation of a 1970s bus station canteen until you realise that it isn't a recreation at all – it has just remained untouched all this time. There's also a good souvenir shop.

Toilets, food and drink, shop, group and school visits, disabled access, tours, events

Ordsall Hall Museum

Taylorson Street, Salford 0161 872 0251 *http://www.salford.gov.uk/leisure/museums/ordsallhall.htm* FREE

Mon-Fri 10am-4pm; Sun noon-4pm

An unlikely place in an unlikely location. This medieval timber-framed house is squashed between a '70s housing estate and an '80s office development. From the main road of Ordsall Lane, the rear of the building looks drab in brick and terracotta. The other side is picturesque in the extreme: a charming vision of Olde Englande, decorated with four-leaf (quatrefoil) panels dating from the 1500s. Inside is the magnificent Great Hall, the lovely Star Chamber, a farmhouse kitchen and an exhibition about daily life in Salford. There are regular events, including family fun days. An old tradition describes how Guy Fawkes met his co-conspirators here to plan the deaths of James I and Parliament in the Gunpowder Plot of 1605 – this probably never happened but makes for a good story. There is a visiting bird of prey that features in the events. The website is excellent and is popular for the ghost webcam: http://www.salford.gov.uk/ghostcam.

Toilets, food and drink, shop, group and school visits, disabled access, tours and events.

Manchester Museum

Manchester University, Oxford Road, University 0161 275 2634 *www.museum.man.ac.uk* FREE *Mon-Sat 10am-5pm, Sun 11am-4pm*

QUICK-FIX

Why visit: visit for the fine collections informatively and entertainingly covering a range of subjects and for the old building with its bridges, galleries and nooks and crannies.

Fully refurbished and fitted out by Ian Simpson Architects, this venerable institution has been an integral part of Manchester life for over a hundred years. The museum is administered by the University of Manchester and though it might be a little way out of the city centre it repays any visit ten times over. It has excellent and well-presented permanent collections, good temporary exhibitions and a charming higgledy-piggledy geography which includes graceful bridges interlocking with the stairways.

The galleries cover archaeology, archery, botany, Egyptology, ethnology, geology, numismatics, Oriental studies and zoology and much else. The entrance is on Coupland Street, which is off Oxford Road, and takes the form of an impressive grey wall which suggests geology and archaeology – a sheer cliff face perhaps or the entrance to an ancient fortress or a mysterious and monumental tomb. This comes courtesy of Ian Simpson Architects. The older elements of the Museum are by Alfred Waterhouse from 1888, and his son Paul who extended the museum in 1912 and 1927.

The Egyptology section is very large. Jesse Haworth, a Manchester textile merchant, and Martyn Kennard were the instigators of the collection, donating their 'finds' in 1890. Today the visitor can see everyday and sacred artefacts from ancient Egypt and an array of 'mummies' – great stuff for both children and adults. The pioneering, if rather unnerving, work of Doctor Richard Neave,

T-rex reigns in the Fossils Gallery

working from the University, has rebuilt the structure of faces dead for 3,000 years. His techniques are now used forensically in criminal cases.

The Animal Life section is especially good. Strung from the roof of the magnificent gallery here is the impressive skeleton of a sperm whale. All around stuffed animals are caught in action-packed poses. Within this department is the Vivarium, a mini-zoo of snakes, lizards and frogs in dramatic landscapes such as a recreated rainforest and a rocky desert. The Fossils Gallery is a favourite amongst all age groups. This explores 3,000 million years of life on Earth and, of course, incorporates a section on dinosaurs, including a cast of a T-rex acquired from South Dakota . The ceiling height dictates that the latter has been positioned in a particularly entertaining Spielberg-esque charging pose. One of the best exhibits here though is the lower trunk and root system of a 200 million year old lycosid tree found in a local coal mine.

The museum is looking to improve and will feature a Manchester Gallery in the coming years. In 2008 one of the North

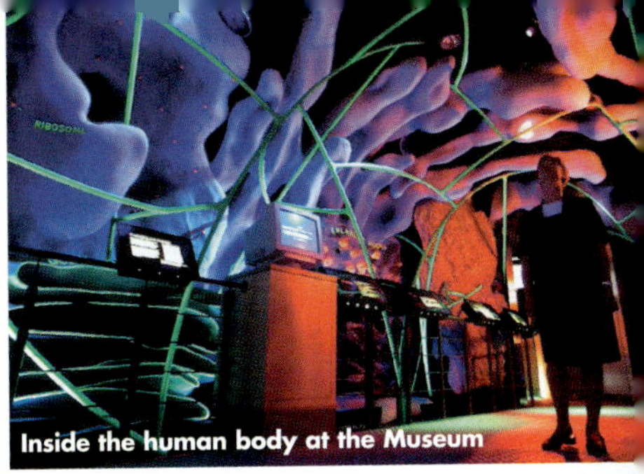

Inside the human body at the Museum

West's most disturbing gentlemen will be returning home from exile at the British Museum. Lindow man will be in town and on display in Manchester Museum. This venerable man was found close to the south Manchester commuter town of Wilmslow. His flesh had been preserved in the peat bog there and he'd been ritualistically beaten, garrotted and had his throat cut. A good story and gore too: the kids will love him.

There is a very good series of weekend events, many aimed at children. *Toilets, baby changing, food and drink, shop, group and school visits, disabled access, audio interpretation, tours, events.*

Tiger, Tiger burning bright in the Animal Life gallery

Museum of Science & Industry 2F

Liverpool Road, Castlefield, City 0161 832 2244 *www.msim.org.uk* FREE *(Except Special Exhibitions) Daily 10am-5pm, closed 24-26 December*

QUICK-FIX

Why visit: this is one of the great Science and Industry museums anywhere in Europe, housed in truly significant buildings with a rich history of their own.

The museum covers seven acres and occupies a number of historic buildings, including the oldest railway station in the world. It is one of the largest museums of its kind anywhere. Exhibitions cover steam engines, space, science, cotton, gas, water, electricity, computers, photography, the history of Manchester and Xperiment! - an interactive science centre.

The Lower Byrom Street Warehouse – the Main Building dates from 1880 and is the principal entrance to the site. Here you'll find the shop with its mix of souvenirs, gifts and books. The main museum café is on the second floor. Down from the entrance is Fibres, Fabrics and Fashion, devoted to Manchester and the cotton industry. This is a bright and busy gallery brought together with great creativity. In the centre is a working exhibition of textile machines. A modern designer or an artist often holds demonstrations in part of the room. For the story of the cotton industry, see pg 22. Close to the café upstairs is the superb Xperiment! This gives children an entertaining and interactive introduction to technology – there is a particularly good under fives play area too. An added bonus, if it tickles your fancy, is the intimate view of Coronation Street from the windows. In the basement of this building, you can find the Special Exhibition, Archive and Collections areas. The most recent gallery in this building is Manchester Science, describing the city's contribution to scientific achievment. The main focus is on the work of John Dalton, James Joule, Ernest Rutherford and Bernard Lovell – all giants of their fields. The holographic displays are impressive although

The Air and Space Gallery

unreliable in terms of always working.

Next door is the Power Hall which contains the largest collection of working steam engines in the world. These are powerful and beautiful. The colliery engine from Haydock dates from the first half of C19, and was never intended for public display yet is ornamented with details such as urns and pillars: a marriage of industry and aesthetics.

The lower part of the hall exhibits early forms of mechanised transport from Manchester, with cars such as Belsize and Crosley and a Model T Ford. The first European plant of Ford was opened in Trafford Park, Manchester, in 1911. Also here are examples of trains built locally. The Beyer Peacock company is represented by a stupendous example of one of the articulated steam engines built for South Africa.

At the lower end of the site, there is a ramp down to Underground Manchester and Making of Manchester. Underground Manchester takes the visitor into a history of sanitation and health and includes a reconstructed 1868 sewer. The Making of Manchester follows the development of the city from prehistory and is clear and precise.

Both galleries finish in an exhibition devoted to the building in which they are housed. The Liverpool Road Station is the oldest railway station in the world and the first passenger railway station. In the second class booking hall there is video to help explain the railway. Upstairs you can gain access to the trackside via an exhibition on photography. In other parts of the building are galleries devoted to gas and electricity.

There is a passage from the station building under the viaduct to the 1830 Warehouse. On the ground floor is the Warehouse of the World which, through a sound and light show, recreates the building in its heyday. Upstairs there is a working reconstruction of Baby, the first modern computer, developed at Manchester University in 1948. It claims this distinction because it was the first with an electronic memory that did not depend on cards punched with holes. Access is provided here on Tuesdays only.

Retrace your steps to the main entrance and cross the road to the Air and Space Gallery – this was formerly a food market from 1876, but now provides a suitably airy structure of iron and glass. Inside there are a large number of aircraft on display, including a Shackleton bomber, a Spitfire, and a Japanese kamikaze plane – unused of course. The major role the city played in aviation history is highlighted and there is also an exhibition devoted to space exploration, housing a section of a Gemini rocket. Also here is the Planetarium which operates on weekends, Bank holidays and school holidays for a small charge.

There is a full programme of events, tours, demonstrations and lectures. This year the crowd pleasing exhibition is Dr Who - Up Close (31 March-5 November). On many weekends there are rides around the site on old steam engines - an entertaining and authentic way in which to conclude a visit to a science and industry museum.

Toilets, baby changing, food and drink, shop, group and school , partial disabled access, audio interpretation, tours, events.

The 1830 Warehouse

Built to the designs of Liverpool architect Thomas Haigh by David Bellhouse and Company, Manchester, this building marks the genesis of rail mania. Completed a little before the station, it is the oldest railway building in the world. Despite almost constant use until the 1970s, much remains as first built.

The warehouse follows the curve of the railway viaduct. It has first-floor double doors opening onto the track. Trucks would have been spun round on a turntable and then pushed into the warehouse. The interior floors were arranged so that a wharf was created with the track sunk into a well, allowing goods to be more easily off-loaded. There were cranes with crane loops in between the doors to provide trackside loading and unloading. Goods unloaded from Liverpool were then transferred to the rear side of the building where they were dropped via cranes to the road level or into carts. Construction was of timber with brick, apart from the basement which was constructed without timber but of brick with cast iron. This level was potentially at risk from flooding.

Pankhurst Centre

Nelson Street, off Oxford Road, University
0161 273 5673 *www.thepankhurstcentre.org.uk*
FREE *Mon-Fri 10am-4pm*

This Georgian building was the home of Emmeline Pankhurst, the woman who made the campaign for women's votes her life's work. From a meeting in this house on 10 October 1903, women members of the Independent Labour Party formed the Women's Social and Political Union. The story of this group, who became known as 'the Suffragettes', is traced in the displays. There's a reconstruction of the Pankhurst's parlour where the first WPSU meeting took place. *Toilets, shop, group, school visits, events.*

People's History Museum 3D

Left Bank, Bridge Street, City 0161 228 7212
www.phm.org.uk FREE *Tue-Sun 11am-4.30pm*

The museum is based around the lives of the working class and their political struggles across Britain, not simply in Manchester. These could seem hopelessly worthy themes but the immediacy of the displays and their great variety manage to tread the difficult ground between information, education and entertainment. Areas covered include the Peterloo Massacre, friendly societies and the trade union movement, the votes for women campaign and working class pastimes incorporating an excellent section on football. You can view the desk where Thomas Paine wrote *The Rights of Man* and there is a good activity sheet for children. The museum is housed in one of the former pumphouses that supplied hydraulic power around the city - this one used to turn the hands of the Town Hall clock and raise the curtain at the Opera House. There's an archive and study centre

Emmeline Pankhurst

Emmeline Goulden was born in 1858. Her mother and father both had radical political beliefs, although this hadn't prevented the latter surveying his sleeping young daughter one night and muttering sadly, "What a pity she wasn't born a lad". Emmeline inherited her parents' radicalism and later married Manchester lawyer Richard Pankhurst, a committed socialist. Both members of the Independent Labour Party, they campaigned on a number of issues, in particular for women's votes. Frustrated with lack of progress, she formed the Women's Social and Political Union in 1903 at her Manchester home. When this body became militant, the term Suffragettes was born. Emmeline had four children, including campaigners Christabel and Sylvia Pankhurst. Richard had died in 1898 and after years of campaigning Emmeline followed in 1928. By this time she'd performed a political U-turn and become a member of the Conservative Party.

People's History Museum

by appointment at 103 Princess Street, City, appropriately this is in the Mechanics' Institute where the Trades Union Congress was founded in 1867. The Museum will be moving to this site during a refurbishment which starts in 2007. *Toilets, baby changing, food and drink, shop, group and school visits, disabled access, tours, events.*

Platt Fields Park

Wilmslow Road, Fallowfield, Manchester

The Gallery of Costume (page 87) occupies the north eastern corner of Plattfields Park. Along Platt Lane, in the park, lies Holy Trinity church, 1845-6 by Edmund Sharpe. From a distance this looks fairly standard but is a real oddball. The building's almost completely constructed out of terracotta, one of two surviving Lancashire 'pot churches'. It came about when Sharpe was encouraged by John Fletcher to display the wide possibilities of terracotta after Fletcher had come across a useful supply of fireclay at his Bolton collieries. Running into the park between the former Unitarian Chapel, now the home of a photographic club, and the south entrance from Wilmslow Road is another oddity, the mysterious Nico Ditch – an Anglo Saxon boundary which ran for several miles across the south of the city. By a coincidence of nomenclature, the notorious German singer and songwriter Nico, at one time with New York's Velvet Underground, passed her last troubled years in Manchester. Platt Fields Park has an exemplary Friends organisation which arranges excellent events.

Manchester's ghosts

Some Manchester spooks prefer obvious places such as the Town Hall or the Cathedral. Others love pubs: more than the usual spirits are said to be found in the Castle (Oldham Street), Night & Day Cafe (Oldham Street), the Old Wellington (Hanging Ditch), the Shakespeare (Fountain Street), Sir Ralph Abercrombie (Bootle Street) and the White Lion (Liverpool Road). Even bars as seemingly prosaic as Brannigans can prove homes for the restless. The very angry ghost at this Peter Street drinking den is perhaps annoyed that his former Methodist, and therefore temperance, hall is now one of the city's rowdiest bars. Even the celebrated psychic Derek Acora was shooed out of the building in a clearly shaken state.

If you want to raise your own ghost in the city, follow these instructions: At night, walk widdershins (dialect word for anti-clockwise, and therefore counter to the sun and therefore wrong) three times around one of the table tombs at the back of St Ann's Church and then put you ear to the tomb. You should be able to hear the dead talking.

You can seek professional help in your otherworldly studies with the Manchester Association of Paranormal Investigators at www.maxpages.com/mapit. For ghost tours, especially at Halloween, contact a city Blue Badge Guide on 07876 235638.

The photograph below was taken in Chetham's Library in 1927. A fake perhaps?

MUSEUMS

THE QUAYS & MANCHESTER SHIP CANAL

2 miles (3.2km) southwest of the city centre
FREE *From the city centre, take a Metrolink tram (Eccles line). The trams run every 15 minutes and provide a stimulating slalom over canals and by offices*

In 1882 Daniel Adamson, an eminent Manchester engineer, organised a campaign for the construction of a canal to allow sea-going traffic to travel inland as far as the city. In 1885 Parliament approved the Ship Canal Act, despite strong opposition from Liverpool Docks and the railway companies. It was these bodies that had given the impetus for the canal through the tariffs they'd imposed on Manchester products, eg it cost 19s 3d to send a ton of cotton from Manchester to Calcutta in 1856 of which 12s 6d was incurred getting it to Liverpool and through the port. Indeed the origin of the rivalry between the cities, and thus Manchester and Liverpool football clubs, lies in the import and export of cotton more than a century ago.

The Ship Canal was the biggest engineering project undertaken in Britain in the C19. It took more than16,000 navvies and six years to excavate the 35 mile (56km), 8 metre deep canal. Opened by Queen Victoria in 1894, the trade the canal generated together with the large industrial area of Trafford Park, which grew along the south bank, delayed industrial decay for many years. But eventually the headwaters became redundant as container vessels grew too large – the last commercial visit was in 1982. Yet around its lower reaches at the Mersey Estuary, the canal is busier than ever. Superlative engineering is still an element. The 92m span lift footbridge at the Quays pictured here was designed by Spanish engineer Casado in partnership with Salford company Parkman.

A visit to the refurbished Quays - the old headwaters – is an essential part of coming to Manchester. The large expanse of water and the natural bowl within which the Quays lie, provides the purest quality of light in the region and some of the best sunsets too. Above all there are the cultural attractions of the Lowry (pg 105) and the Imperial War Museum North (pg 89), which together make this a major centre in which to visit monumental modern

▲ Aerial view of the Quays **The Lowry** on the left and the **Imperial War Museum North** on the right

architecture. In the Lowry is Salford Tourist Information Centre (0161 848 8601). The Salford Watersports Centre (0161 877 7252), with its range of activities for hire, provides another excuse to visit.

On the Manchester United/Trafford side there is a very enjoyable sculpture from SITE – 'Silent Cargoes' – celebrating the former industries of Trafford Park. The sculpture consists of items such as life-sized engines, railway wheels and cotton bales with hats and gloves apparently discarded by workers at the end of their shift.

The change from the busy industrial wharves to the calm of today is dramatic. Where all was work and grime, now you find two cultural centres, housing, offices, restaurants, pubs, hotels, a multi-screen cinema and a shopping mall. Unfortunately much of this is poor quality, such as the lumpen Anchorage office from the late '80s. The number one planning disaster comes courtesy of the shopping mall and its attendant sub-Torremolinos apartment block, which deny a good view of the Lowry. Dock 9 here regularly hosts the swimming section of triathlons, an event which during the 2002 Commonwealth Games was attended by about 100,000 spectators.

A good place to get a hint of the Ship Canal in former times is at Barton Bridge and Aqueduct, five miles west from the city on B5211, close to the Trafford Centre. Here, in spectacular arrangement, you can see the Barton Aqueduct swing 800 tons of water as it carries the Bridgewater Canal across the Ship Canal. This masterpiece of civil engineering is from 1894 by Edward Leader Williams and uses an island in the Ship Canal as a pivot.

Whilst walking the Ship Canal waterside, don't worry too much about falling in. As the Canal was being constructed, a navvy by the name of Laurance fell in and drowned. He was from the Ladywell area and became known as Ladywell Larry. His generous spirit is said to pluck people from the waters should they slip.

Urbis 6B

Cathedral Gardens, City centre 0161 605 8200 *www.urbis.org.uk* FREE *(Except Special Exhibitions) Daily 10am-6pm*

Urbis is local architect Ian Simpson's most interesting and most troubled structure. Externally it's a knockout, sculptural, with a chameleon glass skin, which responds to the changes in the weather's moods, it enlivens and spooks this end of the city centre. Truth is, you could fill Urbis with concrete and it would still be a beautiful form: without any attempt at function, it'd be a great piece of public art. And that's the problem. On the inside Urbis is difficult to use, awkward in the way the different floors work together. In particular the introduction of frosted glass which restricts the view out was a silly idea no matter how clever the arguments put forward in its defence. When people go up they want to look out.

So what is Urbis? It's a visitor attraction with a brief to look at urban culture around the world. The name is Latin for 'of the city'. The reason why it's in Manchester is straightforward. This was the first modern industrial city, and as such it was the first modern city. Frederick Engels (see page 37), the German communist, who lived for more than 20 years in Manchester, recognised the city in this role. By a twist of fate, Urbis is built upon land that Engels knew as Little Gibraltar, then a warren of filthy courts and decrepit housing, which he described in his book *The Condition of the Working Class in England*.

Opened in 2002 Urbis attempts to explore the human response to cities, how people experience and use them by immersing visitors in the experience of the city, the sounds, the sights and the art. It has been a struggle and it's to be hoped that the re-working of levels 2 and 3 might make the mission of Urbis clearer.

The ground floor space introduces the museum and from there a glass elevator (looks like a funicular railway but technically isn't) glides diagonally up the side of the building to the fourth floor. People then work their way back down through the building. The original displays were an essay in how far museum and gallery practice had gone awry in the early years of the decade. This was characterised by an over-reliance and an over-optimism on how far technology could be pushed, with a series of exhibits which were shallow in content and prone to breakdown. If Urbis is to live up to it's external majesty then this is what will have to change after the refurbishment. It'll be worth seeing how it works out. Fortunately there are good people in charge.

These issues aside the tours of the building are interesting, the opening of an evening bar, The Social, in the space occupied during the day by the café, has helped, and some of the temporary exhibitions which take place on level 1 are excellent. To help with running costs and to give themselves higher visibility Channel M, the regional TV, station has taken up large areas of the building - you can pick it up on Sky Digital Channel 203.*Toilets, baby changing, shop, food and drink, schools and group visits, disabled access, tours, events.*

Central art galleries

Castlefield Gallery 3G

2 Hewitt Street, City 0161 832 8034 *www.castlefieldgallery.co.uk* FREE *Wed-Sun 1pm-6pm*

Castlefield Gallery was founded in1984. Led by artists themselves, it provides exhibition space for the Manchester artistic community and for visiting artists with developing reputations.

Toilets, baby changing, group and school visits, disabled access.

Cornerhouse 7G

Oxford Road, City 0161 200 1500 *www.cornerhouse.org* FREE *Tue-Sat 11am-6pm (Thu to 9pm); Sun 2pm-6pm*

The Cornerhouse has three floors of contemporary art galleries, three cinema screens, a bar, café and bookshop. It hosts some of the most thought-provoking, indeed controversial, work in the city. The Cornerhouse also operates an international publications service distributing visual arts books and catalogues. There is a popular bar downstairs and a good veggie-friendly café on the first floor and excellent children's workshops.

Toilets, baby changing, food and drink, shop, group and school visits, disabled access.

Chinese Arts Centre 8B

Market Buildings, Thomas Street, City 0161 832 7271 *www.chinese-arts-centre.org* FREE *Mon-Sat 10am-6pm; Sun 11am-5pm*

The organisation promotes contemporary Chinese arts and the interpretation of Chinese culture in the region. It is committed to developing creative opportunities for artists of Chinese origin and they hold many regular exhibitions, events and workshops. The on-site tea house offers a broad selection of teas to sample and they are also available to take home. There is a shop that sells books, gifts and stationery. The centre is located in the old Market buildings and is a superb refurbishment from one of Manchester's best contemporary architects, OMI.

Toilets, shop, group and school visits, disabled access, events.

CUBE 7F

Portland Street, City 0161 237 5525 *www.cube.org.uk* FREE *Mon-Fri noon-5.30pm; Sat noon-5pm*

The full name is Centre for the Urban Built Environment which says it all. This is a bold venture aimed at explaining how cities work through architecture and urban planning. The building is a fine example of how Manchester's textile warehouses should be converted. This was the work of local architects Stephen Hodder and was superbly handled.

Toilets, shop, group and school visits, disabled access, events.

Temporary exhibition image at the Chinese Arts Centre by Miao Xiaochun

MUSEUMS

Visit Manchester's exhibition centre of city life

URBIS
the city centre

Five floors of exhibitions
Featuring photography, design, architecture, music, contemporary art and much more

The Social at Urbis
Our stylish cafe bar

The Urbis Shop
Packed with original gift ideas

Special events
Including tours, talks and workshops

Family activities
Fun for Saturdays and school holidays

Open daily
10am - 6pm

Next to
Victoria Station

www.urbis.org.uk
0161 605 8200

Parking facilities nearby
at the MEN Arena

Market Restaurant

104 High Street, Manchester M4 1HQ
Tel: 0161-834-3743

Make for the Market...

We are a small and family-friendly restaurant situated in the Northern Quarter close to the former Smithfield Market and the Craft Centre.

We are open for lunch and dinner on Wednesdays to Fridays and for dinner on Saturdays. There is plenty of parking space directly outside the restaurant.

Our menu changes frequently, our wines are reasonably priced and we serve the widest range of bottle-conditioned beers in the City.

Make for the Market - the small friendly restaurant with an atmosphere you will enjoy.

For reservations telephone
0161 834 3743

www.market-restaurant.com

Perigal's 'Fancy Dress Ball'
Salford Museum and Art Gallery

Salford Museum and Art Gallery

Peel Park,The Crescent, Salford 0161 736 2649 *www.salford.gov.uk/salfordmuseum*
FREE *Mon- Fri 10am-4.45pm; Sat-Sun 1pm-5pm*

The first floor art gallery has a collection including Perigal's entertaining painting of the 'Grand Fancy Dress Ball' at the 1828 Manchester Music Festival. This includes portraits of the city's rich and famous all in fancy dress – each bigwig had to pay of course to be featured. There's an interesting reconstructed Victorian street – Lark Hill Place. The Victorian art collection is crammed into one small, rather dismal, room. This is sad as the Gallery has an interesting collection of work with much more in storage. New work by local societies and students is often given unwarranted space. *Toilets, shop, group and school visits, disabled access, events.*

Victoria Baths

Anson Road, Victoria Park 0161 224 2020
www.victoriabaths.org.uk ***£1*** CHILDREN FREE
Apr-Oct, first Sun of each month, noon-4pm

Victoria Baths opened in 1906 as a mini-scandal, having cost Manchester Corporation more than £59,000. This was over budget and twice the cost of usual bath houses of the period. The complex was designed by the city architect, Henry Price. He might have over-spent but he left a civic palace of recreation based around first and second class baths for men, a single more democratic bath for women, Turkish and Russian baths plus a superintendent's living quarters and a laundry house.

The first class baths were intended for the rich gentlemen of nearby Victoria Park, whilst the second class were meant for the terraced house lads, and included household-sized 'slipper' baths for straight-forward washes before most homes featured such luxury. The class distinctions had vanished by WWI but more controversially, mixed bathing had been introduced. The first class pool was frequently floored over and put on dances, lectures and concerts, including the famous swing orchestra of Phil Moss in the '50s. Also in that decade, the first municipal jacuzzi was introduced.

The deteriorating structure closed as a Manchester Council facility in 1993. A vigorous campaign to preserve and re-open the baths began immediately. These efforts paid off when Victoria Baths appeared on BBC2's *Restoration* programme in 2003, in which crumbling UK buildings competed for cash. The baths won the public phone vote easily and collected £3.5m to help restore the Turkish baths area.

The chief attraction on any visit is the fantastical interior weave of terracotta, mosaics, ironwork, woodwork and stained glass (see picture page 116-117). Note the gentlemen playing cricket over the first class entrance and the boxers over the second class entrance. A watery theme is maintained with fishy mosaics on the floor, whilst a stylised version of the ship on Manchester's coat of arms sails through the air in the window over the main pool.

Laurence Stephen Lowry 1887-1976

Born in Old Trafford and locked into the Greater Manchester area for the rest of his life, Lowry was an eccentric artist but not typically so. He was never a fey bohemian, but instead mixed his artistic endeavour with a daytime job as a rent collector. He was also a teetotal, non-smoking, only child bachelor, his odd psyche doubtless the product of a dominatrix mother who ridiculed his art. As a trained artist, his work gradually acquired fame, although it was frequently dismissed by critics as parochial and naïve. Lowry didn't seem to mind. He became a Royal Academician (1962), Freeman of Salford (1962) and Manchester's Man of the Year (1966). His most famous works are the packed scenes of the industrial conurbation (see pages 106-107) he was so familiar with. But it is paintings such as 'Head of a Man with Red Eyes', shown here or the barren, eerie but powerful seascapes such as 'The Sea', below, which reveal a far more complex and gifted artist. Here the influence of Lowry's favourite teacher, Adolphe Valette (see page 108), is most easily appreciated.

MUSEUMS

The Lowry

Pier 8, Salford Quays 0870 111 2020
www.thelowry.com FREE *(donations are welcome)*
The Galleries open Sun - Fri 11am- 5pm, Sat 10am-5pm

QUICK-FIX

Why visit: for the fascinating building and location, and for changing programme of exhibitions and the theatres.

The Lowry was designed by Michael Wilford and cost £94m in total, £64.3m of which came from the National Lottery. For that sort of money you get an art gallery, a restaurant, corporate hospitality suites, a tourist information centre, a publishing house and a study centre. Most importantly in terms of revenue you get theatres, the Lyric with 1,750 seats and the largest provincial stage in the UK, and the Quays Theatre, with a capacity of 460. The Studio,seating 150, has been added recently.

Inevitably, the Lowry has been compared with the Guggenheim in Bilbao, but here the impression is of angles rather than curves. The exterior of the main auditorium of the Lyric Theatre rises in steel panels above a mass of sharp geometric forms, cones, cubes and circles. These latter are swathed in glass allowing a view of people circulating around the interior. The view from the inside out is equally good whilst the vistas through the building are exceptional. Thus the foyer is overlooked by balconies opening from the first floor and the restaurant bar is crossed by a bridge, whilst the outer wrap of the Lyric is punctured by almost deconstructionalist balconies.

On the south-facing side adjacent to the restaurant, the steel cladding rises from the floor through the glass ceiling 20 metres above, to the crown of the building and the sky. The cylinder landmark tower with its trellis top, clad again in steel and housing archive and study areas, actively refers back to the industrial past. The interior colours are robust in deliberate contrast to the shimmering exterior, oranges and deep purples in the entrance areas, royal blues, reds and purples in the theatres.

The art galleries dedicated to Mr Lowry are on the north-facing side of the building to prevent damage from the sunny south, but there is still plenty of natural light streaming in from the neighbouring promenade windows. A variety of the artist's work can be viewed – the classic industrial townscapes and sombre but magnificent sea and moorland pictures, haunting portraits and eerie sketches. Salford began collecting Lowry's works in 1930 and has more than 350. As an introduction there is a permanent Meet Mr Lowry display in the tower. No artist in the world, has so expensive a monument named after him as Laurence Stephen Lowry – the old curmudgeon would have smiled at this. He shares his space with touring exhibitions of varying quality which sometimes hit the heights in terms of quality.

Irony is built in too. A space that is as colourful as an HG Wells dream of the future commemorates a man who inhabited a dark cave of the imagination. A building that needs to attract hundreds of thousands is named after a man who shied from human relationships. And the industrial scenes that drew Lowry so powerfully have disappeared under apartments.

Toilets, baby changing, food and drink, group and school visits, disabled access, tours, events.

MUSEUMS

'Coming from the Mill': all quotations from LS Lowry

1 Chimney: "My ambition was to put the industrial scene on the map". LS Lowry is best known for portraying cityscapes of the industrial North, but his work was remarkably varied and included portraits, landscapes, seascapes, interiors and almost surrealist drawings. He felt that this was his "most characteristic mill scene".

2 Figures: Lowry is best known as the painter of 'matchstick men'. It was a term he hated - he simplified his figures to show them as parts of a crowd rather than as individuals, and could paint in a realistic manner. He said that "the ghostly figures are symbols of my mood".

3 Face of figure: "Crowds are the most lonely thing of all." Lowry rarely painted faces on his figures in his cityscapes, so we read them as part of a crowd rather than individuals. We cannot see their faces, so we read their characters through their body language - with many hunched over, as through walking into wind. Lowry's attitude to workers seems ambiguous, as he does not dignify them nor does he caricature them.

4 Mill: "I did the paintings of factories and industrial workers because I lived on the spot." Lowry came from a lower middle class family, but lived in the industrial suburb of Pendlebury, Salford.

5 Dome in background: "Most of my town and landscape is composite. Made up; part real and part imaginary." Although Lowry observed

the city at work and play, his paintings were not meant to be 'realistic' but imaginative, visionary depictions of an archetypal industrial town.

6 Houses in centre: "I have put most of my tenants in my pictures". Although many people believe Lowry was a 'Sunday painter', he was trained at art school for several years and could draw proficiently. To support himself through his career, however, he kept a part-time post as a rent collector. This allowed him to walk the streets of Manchester and Salford, and provided an endless source of material from his observations of street life.

7 Dog: "I look upon human beings as automatons... they are not free. No one is." Lowry frequently included dogs, which have more of a 'human' character than the automaton-like figures.

8 Walking figures on left: "It's the battle of life." Lowry's figures seem always to be in transit between one location and another, as if forever on the way to and from work.

9 Window of mill building: Lowry never painted inside mills, or people at work in them, choosing to portray the streets where they lived and worked.

10 Horse and cart: By 1930 cars were beginning to become the dominant form of road transport. Lowry almost never painted them, preferring to portray an age that had already passed.

11 Sky: "You never see the sun in my paintings." Lowry's earliest work was dark - they're as though the skies were filled with soot. But his training at art school under an impressionist painter, Adolphe Valette, gave him a sensitivity to effects of light and atmosphere. During the 1920s, Lowry developed his characteristic white backgrounds, and lightened his palette.

12 Grass at front: "I cannot overestimate the effect on me of the coming into this dark city of Adolphe Valette [Lowry's teacher at art school] full of the French impressionists." Even though he was taught by a follower of the impressionists, Lowry's cityscapes seem monochrome and rarely feature strong greens, blues, or yellows. Throughout his career, Lowry only painted with a palette of five colours: white, black, red, yellow and blue.

13 Children: Here, children play on a patch of waste ground. Lowry claimed that he barely noticed the depression of the '30s, and his paintings never simply reflected the time that they were made. But two years after his painting was made, there were hunger marches on the streets of Manchester.

◂ **'Coming from the Mill', 1930 by LS Lowry**

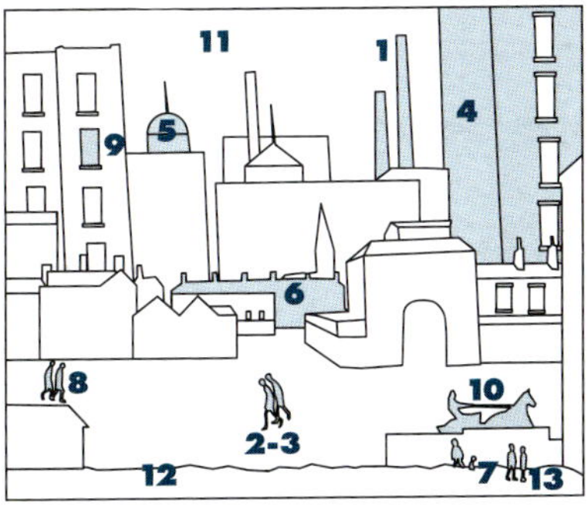

Adolphe Valette

Valette was a French painter who was born in St Etienne in 1876. Awarded a scholarship to Japan, the outbreak of the Russian-Japanese War meant he was transferred to England. After a period in London he came to Manchester working for a printing firm. In 1907 he joined the staff of the Municipal School of Art as a teacher of painting and drawing. His method of teaching students by painting with them was different from the very formal methods of teaching in most English art schools. Amongst his students was LS Lowry, see page 104, who was greatly influenced by the urbane, well-dressed Frenchman. Valette left Manchester in the 1920s.

Although he painted many different themes in many different countries his series of Manchester urban scenes were his finest works. Inspired by Impressionism and finished at a time when horse-drawn vehicles were being super-ceded by cars they capture the spirit of busy, rainy Manchester perfectly. Indeed they are less pictures of things than of atmosphere. In Valette's vision the physical world is dissolved in water and light, edges soften and colours merge. Beauty is distilled from commercial and industrial landscapes, unregarded views are tinged with soft focus lushness. Valette's achievement in these views was such that to date no-one has painted better paintings of the city.

There is a room of his work at Manchester Art Gallery.

MUSEUMS

Manchester Art Gallery 6E

Mosley Street, City 0161 235 8888

www.manchestergalleries.org

FREE *Tue-Sun 10am-5pm*

QUICK-FIX

Why visit: one of the great British provincial galleries complete with lovely buildings and coherent desplays. Good for aesthetes but also for families looking to get their kids into art.

Manchester Art Gallery houses one of the great provincial art collections of the UK. The building is important in its own right. Two of the three parts were by Charles Barry – the architect of the Houses of Parliament. The dignified design reflects Barry's travels in Greece a few years before and was fashionable at the time. Barry's motto was 'Nihil Pulchrum Nisi Utile', which means 'nothing beautiful unless useful.' The building was acquired by the city in 1882, the sale terms requiring an annual £4,000 spend on new works. Round the corner on Princess Street is the Athenaeum by Barry again, now part of the Gallery. It opened in 1837 as a gentleman's club. Barry introduced the Italian Renaissance 'palazzo' to the city with the Athenaeum and this was subsequently copied in warehouses, banks and offices. The Athenaeum witnessed lectures from individuals such as Charles Dickens and John Ruskin.

The third part of the site comprises the new building (completed 2002) by Michael Hopkins Associates. These defer to the art they contain with good grace. In dramatic contrast to the buildings of Urbis or the Imperial War Museum North, this is the architecture of good manners, a masterpiece of understated elegance.

Visitors enter via Mosley Street, as Barry intended. Immediately you find yourself in the hall with, high above, the replica Elgin marbles given by George IV in 1830. The ground floor contains the café, restaurant, shop and the CIS Manchester Gallery devoted to the city's achievements in art and design both past and present.

The first floor houses the permanent collection. The rooms move clockwise from the C18 and include works by Stubbs, Gainsborough, Claude Lorrain, Canaletto, Constable, Turner, Pisarro, Gauguin, Rodin and others. You'll also find one of the nation's best collections of Pre-Raphaelite art: with Holman Hunt's 'Hireling Shepherd', John Everett Millais' 'Autumn Leaves', Rossetti's remarkable 'Astarte Syriaca' and Ford Madox Brown's 'Work'.

The new building contains a collection of British C20 art with works from Stanley Spencer, Lucien Freud, Francis Bacon, David Hockney and Bridget Riley. Here also is the space for visiting exhibitions, large enough to attract the best internationally. The ground floor areas provide educational space. The first floor area between the new building and the Athenaeum contains the Clore Interactive Gallery aimed at 5- 12-year-olds.

The Athenaeum's most dramatic space is the former lecture hall, inserted in 1873 by the firm of Clegg and Knowles. This double height space boasts female personifications of the arts, humanities, science and industry and houses the Gallery of Craft and Design. This contains an international collection of a thousand plus objects including works from Picasso, René Lalique, Fabergé and Conran.

Elsewhere in the Atheneaum, the city's collection of pre-1700s art, including work from Renaissance and Dutch masters, is displayed. Manchester Art Gallery hosts a large number of events so check the website.

Toilets, baby changing, food and drink, shop, group and school visits, disabled access, Braille interpretation, guided tours, events.

The Pre-Raphaelite Brotherhood

Formed in 1848, the 'Brotherhood' of Dante Gabriel Rossetti, Holman Hunt and John Everett Millais was born as a reaction against the perceived excesses of contemporary art. The Brotherhood wanted a return to the more innocent expression of the early Renaissance, before Raphael, particularly they required fidelity to nature: art direct from the source.

'Work' by Ford Madox Brown

This is the artist's masterpiece and one of the most famous works in Manchester Art Gallery. The painting, filled with closely observed detail and symbolism, was begun in 1852, but took 13 years to complete. The artist was being ambitious, and purely of his time, in attempting to capture society, rich and poor, in relation to the benefits of honest physical or intellectual toil, set against the malign effects of a lack of work, either through choice or circumstance. Around the frame Brown has placed relevant Biblical quotations: 'In the sweat of thy face shalt thou eat bread' and 'Seest thou a man diligent in his business? He shall stand before Kings'. The painting was purchased by the gallery in 1885. The words in quotes below are from Brown's own description.

1 The central figure is physical work made heroic. The young navvy is a model of virile health and beauty – a celebration of labour. Nearby is the older navvy 'who does his work and loves his beer'. Brown admired the 'British navvy in the full swing of his activity' and found him just as worthy of artistic depiction as 'a fisherman of the Adriatic'.

2 This is the herb and flower seller who has never been taught to work and who 'with his restless gleaming eyes, he doubts and despairs of everyone'.

3 'The brainworkers, who… are the cause of well-ordained work and happiness in others'. The two intellectuals are Thomas Carlyle – Brown admired his book *Past and Present* – and the Rev. FD Maurice, a pioneer of working class education.

4 The aristocratic gent on horseback is 'honest' and 'true-hearted'. If only he could get to our 'brainworkers' he would be converted to their enlightened thinking, but the way is blocked and his daughter is pointing to an easier route.

5 A ragged group of children, the mother dead (note the baby's black ribbons) and the father a drinker. Thus the ten year old daughter must care for her young siblings, making the best of it in counterpoint to the herb seller, (see above). A paradigm of innocence, the baby, as if in challenge, is the only character in the picture to stare at the viewer directly.

6 This lady's 'only business in life, as yet, is to…look beautiful for our benefit'. Modelled on Brown's wife, she clearly doesn't have enough work to do, but might be reminded of the fleeting nature of beauty if she paid attention to her unworldly lap dog in the red coat who 'will

MUSEUMS

run through that lime' and burn its paws.

7 Behind Miss Lovely is the busybody. Again with no need to work she carries her pamphlets around: this called 'The Bread of Life' which attempts to reform the working class and poor without any desire to learn about them.

8 Along the roadside here are sleeping tramps, examples of idleness and rootlessness. Some are more deserving than others but all desperately need to work to not only sustain their lives but give them meaning.

9 The carpenter is a skilled worker, further up the hierarchy than the navvies, and with ambitions to self-improvement. He dresses in a natty waistcoat, flower in the pocket, and carries a rolled up *Times* under his arm.

10 '[T]he man with the beer tray calling for beer ho! so lustily, is a specimen of town pluck and energy contrasted with country thews and sinews.' This man is another hero for Brown who despite being 'starved, stunted with gin', as a child has found the energy and resourcefulness to become a much respected beer-man.

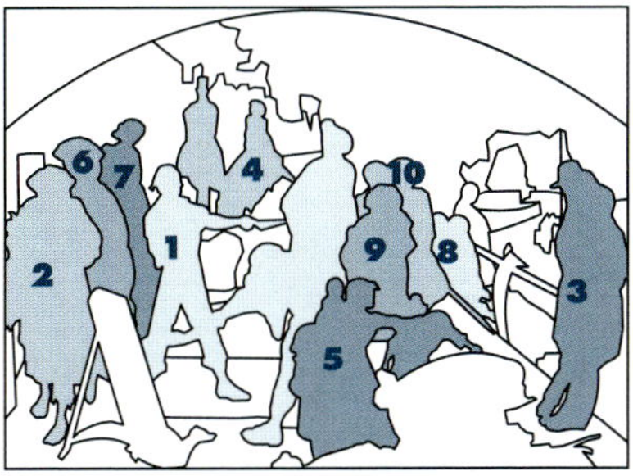

Whitworth Art Gallery

Oxford Road, University 0161 275 7450
www.whitworth.man.ac.uk FREE
Mon-Sat 10am-5pm; Sun 2-5pm

QUICK-FIX

Why visit: because you'll find a comfortable space which caters for all types of visitors with well-presented art, including major works.

Behind the 1885 façade lies a gallery of the 1960 and 1990s. These provide splendid exhibition spaces, spacious and pleasant to walk through, a contrast to the fussy, hot red, terracotta Victorian exterior. The works cover just about every field of the arts. A feature of the Whitworth is the clever curation, with an always stimulating and shifting series of exhibitions from its own and visiting collections.

The gallery was founded under the will of Sir Joseph Whitworth, a self-made millionaire, who is chiefly remembered as the father of precision engineering. He was in many ways the archetypal Victorian entrepreneur, forging his way from humble origins to a knighthood and fame throughout the industrial world: whilst understanding that with wealth came responsibility and the duty to re-invest in the amenity of the locality that gave you the money. His name crops up all over Manchester in buildings and streets named in his honour.

The gallery, owned by the University of Manchester, has one of the chief collections of British watercolours, a collection of historic textiles second only to that of the Victoria and Albert Museum, a collection of engravings and prints, an important collection of wallpapers and excellent work from modern and contemporary artists.

Those represented include Durer, Rembrandt, Hogarth, Piranesi, Mantegna, Cozens, Turner, Blake, William Morris, Madox Brown, Rosetti, Burne-Jones, Van Gogh, Toulouse-Lautrec, Picasso, Henry Moore, Francis Bacon, LS Lowry, Lucien Freud and David Hockney. There are dramatic sculptures from Eduardo Paolozzi and Jacob Epstein.

These are just some of the more famous names, mostly from painting, but you'll find that the aforementioned textile, wallpaperand other exhibits will interest you just as much - such as the James Bond '60s wallpaper pictured here. Of course the gallery can only show a very small percentage of the collection at a time, so it offers access to works in store. Arranged by prior appointment this glimpse into the backstage areas of a gallery is fascinating. Those with an interest in a specific artist also get an unrivalled and intimate view in of the works.

There are many events, including excellent lectures and courses. By the way the on-site cafe was an award winner at the 2006 Manchester Food and Drink Festival.

Toilets, baby changing, shop, group and school visits, disabled access, tours, events.

Gallery Art: Top-left 'Flora', a tapestry by William Morris, **above**, Poverty' by Pablo Picasso, **left**, Arts and Crafts book cover from Walter Crane, **below**,'Lake Lucerne at Sunset' by JMW Turner

The Manchester Art Treasures Exhibition 1857

Manchester was yesterday the scene of an event almost unique in the history of art in England or perhaps the world. An exhibition of art treasures, never before equalled for extent and importance.

The Times, 6 May 1857

2007 marks the 150th anniversary of the first major international art exhibition– the Manchester Art Treasures Exhibition of 1857. In many ways the event was the natural follow-up to the Great Exhibition of 1851 in London, but instead of highlighting industry and technology, it brought together the private art collections of Great Britain. The Exhibition held a third of the country's art treasures, including works from Queen Victoria and Prince Albert who both visited. Held in a single huge building in Old Trafford designed by local architect Edward Salomans, during its 142 days of operation more than 1.3 million people from all sections of society visited. The Exhibition was the first occasion in Britain in which the national art treasures were presented in a 'palace of art'. It was the inspiration behind the creation of the National Gallery in the capital.

The public response was gratifying because one of the express aims of the exhibition had been to bring art to the masses. When Mr CJ Deane had come up with the idea in March 1856 he wished 'to promote among the people a knowledge of those great masterpieces of the human genius through the contemplation of which the popular taste might be elevated and refined.'

Artists represented at the Exhibition included Michelangelo, Bellini, Titian, Rubens, Rembrandt, Holbien, Turner and so on. An unfinished work by Michelangelo, now at the National Gallery, gained the name, the 'Manchester Madonna', at the event.

The only real memorial left from the event is the Hallé Orchestra. German musician, Charles Hallé had assembled a group of musicians to entertain the guests for the Exhibition. The response encouraged him to form an orchestra which became the Hallé.

‹ **Exhibition catalogue:** the catalogues of the day were spectacular in the way they looked and the effort taken to produce them. The Art Treasures Exhibition catalogue included full engravings of works featured, with beautifully worded descriptions of the artists and their art.

▲ From 6 October 2007 to 27 January 2008 Manchester Art Gallery will be holding a major exhibition based on the 1857 event. This will feature the **Manchester Madonna 'Virgin with Child'** on loan from the National Gallery

▲ Queen Victoria and Prince Albert at **Manchester Art Treasures Exhibition**

The Exhibition Timeline

Victorian energy unleashed

1856

March – the Exhibition is proposed in a series of meetings
May – Royal assent given
June – Old Trafford site chosen
August – first pillar raised from the ground

1857

February – 6000 VIP visitors view the nearly completed building
Spring – a building of brick, glass, iron and stone, measuring 700ft in length, 104 feet broad, 65 feet high with a central nave and two aisles is completed and fitted out, incorporating an organ and and space for an orchestra of 100 performers and 500 vocalists
May 5 – The Exhibition opens
September 23 – Exhibition closes after receiving 1, 336,715 visitors

1858

May – the site is cleared and no trace of the Exhibition remains

MUSEUMS

First Church of Christ Scientist – Edgar Wood Building

Daisy Bank Road, Victoria Park.
This remarkable church was designed by Edgar Wood in 1903. Architectural critic Nikolaus Pevsner described it as 'a pioneer work, internationally speaking… and it stands all on its own in England'. Working predominantly in his beloved Arts and Crafts style, Wood pushed and distorted the building through Art Nouveau to an Expressionism of the type that became fashionable in Germany 20 years later.

After entering through the sturdy perimeter wall, visitors find themselves in a triangular space between the diagonal arms of the former reading room and hall. Directly ahead is the white rendered gable of the main building with its exaggerated up thrust. Tucked away like a spire that never grew up is the chubby round brick tower with a conical roof. The main door of the church is a sweet curve of red brick under a vast cruciform window. Inside the highlights include the fascinating and complex pattern formed by the organ screen and the green Norwegian marble of the piers.

Sadly much of the original and exquisite furniture has been lost, although some survives in Whitworth Art Gallery.

Arts and Crafts & Art Nouveau

A lot remains in the city of that interesting period in design and architectural history from the late C19 and early C20. This was when the solid craftsmen virtues of the Arts and Crafts Movement, as espoused by William Morris, started to loosen into the sinuous, sensuous Art Nouveau style, characterised by the dismissal of the straight line and an embracing of flowing movement.

In Britain, Glasgow's Charles Rennie Mackintosh is famous for his work in the period. Manchester has the remarkable practice of Edgar Wood and James Sellars, which spanned Arts and Crafts, through Art Nouveau and touched the Modern Movement (see panel, left). Wood also worked in nearby Middleton. Knutsford, meanwhile, has the maverick Manchester businessman Richard Harding Watt to thank for several unusual buildings (see the Regiobnal Sightseeing section).

Aside from such specialists, Art Nouveau's arrival in Manchester coincided with the boost to the economy given by the Ship Canal from 1894. The warehouses and

Victoria Baths

other commercial buildings of the period frequently carry entertaining glimpses of the style. This is usually in decoration only, on tilework, wrought iron or stained glass - as though the style was too frivolous, too Gallic-tinged to attract the serious businessmen of Manchester to commision whole buildings. Good examples include tile work on Prince's Buildings (Oxford Street), iron work at John Ryland's Library (Deansgate), glass at the Rossetti Hotel (Piccadilly) and the superb and artfully tortured iron gate and lamp between Lancaster House and India House on Whitworth Street from Harry S Fairhurst.

Outside the centre on Hathersage Road is Victoria Baths (see page 103). Presently campaigners are working hard to preserve one of the best ensembles from the period, by Henry Price, 1906 and there are regular open days. Another eye catcher is the splendid wood, tile and glass at the Lamb Inn, Eccles (0161 789 3882) – close to the Metrolink station. Manchester Art Gallery and Whitworth Art Gallery contain examples from the period in their collections - the latter has examples of Edgar Wood furniture.

Blackwell House – Manchester in the Lakes

When Edward Holt, Manchester brewer, decided to go second house hunting in the Lake District in the 1890s, his architect Baillie Scott excelled himself. Baillie Scott was one of the foremost designers in the Arts and Crafts style and gave Holt a house of contrasts. Externally it has an updated Tudor feel, inside it is joyful play of space, light and textures. The three showpiece rooms include the Main Hall, the Dining Room and the White Drawing Room.
This last is glorious, with light flooding in from windows framing views of lake and mountains. On a bright day, it's difficult to know where the room ends and the outside world takes over. The detailing of the slender columns, the moulded plasterwork and white tranquility of the room makes for a sublime space even on days busy with visitors. The wood carving at Blackwell is from Arthur Simpson of Kendal, who also designed the sweet, sweet carving at St Margaret's in Prestwich, close to the north gate of Heaton Park. This was also under Edward Holt's patronage as well as that of another Manchester brewer, Hubert Wilson. Meanwhile a third brewer, Henry Boddington, was providing Pownall Hall, Wilmslow – presently closed to the public but with another beautiful Arts and Crafts interior. We should raise our glasses.

SIGHTSEEING

Japanese Gardens, Tatton Park

Regional sightseeing

The sightseeing in this section conforms to the Greater Manchester region and a little beyond, with the exception of the final pages. This area shows great diversity of human and natural landscapes. The works of man vary from stone to brick, from slate-roofed terrace to thatched cottage, from towering mill to stately home. Nature expresses itself from the north to the south east with tough millstone grit moorland followed by limestone uplands. To the south lies a gentle rolling countryside of villages and meadows. If you enjoy walking you should consider purchasing the Ordnance Survey maps to the area, particularly the Landranger series. Maps 109, 118, 110 and 103 will prove the most useful. With a scale of 1.25 inches to a mile or 2cm to a kilometre, these maps cover the region in detail and include footpaths.

SIGHTSEEING

Stately homes and gardens

Adlington Hall

Mill Lane, Adlington, Macclesfield **01625 829 206** *www.adlingtonhall.com* FREE

Open by prior arrangement

Still in the private ownership of the original family, a branch of the Leghs, this is a house with a split personality, part black and white Elizabethan and part Georgian. There are three major rooms to visit, including the Great Hall with its superb murals.

Toilets, food and drink, shop, group and school visits, disabled access, guided tours and events.

Arley Hall

Arley Estate, nr Northwich, Cheshire **01565 777 353** *www.arleyhallandgardens.com* ***Gardens and chapel: adults £5, children £2.50, family £12 Hall: adults £2.50, children £1, family £7***

Apr-Sep, Tue-Sun (and Bank Holidays) 11pm-5pm; Hall open Tue and Sun only noon-5pm

A Tudor mansion set within 12 acres of award-winning gardens, Arley Hall, with its ancient history and over 100 acres of gardens and parkland, has been owned and run by the same family for more than 500 years. The present hall is built in the Victorian Jacobean style and each of the rooms has an individual character and charm with notable plaster work and panelling. The small but perfectly formed gardens are the best part of any visit and considered not only one of the best in Britain but amongst the best in Europe. Arranged in a series of 'green rooms', features include a Herb Garden, Flag Garden, the Kitchen Garden and the Walled Garden. The standout feature is the Herbaceous Border, which was the first of its kind in the country from 1849. The view along the Lime Avenue to the clock tower and the old barns is exquisite.

Toilets, food and drink, shop, group and school visits, disabled access, guided tours and events.

Arley Hall

Bramall Hall

Bramhall Park, Stockport **0845 8330974** *www.stockport.gov.uk/heritageattractions* ***Adults £3.95, children £3, family £11 (Mondays £2 for everybody)*** *Easter to Sep Mon-Sat 1pm-5pm, Sun and Bank Holidays 11am-5pm; other times ring ahead*

Black and white timber-framed Elizabethan manor house set in a 60-acre park overlooking Victorian landscaped gardens and the lush Ladybrook Valley. Bramall Hall was remodelled in the C19 but retains many original features. In brief it is one of the region's grandest timber-framed buildings. Built in the traditional local style, the framework is made with oak timbers, joined together using mortice and tenon joints and held in place with oak pegs. From 1066, for the first 800 years, just three families owned the estate: the Masseys, the de Bromales and the Davenports. The house was received into local authority control in 1935. The east front provides the finest view of the house. The most notable features are, perhaps, the religious paintings in the chapel and the intricate C16 wall paintings above. These are regarded as some of the most important in the country – composed of vegetable dyes, they depict birds, animals, flowers and demons. They alone make the journey here worthwhile. C19 living is well documented in the servants' quarters and is brought to life with period tours from the 1890s. The grounds are a great place to take a stroll with adventure playgrounds for kids and outdoor events in summer.

Abney Hall

Toilets, baby changing facilities, café, shop, group and school visits, disabled access, guided tours, video, special events.

Also nearby is **Abney Hall**, off Manchester Road (B5095), Cheadle. Built in 1847, this ornate Gothic Revival hall has hosted Disraeli, Gladstone and Prince Albert in its time, not to mention Agatha Christie, who regularly visited the house as a child and based the character Miss Marple on the Governess. The gardens and fishing ponds are open year round to the public, the hall infrequently and for a small charge.

Bramall Hall

SIGHTSEEING

Dunham Massey Hall

Charcoal Lane, Altrincham **0161 941 1025** *www.nationaltrust.org.uk* ***House and garden: adults £7.50, children £3.75, family £18.25 National Trust members free. Car park charge***
Mar-Oct: garden 11am-5.30pm, house Sat-Wed noon-5pm. Park open all year 9.30am-7.30pm

QUICK-FIX

Why visit: for the walks in the deer park, the house interiors and the fine gardens.

Smaller then Lyme Park or Tatton Park but still one of the big three stately homes now open to the public in Manchester's southern hinterlands. The house is of red brick with the centre of the façade stone-faced. It is a handsome building, plain and strong with elements dating from the C17, although most of the building is early the C18. The house was opened to the public on the death of the Earl of Stamford in 1976. The rather severe interior is perhaps a reflection of the last Earl's bachelor status. The most famous feature of the house is its collection of Huguenot silver.

The garden is lovely and large and contains an exquisitely kept parterre, an aromatic orangery and a busy Edwardian water garden. Outside the garden is the informal parkland area, which stretches over a couple of hundred acres. To add grace to the landscape of grass and tree, there is a herd of fallow deer which regenerates itself – every year there are up to 20 fawns produced. Close to the house is an attractive and working Elizabethan water mill. The Coach House features a permanent display on the park's natural history. You'll also find a restaurant/café, shop and art gallery. Good lunches can be had if you follow the cinder path near the Mill to Little Bollington and the attractive Swan with Two Nicks pub
Toilets, baby changing, food and drink, shop, group and school visits, disabled access, Braille interpretation, guided tours, events.

Dunham Massey Hall

Heaton Hall and Park

Prestwich 0161 773 1085 *www.manchester.gov.uk* FREE *Hall: Wed-Sun (bank holiday) 11am-5.30pm; farm centre: 10.30am-6pm (3.30pm); park 7.30am-9pm*

QUICK-FIX

Why visit: for the views from the Temple, pictured here, the many activities and the absolutely delightful house interiors.

Owned by Manchester City Council, Heaton Hall and Park are at last undergoing a drawn-out refurbishment. The estate covers a massive 600 acres and has one of its principal entrances conveniently situated over the road from the Heaton Park Metrolink stop just 15 minutes from the city centre. There is a new regional centre of excellence for bowls – the Commonwealth Games event having taken place here. The house is not huge but it is considered to be one of the best neo-Classical homes in the country. It was built in 1772 for the Earl of Wilton by James Wyatt. It is a building of lovely symmetry: end pavilions and colonnades linking to a domed central block guarded by life-size bronze lions. The interior is superb, a sublime harmony in natural wood and pastel shades. The Cupola Room above the Salon is simply gorgeous, displaying a complex of delicate patterns and deities by Biagio Rebecca.

Outside, 100 metres to the north east, is the Temple of the Winds. This restored delight offers a wonderful belvedere, south across the city and east and north to the Pennine Hills. Another restored beauty is the Dower House near the car park accessed from Bury Old Road. This has a beekeeping display and is a lovely Classical structure. Down by the lake you can see part of the façade of the old Town Hall of Manchester, re-erected on this site early in the C20. The restoration has reached the cafe here. Not far away a stone marks the spot were Pope John Paul II preached to more than a quarter of a million people in 1982.

If you feel in the need of some recreation, there is fishing, bowling, golf and an excellent pitch and putt course. You can also find a good Pets Corner and a Farm Centre. A new adventure playground close to the Dower House is filled with good stuff for the kids including an absolutely huge slide. On certain days you can take a trip on the old trams that run through the lower end of the park from the Boating Lake to the Middleton Road entrance. Tucked away in the wooded area to the west of the house is the excellent walled garden maintained by the volunteer Friends of the Park which always has something of botanicl interest on display. Heaton Park has a place in sporting history too. Horse races were held in the park in the C19 until the crowd became too riotous and drunken. The organisers then moved the races to Aintree, near Liverpool. The Grand National, in part, owes its origin to this large public estate. *Toilets, baby changing, food and drink, shop, group visits, disabled access, guided tours, events.*

SIGHTSEEING

Lyme Park

Disley, Stockport **01663 762 023**

www.nationaltrust.org.uk ***House and gardens: adults £7, children £3.50, family £17.50, National Trust members free. Car park charge*** *Mar-Oct: house Fri-Tue 1pm-5pm; gardens 11am-5pm. Deer park: Apr-Oct 8am-8.30pm, Oct-Apr 8am-6pm*

QUICK-FIX

Why visit: for one of the most spectacular sites of any of Britain's stately homes, but also for the garden, the walks and house which contains one of the most delightful of courtyards.

SIGHTSEEING

Lyme Hall and Park are perched on the edge of Pennines. Their situation in a bowl below the higher hills but still far above the Manchester and Cheshire plains give the house and gardens power and dignity. The place is particularly attractive to the costume drama hunter through its role as the home of Mr Darcy in the 1990's BBC production of *Pride and Prejudice*. The family of Lyme were the Leghs. The building is composed of Elizabethan elements with later alterations, particularly by the celebrated architect Giacomo Leoni in the 1730s. The result is a handsome house built around a lovely rusticated Renaissance courtyard. Highlights of the interior include Grinling Gibbons woodcarvings, Mortlake tapestries and a splendid collection of clocks. High in the building is the bedroom that housed Mary Queen of Scots. When the weather was unsuitable for a perambulation around the gardens, the impressive space of the Long Gallery was used. The house is set in 1,377 acres of parkland containing red and fallow deer. There are also formal gardens containing fine plant specimens and a Dutch walled garden. A lake fronts the house, the portico for which boasts a proud Neptune, trident in hand. From the Elizabethan viewing tower to the north, there are wide views from the Pennines in the east to Manchester in the northwest. There is a café and a shop. You can get fishing and horse-riding permits and there is an adventure playground and an orienteering course.

Toilets, baby changing, food and drink, shop, group and school visits, disabled access, Braille interpretation, guided tours, events.

Lyme Hall and Park

Smithills Hall

Smithhills Hall

Smithhills Dean Road, Bolton 01204 332377

Adults £3, concs £1.75, family £7.50

Apr-Sep: Tue-Sat 11am-5pm; Sun 2pm-5pm.
Oct-Mar: Tue 1pm-5pm; Sat-Sun 2pm-5pm

Excellent though slightly rundown- half-timbered and stone mansion with many original features from the Medieval, Tudor and Victorian Arts and Crafts periods. In addition to the furniture and artefacts permanently housed at the Hall, there are changing exhibitions and displays throughout the year. There's also a good story concerning Protestant martyr George Marsh. Marsh stamped so hard his refusal to turn against his religious beliefs that an imprint of his foot was left in the flag stones. Events take place regularly in the Hall and grounds.
Toilets, baby changing, food and drink, shop, group and school visits, disabled access, guided tours, events.

Hall I'th Wood

Green Way, off Crompton Way, Bolton 01204 332370 *www.boltonmuseums.org.uk* ***Adults £2, concs £1, family £5***

Apr-Oct: Tue-Sat 11am-5pm; Sun 2pm-5pm

An attractive part-timbered, late medieval merchant's mansion dating from 1530 to 1648. The Hall is furnished with C17 and C18 furniture and also includes pictures and ceramics. It is here that Samuel Crompton invented the Spinning Mule in 1779. This was one of the key inventions of the early industrial age and helped push textile production to new heights. Crompton was always worried that people might steal his ideas before he could apply them and thus gain the credit and money he was due. To scare intruders off he used to play a violin very badly at night to make the Hall sound haunted. *Toilets, school and group visits, guided tours, events.*

Hall I'th Wood

Tatton Park

Knutsford, Cheshire **01625 534 400** *www.tattonpark.org.uk* ***Garden and mansion: cars into the park £4. For a visit to any two attractions from mansion, garden, farm or Tudor Old Hall, buy the Discovery Saver Ticket: adults £5, children £3, under-5s free, families £13.50. Individually, the prices for each attraction are £3.50 for adults and £2 for kids.*** *Park: Mar-Oct 10am-7pm daily; Oct-Mar 11am-5pm Tue-Sun. Mansion: Mar-Oct 1pm-4pm Tue-Sun. Gardens: Mar-Oct 11am-5pm Tue-Sun; Oct-Mar 11pm-3pm Tue-Sun*

QUICK-FIX

Why visit: principally because of the outstanding garden but also for the events and children's activities.

Set in the calm beauty of the gently undulating Cheshire countryside and within its own 1,000 acre deer park, Tatton Hall and its attractions are as pretty as they are popular - and this place is the most visited National Trust property in the North of England. The house, park and gardens are owned by the National Trust, and the site is the most visited of any NT property. The elegant Georgian mansion is by Samuel and Lewis Wyatt and was formerly the home of the locally – and occasionally nationally – important Egerton family. Amongst many qualities, the house has fine furniture and decorations and a large and interesting library.

Without a doubt though the principal glory of Tatton Park, is its exceptional garden, said to be amongst the top ten in the country. There are 50 acres of formal garden crammed with variety and beauty at all times of the year, autumn being particualrly pleasing. The Japanese Garden, 1910-12, is the oldest and best designed by the Japanese themselves in the West. Because it was a

SIGHTSEEING

Tatton Hall

Tatton Hall interior

Japanese team who installed the garden you can be forgiven for thinking yourself lost in the hills above Kyoto, well sort of. The garden features architectural detailing such as a graceful bridge and a Shinto temple. The parkland is wonderful for a stroll at any time of the year. This has free access via various public paths but the best way to enter is from the top of King Street in Knutsford. The park has two large meres and there is swimming, sailing, fishing and riding. You can also visit the C15 Old Hall and the Home Farm. Refreshments are available in one of the stable buildings. There is a gift shop and a garden shop where, inspired by the gardens here, you can take something home for your own green space.

Tatton Park hosts events most weekends. The Christmas ones can be magical, especially for children with Father Christmas ensconced on bales of hay in the farm and donkeys and sheep not far away. The Hall is lit beautifully at this time too. In summer there are outdoor classical concerts regularly featuring the Halle Orchestra. Meanwhile the annual Royal Horticultural Society Flower Show in July has over the past couple of years become one of the great social gatherings of the North as competitors seek to out-do one another with extravagant floral displays in equally extravagant and creative surroundings. On the foodie side of things Tatton hosts one of the North West's Food Lovers Festivals which showcases the immense amount of good grub grown, reared and produced in the region. This takes place in October.

Toilets, baby changing, food and drink, shop, group and school visits, disabled access, guided tours, events.

Classical concert finale

SIGHTSEEING

Secret gardens

Well maybe not too much of a secret, but a testament to hard work and clever green fingers. If you hanker for the horticultural then check these out.

Dunge Valley Hidden Gardens and Hardy Plant Nursery

Windgather Rocks, Kettleshulme, nr Whaley Bridge, Cheshire **01663 733787**
www.dungevalleygardens.co.uk

Back in 1984 when Manchester was pulsing to New Order's 'Blue Monday', a less hedonistic movement began up in the Pennine Hills east of Macclesfield. Deep in a wooded gully, a spectacular garden began to take shape as hundreds of rhododendrons, azaleas, magnolias and other acid-lovers were planted into the barren soil amidst a lattice of winding paths and bridges.

Twenty years on, this bleak, forgotten valley has metamorphosed into a lush, fertile plant-lover's paradise. As you follow the woodland upwards, the drama of the near-vertical, ivy-covered banks and the exquisitely scented evergreen shrubs gives way to views across the moorland and the racing skies. Closer, the attention to detail is captivating, with leathery leaved rhododendrons, curly fronded ferns and delicate blooms. In spring the ground is crammed with naturalised bulbs, and the bog gardens formed by the meanderings of the stream teem with a mix of wild and cultivated plant varieties. Pay a visit to the on-site shop if you have time, but definitely park yourself on the delightful terrace and enjoy the home-made snacks and meals.

Fletcher Moss and Parsonage Gardens

Wilmslow Road, Didsbury **0161 998 2117**

A delightful part of the city, five miles due south from the centre. The Parsonage Gardens next to the Old Cock Inn comprise a high-walled garden of roses, rare trees, shrubs and plants, an orchid house and herbaceous border. The lovely old house formerly belonged to an eccentric alderman of the city, Fletcher Moss, who bequeathed this and the Botanical Gardens for public use in 1919. Under an old yew in the gardens is his pet cemetery. Across Stenner Lane is the handsome St James Parish Church, which contains an impressive memorial to the Mosley family from 1612.

Fletcher Moss Gardens

Round the corner are the small but perfectly formed Fletcher Moss Botanical Gardens. The main feature is the lovely rock garden with rare plants, pools and waterfalls, which occupies the south facing slope. A walk across the old flood plain, through the walkways winding between willows to the levee of the River Mersey, is also recommended. You can then follow the river west to Chorlton and Sale Water Parks.

Within Fletcher Moss is a café with a terrace overlooking the gardens. This is a wonderful place to take refreshment during sunny summer days. The homemade cakes are particularly recommended. In the same building, a group of local ladies met together in 1890 to campaign against the craze for egret feathers from Florida that was driving the bird close to extinction. This meeting led to the formation of the Royal Society for the Protection of Birds.

Hare Hill

Off B5087, close to Alderley Edge, Cheshire **01625 584412** *www.nationaltrust.org.uk*

This National Trust property (£3.20 adults, £1.50 children) is the cultivated and propagated antidote to the untamed woods of Alderley Edge on the hillside above. Hare Hill is an artificial landscape of clipped hedges and herbaceous borders with a glimpsed and then found pergola providing an architectural element to the gardens.

An especially good time to visit is May when the rhododendrons and azaleas light up this little Garden of Eden. Indeed a great part of Hare Hill's charm lies with its secluded position hidden behind a handsome brick wall apparently unconnected to any large house or major property. Arrive early and you might even get the place to yourself. If any Hollywood director were looking for the perfect movie set for a reworking of *The Secret Garden* or *Tom's Midnight Garden* they wouldn't have to look much further.

Vicarage Botanical Gardens

Off the A6144, Manchester Road, Carrington
0161 775 2750
www.vicaragebotanicalgardens.co.uk

An unlikely location: a barren avenue of sewage works, electricity substations and chemical plants doesn't seem the obvious place for garden-lovers. But a stone's throw from the corporate fortresses and the acrid smell of heavy industry lies a jewel-like garden that rivals some of the region's best. This is a secluded *Alice in Wonderland* garden of formal evergreen hedges, clematis-laden pergolas, and little woodland paths. Created over the last 18 years by a Christian community, the place provides peace and serenity, in spite of the distant crackle of pylons and the occasional chemical plant rearing its head out of the trees. Indeed, such is the magic of this place that its outsize industrial neighbours only add to the charm.

Despite being only five acres in size, the network of meandering paths, pools and hidden glades in the woodland garden seem to stretch for miles. It's quite possible to get pleasantly lost amongst the ferns, shrubs and foliage. The gentle changes in level with swamp-like ponds and mature trees generate a dreamlike, jungly atmosphere, overlaid with the constant sound of birdsong and the flitting of bees and butterflies.

The garden is free to enter and the friendly, well-priced teashop serves home-made scones, although there is lots of lawned space for picnics. Garden centre addicts can get their fix from a well-stocked nursery offering cheap, well-grown plants. The website provides a good introduction to the joys of this unlikely place.

Walkden Gardens

Walkden Gardens

Jct of Derbyshire Road/Marsland Road, Sale

So well hidden that even local residents don't know they exist, these magical gardens have recently enjoyed a facelift thanks to the energies of a group of volunteers. Created in the 1970s on land left to the council by Harry Walkden, a keen gardener and hybridist, the seven-acre site is laid out in the style of Hidcote Manor in Gloucestershire, with a series of outdoor rooms connected and unified by hidden paths and mature beech hedges. The design places the emphasis on long vistas and quirky angles, with something to delight around every twist in the path. An enclosed theatre lawn with a raised turf stage leads to a box-edged fuchsia garden, a newly restored laburnum arch and a well-kept central border. The cherry walk and circular beech exedra underplanted by hundreds of naturalised bulbs are enchanting in the spring, and the many trees give the space presence.

Much restoration and renewal is taking place. 2005 saw the installation of Dovecote Garden around the Grade II listed dovecote rescued from doomed Sale Old Hall. With summer music events, weekly tai chi sessions and a myriad secret places to sit and muse, doze, picnic or play hide and seek, it's the perfect example of an urban park.

Wythenshawe Hall

Wythenshawe Hall and Gardens

Altrincham Road, Wythenshawe 0161 998 2331 *www.manchestergalleries.org* FREE *Hall: Easter-Nov, Wed-Sun 10am-5.30pm, (open Bank Holidays). Gardens free access, any time*

250-acre Hall and Park of the Tatton family, now under the ownership of the City Council. Much of the house dates from the C16, the most notable rooms being the dining room and the drawing room. There is an impressive statue of Oliver Cromwell opposite the front of the house in the park. The reason for him being here is that the house was besieged during the English Civil War by Parliamentarian forces. The statue used to reside in the city centre but for dubious reasons, some political, was removed down here. It's time Olly went back, he had a fine position outside the Cathedral. The best part of any visit to the park is a look around the Horticultural Centre. Here, within a walled garden, lie huge glass houses with collections of cacti, succulents, bananas, palms etc. There are also good outdoor areas with raised flower beds. Given the nature of the facility this works in rain or shine. Other parts of the park have pitch and putt, all-weather football, a children's playground and farm which kids can visit. *Toilets, baby changing, food and drink, shop, school visits, disabled access, guided tours, events.*

Public buildings, museums and art galleries

Bolton Museum and Art Gallery

Le Mans Crescent, Bolton 01204 332209 *www.boltonmuseums.org.uk* FREE *Mon-Sat 10am-5pm (closed for Bank Holidays)*

Almost of city size, this museum makes for a good excursion from Manchester. It's very handsome too, occupying part of a fine piece of civic planning from the first half of the C20. There are touring exhibitions of paintings, photography, sculpture and contemporary ceramics. In the museum there is an aquarium, a Wildlife on your Doorstep exhibition, Ancient Egyptian treasures and an exhibition on British archaeology. Bolton-born Thomas Moran's celebrated painting 'Evening Camp, Nearing the Upper Colorado River,' 1882, a hymn to the undeveloped American West, is tremendous when on display. The collections in Bolton also contain The collection includes the remarkable Bowyer Bible of 45 volumes from the beginning of the C19. Bowyer sought to illustrate every aspect of the Bible world by hunting all over Europe and Britain for appropriate images – the prints and engravings he eventually obtained included some by Rembrandt and Durer amongst others.

Toilets, guided tours, events, disabled access, shop.

Bolton Town Hall

Bolton Town Hall

01204 364 333 *www.visit-bolton.com* FREE

Informal visits welcome, but phone for guided tours

One of the three great Victorian Town Halls in the area along with those of Manchester and Rochdale. Unlike the other two, however, this is Classical in inspiration. The building dominates the town centre with its six-column Corinthian portico reached by a wide staircase and its tower given a French cap and cupola. Inside is the impressive Great Hall with an organ gallery supported on male figures: Atlantes. It was the work of William Hill of Leeds – no relation of the famous bookmaker. The Town Hall was opened in 1873 but the first suggestion to build such a grand building was made in 1863 during the height of the Cotton Famine. The blockade of Southern States by the Union cut off the supply of raw cotton to Lancashire. With so many mills silent, it was thought that such a major project could provide employment for hundreds of the needy.

Toilets, shop, group and school visits, disabled access, guided tours, events.

Bury Art Gallery, Museum and Archives

Moss Street , Bury 0161 253 5878

www.bury.gov.uk FREE

Tues-Fri 10am-5pm, Sat 10.am-4.30pm

Victorians with wealth were supposed to give generously of their money. The children of Bury paper manufacturer Thomas Wrigley were especially generous. In an elegant Edwardian building constructed especially for Wrigley's collection Bury has over two hundred oil paintings, watercolours, prints and ceramics. The oil paintings include Turner's 'Calais Sands', Landseer's 'The Random Shot' and Constable's 'Hampstead Heath'. There are also C20 paintings by artists such Burra. The small museum on site is less interesting, although family events are fun.

SIGHTSEEING

Bury Art Gallery

East Lancashire Railway

East Lancashire Railway

Bolton Street Station, Bury 0161 764 7790
www.east-lancs-rly.co.uk ***All line round trip: adults £11, concessions £7.40, under-fives free, family £23*** *Trains run every hour. Sat 9am-5pm, Sun and Bank Holidays 10am-5pm*

Volunteer-run attraction. For a modest price, take a journey in a steam train, or sometimes a veteran diesel, the eight miles or so up to Rawtenstall and back. During the journey you can partake of refreshment in the little buffet bar. The journey is a pleasant one with the Irwell Valley narrowing and the hills and moors pressing in. You can take a bicycle on the train for free. Special events include Santa Specials, Thomas the Tank Engine Days, and drive-an-engine-yourself sessions. The East Lancs affords good opportunities to visit several of the Irwell sculptures (see pg 119).

Toilets, baby changing, food and drink, shop, group and school visits, disabled access, guided tours, events.

Ellenroad Engine House

Elizabeth Way, Milnrow, Rochdale
01706 881952 *www.ellenroad.org.uk*
Adults £2, concessions £1
First Sun in the month except Jan, noon-4pm

The 1892 Ellenroad Mill has gone but its Engine House remains and holds inside the Alexandra and Victoria engines – the largest steam mill engines in the world. When the site is open, the display of power from these steamed-up leviathians is awesome. There's a pleasant picnic area too in the shadow of the 60m (200 foot) chimney.

Toilets, food and drink, shop, group and school visits, disabled access, guided tours, events.

East Lancashire Railway

East Lancs walk

You can use the East Lancs railway to enjoy this walk. The length is about 5km (3 miles) and involves a climb of around 200m (650ft). It also involves several transport methods, good grub and splendid views.

Take the tram from Manchester city centre to Bury which takes twenty minutes or so. From Bury tram station follow the signposts to the East Lancs Station on Bolton Road where you can take a train north. This is a ten minute walk maximum. The East Lancs Railway is the type of volunteer run attraction that gives underfunded tattiness a good name because there is such love built into it.

The trains have period interiors which are basic but atmospheric and there's always a snack bar on board for drinks and sweets. After leaving Bury you start to climb into countryside and after the pretty stop at Summerseat you reach Ramsbottom (see page 147), fifteen minutes after you started out.

Ramsbottom's (see page 147) a charming Pennine town. The station is as pretty as a picture and looks just like the one in the Railway Children – remember time stopped on the East Lancs at least 60 years ago.

You might want to inexpensively stoke up, to use a railway analogy, at the fast food stall by the level crossing which provides the Lancashire speciality of black peas. Remember to saturate them in vinegar or add mint sauce to really make them zing.

At the level-crossing, close to the food stall, turn left up Bridge Street. This street has a good chippy, a top notch ice cream shop and traditional cream tea café called Baileys. At Market Place, which sports Edward Allington's huge 'Tilted Vase' sculpture, cross carefully over to Carr Street straight ahead and continue up. Carr Street climbs past an old mill lodge on the right – good duck-feeding territory – to the Rose and Crown pub and then turns sharply left and becomes Tanners Street. Follow this up to Rawson's Rake and turn right up the latter which is an extremely steep lane.

As you climb you'll begin to see your destination, Peel Tower, straight ahead and high above. Continue past Eammanuel Church to the Shoulder of Mutton pub in Holcombe village which provides good family food. Cross carefully over the busy road (the B6214) after the pub into Cross Lane.

Follow Cross Lane and, just before it becomes cobbled, turn right along the track called Moorbottom Road. Just a few metres down, another track opens on the right, which takes you to the tower. You can either choose this (the sensible option) or take the more informal route directly up.

When you reach the tower you are 330m (1100ft) above sea level. The 36m (120ft) tower here was built in 1852 to mark the achievements of local man and important politician Sir Robert Peel, the man who created the modern police force. The Tower is usually closed but if the flag is flying then you can toil up the 148 steps. Call Bury Tourist Information, 0161 253 5111, if you want to make sure you visit on an open day. From the top, if the weather is behaving itself, you can see as far as the Lake District. To return simply retrace your steps back down to Ramsbottom.

SIGHTSEEING

Fairfield Moravian Settlement

Fairfield Square, Droylsden 0161 370 3461
www.billnkaz.demon.co.uk/moravian.htm
£1. Call to arrange guided tour

The Moravian Church was founded in 1457 in the Czech Republic by those disenchanted with the Catholic Church. This settlement dates back to 1785 when the local Moravians established their community a few miles from the city. Well preserved and now surrounded by the suburbs, the settlement, with its cobbled streets, attractive houses, church and segregated graveyard retains the tranquil atmosphere of the late C18. In the graveyard there are no standing headstones - just simple plaques laid in rows. Married couples share the same grave, single men to one side, single women to the other.

Toilets, guided tours, group and school visits.

Fairfield Moravian Settlement

Gallery Oldham

Greaves Street, off Union Street, Oldham
0161 911 4657 *www.galleryoldham.co.uk*
FREE *Mon-Sat 10am-5pm*

This smart, multi-million pound home designed by Pringle, Richards, Sharratt houses a permanent collection of work, including paintings by Dante Gabriel Rossetti, Sickert and Hockney. There are temporary exhibitions too. Be sure to check out the extraordinary metres-long panorama taken in 1879 by Mr Knott. The light installations by Peter Freeman are enjoyable including the spooky *Light Shift* pieces in the lifts.

Toilets, baby changing, food and drink, shop, group and school visits, disabled access, audio interpretation for adults and children, guided tours, events.

Gallery Oldham

SIGHTSEEING

Hat Works

Wellington Road North, Stockport 0845 833 0975 *www.hatworks.org.uk* FREE ***(except special events. Guided tours £2 per person)***

Mon-Fri 10am-5pm; Sat-Sun 1pm-5pm

Housed in a former mill in the town centre, this museum traces the history of hat making from a cottage industry using beaver and otter fur to today's fashion designs. There are permanent and temporary exhibitions and a family space with seating, mirrors and a range of headgear to try on. The mill also holds a large collection of hat making machinery in full working order.

Toilets, baby changing, food and drink, shop, group and school visits, disabled access, guided tours, events.

Museum of the Manchester Regiment

Town Hall, Market Place, Ashton-under-Lyne 0161 342 2812 *www.tameside.gov.uk* FREE

Mon-Sat 10am-4pm

A complete history of the Manchester Regiment from the Napoleonic Wars to their amalgamation in 1958. During the First World War, the Manchesters suffered some of the worst losses of any British regiment. Amongst the casualties was poet Wilfred Owen, killed shortly before the Armistice. He is remembered, along with his comrades in the Regimental Chapel, in Manchester Cathedral.

Toilets, baby changing, group and school visits, disabled access, guided tours, events.

Portland Basin

Portland Basin

Portland Place, Ashton-under-Lyne 0161 343 2878 *www.tameside.gov.uk*

Housed within a C19 Ashton Canal Warehouse, this museum combines a lively modern interior with a peaceful canal side setting. Inside the museum you can walk down a 1920s street and experience the lifestyle, industries, crafts and trades of the area. There are lots of hands-on activities including remote controlled boats.

Toilets, baby changing, group and school visits, disabled access, events.

SIGHTSEEING

Hat Works

Quarry Bank Mill

Styal, near Manchester Airport **01625 527 468**
www.nationaltrust.org.uk ***Adults £9, children £4.70, family £20, under 5s and National Trust members free*** *Mill: Apr-Sep every day 10.30am-5.30pm; Oct-Mar Tue-Sun 10.30am-5pm. The Apprentice House and the Garden have slightly reduced hours compared to these.*

QUICK-FIX

Why visit: because this is one of the best working mill museums in the country, with a strong events programmes and interesting surroundings.

One of the best days out around, this museum is housed in a 200-year-old spinning mill deep in a picturesque dell. The museum is fully working with skilled demonstrators operating original machinery and giving a display of the different processes needed to take cotton from raw material stage to finished product. This involves carding, spinning and weaving. It is a fascinating process to watch. In the museum shop you can buy some of the items made in the mill. The water wheel, installed 1850, is said to be the largest working example in the country. A short walk away is the Apprentice House where the pauper children were housed whilst they worked at the mill. The model village of Styal is in itself worth a visit. Totally unspoilt, it has handsome stone houses, a school, a shop and a church. There are also the very attractive 250 acres of Styal Country Park, with its river and woodland walks. There is a licensed restaurant at the mill.

Toilets, baby changing, food and drink, shop, group and school visits, disabled access, guided tours, events.

SIGHTSEEING

Rochdale Pioneers Museum

Toad Lane, Rochdale 01706 524 920
http://museum.co-op.ac.uk/ ***Adults £1, concessions 50p*** *Tue-Sat 10am-4pm; Sun 2pm-4pm*

This museum is housed in the original building where Britain's first successful working class co-operative began in 1844. This museum provides an insight into the principals and ideals of co-operative philosophy.
Toilets, shop, group and school visits, disabled access, audio interpretation, events.

Rochdale Town Hall

The Esplanade, Rochdale 01706 356 592
www.rochdaleonline.org FREE *Ring ahead for details of guided tours or just take a chance and have an informal look around*

Magnificent Gothic Victorian Town Hall: a sumptuous display of civic pride and C19 wealth. The building is set off by the grand civic space it has been given, the gardens on three sides and the parish church high on the steep bank behind. It was built between 1866 and 1871 to the designs of William Crossland. The building is 100m long. The tower is 50m tall. The latter used to be taller and had a spire constructed of wood, but this burnt down and was replaced with this better stone version, in 1883, by Alfred Waterhouse, the architect of that other Gothic masterpiece, Manchester Town Hall. The interior has a giant staircase leading up to the Great Hall with a hammerbeam roof, a large mural of the Magna Carta and stained-glass windows depicting British monarchs. It is said that Adolf Hitler had wished to requisition these for transport back to Germany if he'd won World War II.
Toilets, group and school visits, guided tours.

Setantii

Tourist Information Centre, Ashton-under-Lyne 0161 342 2812 *www.tameside.gov.uk* FREE
Mon-Fri 10am-4pm, Sat 10am-1pm

Based in the refurbished Tourist Information Centre, this hourly interactive, walkabout exhibition starts its journey 2,000 years ago when the Setantii branch of the Brigantes tribe inhabited Tameside and Greater Manchester. The tour depicts the area and its inhabitants through time zones. It ends in a tribute to modern-day Tameside and some of its more famous citizens, such as Margaret Beckett MP and Mick Hucknall of Simply Red. Kids love the ghost stories told in the crypt as well as the more hands-on exhibits. Members of the Manchester University Archaeology Department are on hand to show how and where to begin to trace ancestors.
Toilets, shop, group and school visits, disabled access, audio interpretation, events.

Rochdale Town Hall

Staircase House

30-31 Market Place, Stockport **0161 480 1460**
www.staircasehouse.org.uk ***Admission (all ages) £3.50, under 5s free*** *Mon-Sat noon-5pm, Sun 1pm-5pm*

A recent attraction for Greater Manchester and a very worthy one too. It claims to be interactive in the old sense of the word, instead of banks of computer terminals with half of them out of action, this is a real hands-on experience with visitors being encouraged to wander around the house and touch the exhibits. You can turn back the sheets in a four poster from the 1600s or try your hand at writing with a quill. An audio guide comes with the entry price to help bring the building alive. It might come alive with other things too as the place has some very active ghosts. The cruck framed house dates back to the 1460s and is one of the oldest merchant's houses in the country. The Jacobean newel staircase, which gives the building its name, was added in 1618 and is only one of three in the country.
Toilets, baby changing, food and drink, shop, group and school visits, disabled access, events.

Staircase House

Stockport Air Raid Shelters

Chestergate, Stockport **0161 474 1940**
www.stockport.gov.uk/heritageattractions
Adults £3.95, children £2.95
Mon-Sun 1pm-5pm

Odd and interesting museum housed in former tunnels carved out of the soft red sandstone. These were designed to protect thousands of people for prolonged periods of

Stockport Air Raid Shelters

SIGHTSEEING

time from the threat of German air attack. The visit involves a descent into the 1940s gloom to experience the sights and sounds of the Home Front. There are special explorer tours that penetrate deeper into the network and involve hard hats, lamps and sensible shoes – ring ahead for the times of these. Souvenirs and wartime memorabilia on sale.

Toilets, shop, group and school visits, disabled access, guided tours, events.

Touchstones Rochdale

The Esplanade, Rochdale 01706 864986

www.rochdale.gov.uk/touchstones FREE

Mon-Fri 10am-5.30pm; Sat, Sun & Bank Holidays 11am-4.30pm

The centrepiece of this reinvented former library from 1903 is the smart new museum. Reached through a Time Tunnel, the museum depicts the social history of Rochdale via a series of colour-coded areas. Same Difference highlights the changing face of daily life through its fine collection of ephemera and Rochdaliana, housed in real shop, pub and cinema interiors – there's even the chance to cuddle up to a Gracie Fields film in an original 'loveseat'. Slightly less comfortable is the authentically chilly recreation of a wartime air-raid shelter. People and Places celebrates the town's most famous sons and daughters. The town's art collection is also located here, together with the local studies department. There is a good café-bar too.

Toilets, baby changing, food and drink, shop, group and school visits, disabled access, tours, events.

Touchstones Rochdale

Wigan Pier Experience

Wallgate, Wigan 01942 323 666

www.wiganpier.net ***Adult £5.25, concessions £4.25, family £14.50***

Mon-Thu 10pm-5pm; Sat-Sun 11pm-5pm

This is a series of attractions located in and around cotton mills and canal wharves a short walk from the centre of Wigan. The Pier was always a joke – the small, mucky, industrial wharf ironically compared to the great seaside piers at resorts such as Blackpool. The Wigan Pier Experience gives an insight into the town's industrial past. The emphasis is on recreating the sights, sounds and atmosphere of the past. Boat trips on the redeveloped Leeds and Liverpool Canal are also available.

Toilets, baby changing, food and drink, shop, group and school visits, disabled access, guided tours, events.

Wigan Pier

Churches

There are numerous exquisite places of worship to visit around the area. Many of these trace their origins back to medieval times or earlier. In many, despite the secularisation of society and, on occasion, unfortunate restorations, the atmosphere of generations of lives coming and going is as tangible as the dust floating through the nave. Some of the churches will be locked, some will be open – please make sure you telephone ahead.

Five miles northwest of the city, just off a road named for The Beast, the A666, lies one of the greatest of all British Victorian churches (usually locked tighter than the gold vault of the Bank of England). This is **St Augustine**, Pendlebury, by GF Bodley (0161 727 8175). Dressed in brick to deny luxury, it looks austere glimpsed from the roadside (see page 39 for a picture). But as you get closer, the building grows in dignity and power. It is the scale and the simplicity of the design that is impressive – a rhythm of window and piers on one large, inverted ark. Inside the simplicity is continued with the only division, the row of internal buttresses moving towards the screen and the sanctuary. The money for St Augustine's was provided by the Heywood family. It was formerly known as the Miner's Cathedral, but all the pits in the area have now closed. Nikolas Pevsner called it "one of the English churches of all time".

Other churches include **Emmanuel Church**, Didsbury (0161 445 7863), four or so miles south of the city, which contains wonderful William Morris stained glass from 1889. This church also broadcasts the world's oldest continuous radio programme: Radio 4's five decades old *Daily Service*.

St Mary, Cheadle (0161 428 8050), lies six miles south of the city centre in a prominent position on the main high street. It dates chiefly from the 1500s and includes fragments of the ancient screen and prone effigies of knights in the Brereton Chapel.

In Stockport, seven miles out, is the massive church of **St George** (0161 480 2453), designed by Austin and Paley in 1896-7 and a model of crisp, majestic beauty.

St Augustine

Again in Stockport, in a pleasant situation on the River Goyt, lies the simple **Chadkirk Chapel**. Part of this building is timber framed and dates from the C14.

To the east of the city, the parish church of **St Michael**, Ashton-under-Lyne (0161 343 4305) again occupies a fine position in the town. Here the highlights include a splendid set of late medieval stained glass depicting the life of St Helena in 18 scenes. The nave interior contains wooden galleries, box pews and a three-decker pulpit. **St Lawrence** in Denton is an interesting timber-framed church from the late Middle Ages.

Five miles beyond Ashton, the tower of **St Michael in Mottram** (01457 762268) dates from around 1486, whilst the superb view into the hills of the High Peak is the best from any local parish church. Six miles north east of the city centre is the delightful wooden towered church of **St Leonard**, Middleton (0161 643 2693). Most of the present building dates from 1524, but includes a tower and porch from 1412 and there is a repositioned Norman arch and some Norman piers from around 1100. Most of the 1524 work was paid for by Sir Richard Assheton, the hero of Flodden Field, where the English defeated the Scots. On the south wall in the sanctuary there is a war memorial window with the names of local men who took part in the battle – the oldest such memorial anywhere. There is a good medieval screen with stalls and misericords.

In Stand, six miles north of the city, lies **All Saints** (0161 766 2619), from 1822 in fanciful Gothic by Charles Barry, who would later design the Houses of Parliament. The outstanding feature here is the dramatic porch under the tower.

Two miles into the city from Stand lies **St Mary**, Prestwich (0161 773 2912). This church, with elements dating from the later Middle Ages, has an east end designed by Paley and Austin from 1888-9, one of the most original of architectural practices working in England at that time. The church is well placed above Prestwich Clough.

A mile east, **St Margaret's**, Prestwich (0161 773 2698) provides one of the best collections of woodwork in the region. Here craftsman Arthur Simpson on behalf of brewers Holt's and Wilson's provided between 1899 and 1920 an essay in the joys of the Arts and Crafts movement .

A suburb of Bolton, Deane, contains **St Mary** (01204 61819), a model of the medieval north country church – long, low and embattled. Wigan parish church of **All Saints** (01942 244 459) has C13 elements and a pretty location right in the centre of town.

St Mary (0161 281 5739) in Eccles, four miles due west of the city centre, is another gem – this time tucked away from the town centre. The site is ancient, dating from the 1100s, although most of the church comes down from the C15, C16, and C19. There are early stained-glass remnants and a moving group of stone effigies from around 1600 of Richard Brereton, his wife and baby.

On Chapel Street, Salford, close to the city centre, lies the **Catholic Cathedral** (0161 834 0333) of 1885 by Weightman and Hadfield. This has a beautifully sharp spire and an impressive east window.

The best steeple in the area, though, is that of **St Mary**, Hulme, one and a half miles south of the city. The church, now flats, was built in 1858 by JS Crowther. Its spire is exceptionally elegant and slender.

Further out from the city, south in Cheshire, are the delightful country churches of **St Mary** at Rostherne (01565 830 595) near Tatton, and **St Mary**, Nether Alderley (01625 583 134) near Alderley Edge. The first of these hangs above Rostherne Mere. Centuries ago, one of the church bells came away from its ropes and rolled into the mere. After this had happened three times, the local workmen decided to leave it there. Legend says that at dawn on Easter Day, a mermaid swims into the mere through a channel from the Irish Sea and rings the bell. She then sits on the bell, combs her hair and sings.

SIGHTSEEING

St Mary, Cheadle

Peckforton Castle

Prehistory, Romans, castles

There are very few traces of our prehistoric brethren across the Greater Manchester. There were Bronze Age mines at Alderley Edge but it is difficult to say what is exactly left from that era. The most tangible remains are the tiny remnants of a stone circle and enclosure on Turton Heights, north of Bolton, and the traces of an Iron Age hillfort at **Buckton Castle**, on Buckton Moor, above Mossley. Both these places, with the aid of an Ordnance Survey map, provide good walks. The closest prehistoric monuments of the first order lie in the Peak District National Park. 25 miles southeast is **Arbor Low**, a Neolithic henge monument, signposted off the A515.

The Roman period leaves us with a little more. Aside from the part reconstruction of the **Manchester Fort** (see pages 16 and 65), there is the dramatic fort site at **Castleshaw** off the A62 in Saddleworth. Again the remains aren't huge, but the shape of the fort can be made out and there is an excellent series of display boards describing the former buildings. The situation of the fort, high in the hills on a shelf below the pass over Standedge and over the later reservoirs, provides a wonderful summer picnic spot. The original name seems to have been Rigodunum – the Fortress of the King – and we know from tiles found at the site that some of the soldiers stationed here were from Braga in Portugal.

Best of all is the Roman Road – although some doubt this provenance – that clambers over **Blackstone Edge** six miles northeast of Rochdale on the A58. See next page. Another superb Roman road to follow is the one over **Doctor's Gate**, parallel to the Snake Pass, A57. The best place to follow the road is from Old Glossop, up the valley of Shelf Brook.

Castles are a problem. There aren't any left in Greater Manchester, unless you count the C19 reconstruction of **Liverpool Castle** in Rivington Park, west of Bolton, the foundations of **Bury Castle** in the town of the same name and, most authentic of all, the ruins of a fortified tower house – akin to the Pele Towers of the Border country – at **Radcliffe**, ten or so miles north of the city. Otherwise take the short trip – 20 miles – into the Peak District, to Castleton, and visit the dramatically situated, romantic ruin of **Peveril Castle**. 30 miles southwest, in Cheshire, another fine ruin guards the Peckforton hills at **Beeston**. This has a good events programme, caves and a splendid elevated position. Nearby is **Peckforton Castle**, a Victorian dream of a medieval fortification, 1844-50, by Anthony Salvin.

Recent public art

Not since Victorian times has so much public art been produced. Every recent major private or public scheme has had its own culture budget, which has usually given us some sort of public art. Manchester even hosted the international CowParade event in 2003 to great success and you can still see some of these beasts around the city.

The big daddy of recent works is **'B of the Bang'** designed by Tom Heatherwick, darling of the UK art world and a former Manchester graduate. Located in Sport City, a couple of kilometres to the east of the city centre and cheek by jowl with the City of Manchester stadium, this is the tallest sculpture in the UK at 56 metres (180ft). It also weighs 180 tonnes and leans at an angle 10 times more acute than the Leaning Tower of Pisa. Stand beneath it and this masterpiece wobbles. This has been a problem as some of the spikes have fallen off - still you might expect the odd hitch when you attempt something which has never been attempted before. The work was commissioned to commemorate the 2002 Commonwealth Games and the name comes from athlete Linford Christie's description of how he began running at the 'b of the bang' of the starting pistol.

Nearby at the Regional Athletics Centre is Colin Spofforth's best work thus far, **'The Runner'** (2003), which shows the tensed body of the athlete as he crosses the finishing line – a nice complement to 'b of the bang.'

Running north of the city is the **Irwell Sculpture Trail** (www.irwellsculpturetrail.co.uk) – the largest public art scheme in the United Kingdom, with over 50 regional, national and international artists of variable quality represented along 30 miles (50km) of trail. This follows footpaths stretching the course of the River Irwell from Salford Quays to Bacup in the north.

Four of the best are Ulrich Ruckriem's **'Untitled'** at the former Outwood Colliery, Radcliffe, which is made up of ten huge granite blocks. David Fryer's **'Picnic Area'** is a six-metre-long mousetrap with the spring poised ready to slice you in two at Burrs

'B of the Bang'

Country Park north of Bury town centre. Close by in the same park is Julie Edwards' **'Stone Cycle'**. The circular layout of the sculpture covered with symbols that hint at the passing of time, people and industry. One of the most intriguing is Richard Cainks **'In the Picture'**, a picture frame twice human height which turns the scene beyond of river, woods, hills, fields and farms into a gallery exhibit. This work is deteriorating fast so get along to it soon.

Other public art hotspots include Trafford Park with Brian Fell's towering chains, **'Skyhooks'**, on Trafford Road, and Site's **'Silent Cargoes'** on Trafford Wharf. Some of the best public art in the North West is in Blackpool and is produced by Manchester artists. Two show-offs are **'High Tide Organ'** and **'They Shoot Horses Don't They?'** The first, by Liam Curtin, uses the incoming tide to produce haunting sound, and the second by Michael Trainor is the biggest mirror-ball in the world.

See the Walks (page 62) for the Northern Quarter artworks.

Country walks and parks

There are a number of lovely country trails and parks within the area. The list below is not exhaustive but highlights the best. Again take a map and discover some walks for yourself. The most impressive walking areas lie among the moors of the Pennine Hills, curving from north to southeast around the city. The area below conforms more or less to the Greater Manchester county boundary.

Eight miles due north of the city centre, midway between Bury and Rochdale on the B6222, lie the lovely woods of **Ashworth Valley**, rising past the excellent Egerton Arms pub on School Lane to Owd Betts on the A680. The walk along Cheesden Brook which leads off northwest from the main valley is filled with an empty grandeur and the evocative remnants of former industry. Two and half miles northwest of Rochdale, where the B6377 meets the A671, is the romantic, rocky chasm of **Healey Dell** with its disused but spectacular railway viaduct. There is easy access to the open moors here and at the lonely **Watergrove Reservoir** above the old stone-built village of Wardle, northeast of Rochdale. Further round again and on the B6255 lies popular **Hollingworth Lake**. Almost a mini-resort with its boatyard and amusement arcade, this was formerly called the Weaver's Seaport, as those who didn't have the time to make it to Blackpool would spend their days off 'at t'lake'. Nearby there are marvellous walks to be taken up to **Blackstone Edge**, off the A58, see the walk described on pages 149-151.

In between Rochdale and Royton off the A671, and only seven miles from the city centre, is **Tandle Hill Park** crowned by an obelisk. The beech woods here are superb. They were planted to prevent Chartists from drilling on the previously open ground in the C19. The whole area around **Saddleworth** and the villages of Delph, Denshaw, Dobcross and Uppermill are worth a close look. Delph and Dobcross are particularly pretty. The most dramatic area of Saddleworth, perhaps of the whole Greater Manchester area, are the high hills, cliffs and reservoirs at **Dovestones** on the A635, 14 miles from the city centre. A good walk starts from Saddleworth township up to Pots and Pans, the crags above.

Rivington: a nineteenth century view

Southeast of Hyde are two attractive country parks, one upland, one lowland. **Werneth Low Country Park**, off the A560, offers the views, Etherow Country Park, off the B6104, offers the prettier woodland walk. The walk along the Peak Forest Canal at Marple Locks on either side of the A626 combines water and barges with woods and views. East of this point there is superb walking country.

Similarly the upland walks around **Lyme Park** (see page 124) are beautiful. Something for the children is provided at **Bruntwood Park** off the A34 in Cheadle, with an adventure playground and pets corner. 12 miles due south of the city, off the B5087, through the village of **Alderley Edge** lies the Edge itself. With its legend of a wizard guarding the sleeping King Arthur and his knights, this is a magical place. Two excellent children's books are placed on the Edge: The Weirdstone of Brisingamen and The Moon of Gomrath, both by Alan Garner. There's a magnificent view northeast from the red sandstone outcrop and interesting woodland walks.

At **Quarry Bank Mill**, Styal, a mile from the airport off the B5166, there are fine woodland walks alongside the steep valley of the River Bollin. Just four or so miles south of the city, the line of the River Mersey from Didsbury, past **Chorlton Water Park** to **Sale Water Park**, offers a pleasant walk with a watersports centre at the latter.

Due west of the city the landscape for many miles is extremely flat and was once part of Chat Moss – one of the most impenetrable swamps in all England. Another five miles further on between Leigh and Wigan lies **Pennington Flash**. The Flash, all 70 hectares of it, was created by the ground slowly slumping into the old mine workings in this area. The lake and its surroundings are the best place for bird watching in Greater Manchester. There is also sailing and a children's play area. North east of Wigan town centre lies **Haigh Country Park**, which provides good walks, a mini-railway, model village, walled gardens, craft centre, café, gift shop and children's play area.

Perhaps the most interesting of the country parks is **Rivington and Lever Park**, northwest of Bolton off the A673. These are the former gardens and estate of the Bolton entrepreneur William Hesketh Lever, Lord Leverhulme – his name is still commemorated in the company Unilever. At Rivington there is a reconstruction of Liverpool Castle, the Great House Barn with its huge medieval cruck beams, shop and art gallery and, high on the moor, Rivington Pike Tower, built in 1773. Barrow Bridge, closer to Bolton, is a charming village through which access to the crest of Winter Hill can be gained. Three miles north of Bolton off the A676, Bradshaw Road, lies **Jumbles Country Park**, which comprises 250 acres of reservoir and countryside.

Three small towns

There is always a temptation to visit the big towns. This small section looks at two small towns nearby, each with a different personality and each replete with its own quirky interest. Other little towns worth a close look are Delph and Dobcross in Saddleworth, Marple with its canal and locks east beyond Stockport, Lymm with a dam and lakes right in the town centre and Middleton with its hil top church.

Knutsford

'Let every dawn of morning be to you as the beginning of life and every setting sun be to you as its close' **Text from the Ruskin Reading Room, Drury Lane, Knutsford**

01565 632611 Tourist info. *16 miles (25km) south west of the city on the A50. Direct train connections from Piccadilly Railway Station.*

This prosperous town in north Cheshire is a gem. It is the embodiment of the lowland English market town with the added bonus of containing some of the most eccentric buildings in Britain. The town is grouped around King Street and Princess Street.

King Street is a thoroughfare that has one of those splendid English haphazard harmonies of buildings from throughout the last 250 years. It also has a range of shops and eateries and a very good antique shop for knick-knacks. The north end of the street leads into Tatton Park. Halfway along King Street is the swanky Belle Epoque restaurant under the Gaskell Memorial Tower. This building introduces the visitor to Richard Harding Watt's eccentric buildings. Watt (1842-1913), a millionaire Manchester glove manufacturer, had a very personal vision of Mediterranean architecture – this he imposed on lucky Knutsford. He also adored birds – his buildings are covered with projecting stones to allow them to perch. Other examples of Watt's architecture include the Ruskin Reading Room in Drury Lane and the houses on Legh Road, which have been called 'the maddest sequence of villas in all England'. This became suburban Shanghai for the Spielberg film *Empire of the Sun*.

Knutsford is also well-known famous as *Cranford*, the town in the novel of the same name by C19 novelist Elizabeth Gaskell. Gaskell, although more associated with Manchester through novels such as *North and South*, was brought up in the town and her grave lies in the cemetery of the Unitarian Chapel on Brook Street. Every first Saturday in May, the May Day celebrations are held – the most charming carnival procession in the North West.

Knutsford: a house by Richard Harding Watt

SIGHTSEEING

Middleton

'A subborn people with a wooden steeple'
Traditional description of Middleton folk

01706 924928 Tourist info *On the A664 Rochdale Road, four miles from the city centre. Nearest Rail Station is Mills Hill.*

All the interest of Middleton lies around the Parish church and Long Street, up from the dreary shopping mall. Like Knutsford, it contains interesting and innovative architectural work from around 100 years ago. Instead of a maverick glove manufacturer we're dealing with a very gifted architectural practice, of Edgar Wood and JH Sellars. Unlike Knutsford, this little town, in Manchester's inner sprawl, is struggling to come to terms with the decline of traditional industries. The parish church of St Leonard (0161 643 2693) is special. The weather boarding on the tower dates from 1667 when new bells were hung. Most of the present building dates from 1524 but includes a tower and porch from 1412 plus some Norman vestiges from around 1100. Most of the 1524 work was paid for by Sir Richard Assheton, the hero of Flodden Field, where the English defeated the Scots. On the south wall there is a memorial window with the names of local men who took part in the battle- the oldest such memorial anywhere. From the churchyard to the south, there is a robust, view across the valley of the river Irk. This captures some of the spirit of old industrial Lancashire. Down the steep hill, east from the church, lies the restored Old Grammar School of 1586, this was the school of the C19 Middleton radical Samuel Bamford who provided the best eyewitness account of the Peterloo Massacre in Manchester in 1819. Wood and Sellars' buildings in Middleton include Long Street Chapel, which contains some exquisite Arts and Crafts meets Art Nouveau designs in its details and the plans. Nearby are several houses built by the practice – a trail leaflet can be picked up from the Middleton Library. Also see page 116. Close to Long Street chapel is the Old Boars Head, at least half a millennium old, and full of charm. As a bonus it serves ales from the nearby JW Lees brewery

Ramsbottom

'What's Ramsbottom like? Wet and windy'
Traditional music hall joke about the town.

'Valley of the wild garlic'
The Anglo-Saxon origin of the town name.

0161 253 5111 Tourist info. *The best way to visit Ramsbottom is via the East Lancs Railway on a weekend. Take the Metrolink to Bury and walk the quarter of a mile to the Bolton Street terminus of the heritage railway. The town lies on the A676 four miles north of Bury.*

Ramsbottom may be less than 25 miles (40km) as the crow flies from Knutsford but it is totally opposite in character. This is a no-nonsense stone-built Pennine hill town. The roads out of the town east and west are impossibly steep. In the Market Place is the Grant Arms, which commemorates and was owned by the chief bigwigs of C19 Ramsbottom, the Grants, who Charles Dickens immortalised as the Cheryble brothers in *Nicholas Nickleby*. These mill owners made sure of the profits of their pub by part paying their workforce in tokens redeemable for beer in the Grant Arms. Ramsbottom is placed on the Irwell Sculpture Trail and in the Market Place is the wonderful *Tilted Vase* by Edward Allington. This two-ton sculpture is classical in shape to reflect the surrounding buildings but also bolted together to reflect the old industries. The excellent fish and chip shop on Bridge Street is worth a visit, as is Bailey's Tea Shop on the same street. At the other end of the scale, this tiny town has one of best independent restaurants in the region, called Ramsons. Located in the Market Place, all their food and drink is organic. A very steep but very pleasant walk west up Tanners Street and then the Rake leads to lovely Holcombe Village and good food and drink at the Shoulder of Mutton pub. A further climb takes the visitor to the Peel Monument on Holcombe Moor. Even from the foot of the 39-metre tower there are spectacular views over Manchester to North Wales. The tower was erected in 1852 in memory of Sir Robert Peel, the Bury-born PM, founder of the modern police force and the man who repealed of the Corn Laws.

Room at the top

The Moors

'Moors are a stage for the performance of Heaven, any audience is incidental'
Ted Hughes

The Pennine Hills surround Manchester on three sides, at their closest a mere 10 miles (16km) away. Most of these upland areas are characterised by the vast spaces of the Moors, often forming a series of plateaux wide open to all that the elements can throw at them. Often the plateaux break and crash into deep ravines and dells, where scrub woodland fights with ferns and nettles. The edges of the heights themselves are frayed into crags such as those at Cown Edge Rocks near Glossop or the pithily named Windgather Rocks at Kettleshulme. In fine weather, the Moors are beautiful and dramatic, mingling fresh air with long views and sheep. On some days a silence seems to descend, broken only by skylarks or a gentle breeze whispering through the coarse grass. On several of the Moors, east of the city, the heather burns purple in late summer.

But there is something ambiguous about the Moors too. If there is beauty here it is imperfect. This is no Alpine idyll or lowland English pleasantry. In bad weather, there is a dark primeval quality, which has fascinated writers for centuries. It's as if the Moors have their own personality: one traumatised by the human abuse of deforestation, quarrying and industry. Emily Brontë understood this well in *Wuthering Heights* – set on the Haworth Moors 25 miles northeast of the city. So did Ted Hughes who captured the raw, hard beauty of the hills in *Remains of Elmet*, from which the introductory quotation to this description comes.

Of course, the name Moors is tarnished in Manchester with the word murderer. Saddleworth Moor was the chosen location for Ian Brady and Myra Hindley when they buried their child victims in the '60s. One body remains lost up there. As do others from other times. In the deep peat pleats around Kinder, Bleaklow and Black Hill are the scattered wreckage of a large number of planes, including Spitfires, Lancasters, several US Liberators and a Superfortress.

Sometimes it feels appropriate that a common bird call up here is the cry of the curlew: if all that is cold and sinister about the Moors could be caught in one sound it is that. Yet similarly all that is bright and fresh about the Moors is contained in the twitter of the skylark. The Moors are about extremes.

If there is time, every visitor should take the opportunity to claim their own bit of the southern Pennines. The walk on the next page will let you achieve this.

Take it to the Edge

This country walk offers a Roman road, Robin Hood, beer, books and the ragged rocky peak of Blackstone Edge hanging over the small Pennine town of Littleborough. It's not the prettiest walk in Greater Manchester, although there is prettiness along the way, but it provides a distinctive introduction to the gritty nature of this region. That's the real reason why we chose this route, visitors couldn't be anywhere else. As a country walk it gets to the soul of Manchester and the surrounding area better than any preserved National Park or gentle Cheshire lowland walk could ever do. It's tough, even hard, yet spectacular.

In its toughness it reflects the experience of so many people in this area. Children from the 1960s to the 1990s in places like Littleborough grew up amidst a mass extinction. This region and these hills suffered and rejoiced in a longer period of industrialisation – almost three hundred years - than anywhere else on the planet but thirty years ago heavy engineering and the textile trade was in terminal decline. A child was surrounded by empty mills, mouldering mill lodges, Cyclopean revetments on river embankments, and shattered railways leading nowhere. Spouting literally out of the ground were the rusted remnants of machines and engines.

Most of this has now gone or been smoothed over. Yet on this walk if you look carefully you will still see the evidence, massive walls in seemingly inappropriate places, a landscape occasionally pitted and pock marked with old workings. Today age lends these features charm and scarcely hints at the lives they supported and the industrial society they helped pioneer.

The route

When you get off the train at Littleborough station (see boxout next page) you can see your destination, the craggy head of Blackstone Edge, 3.5km (2miles) away.

Take the stairs down from the platform and turn left through the tunnel under the platform and on to Canal Street. Cross over to Rochdale Canal and follow the tow path left to the first lock. Cross the canal here and the path takes you left and then right past a row of terraced houses. The path joins Shore Lane, turn right and continue past the Fothergill's factory on the right and one of the Rochdale Canal reservoirs on the left. Continue until the lane meets the meander of the stream – Ealees Brook. A short way ahead take the first path up steps on the left of the lane. This crosses over one of the disused feeder channels for the Rochdale Canal and climbs through the fringes of a wood towards a group of buildings, bear left before the buildings and then right through the hedge and follow the path down to

Shore Lane Brook. Follow the path along this delightful valley of heather, ramson, birch, alder and scrub oak to the equally delightful Owlet Hall.

This old yeoman's house sports the mullioned windows and tough bones of typical Pennine architecture and shows how wealth was growing along with the significance of the textile trade in the C17 and C18 centuries. The name is probably nothing to do with owls but more with alders, the native tree which flourishes locally and provided a perfect wood for tool handles, clogs and charcoal. The dialect word for alder is owler.

Practicalities

This is a tough walk, six miles in length and rising 472m (1548ft) above sea level. It will take at least four hours to complete, more with lunch at the White House pub.

Throughout the day there are usually two trains an hour from Manchester Victoria to Littleborough. These take less than 30 minutes. Sample Saturday services might be the 10.54am from Victoria arriving at 11.16am, with return trains, to allow time for the walk and lunch, from Littleborough at 4.45pm.

For those of a less active disposition they might want to leave the train at Smithy Bridge, the station before Littleborough, and walk up to Hollingworth Lake for a leisurely stroll, an ice cream and some very good fish and chips.

By car you can park at Littleborough station, or if you choose the easier option, at Hollingworth Lake Visitors Centre. If you park at the latter you can follow a path away from the lake along the valley bottom to join the route described here from the point where it leaves Shore Lane and climbs the hillside.

Dogleg through the gates, to the right and then left around Owlet Hall and follow the stream valley to a track crossing in front of you. Turn left alongside the pylon line to the minor road and the tiny community of Lydgate. Turn right along the track in front of the row of houses and then alongside the field wall (not the minor road that veers left in a similar direction). Ahead the rocky crown of Blackstone Edge is clearly visible. The track turns into a path and reaches the car park at the foot of another track which attacks Blackstone Edge head on. Follow the track and as you climb you will find traces of a paved road with kerbs and a central groove. This is either the best preserved and most spectacular Roman road in the UK or a seventeenth century packhorse route, the debate still rages. The groove was probably intended to provide drag for a cart's brake pole. At the crest of the hill a clear path opens to the right. This is the Pennine Way and we turn south along it. The tall stone at the turn point here is the Aiggin Stone, marked with a cross and a waymarker over what can be treacherous and lethal moorland in winter. The name might be derived from the French aiguille or a needle, but then again it might not.

On the approach to the crest of Blackstone Edge the land turns into the surface of the moon, a barren rockscape reaching to the tors on the Edge itself. The Pennine Way follows a route east of the summit, our path is to the highest rock outcrop by the best route the walker can find. If you love rock hopping this is perfect terrain.

The highest point marked by the concrete triangulation station is called Robin Hood's Bed. You are now 472m (1548ft) above sea level. The rocks, the landscape and, above all the views, are spectacular. The wind from the west is usually spectacular as well. Blackstone Edge isn't the highest point in Greater Manchester, that lies south east and is an inconspicuous boggy lump amidst high moorland. This destination is more impressive in appearance and for views and access. On a clear day the Welsh mountains can be seen to the south west. In, more or less, the same direction, 17 kilometres away,

the tall buildings of Manchester city centre, particular the 177m Hilton Tower rise from the Lancashire Plain (on page 34 the hills glimpsed in the distance include Blackstone Edge). To the east the moorland stretches down into Yorkshire. The Pennines always have their sheerest escarpment and highest peaks in the west of the range.

The name Robin Hood crops up in many places across Britain and especially across the Southern Pennines. Many believe the name predates the legendary outlaw of the Middle Ages and stretches back to Robin Goodfellow, a wild pre-Christian diety of wood and moor.

There are many stories about the Edge. The strangest states that if you get lost in the rocks beneath the crest you may be overwhelmed by ecstatic yelps and screams which suddenly cease as quickly as they swept over you. Then again the place has been known as a refuge for lovers.

The best return route is via refreshment and the White House pub. In 1724, *Robinson Crusoe* author, Daniel Defoe, might have had a terrible fright when he crossed Blackstone Edge in a snowstorm but he had this to say, 'as in all those northern countries, the people had

an extraordinary way of mixing the warm and the cold very happily together; for the store of good ale which flows plentifully in the most mountainous part of this country, seems abundantly to make up for the inclemencies of the season, or difficulties of travelling.'

Retrace your steps to the Aiggin Stone and continue on the Pennine Way to the A58. Clearly visible up the hill to the right is the White House pub. Here you can enjoy a good lunch and fine ales. When you've eaten or drunk your fill, totter carefully back down the A58 to the first path leading off to the right. This is a bridleway, and another old packhorse route, back down to Littleborough. Keep left when smaller paths break off to the right. After a small pond which fills an old quarry, bear left back to the A58. Cross over to the minor road which is Blackstone Edge Old Road. Follow this back through Lydgate and over Gatehouse hamlet back to the A58 at the handsome Rake Inn. The A58 takes you back to Canal Street and the railway station.

If you continue under the viaduct and past the church you will come to the main square of Littleborough. On the right hand side is the best second-hand book shop in Greater Manchester, Kelsalls. This is a fascinating warren of antiquarian and second hand books that is worth the journey from Manchester alone. If you have time you could lose a couple of hours in here. Perhaps you might want to reward your efforts with a slim volume of heroic poetry in tribute to the day and yourself.

Love **by Robert Indiana washed by the Cascade at Chatsworth House**

Hit the North

A glance at a UK map shows Manchester is in the centre of the island. The motorway system serves the city well, with the main east-west artery, the M62, connecting Manchester to Liverpool and the cities of Yorkshire, whilst the M6 links the city to north and south. The rail system also connects Manchester with the rest of the country, whilst you can fly from the Airport to most other airports in the British Isles.

Visitors should do what the locals do and take advantage of this. Manchester is lucky in terms of access to the best of Britain. The city is within an hour and a half drive of great cities, great landscapes and great theme parks. You can get long views from high hills, top class art and go down a big dipper, all on the same day - if you're stout of character and eccentric in habits.

This part of the book looks at that wealth of tourist potential on the Mancunian doorstep whether it be the mountains of the Lake District or Snowdonia, the gentler hills of the Yorkshire Dales or the Trough of Bowland, or the powerful city scapes of Liverpool and Leeds. Given that 2008 is the Capital of Culture in the former city we pay special potential to Liverpool and it's welcome, if overdue resurgence. Forget those stories of the Scouse-Manc rivalry, for our part we can see through it all to the valuable stuff beneath. Bless us eh? Finally we walk you through the major visitor attractions, such as theme parks, in the near North.

pop boutique
YEAH!

Wasdale Head

The Lake District

The Lake District has captured the poetic imagination of the world ever since the great romantic poets of the late C18 and early C19 discovered within it a balance of nature: lakes, mountains, forests and meadows. William Wordsworth, Samuel Coleridge, Robert Southey, and later John Ruskin, Beatrix Potter and others, penned verses and books to celebrate the area, and visitors have been pouring in ever since.

Judicious use of Ordnance Survey maps allows the walker to find empty corners in this popular district: the key is to pick the peripheral areas. Making the extra effort to get over to Wastwater, Ennerdale, Buttermere and Bassenthwaite pays dividends in terms of isolation. Wasdale Head beyond the furthest shore of Wastwater has the most profoundly grand landscape in all England, see the picture above, but without the softening elements of the meadows and woods of elsewhere in the Lake District. The walk up the mountains of Great Gable and round to Pillar is majestic here. The highest mountain in England, Scafell Pike (977m-3206ft), can be accessed from Wasdale Head too.

The High Street fells along to Haweswater and down to Kentdale and Longsleddale is the land of waterfalls, golden eagles, deer and very few people. It's also where the water comes from when you turn on the tap in Manchester. Both Haweswater and Thirlmere are city reservoirs. The water that comes out of your tap in this city comes from 80 miles (100km) north.

Another much underestimated area is Furness, south of Coniston, where the hills are gentler but the sea inlets and wooded valleys compensate. The little town of Cartmel in this area is exquisite, a jumble of streets around a mighty priory with the Michelin starred L'Enclume restaurant not far away. It has also the prettiest race course (for horses) in these islands.

History is everywhere, from Castlerigg Stone Circle near Keswick and the Roman fort at Hardknott to Wordsworth's Dove Cottage at Grasmere. There are numerous tourist hotspots: one of the more unusual is the sculpture trail in Grizedale Forest. Easy day excursions can be made via train from Manchester to Windermere. Bowness, a mile or so south west of Windermere, is a pleasant town with a waterfront offering lovely boat trips.

The Peak District

Cheek by jowl with Manchester to the east is the Peak District National Park. This is riven in two by the Dark Peak and White Peak. The Dark Peak is dominated by Kinder Scout, 636m (2088ft) of rock and peat stretching out towards Bleaklow and Black Hill. The tiny village of Edale is in its shadow, and is the start of the 270 mile Pennine Way. Glossop is the main centre in the north, and easily reached by train from Manchester. Nearby are the handsome townships of Hayfield and New Mills, the latter with an impressive gorge and award-winning Millennium Footbridge. The main road from Glossop to Sheffield goes over the aptly named Snake Pass. On the other side is Ladybower Reservoir in the Derwent Valley, a monument to Victorian civil engineering. This is a great walking and mountain-biking country- you can hire bikes at the Derwent Dale car park. A few miles to the south is pretty Eyam, where a C17 plague wiped out much of the population.

The White Peak is a limestone region famous for its caves. Tideswell in this geological area has a beautiful church often called 'the Cathedral of the Peak'. Religion plays a part throughout the Park and the high summer well-dressing ceremonies provide a continuous link back to Pagan times. Buxton in the south of the district is a former spa town, reached by train from Manchester, with a splendid opera house.

In the centre of the Peak District is Mam Tor, ('the shivering mountain', so-named because of the frequent landslips), capped by an Iron Age hill fort, and Castleton with its dramatic caves and castle. Speedwell Cavern here offers an underground boat ride. Two further highlights of the Peak District are Chatsworth and Dovedale. The first is the Duke of Devonshire's impressive stately home in stunning landscaped grounds near the River Derwent at Baslow, while in the far south of the park is Dovedale, a beautiful river gorge studded with caves and forests, where angling was developed into an art form by Isaak Walton. The next valley over, the Manifold, is as beautiful but less used.

Just outside the Park to the south east is Matlock Bath in its deep gorge. The attractions here include the Heights of Abraham with its caves and cable-car ride.

Mam Tor broods in the sunshine

WORLD MUSEUM Liverpool
BRING YOUR
MUMMY
GET WRAPPED UP IN WORLD MUSEUM LIVERPOOL
www.worldmuseumliverpool.org.uk
WALKER ART GALLERY
FAMOUS FACES
www.thewalker.org.uk
Lady Lever Art Gallery
www.ladyleverartgallery.org.uk
MERSEYSIDE MARITIME MUSEUM
LIFELINES
A STORY OF MERCHANT SHIPS AND SEAFARERS
www.merseysidemaritimemuseum.org.uk
08 Liverpool EUROPEAN CAPITAL OF CULTURE
FREE ENTRY
NATIONAL MUSEUMS LIVERPOOL

Bowland and the Yorkshire Dales

The Trough of Bowland lies thirty or so miles north of Manchester in Lancashire. This is a relatively unvisited area of splendid hill country marked out by the classic rounded shapes of the Pennine hills. One of the communities here, pretty Dunsop Bridge, has been identified by Ordnance Survey (the main mapping organisation of the UK) as the exact geographic centre of the country. So expect to get your sense of equilibrium restored here. Good villages to visit include Dent and Slaidburn, whilst the road north west to Lancaster over the Trough itself is hard to beat on a sunny day. The grandest property is Stoneyhurst College, associated with Arthur Conan Doyle, Gerard Manley Hopkins and JRR Tolkien - the main approach to the buildings is breathtaking. Nearby Clitheroe has the smallest castle keep in England but also a butchers shop and a wine shop with a national reputation. Brooding over Citheroe is Pendle Hill with its occult associations.

Further north and east over the River Ribble lies Skipton with its impressive castle. North of the town lies the Yorkshire Dales National Park. The Dales are simply delightful, lush with the greenest of green valleys under rounded moorland hills of skylark and heather. The white limestone cliffs and the deep caves provide added attraction, as do the almost absurdly pretty villages. In two places the hills rise to peaks, at Ingleborough and Pen-y-Ghent – both of which make excellent walks. Malham is a popular tourist spot with Gordale Scar and the tarn. More interesting towns lie deeper into the park such as Hawes and Askrigg in Wensleydale, which also features the mighty Middleham and Bolton Castles. Just outside the Park south west is Kirby Lonsdale with a fine church and Ruskin's View. This was the favourite view of art critic John Ruskin. It balances fells, river, woods and meadows in perfect counterpoint. There's a couple of good pubs, The Sun and the Snooty Fox, plus a good chippy in Kirby too.

Bolton Castle

The Great Orme and Llandudno Pier

North Wales

When Edward 1 conquered North Wales in the late 1200s he may have sealed the fate of a once proudly independent nation but he left Wales with an astonishing legacy in fortifications. Conwy, Beaumaris, Caernarfon and Harlech castles are the most impressive castles in Britain, some say Europe.

Conwy castle, in particular, an hour and three-quarters away by train from Manchester, is impressive. The town beneath is fascinating too: walled, with good buildings and a pleasant harbour. A little north is the elegant seaside resort of Llandudno, with its lovely beach, superb pier and the fabulous Orme: a rocky mountain headland climbed by exhilarating tramcar. Again there are direct train services from Manchester. South of Conwy is Bodnant Garden, a spectacular and award-winning creation clambering over hilly country.

Portmeirion

Except for Llandudno the other seaside resorts are tacky (how many caravan parks can there be in one small country?) so head for Snowdonia. Here you'll find climbing, walking and canoeing as good as anywhere in Britain. This area is defined by lakes and tumbling streams under tall mountains, with gentler walks in the valleys. Some of the sights not to be missed include Betwys-y-Coed, with its rapids and waterfalls, Portmeirion, the Italianate folly designed by Clough-Ellis in mimicry of Portofino, the beaches at Red Wharf Bay on Anglesey and the hill fort at Tre'r Ceiri on the Lleyn Penninsula. The further west you go, the more dominant the Welsh language becomes. Overseas visitors often remark how strange it is to find just 80 miles or so from Manchester city centre people who, in unbroken tradition, have spoken a language that predates the world-dominant English.

The island of Anglesey offers a gentler alternative to Snowdonia and also access, via Holyhead, to Ireland. The landscape might be gentler but remains unmistakeably that of the Celtic far west of the United Kingdom.

The Lancashire coast and the resorts

Silverdale

The Lancashire coast west of Manchester might appear flat at first glance but don't be fooled. North of Liverpool at Crosby and Formby huge sand hills crowned with pine have been carved by long shore drift. The walks through these are rewarding and involve, at Formby, a red squirrel sanctuary. At Crosby, Antony Gormley's *Another Place* makes any visit special, here a 100 mysterious life size metal figures appear in and out of the sea as the tide changes.

The resort of Southport has the wrought iron clad, tree-lined boulevard of Lord Street, the Botanic Gardens, the Lawnmower Museum (they even do lawnmower demonstrations – the excitement gets too much, honestly). Over the Ribble estuary is brash Blackpool. Of course the place is unashamedly vulgar, with its Golden Mile of sand, promenade, trams, hotels, zoo, tower and ballroom, three piers, amusement arcades, cabaret bars and theatres. It extends the holiday season each year with its annual illuminations. Blackpool is a snob's nightmare, but for any overseas visitor who wants to make a fun study of an essential part of the British psyche, it is irresistible. You just have to suspend any good taste you thought you had, knot a handkerchief on the head and plunge in. If the beach gets boring or the day is cold try the 148m (518ft) Blackpool Tower (01253 292029 www.theblackpooltower.co.uk). The Pleasure Beach is described on page 168.

Further north is Lancaster. This is a fiercely impressive castle, that doubles as a tourist attraction and an HM Government prison. The Georgian Quayside makes for a lovely walk. On a hill to the east lies the Ashton Memorial in Williamson Park - the largest folly in the country. There is a Butterfly House here and good views of the Lake District. The fabulous John O'Gaunt pub and Atkinsons, the unchanged C19 purveyor of teas and coffees – blended on the premises – provide an excuse to pause further.

But back to landscapes. The area a few miles north of Lancaster around Arnside and Silverdale is a cutsy limestone wonderland with delightful wooded walks over Morecambe Bay. There are direct trains from Manchester to Silverdale and Arnside.

LANDSCAPES

Another Place by Antony Gormley

View to the Pier Head from Albert Dock

5 Liverpool myths (as told by Scousers)

Liverpudlians are the funniest people in the country/world/galaxy/universe
No. Funny, but too sentimental. Lancastrians (Lancashire of the pre-1974 boundaries which includes Manchester and Liverpool, but in this case excludes Liverpool, if you follow) are the funniest because they combine wit and absurdity with much less emotion. Oddly Yorkshire people have no sense of humour at all.

Liverpool people are the friendliest in the world
Possibly true. Unless you support Manchester United (although Everton FC fans don't care).

Liverpool has some of the best architecture in the country
Yes, indeed.

Liverpool is hated by the rest of the country
Not at all, lots of Liverpudlians have moved out of the city and they still remain in love with the place.

Liverpudlians are talented over-achievers
True. The number of Scousers who've made a national and international impact is impressive – must be because they're so funny and friendly.

Liverpool

The land that Time finally remembered

Manchester and Liverpool used to be equals in economic muscle, Liverpool occasionally even had the upper hand. Then when the Atlantic trade died after World War II and European trade grew, the city found itself a dead end on the wrong side of the country. The death of the docks coincided with the decline of manufacturing. Manchester went through similar problems but rode the storm better because of better management and the good fortune of lying at a natural crossroads.

Some Liverpool facts: there are more listed buildings of architectural merit in Liverpool than anywhere outside London, there are more green spaces then anywhere outside the capital, there used to be 35 miles of wharves, between 1830 and 1930 nine million people emigrated to the New World from Liverpool. And all of this was founded in the eighteenth century on Liverpool traders shipping millions of slaves across the Atlantic.

The result of the wealth the city

Catholic (foreground) and Anglican Cathedrals

generated in the past is a quite spectacular city centre. And, happily, the present is beginning to make up ground on the old days. A renaissance is underway, cranes dominate the landscape as a new retail heart worth £1bn starts to become reality. In these circumstances the award of Capital of Culture for 2008 was more than justified. Events such as the Biennial Festival (next held in autumn 2008) were already evidence of a city re-engaging with the modern world.

As were the exceptional galleries and museums of the city and its region, the National Museums Liverpool - www.liverpoolmuseums.org.uk. These include the Walker Art Gallery, Merseyside Maritime Museum, the National Conservation Centre, the Lady Lever Art Gallery in Port Sunlight and the World Museum Liverpool. The first five of these are amazing. The Walker, in particular, is a must visit, the best provincial art gallery in the country with old masters and modern works. Sadly the World Museum Liverpool is dreadful, another example of modern museum practice losing its direction and dumbing down.

But that's about it as far as bad news for the visitor goes. The city has two remarkable cathedrals. The Roman Catholic, from 1967 and the Anglican Cathedral, finished 1978, the pair are connected by Hope Street – which is a pretty coincidence. The former is by Sir Frederick Gibberd and is famous for its stained-glass windows and huge altar. The latter, by Sir Giles Gilbert Scott, took 75 years to build, and is the largest Anglican

5 Liverpool myths (as told by non-Scousers)

Liverpool relies on the Beatles too much
Yes and no, after ignoring the Beatles' popularity in official circles until the eighties, the City authorities then became too enthusiastic. If you've got it flaunt, but in truth the city's much better than some dated moptops.

Liverpudlians are always whinging
True. When Conservative MP Boris Johnson made some throw away comments in 2004 about Scouse victim mentality he had to visit and apologise. This made the city look silly. Why this chip on the shoulder exists is hard to fathom, possibly it's tied in with the economic decline in the seventies and eighties. Or perhaps they just like moaning. There's only very good or very bad in Liverpool, no middle ground.

It's hard to organise events in Liverpool because everybody's shouting so much about 'der people, what are dey gettin' out of it?'
Er…no comment. Capital of Culture's going to be great. We're sure of that in Manchester. Honest. No, really.

Liverpool has a lot of crime?
Nope. Many other cities in the UK come out worse across a range of statistics including car crime.

Manchester is a much more dynamic, diverse and interesting city
So true (this is a Manchester guidebook you know).

Check out page 34 for what Mancunians think about themselves.

The Liver Building

Scouse

The proper adjective for a person from Liverpool is a Liverpudlian, but the less polite, if latterly more common, nickname is Scouser. This derives from the stew the city is associated with. Scouse is a type of lamb stew (although there are many variations) which was traditionally the food of poor families around the docks in Liverpool. The real name for the dish, lobscouse, is Scandinavian or German in origin. Evidently the locals adopted the dish from visiting sailors, the lob syllable was dropped and the nickname followed.

Cathedral in the world – a gargantuan tribute to the power of the Almighty or if you're not a believer, a gargantuan tribute to the human spirit. The view from the tower is spectacular. The spooky adjacent graveyard, St James' is essential for any visitors with a Goth frame of mind.

The city centre still has its Georgian squares and terraces too, plus grand Victorian and Edwardian warehouses. When you step out from Lime Street Station, the first sight that greets you is St George's Hall from 1856. Wow is the only reaction.

The tang of the sea is never far away. The ferry trip, a mile over the River Mersey

Keep an eye on this group, they might be big one day

to Birkenhead is recommended. The three buildings of the Pier Head – the Liver, the Cunard and the Port of Liverpool buildings (known locally as the Three Graces) – sum up the wealth of the British Empire in its Edwardian heyday 100 or so years ago.

Along from the Pierhead is Albert Dock. This was designed by Jesse Hartley and built in the 1840s. It decayed in the C20 and was revived in the 1980s. It houses the Tate North art gallery, the Merseyside Maritime Museum (and nearby the Museum of Liverpool Life), The Beatles Story, plus bars, restaurants and shops.

For many, Liverpool and The Beatles are one and the same thing – the band, now 37 years defunct, still attracts 600,000 visitors a year. The Cavern on Mathew Street, demolished in the 1970s, has been re-excavated and reopened. The best way to relive Beatlemania is to take a trip on the Magical Mystery Tour, which visits Penny Lane, Strawberry Fields and other Beatle's landmarks. There is also the aforementioned Beatles Story at Albert Dock and a Beatles shop on Mathew Street. On the last Bank Holiday weekend of August the Beatles Festival takes place. During the 2007 Festival the Hard Days Night, a Beatles themed hotel, on North John Street opens.

In a different tradition, on Hope Street is the fabulous Art Deco Philharmonic Hall, home to the Royal Liverpool Philharmonic Orchestra. Two of the best choices for food and drink lie close by. The Philharmonic pub, opposite the Hall, dates from 1900, and is simply (or perhaps we should say extravagantly) the most ornate pub in the UK. Still on Hope Street is the The London Carriageworks which provides superb, original and exciting grub from Paul Askew.

Then there are two football clubs. Apparently. Both with museums. Apparently. As a Manchester guide we're frankly not interested. Oh, go on then. The teams are Liverpool and Everton, and they gaze at each other across Stanley Park.

This sort of joshing between Manchester and Liverpool comes naturally. Due to proximity and competition ithe two cities have always been wary of each other – see page 98 for a key example of this. But in many respects they are two peas in a pod, cities with a western outlook, open to the immigrants that have come in over the centuries and with a more radical and egalitarian mindset than the rest of England. Livercunians, Manpudlians you might say.

For information about Capital of Culture events try www.liverpool08.com

St George's Hall

Leeds and West Yorkshire

Over the Pennines east from the city lies the bustling city of Leeds. This is Manchester's only really commercial rival in the North but is much smaller. Still there's a lively cultural life, good museums and shopping as well as a much reduced Leeds United Football Club, a Test cricket ground, good rugby, Opera North and the West Yorkshire Playhouse. Its well-appointed city centre has spectacular arcades in which to shop. The Corn Exchange is another retail favourite. Roundhay Park is a fine and very large public amenity whilst the Royal Armouries and Thackray museums will entertain militarily or medically depending on what you like.

Bradford lies in the shadow cast by Leeds. Famous for being the curry capital of Britain, the main tourist attraction is the National Museum of Photography, Film and Television. Between Bradford and Halifax is Saltaire, founded as a model industrial village by philanthropist millowner Sir Titus Salt, and now home to the David Hockney Gallery.

In between Manchester and Bradford, and easily accessed on the line from Manchester Victoria, visitors will find lots of tough boned but attractive stone towns such as Hebden Bridge and Todmorden. Hebden Bridge has a famously leftfield community of hippies and lesbians, so expect lots of kooky gift shops. A steep walk takes visitors to Heptonstall, a lovely Pennine village, which contains in its romantic graveyard the tomb of American poet Sylvia Plath. Plath committed suicide whilst married to local poet and future laureate, the late Ted Hughes. A few miles east is Halifax with Eureka! one of the finest children's attractions in Britain, suitable for all ages from 2-14. The nearby Piece Hall is a spectacular Georgian cloth hall.

Chester v York

For that classic 'olde' county town experience from Manchester visitors have two choices in major league tourism: Chester and York. Both are easily reached by train from the city – Chester in just over an hour, York in an hour and a half. So which is it to be if you have one day and have to choose one or the other?

Let's consider Chester first. Founded by the Romans in the first century as Deva, it became a legionary fort for the XXth Legion, strategically placed to control North Wales and North West England with sea access via the River Dee. It continued as an important city until the C17, when the Dee silted up, and Liverpool supplanted it as a trading port. Today it is a prosperous small city with enough history and good shopping to drag in tourists from around the world.

One of the qualities that makes the place special is the complete circle of defensive walls. A stroll around these takes an hour or so and always presents something of interest. Roman traces include an amphitheatre, bath houses and temples. The Grosvenor Museum has the full story of Deva and is full of great finds. The Cathedral was once an abbey, and it shows – with cloisters to one side, and extensive grounds beyond the Close. The most remarkable medieval feature though is The Rows, a unique system of covered walkways with shops on two levels (a proto shopping mall, almost) from three quarters of a millennium ago. If all this gets too much and you feel like a lie down, then you could stop over at one of the country's top hotels, the Grosvenor. You will need a full wallet though.

A little way outside Chester is Chester Zoo, the North's premier zoo set in 110 acres, and with a fine record of breeding endangered species. A little further north again is the Blue Planet Aquarium, one of the best of its kind in Britain and excellent for families. Chester Races, just outside the walls, lays claim to being the most glam in

The Rows, Chester

the North. Although the folk at York races say the same.

So how does York compare?

Well first off, it has the mightiest medieval Cathedral in the whole nation: York Minster. If architecture can ever be art rather than craft then this whole building is a masterpiece in masonry. And wood. And glass. The crypt is also special. Just as Chester was a Legionary fortress, York, or Eboracum if you prefer the Latin, madam, was home to the VI Legion. The difference is that York has always been on the main road from London to Scotland and thus been forced to play a central role in British history up until the Industrial Revolution, when its importance declined. Because of this the crypt in the Minster displays the remains of the legionary headquarters where Constantine was crowned Emperor whilst campaigning in Britain. He would turn the Roman Empire Christian and thus history would enter a new phase. If you like your history large, this is about as big as it goes.

Aside from the Minster, the streets of York are truly charming, a gorgeous mish-mash (and mix-match) of buildings where hundreds of years of differing architectural fashions lie cheek by jowl. The Shambles area is particularly good. Then there's the National Railway Museum, a good art gallery, a fine castle (Clifton Tower), city walls and adorable spins down the river on a variety of river craft (although Chester has this too). The only drawback is the 500 different types of ghost walk (well almost that many) which you keep bumping into.

So which should it be for that day trip? Chester or York?

There can only be one winner.

It's York every time. It feels bigger, more significant and loses no points for prettiness. The restaurants are better too. So whether it's for a day trip or a dirty weekend in a four poster bed, go east. *Manchester, the Complete Guide* has spoken.

York Minster

Major Attractions

These are the main theme parks and attractions within 50 miles of Manchester including the two supernova theme parks of Alton Towers and Blackpool Pleasure. If you want organised days out on supervised sites these are the places for you.

Theme parks

Alton Towers (Alton, off B5032, signposted from the north off Junc 28 of M1 or Junc 16 of M6, Staffordshire. www.altontowers.co.uk) Adults £32, children 12 years and over £24, children between 4 and 11 years £12, family £89. Alton Towers combines fun and thrills with several laid-back attractions. There's the recent Charlie and The Chocolate Factory ride plus older favourites such as Oblivion (which leaves your stomach about 20 metres behind) and Nemesis (which leaves all your spatial awareness about 20 metres behind). If it all gets too much, there're the beautiful gardens in which to retreat.

Blackpool Pleasure Beach (Ocean Boulevard. www.blackpoolpleasurebeach.com) is the other heavyweight of northern fun and the favourite of this guidebook, because it's not only fabulous in its own right but also surrounded by the other attractions of Blackpool and next to the sea. It's got other strengths too such as the curious price structure whereby it's free to enter and then you pay for each ride separately. But if you do plan to stay you might want to invest in the unlimited ride wristbands which also get you into the on-site shows –wristbands start from £25. The standout ride is the Pepsi Max, which climbs 72 metres (235ft), and turns confirmed atheists evangelical. Not so far away is Valhalla, a water ride in the dark with twists and turns and a fire to spice things up. There are also ice shows, circus musicals and illusion acts.

The Pepsi Max, Blackpool

Animal Attractions

Blue Planet Aquarium (Longloomes Road, Cheshire Oaks, Ellesmere Port. www.blueplanetaquarium.com) Adults £9.95, children £7.50, under 3s free, family tickets £34. An exceptionally good aquarium with, as its main highlight, the 71 metre underwater walk surrounded on each side and above by sharks, stingray and other oceanic exotica. Elsewhere there are a range of habitats and rockpools, including ones for freshwater fish plus one that focuses on swamps so don't get bogged down there.

Chester Zoo (Near Bache, Chester (off A41). www.chesterzoo.org). Adults £14.95, children (3-15 years old inclusive) £10.95, family ticket £49.50. Off peak, Oct-March, adults £10.50, kids £7.50, family £34. Prices are subject to change. The biggest zoo in the country, covering 110 acres with 7,000 animals including many endangered species. Every visitor to the region might want to come and enjoy this superbly managed zoo with everything from elephants to orang-utans plus jaguars, rhinos, Red River Hogs and Blue Throated Macaws.

Martin Mere Wildlife and Wetlands Trust (Burscough, Ormskirk, Lancashire. www.wwt.org.uk/visit/martinmere/). Adults £6, children £3.80, under 4s free, family £15.55. The area covered by Martin Mere is 376 acres: a massive man-made wetland of ponds and marsh. From the viewing areas thousands of native fowl of the watery kind can be viewed as well as geese, swans and, not very Lancashire, flamingos.

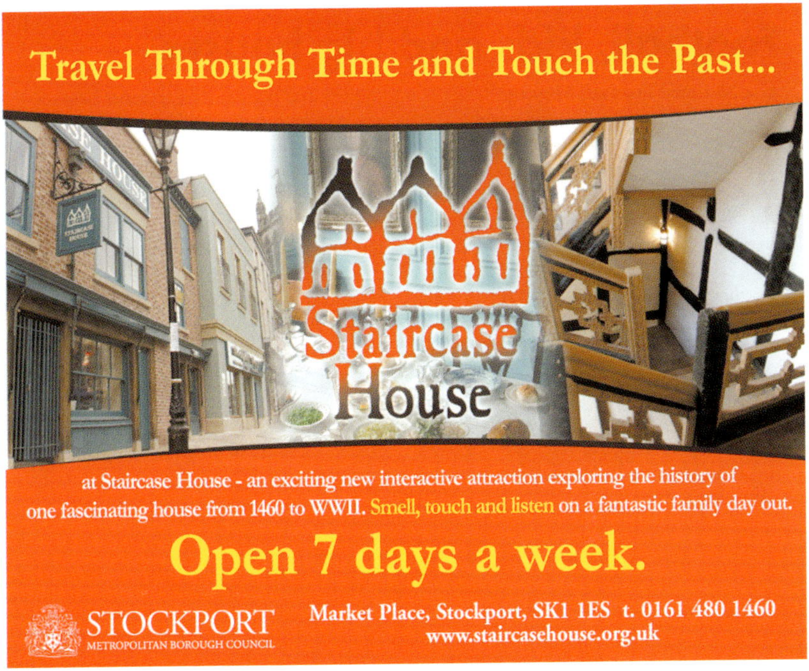
Travel Through Time and Touch the Past...
Staircase House
at Staircase House - an exciting new interactive attraction exploring the history of one fascinating house from 1460 to WWII. Smell, touch and listen on a fantastic family day out.
Open 7 days a week.
STOCKPORT
METROPOLITAN BOROUGH COUNCIL
Market Place, Stockport, SK1 1ES t. 0161 480 1460
www.staircasehouse.org.uk

The University of Manchester
The Manchester Museum
MANCHESTER 1824
The Manchester Museum
• Fun-packed events for all the family
• Hundreds of displays from Archaeology to Zoology
• Café with children's menus
• Free admission
• Open every day
The Manchester Museum, The University of Manchester, Oxford Road, Manchester M13 9PL
Tel 0161 275 2634 Email museum@manchester.ac.uk www.manchester.ac.uk/museum

Football, kids and big houses

The National Football Museum (Sir Tom Finney Way, Preston. www.nationalfootballmuseum.com) Free. Preston was one of the founders of the Football League in 1888 and deserves to host the National Museum. The museum is split into three sections: the First Half, the Second Half and the Hall of Fame (which should of course be called Extra Time). The First Half looks at how the game developed and spread, and the Hall of Fame looks at the great players. In the Second Half, you can have a go at table football and then watch as your game is played back on screen. Or become a guest panellist with Gary Lineker and Alan Hansen on *Match of the Day*.

Eureka (next to Halifax railway station, West Yorkshire. www.eureka.org.uk) All tickets £6.95, ages 1-2 £1.95, under 1s free, family ticket £29.50. A museum especially for children, it even has its own nursery and holiday club. Justifiably award-winning, there're over 400 exhibits of hands-on museum fun for children ages 3-12 years arranged around four main galleries: Me and My Body; Invent, Create, Communicate; Living and Working Together; and Our Global Garden. Filled with clever tricks, these otherwise dry and worthy subjects are brought to life in a way which captivates young minds. In Me and My Body, giant models and hundreds of activities help you to find out all about your body, how it works, and how to look after it.

Magnificent houses are dotted across the North, some are covered in earlier sections of this book. But if you had to choose one further afield to visit for the day then it would have to be **Chatsworth House** (North off the B6012 in the Peak District National Park). House and garden: adults £11.50, children £4.40, family £27.50. The attractions at Chatsworth includes a house, garden, farmyard, adventure playground, gift shops and restaurant. But some house, some garden, both are worthy of royal palaces. The house is a masterpiece of early eighteenth century architecture containing one of the finest private art collections anywhere with many Old Masters. It represents 4,000 years of European culture and expert craftsmanship from Greek statuary to modern paintings. Chatsworth doesn't rest on its laurels either but still adds to the art collections, as the picture of the Robert Indiana work shows on page 152. The garden is equally stunning, landscaped by Capability Brown and later Joseph Paxton – Paxton's work in Birkenhead Park, across the Mersey from Liverpool, inspired Central Park in New York. The water features in the garden are the best in the UK.

Chatsworth House interiors

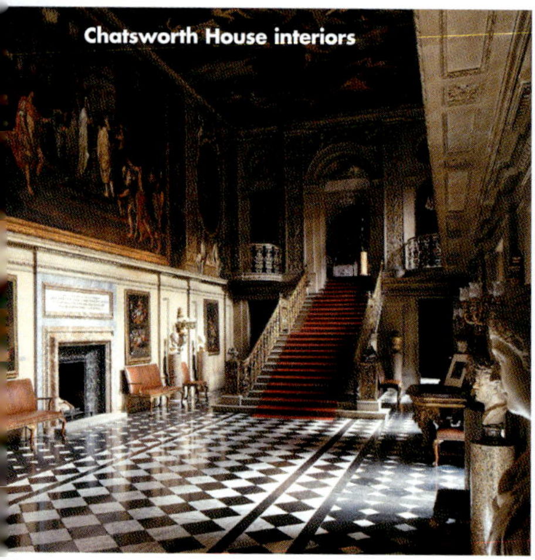

MANCHESTER AIRPORT

Manchester Airport

Manchester Airport is the largest in the UK outside London: 22 million passengers use it each year. The airport flies to over 200 destinations worldwide and is used by more than 300 tour operators and 100 airlines. It is the largest municipally owned airport in the country and is jointly owned by the ten local authorities of Greater Manchester.

The Aviation Viewing Park

Wilmslow Old Road, off the A538, close to Jct 6, M56. Turn down Sunbank Lane to the Romper pub, then turn right on to Wilmslow Old Road and follow it to the end. **0161 904 9460** *8.30am-until dusk everyday except Christmas Day.*
£3 per car and driver, plus £1 per passenger (under 4s free), £2 motorbike and rider, £1 cyclists and walkers

Passes: Midweek Pass 6/3 months £40/£25, Any Day Pass 6/3 months £60/£40. Season ticket passes can be purchased at the entrance kiosk via cash or cheque.

The Aviation Viewing Park is the perfect place to watch the airport's many and varied aircraft take off and land. There are several raised earth platforms so you can see directly over the security fence. The party atmosphere on hot Bank Holidays with families picnicking is lovely. Also on-site is a Visitor Centre, a snack bar and a shop. The Visitor Centre provides an excellent educational resource, with information and displays. The stock in the shop (0161 904 9935) includes make-your-own and die-cast models from £1.99 to £99, thousands of postcards of different types of commercial planes plus gizmos for tracking flights and listening to air traffic controllers. There's a dedicated selection of Concorde memorabilia and gifts of Concorde memorabilia and gifts. *For tours of Concorde see next page. Toilets, shop, food and drink, pram and disabled access.*

Concorde

Manchester Airport is home to Concorde G-BOAC, the flagship of the British Airways Concorde fleet. On selected dates during 2007, the world's most famous aircraft will be open for public guided tours. Concorde at Manchester has the only fully accessible Concorde flight deck in the UK. Manchester Airport now offer a range of four guided tours on board Concorde G-BOAC,– pre-booking is essential for all

All Manchester Airport details correct at time of publication

tours. Please call **0161 489 3932** for details. Gift vouchers available as well. Full details of Concorde open dates and how to go on board can be found at *www.manchesterairport.co.uk/concorde.*

The Classic Concorde Guided Tour

- welcome briefing and short audio/visual show
- guided tour underneath the aircraft to find out more about the remarkable engineering technology
- on-board tour, with a chance to sit in the leather seats in the front cabin. Learn about some of the aircraft's famous passengers and see where the Queen used to sit when she flew on the plane
- a brief glimpse inside the flight deck – the only fully accessible Concorde flight deck in the UK
- presentation of a certificate to commemorate your visit

Classic Tours cost £12 per person (plus entry to Aviation Viewing Park) and last around 40 minutes

Technical Concorde Tours

- in-depth look at the technology and aviation engineering
- welcome briefing
- guided tour underneath the aircraft plus complete on-board tour with extended time in the flight deck and cabin
- presentation of a commemorative certificate.
- suitable for age 12 plus
- smaller tour groups

Technical Tours cost £20 per person (plus entry to Aviation Viewing Park), and last about one hour 15 minutes

VIP Champagne Celebration Specials

- An ideal gift for Christmas, Fathers Day or any special occasion
- Welcome briefing on the DC-10 exhibit with audio-visual show
- Extended tour of Concorde with extra time in the cabin and flight deck
- Celebratory glass of champagne or orange juice
- Presentation of certificate alongside Concorde
- Strictly limited availability – only 12 per group
- Suitable for age 12 plus
- Free parking

These tours cost £30 per person (plus entry to the Aviation Viewing Park). Allow around 2 hours

New for 2007 – Three Aircraft Enthusiast Tour

This provides an opportunity to board three aircraft in one day. *The tour lasts approx 2 hours and costs £26 per person (plus entry to the Aviation Viewing Park).*

Private Group Tour

Concorde G-BOAC is now available for private tours for group bookings. *Please call 0161 489 3932 for details.*

Walk down the aisle

Concorde is an extraordinary setting for a wedding celebration. Take your vows on board and enjoy professional help from staff in planning and preparing for the big day. *To discuss individual requirements please call our wedding co-ordinator on 0161 489 3932.*

Corporate High Fliers

Limited number of exclusive corporate event packages are available every year. The bespoke packages allow exclusive access to Concorde, backed by VIP service.

For more information on the Concorde Experience or for a Corporate Pack please call 0870 242 1491

How to get to the Airport

Manchester is the UK's third busiest airport. This means approximately 80,000 car journeys a day to and from the airport. This has a major environmental impact, which is why the Airport is aiming to reduce car use by 40%.

The key to this is The Station which connects rail, bus, coach and cycling facilities all under one roof. It's only five minutes away from Terminal 1 and 2 and ten minutes from Terminal 3 and is the best way to get around.

Visitors will also find here a choice of retail and catering outlets, a 24 hour ticket sales facility located centrally at the station, 'Real Time' systems providing up to date travel information, dedicated waiting areas with comfortable seating, full accessible, car and taxi drop off.

By Road

Follow the signs on the M60 and then onto the M56 for Manchester Airport. From Manchester city centre take A5103, Princess Road/Princess Parkway, to its junction with the M56 and turn off for the Airport as signposted at Junction 5. There are a range of car parking facilities at the Airport. These can be booked online at *www.manchesterairport.co.uk/app/CarParkBooking*

By Rail

From Manchester Piccadilly to the Airport there are 6 trains an hour throughout the day (Monday–Saturday) with at least 4 an hour on Sundays. Local destinations include Salford Crescent, Bolton, Stockport and Wigan. More distant destinations include Preston, Lancaster, Blackpool North, Sheffield, Newcastle and Liverpool.

Useful contacts for passengers:
National Rail Enquiries
08457 48 49 50 *www.nationalrail.co.uk.*
GMPTE Local Transport Enquiries
0161 228 781 *www.gmpte.com*

By Bus and Coach

Manchester Airport has established partnerships with many bus operators, running local services as often as every 10 minutes, from early in the morning till late at night. Key destinations include Manchester city centre, The Trafford Centre, Altrincham, Sale, Hale, Northenden and Stockport.

For all bus enquiries call: 0161 228 7811
National Express serves over 50 destinations from Manchester Airport Call **08705 80 80 80** or visit *www.nationalexpress.com*

By Bike

At Manchester Airport Station there is a state of the art cycle centre where any cycling queries you may have can be answered.
Please telephone the Cycle Centre: **0161 489 3487** For further details visit *www.manchesterairport.co.uk*

Shopping at the Airport

There's a lot of shopping to be done at Manchester Airport and there's going to be a lot more soon.

For a full list of shopping and catering outlets at the airport check out www.manchesterairport.co.uk especially if you want to check out special offers available before you fly. The website will also give you information about the variety of shops at the airport and where to find them. Here are a few examples of the range on offer.

All'Ombra sells both sunglasses and accessories and is a good place to find fashion and sports sunglasses from top designers. Located in Terminals 1 and 2 after security, everything is tax free and available to all passengers regardless of the destination.

Alpha Airport Shopping offers a wide range of duty free spirits, cigarettes and tobacco for passengers traveling outside the EU as well as fragrances and cosmetics, wines, spirits, champagne and confectionery plus designer sunglasses, bags, jewellery and watches, for people travelling within the EU. Alpha is also home to some exclusive products such as fragrance and cosmetic travel sets, export strength spirits and confectionery gift packs. Some of these become available before they hit the High Street so you can stay ahead of trends without breaking the bank. Alpha provides collect on return and home delivery services.

The exciting new **Hamleys** store has more than 300 types of tax free gifts and toys, including a wide range of classic

favourites, such as Hamleys' own soft toys and bears, pre-school toys, family and travel games, outdoor activities, educational toys and arts and crafts.

Dixons Tax Free supplies audio-electrical goods, selling a variety of tax-free products including I-pods, MP3 players, digital cameras, laptops, TVs and DVD players. These can be delivered to a customer's home on your return from holiday. By checking on line - www.dixonstaxfree.co.uk - people can pre-order a product so they know it will be waiting for them when they get to the airport. Dixons are located in every terminal and once you are through security everyone can shop at Dixons tax-free, no matter where they are travelling to. Remember Dixons also provides home delivery.

Goldsmiths is a well-known High Street brand but here the products are tax-free. This premium jewellery shop offers an extensive range of men's and women's watches, jewellery and ornaments from brands such as Tag, Armani, DKNY and Swarovski. All products are available to all passengers at tax-free prices.

Near or far, business or leisure, Manchester Airport brings the world closer with over 200 destinations worldwide

Trendy
Catania
Figari
Ibiza
Newquay
Lamezia
Perpignan
Shannon

City Breaks
Amsterdam
Barcelona
Berlin
Bratislava
Budapest
Cologne
Dublin
Dubrovnik
Helsinki
Krakow
Madrid
Milan
Nice
Palma
Paris
Prague
Reykjavik
Riga
Rome
Valencia
Venice
Vienna
Warsaw

SKI/WINTER
Bolzano
Chambery
Enontekio
Geneva
Grenoble
Innsbruck
Inverness
Ivalo
Kuusamo
Lyon
Rovaniemi
Salzburg
Sofia
Toulouse

Long Haul
Abu Dhabi
Antigua
Aruba
Atlanta
Banjul
Barbados
Boston
Calgary
Cancun
Cape Town
Cayo Coco
Chicago
Damascus
Dhaka
Doha
Dubai
Eilat
Goa
Holguin
Houston
Huatulco
Hurghada
Islamabad
Jeddah
Johannesburg
Karachi
Lahore
Las Vegas
Luxor
Male
Marrakech
Marsa Alam
Mombasa
Montego Bay
Montreal
Nassau
New York
Orlando
Philadelphia
Phuket
Puerto Plata
Puerto Vallarta
Punta Cana
Salvador
Santa Clara
Sanya (China)
Sharm-el-Sheik
Singapore
St Lucia
Toronto
Vancouver
Varadero

For further destinations and information click www manchesterairport.co.uk

AIRPORT

FOOD&DRINK

Room Restaurant in the mighty space of the former Reform Club

Star quality.
Michelin-starred Paul Kitching
Star quality needn't cost the earth when you savour superb food conjured up by Greater Manchester's only Michelin-starred chef.
At the region's most acclaimed restaurant enjoy five course dinners every Tuesday for £30, three course lunches every Friday and Saturday for £22 and prix fixe dinners Wednesday to Saturday from £40.
Juniper
www.juniper-restaurant.co.uk
0161 929 4008
21 The Downs, Altrincham WA14 2QD
Prices correct at time of going to press.

OPEN
EVERY DAY
金煌
大酒樓
GLAMOROUS
CHINESE RESTAURANT
Wing Yip Business Centre
1st Floor, Oldham Rd, Ancoats,
Manchester M4 5HU
FREE SECURE PARKING
As one of the biggest Chinese restaurants in the UK, the Glamorous occupies two expansive air-conditioned floors and offer dining services for up to 600 people.
Telephone 0161 839 3312 Fax 0161 839 8233
www.glamorous-restaurant.co.uk

Introduction

Manchester has great variety of food and drink with over 30 different national cuisines on offer. There is nowhere in the UK that can rival the choice available across the mile or so of the city centre. The city can also boast the biggest urban Food and Drink Festival in the country, which takes place every October.

Restaurants

With the exception of Juniper all these restaurants serve vegetarian options. Also check out the different types of cuisine in the Chinatown, Rusholme and Vegetarian sections. All the venues are in the city centre unless stated. For a fuller and more detailed guide, pick up the latest copy of *City Life* Food & Drink Greater Manchester (£5).

Smart, chic or highest priced

You might want to put on your sassiest outfit for these venues, especially at weekends.

The French Restaurant 5F (Midland Hotel, Peter Street. 0161 236 3333) has Edwardian scale and wonderful French food. This is the classic 'old school' restaurant of choice for many experienced Mancunian gastronomes. The service from long-serving Bruno Lucchi is superb, filled with charm and care. **Juniper** (21 The Downs, Altrincham. 0161 929 4008 www.juniper-restaurant.co.uk) is the only Michelin starred restaurant in Greater Manchester and the food, from genius Paul Kitching, is probably the best contemporary cooking in the region. They have a long roster of set meals and special events. A typical main might be Best end of lamb, salted peanuts, spring cabbage, bacon, new potatoes, rosemary and white chocolate glaze, leek strips, curried turnip and lemon puree. The only sad thing is that Juniper lies 8 miles (13km) southwest of the city centre in Altrincham. **Lounge Ten 6D** (10 Tib Lane. 0161 834 1331) offers French food and extravagantly decadent décor such as the Vivienne Westwood designed ladies toilets (but watch out for the Roman orgy scenes). A real eating out occasion, worth dressing up for, with good food and signature homemade bread. With live entertainment on most nights this is a true Manchester original. **The River Restaurant 4C** (Lowry Hotel, Dearman's Place. 0161 827 4041) at the Lowry Hotel is run by star chef Eyck Zimmer who makes sure that the five star hotel has a restaurant to match its aspirations. Zimmer brings in a whole variety of influences and then twists them to create something very distinctive. His is the most exciting cooking for innovation and balance within the city centre by a long way. **Room 6D** (81 King Street, City. 0161 839 2005) With the most spectacular restaurant interior in the city, Room does a

Room

FOOD&DRINK

Akbars

topsy turvy teasing world of nudge nudge wink wink food. Dish descriptions don't match the food itself but if you can put up with this then dishes are splendid such as oxtail and quail egg (called corned beef hash - honest). **Samsi 7F** (36 Whitworth Street. 0161 279 0022) is a proper sushi restaurant with careful attention to detail in the cooking and the layout. **Stock 6C** (4 Norfolk Street. 0161 839 6644) is the finest top-notch Italian restaurant in the city centre. The décor is unusually good, as the restaurant sits under the dome of the former Stock Exchange. Chef Enzo Mauro's cooking is marvellous.

Mid-price excellence

You might still want to dress up but these places are a little more laid back.

Akbar 2B (83 Liverpool Road. 0161 834 7222) is a smart and superb Indian restaurant with freshly baked naans from the oven and well balanced flavours underscored by nuance rather than bite-your-head-off heat. The karahis and the handis are divine. **Assembly** (Lapwing Lane, West Didsbury. 0161 445 3653) is a good-looking venue with an easy-going attitude. With a British-going-on-Mediterranean menu it is a great place to chill and chat. **Cafe Jem'n'I**(1c School Lane, Didsbury. 0161 445 3996). Jem is a real gem on the food and drink scene. Since it's expansion Jem O'Sullivan's cooking has hit the heights. Definitely worth seeking out and savouring. with a Modern British menu and an innovative approach this place makes for a fabulous excursion out of town. **Cafe Istanbul 4D** (79 Bridge Street. 0161 833 9942) is a family-run independent Turkish restaurant with good service and a progressive attitude. Recently refurbished, this restaurant provides the best Turkish cuisine in the region. **Choice 2G** (Castle

Obsidian

FOOD&DRINK

Quay, Castlefield. 0161 833 3400) is a fine purveyor of Modern British food with elegant and gentle décor in a former warehouse in the pretty Castlefield area. There's also a good bar here for lounging and lazing with live piano music. **Dilli** (60 Stamford New Road, Altrincham. 0161 927 9219 www.dilli.co.uk) is an ambitious south Manchester restaurant which looks sharp and provides excellent service. The food from Kuldeep Singh is cooked according to Ayuvedic principles to help keep the body in equilibrium (apparently) and provides an upmarket alternative to predictable Anglo-Indian favourites.

Dimitris 3F (1 Campfield Arcade, Deansgate. 0161 839 3319) is a Greek favourite with a loyal following, and good for summer eating in the glassed-over arcade of the old market hall. The Mega Meze – a Mediterranean banquet of meat, vegetables or seafood – is good value. **EastZEast 8G** (Ibis Hotel, Princess Street. 0161 244 5353 www.eastszeast.com) is a refreshing, recent Asian restaurant which gives curry connoisseurs an excuse to forego Rusholme and enjoy some fine original cooking. It was the Food and Drink Festival Restaurant of the Year 2006

Evuna 4F (277-9 Deansgate. 0161 819 2752) is one of the outstanding wine restaurants in the North. It has enough bottles of Spanish wine making excellence (around 600 representatives) to make Bacchus weep for joy. **Fat Loaf** (62 Green Lane, Ashton-on-Mersey, Sale. 0161 972 0397) is a tiny, homely affair with good service and a down-to-earth but skillfully put together Modern British food. **Gaucho Bar and Grill 5C** (2a St Mary's Street, off Deansgate. 0161 833 4333) sits in a very big, former, Methodist church hall. This Argentine restaurant serves steaks almost as big as the building – the Lomito de cuadril weighs 950g. Worth going if you're very hungry or fattening up for a world title fight at the nearby MEN arena. **Greens** (43 Lapwing Lane, West Didsbury. 0161 434 4259) is perhaps the best vegetarian restaurant in the UK. It provides veggie nosh of a range and variety that isn't approached elsewhere, so much so that it even appeals to meat eaters. Maybe that's the secret: the proprietors are carnivores. **Grill on the Alley 5D** (5 Ridgefield2 Lloyd Street, Albert Square. 0161 817 4110) is an essay in professionalism: handsome, efficient, savvy and great for people watching. The food is good too, as is the buzz of life in this popular venue. Great for steaks, pies and puddings. **Isinglass** (46 Flixton Road, Urmston. 0161 749 8400) has a menu dictated by the seasons and whether the food is produced in the UK. Chef Lisa Walker displays creativity and strength of character with dishes such as blue pig rare breed pork sausages with creamy mash, onion and sage stock gravy or gooseberry and elderflower jelly, honey spiced sponge and whipped cream. **Koreana 4D** (40a King Street West. 0161 832 4330) is a long-celebrated and family-run restaurant.

Recipe for success

Manchester has always had its gourmands. In 1769, local superwoman Elizabeth Raffald published *The Experienced English Housekeeper*, which ran to 13 editions and was pirated 21 times. It was the first mass popular cook book in English with full recipes, preparation suggestions and menu recommendations. The suggested second course of a grand dinner consisted of: roast hare, transparent pudding covered with a silver web, snowballs, moonshine, rocky island and burned cream, mince pies, creerant with hot pippins, crawfish in savoury jelly, snipes in ditto, pickled smelts, marble veal, collared pig and potted lamprey, vegetables etc, stewed cardoons, pompadour cream, macaroni, stewed mushrooms and dessert.

Marmalade

An interesting dish to try would be the Dolset Bibim Bab, a speciality rice dish served in a hot stoneware pot. The lunchtime take-aways in sandwich boxes are legendary. **The Lime Tree** (8 Lapwing Lane, West Didsbury. 0161 445 1217 www.thelimetreerestaurant.co.uk) offers Modern British suburban bliss with calming woods, whites and greenery, and superb food. It is the sort of place that encourages people to return again and again. The food is always competent and frequently hits the heights with a mixture of robust cooking and delightful presentation.

Livebait 5E (22 Lloyd Street, Albert Square. 0161 817 4110) has a smooth and sharp interior of glass and tile with superb seafood. For sheer extravagance, try the groaning Livebait platter for two. **Luso 4D** (63 Bridge Street, City. 0161 839 5550) is run by Carlos and Jane Cortes and the city's first Portuguese restaurant this also features dishes from Brazil, Japan and Goa. It's a popular and lovely little place, the salt cod with a poached egg, crushed new potatoes plus black olives and spring onions is good.

Marmalade (60 Beech Road, Chorlton. 0161 862 9662) is a clever venture that aims to provide a good British alternative to the countless neighbourhood bistros in France. There are excellent meat dishes and an interesting range of drinks both alcoholic and non-alcoholic. **The Market Restaurant 9B** (104 High Street. 0161 834 3743) was the Restaurant of the Year in 2005 and is a labour of love for the proprietors – a twenty six year labour of love. It occupies an eighteenth century building and has a lovely atmosphere. The food is attractively presented and carefully put together. The menu changes frequently and there are good events. **Northern**

Livebait

FOOD&DRINK

wagamama
delicious noodles | rice dishes
freshly squeezed juices
wine | sake | japanese beers
manchester spinningfields
1 spinningfields square
tel • 0161 833 9883
manchester printworks
corporation street
tel • 0161 839 5916
positive eating + positive living
wagamama.com
uk | ireland | holland | australia | dubai | antwerp | auckland | copenhagen | istanbul

Sam's Chop House

Quarter Restaurant and Bar 8B (108 High Street. 0161 832 7115). This place is the neighbour of the Market Restaurant and the neighbour in this book too. It's a handsome devil with big windows overlooking the fancy façade of the old fish market opposite and a good menu that never over-elaborates yet provides variety. **Obsidian Bar and Restaurant 6E** (18-24 Princess Street. 0161 238 4348) was the Newcomer of the Year 2004, and it's got the looks, the food and the drink. The food mingles robust Modern British flavours with more subtle tastes. There are excellent, lighter lunchtime options too including tapas, soups, salads and sandwiches and chef Adrian Bailey has even reintroduced haggis to the menu. The bar area is very sexy. **Piccolino 6D** (8 Clarence Street. 0161 835 9860) is perfect for an afternoon shopping break or an evening schmooze. It is a lively, friendly operation with good Italian standards on the menu. The place is always popular but slows things down with a singer on Sundays. **Rhubarb** (167 Burton Road, West Didsbury. 0161 448 8887). Run by the husband and wife partnership of Mark and Lisa Ramsden, this was *City Life* Newcomer of the Year 2003. What sets it apart is attention to detail, the food a model of discipline and control allied with real skill and innovation. **El Rincon de Rafas 4E** (Longworth Street, off St John's Street, off Deansgate. 0161 839 8819) is the best Spanish restaurant in town. Hidden away off Deansgate, it creates a genuinely Spanish feel with its music and entertainment as well as the fine tapas and mains.

Sam's Chop House 6D (Back Pool Fold, Chapel Walks, off Cross Street. 0161 834 3210) is the best for classic and contemporary British cuisine in the city. Try Sam's famous corned beef hash, the grilled kippers, rib of beef, suckling pig, home-made steak and kidney puddings, steamed jam sponge pudding and British cheeses. The interior is warm with wood, stone and brick dominating. It even serves its own ale. And with a superior winelist, this is a real *City Life* guidebooks star. **San Carlo 4D** (40-42 King's Street West. 0161 834 6226) has a bright interior and a buzzy ambience. There's a full à la carte menu but also a chalkboard from which guests can choose an array of daily specials. San Carlo is very good for market-fresh fish and seafood. **That Café** (1031 Stockport Road, Levenshulme. 0161 432 4672). Chef Alison Eason has created one of the best value Manchester food venues. Expect innovation in the dishes. There are good deals on Sunday lunches.

Value destinations

These places have both decent food and lower prices – usually £15 per head or less. Some are coffee shops and cafes and may not serve alcohol. Also look through the Chinatown, Rusholme and Vegetarian sections below. Most pubs serve food that comes into this category too.

Aladdin (529 Wilmslow Road, Withington. 0161 434 8588/8558) offers excellent, laid back and unpretentious Middle Eastern food in a bring-your-own-bottle venue. **Barburrito 8D** (1 Piccadilly. 0161 228 6479) was the 2006 Manchester Food and Drink Festival Newcomer of the Year. It deserves it. Food comes canteen style and is centred around Latino staples such as quesadillas, tacos, burritos and nachos and very much less traditional Latin American food such as carrot cake. For a light lunch or hot takeaway, this is as good as it gets in Manchester. **Croma 6D** (1 Clarence Street. 0161 237 9799) is spick and span and open plan with truly excellent pizzas and wonderful, warm service. It's the best pizzeria in the city. **Fitzpatrick's Herbal Health** (5 Bank Street, Rawtenstall. 01706 211152) is 15 miles (25km) out of the city but is Britain's last original temperance bar, calling itself 'the pub with no beer'. Dispensed from china or glass kegs and served with a frothy head, you can indulge in dandelion and burdock, black beer and lemon, sarsaparilla and others. **Katsouris 5D** (Deansgate. 0161 819 1260) provides the best meaty and veggie hot sandwiches around. Take a spicy chorizo bap, the meat heated on the hotplate, and enjoy. Wow. **Love Saves the Day 3G** (345 Deansgate. 0161 834 2266) is a trendy bistro and coffee shop with good food, exceptional wines and great events. **Oklahoma 8B** (14-16 High Street) was winner of the Coffee Bar of the Year 2003 and is an absolute original with good coffees, smoothies, toasties and so on. You have to see it to believe it. There's a wonderfully kitsch shop here and a music store too. **Persia Grill** (Barlow Moor Road, opp. Southern Cemetery, Chorlton. 0161 860 6864) is a little gem, a family run venture with astonishing service. The décor is spot on, filled with heavy wooden furniture, kilim, flowers and illustrations of Persian figures of antiquity and legend. Expect

Barburrito

Getting High

High Street around the junction with Thomas Street **8F** is the most entertaining and determinedly independent food and drink destination in the North of England. You get it all here, a curious and joyous variety of venues: from fine dining to fast food, from trendy cocktails to pints of bitter. Facing each other across the junction of the two streets are **Bluu** and **Hunters**. The first of these was the Manchester Food and Drink Festival Bar of the Year 2005 and the second is the nuttiest curry café in the known world with game, such as venison and quail, on the menu. North on High Street is the **Market Restaurant**, the Manchester Food and Drink Festival Restaurant of the Year 2005, margaritas bar **Rodeo**, sassy and sexy cocktail trendsetter **Socio Rehab** plus the very handsome **Northern Quarter Restaurant and Bar**.

Meanwhile **Oklahoma**, the most eccentric coffee shop you'll ever encounter lies a little way south down High Street. Next to Hunters but on Thomas Street is the Manchester Food and Drink Festival Bar of the Year 2006, **Odd Bar**, with one of the best interiors around and bargain food to match. Over the road is the **Bay Horse** with its red pool table and laid-back vibe. In the other direction next to Bluu, is the **Chinese Arts Centre** with an amazing selection of teas. Opposite the latter is **TV21**, a crazy new TV themed drinkerie and **Trof**, a very well designed newcomer for both food and drink. Two minutes away lies the **Hare and Hounds**, a proper pub with its Wednesday night sing-a-long. Also nearby are supercool **Common** bar on Edge Street and the veggie **Earth Cafe** with great smoothies in the Buddhist Centre on Turner Street.

simple taste-filled mains such as Shishleek and lovely tea from the huge samovar. **The Royal Exchange 6C** (Entrances Cross Street, St Ann's Square. 0161 932 6795) is one of the most impressive interior spaces in the North. The sandwiches and other dishes are never spectacular but the surroundings are. **Shlurp 5D** (Unit 2, Brazennose House East, Brazennose Street. 0161 839 5199) is the best soup bar in the region. **Slattery** (190 Bury New Road, Whitefield. 0161 767 9303) was winner of the Coffee Shop of the Year award in 2004 and this patisserie, chocolaterie and coffee shop lives up to its reputation. **Suburb 5C** (63 Deansgate. 0161 832 3642). Forget the chain coffee bars, this exceptional caffeine filling station is effortlessly cool in décor, mood and music. Suburb deservedly won *City Life* Coffee Bar of the Year 2005. **Tampopo 5E** (16 Albert Square. 0161 819 1966) is Manchester's original 'noodle bar'. Look out for huge bowls of Ramen (Japanese noodle soups), fried noodle and rice dishes, speciality sauces and soups. It's a popular Mancunian destination.

City centre fish and chip shops

For a genuine fish and chip experience, try the following places for take away or eat in: **The Hut 3F** (27 Liverpool Road), **Harry Ramsdens** (Water Street. 0161 832 9144), **Kingfisher Fish Bar 9B** (43 Tib Street. 0161 834 3332), **Portland Plaice 7E** (Portland Street. 0161 237 1002). Mossley, 12 miles (19km) east of the city, lays claim to giving birth to the chippy in 1863, courtesy of John Lees, as an offshoot of a pig trotter and pea soup operation.

Chinatown 7E

Based around the ornate Chinese Arch in the city centre, there are many different types of cuisine to sample, but the principal ingredients come from Canton. With such a range of eateries, perhaps the best idea is to go for a stroll and take your pick. The buffet deals for around £5-£10 are very good value if not the best in terms of cooking.

Tampopo

Greens

If you just want a quick bite, be sure to grab a honey bun or chicken curry pastie from **Ho's Bakery** (Faulkner Street). For a longer shop, try **Hang Won Hong** supermarket (George Street). There are several good restaurants: **Red Chilli 7E** (70 Portland Street. 0161 236 2888) provides Szechuan and Beijing cuisine. This is not for the faint-hearted with dishes such as pork stomach shreds, sea cucumber and lung slices but in many ways it's the most surprising and satisfying of all the Chinatown venues at present. **Wing's 5D** (Lincoln Square. 0161 834 9000) is a new top flight restaurant, a short walk from Chinatown with a relaxed attitude, modern clean design, a good wine cellar and good traditional and modern Chinese dishes. **Yang Sing 7E** (34 Princess Street. 0161 236 2200) is a Manchester institution. It was established in 1977 by Tim Kwan Yeung and then run through the partnership of sons Harry, the celebrated chef, and Gerry. But not everything has been plain sailing – in 1997, the present Princess Street building was gutted by fire. After a couple of years, the restaurant returned in substitute premises and on a huge scale: three kitchens, two restaurant floors, banqueting and conference facilities.

Wings

Rusholme

With the largest concentration of Asian (or Pakistani to be more precise) food outlets in the UK, Manchester's 'curry corridor' or 'curry mile' in Rusholme is a must visit for lovers of Eastern flavour. Rusholme lies two miles south of the city centre. Try the **Sanam Sweet House** (0161 224 3852), the award winning **Darbar** (0161 224 4394), the **Dil Dar** (0161 248 8880), the **Lal Haweli** (0161 248 9700) with its resident magician most nights, the **Hanaan** (0161 3565 4786) or the **Sangam** (0161 257 3922) and ask about the links with the obstinately popular Take That.

Northern Quarter curries 8C

Perhaps the best value food can be found in the cluster of Asian cafés around High Street and Church Street. For £3-£4 you get a stomach-busting portion of curry, but beware: most close between 6pm and 7pm. Try **Hunter's BBQ** (0161 839 5060), **This'n'That** (0161 834 7925), **the Yadgar** (0161 834 7925), **Little Aladdin** (0161 835 2606) and **Kabana** (0161 835 2447).

Vegetarian

Manchester's history as a vegetarian friendly city goes back a long way. The mass Western vegetarian movement began here in 1809 inspired by the sermons of a local preacher called, of all things, the Rev. William Cowherd. Accordingly the **Vegetarian Society's** HQ is still based in Altrincham (Parkdale, Dunham Road. 0161 925 2000. www.vegsoc.org.Email:info@vegsoc.org) and hosts various gourmet evenings and popular Cordon Vert cookery courses. A call here will elicit a friendly response. Vegetarian venues include **Earth 8B** (16/20 Turner Street. 0161 834 1996), part of the Manchester Buddhist Centre, offering a haven of calm and serenity. The food wins rave reviews from regulars and newcomers. **Eighth Day** (111 Oxford Road, University. 0161 273 1850) is a cafe and shop that makes looking for a vegetarian meal option a real pleasure. **Greenhouse** (331 Great Western Street, Rusholme. 0161 224 0730/ 0800), offers wholesome, large helpings of food. The real standout vegetarian venue is **Greens** (43 Lapwing Lane, West Didsbury. 0161 434 4259), see above page 181.

Markets

There are four main markets to look out for. Every second Fri-Sat of the month, the **Farmers' Market 8D** visits Piccadilly Gardens. Here you'll find a fantastic array of North West produce, including cheeses, preserves, meats and much else.

The three best traditional markets are in the Greater Manchester towns of **Bolton, Bury** and **Stockport**. The first two have exceptional fish markets – the noise on a Saturday as traders try to sell off the week's catch at bargain prices is terrifying. Also keep a look out for the Continental **Christmas Markets** in Albert Square **5E** and St Ann's Square **5C**. There's always a food market during the October Food and Drink Festival too.

FOOD&DRINK

Bar land

Due to the number of bars across the city, this selection only refers to city centre premises. There is an astonishing range from the strictly student through the gay and grungy to the glam and neo-cabaret. Many have DJs on the weekend. Nearly all are free to enter, many up to 2am or later. For the Gay Village venues see pages 264-268.

The 'Fun' Zone 4E

'Fun' in inverted commas. This is Peter Street running into Quay Street and is the brazen, good time party place for the weekend. It's not for the style gurus or grunge fans, but for those who like to flaunt it high-street style. The women go décolletage with micro minis and the men loll around with their shirts hanging out. It can be very raw but it's also democratic, and several bars have a surprisingly mixed age range. The main venues are **Brannigans** (0161 835 9697), with live cabaret and music, **Bar 38** (0161 835 3076), with the grassed area in front, **Life Café** (0161 833 3000), with frequent live music, and **Teasers** (0161 8333118) with bar girls and boys in very tight, tiny costumes.

The Locks & Castlefield 2G/3G

There's an eclectic mix of venues at Deansgate Locks comprising of six bars and one comedy club strung underneath a railway viaduct accessed by a boardwalk over the Rochdale Canal. **Loaf** (0161 819 5858) is the most popular bar, and is chic, smart and huge, with nightclub included, but beware the queues and the door can be choosy regarding dress code. For more relaxed venues, try **Fat Cat Café** (0161 839 8243) with its cocktail menu and more progressive music policy and **Baa Bar** (0161 832 4446) with its unisex toilets and a constellation of disco balls. **Dukes 92** (0161 839 8646) in the canal basin has the

Cloud 23 4F

Hilton Manchester, Deansgate, City. 0161 870 1600

Beautifully designed cloud tickling bar on the 23rd floor. Great views south, north and west with good seating in the crisp interior. The drinks prices are as sky high as the location. And despite the bars failings, closed at lunch, badly managed queues downstairs, every visitor and local should take at least one trip up the super-charged lift.

best outside drinking area in Manchester and a cheese and pate menu. If you want it intimate and fun try the glorious and tiny **Lava** bar (0161 833 2444), in Middle Warehouse.

Northern Quarter 8B/8C/9B/9C

This is the dark, creative heart of the city and the place to head for independent, non-mainstream bars with good music and good beers and other drinks. Anybody who hankers for the *joie de vivre* of those who think differently should make this area their first port of call. **Centro** (Tib Street. 0161 835 2863) is the place to go for rare beers, rare music and good food. **Bar Fringe** (Swan Street. 0161 835 3815) has a superb beer range whilst **Cord** (Dorsey Street. 0161 832 9494) offers something intimate and quirky and is filled with Manchester's music set. If street art was a bar then that would be pared-down **Common** (Edge Street. 0161 832 9243) round the corner from Cord. **Dry Bar** (Oldham Street. 0161 236 9840) is the venue formally owned by Factory Music, which in1989 changed Britain's bar scene for good with the industrial design from Ben Kelly. **Night and Day** (Oldham Street. 0161 236 4597) is the live music dive that visitors to Manchester should seek out. It's a proper rock and roll bar with music every night. Brazilian MTV on a trip to town christened the place 'the best guitar music venue in the world'. Mind you they'd had a bit to drink by the time they'd left. See Jazz and Clubbing sections for details of Matt and Phred's Jazz Club. **Trof** (6-8 Thomas Street. 0161 8333197) is handsome new addition with great decor, good food and rare beers. Just over the alleyway **TV21** (10, Thomas Street. 0161 839 5021) is a crazy new TV themed addition to the Northern Quarter party with memorabilia and neon lighting to match.

The Printworks 7B

Northeast of Exchange Square you can find the vast Printworks. This old printing complex is beloved of mainstream night-goers (don't expect the cool crowd). The complex includes **Hard Rock Café, Henry J Beans, Nando's, Norwegian Blue, Opus, Tiger Tiger** and **Waxy O'Conners**.

Panacea

Others

You may want to check out these other bars too. **Grinch 6C** (5-7 Chapel Walks, off Cross Street. 0161 907 3210) is a good local independent that serves cosmopolitan cocktails. **Kro Bar** (325 Oxford Road, near the University. 0161 274 3100) is the best place if you're thirsty and hungry and lost at University.**Mojo 4D** (Back Bridge Street. 0161 839 5330) is a rocking bar with a great soundtrack of bouncing guitar classics. But first you have to find it. **Odder** ((14 Oxford Road, Manchester. 0161 238 9131), the sister of Odd bar in the Northern Quarter has arrived on Oxford Road opposite the current site of the BBC. Downstairs the decor is almost subdued, upstairs it's a riot of fun, colour and comfy seating. There's decent food too. **Panacea 5D** (John Dalton Street. 0161 833 3000) has a bar of onyz which stretches as far as the eye can see. It's for dressing up and showing off with a blonde on your arm who's at least 18 years younger than yourself, whilst a Ferrari waits outside. **The Living Room 5C** (80 Deansgate. 0161 832 0083) is smart with pretensions to exclusivity, good food, and 100 cocktails. **The Temple 6G** (Great Bridgewater Street. 161 661 0295) is a pleasant converted gents urinal. Indeed. **Tribeca 8F** (Sackville Street, City. 0161 236 8300) is a Village venue with, in the basement, a sister venue called Bed where you dine horizontally.

The Crown and Kettle

Quirks and quarts

Pubs are often the home of eccentricity. The Church Inn (Uppermill, Saddleworth, Oldham. 01457 874626) sums this all up. This has its own micro-brewery with a head brewer who is a Morris dancer. The group practices outside the pub on Thursday around 8/8.30pm, there is a collar on the wall for gurning through (pulling a mad face), the handbells on display are the training set for the local bellringers, whilst outside is a menagerie of geese, rabbits, horses etc. You can even hire part of the pub grounds as a grave plot should you wish to make a permanent residency in the hopefully distant future. There are frequent events too, whilst the Church is also excellent for moorland walks. Other outposts of eccentricity include the Queens Arms (4-6 Honey Street, Red Bank. 0161 834 4239) with its Thursday Viking Re-enactment Society, the Britons Protection **3G** (50 Great Bridgewater Street. 0161 236 5895) with its Grateful Dead Society meetings and Comedy Balloon nights, and Ye Olde Man and the Scythe in Bolton (6-8 Churchgate. 01204 527267) with a whole range of lunacy, run by a bonkers landlord.

FOOD&DRINK

City centre pubs

'There is nothing which has yet been contrived by man, by which so much human happiness is produced as by a good tavern or inn'
Samuel Johnson

It has been said that the two most important institutions in England's history have been the pub and the church. With church attendance now tinier than minuscule, that leaves the boozer. As a complement to the ever-growing tide of bars (and as a welcome alternative to the increasing numbers of big bland chain bars), pubs can't be beaten. They are still the third place – a public house away from the stresses of both work and home. Manchester and area has some wonderful examples which repay long, slow examination.

Organised pub tours

There are regular pub tours from 6.30pm at the Manchester Visitors Information Centre in St Peter's Square. Phone 0787 623 5638 or email jgschofield@btinternet.com for further information. These entertaining and informative tours tell the story of Mancunian drinking over the centuries and conclude with short, fun quiz based upon the commentary.

Ape and Apple 5D (John Dalton Street. 0161 839 9624) is a smart Joseph Holt house with good Holt's beers and decent food. **The Britons Protection 3G** (50 Great Bridgewater Street. 0161 236 5895) is a multi-roomed gem full of elegant wood, tile and plaster detailing covering 200 years of pub history, with over 175 whiskies and bourbons. Good food too. **The Castle Hotel 9C** (66 Oldham Street. 0161 236

Knott Bar

2945) boasts an interesting period interior and retains the atmosphere of a village pub. **The Circus Tavern 7E** (86 Portland Street. 0161 236 5818) is so tiny that only one bar person can fit behind the bar. It's a 200-year-old surviver and definitely worthwhile seeking out. **The City Arms 6E** (48 Kennedy Street. 0161 2364610) has one of the best ranges of beer in the city and is an attractive homely place. **The Crown and Kettle 9B** (2 Oldham Road. 0161 236 2923) returned to the land of the living in late 2005 after fifteen years as a vandalised hulk. The ales are one reason to go, the amazing pendent adorned ceiling are another six or seven reasons. **Hare and Hounds 8B** (46 Shudehill. 0161 834 9088) has splendid period interior, good beers and on Wednesday a sing-along session at the stand up piano. **The Kings Arms 2B** (Bloom Street, Salford. 0161 839 4952) is an innovative pub with an excellent range of beers, great jukebox and live acts, including a resident theatre company. **Knott Bar 3G** (374 Deansgate. 0161 839 9229) is an excellent real ale bar serving the Marble micro-brewery's own lovelies but also regional guest ales. Great jukebox, interesting shape, upstairs terrace drinking area and good food. **Marble Arch 9A** (73 Rochdale Road. 0161 832 5914) is a classic Victorian pub with one of the region's finest micro-breweries. The Marble has tiled splendour, a vaulted ceiling and floor. **Old Wellington Inn 6B** (New Cathedral Street. 0161 830 1440) is half timbered and dates from the 1530s. Entwined with the Old Wellington, **Sinclairs Oyster Bar 6B** (New Cathedral Street. 0161 834 0430) dates back to the 1730s and was moved brick by brick after the IRA bomb of 1996 to its present location. It's a wonky pub with an up and down interior stuffed with comfortable nooks and crannies. It also serves good ales and great oysters, including local dish steak and oyster pie. The Samuel Smith's beer is very cheap. **Peveril of the Peak 6G** (127 Great Bridgewater Street. 0161 236 6364), with its splendid green tiles on the exterior, is a friendly and popular pub with a pool table, a good jukebox, an exquisite bar and table football.

Gastro-pubs

These are the new flavours of the moment, with good-quality, restaurant-standard food and good booze – usually in a perfect old pub. Some of these lie outside the city centre.

The Arden Arms (23 Millgate Street, Stockport. 0161 480 2185) is an eighteenth century coaching house with lots of period detail and very good food Modern British food too. **The Bridge 4D** (Bridge Street. 0161 834 0242). Bridge Street is turning into a cool part of town, and this traditional boozer has been given a major overhaul by established Manchester chef, Robert Owen-Brown. His take on Modern British cuisine here is exceptional and very good value. The function room here is a dream of what such rooms should look like and the events, often themed on a film, are great value. **Ox Hotel 2F** (Liverpool Road. 0161 839 7740) provides an interesting twist to the traditional pub with restaurant-quality food and a good range of drinks – both ales and wine. It's all very comfortable and they also have bedrooms if you feel you can't tear yourself away. **Mr Thomas's Chop House 5D** (52 Cross Street. 0161 832 2245) is a tiled delight with waiter service to the tables for drinks and wonderful, very genuine, British food. This is the sister establishment to Sam's Chop House (see page 145). **The White Hart** (51 Stockport Road, Lydgate, Saddlworth, Oldham. 01457 872566) is 12 miles (19km) from the city centre and makes for a fine excursion. There are special events, special drinks and special in-house sausages. The Sunday roast is exceptional, as is the lofty hill-top location. There are good bedrooms too.

Pubs outside the centre

Bolton: Old Man and the Scythe (6-8 Churchgate, Bolton. 01204 527267) is a contender for oldest pub in the area. Some parts allegedly hail from C14, and there's a resident ghost. **Bury:** Trackside (Bolton Road Station, Bury.) offers

Deansgate drinking in the 1880s

FOOD&DRINK

Inn (Elbut Lane, Birtle. 0161 764 3620) – stone country pub. **Delph:** Royal Oak (Th' Heights, Broad Lane Heights, above Denshaw Road, Delph. 01457 874460) – hill-top country pub. **Denshaw**: Rams Head (Ripponden Road, Denshaw, Saddleworth) – traditional country pub. **Eccles**: The Lamb (33 Regent St, Eccles. 0161 789 3882) is a town pub but also a spectacular Edwardian gin palace. The Grapes (431 Liverpool Road, Eccles. 0161 789 6971) is another carved wood and etched glass delight. **Heaton Norris**: Nursery Inn (Green Lane, off A6, Heaton Norris. 0161 432 2044) has a gorgeous interior and a range of sports and events – past winner of National Pub of the Year. **South Manchester**: The Beech (72 Beech Road, Chorlton. 0161 881 1180) – snug boozer. The Station (682 Wilmslow Road, Didsbury. 0161 445 9761) – unpretentious boozer. **Mellor**: The Oddfellows Arms (73 Moor End Road, Mellor. 0161 449 7826) – village country pub. **Middleton**: Old Boar's Head (Long Street. 0161 643 3520) is an ancient half-timbered pub. Tandle Hill Tavern (14 Thornham Lane, Slattocks. 01706 345297) country pub. **Rochdale**: The White House (A58, Blackstone Edge. 01706 378456) is right on top of the pass out of Lancashire- 369 metres above sea level, with good food too. **Saddleworth/ Uppermill**: Cross Keys (Running Hill Gate, Uppermill. 01457 874626) classic country pub. **Stalybridge**: Stalybridge Buffet Bar (Rassbottom Street. 0161 330 6776) famous boozer on the railside direct from Victoria Station. **Stockport**: Queens Head (12 Little Underbank. 0161 480 0725) has ghosts, atmosphere and the smallest urinal in England. Blossoms (2 Buxton Road, Heavily. 0161 477 2397) is a classic multi-roomed local. **Stoneclough**: Lord Nelson (Kearsley Hall Road. 01204 579302) provides top food, very reasonably priced from Robert Owen-Brown.

15-17 Chapel Walks
(next to Sam's
Chop House)
Manchester, M2 1HN
T: 0161 819 1997
E: info@bacconline.com
www.bacconline.com
BACCHANALIA
RESTAURANT + BAR

Family run business established for 46 years
The Rice Bowl
lunch time,
evening and
á la carte
menu's
available
33a Cross Street
City Centre
Manchester
Tel: 0161 832 9033
www.the-rice-bowl.com

Slattery
PATISSIER & CHOCOLATIER
Dining Room
Conference Facilities
Wedding Cake Showroom
School of Excellence
Gift Shop
Slattery Patissier & Chocolatier
197 Bury New Road, Whitefield
Manchester M46 6GE
0161 767 9303
www.slattery.co.uk

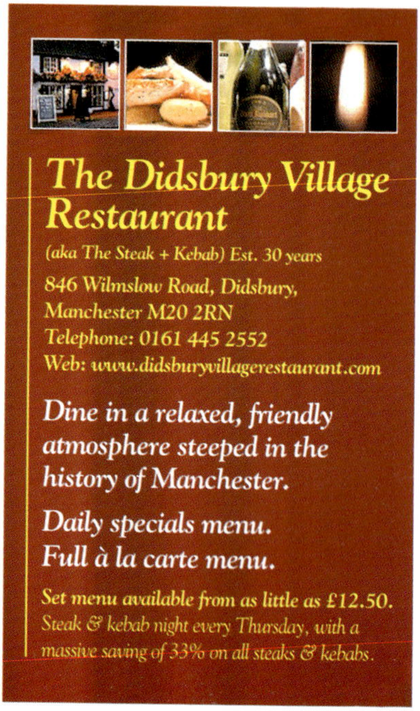
The Didsbury Village
Restaurant
(aka The Steak + Kebab) Est. 30 years
846 Wilmslow Road, Didsbury,
Manchester M20 2RN
Telephone: 0161 445 2552
Web: www.didsburyvillagerestaurant.com
Dine in a relaxed, friendly
atmosphere steeped in the
history of Manchester.
Daily specials menu.
Full à la carte menu.
Set menu available from as little as £12.50.
Steak & kebab night every Thursday, with a
massive saving of 33% on all steaks & kebabs.

Full pint

The Manchester area is the capital of UK beer. There are four major family breweries and around 20 micro-breweries – London has just one family brewers and 11 micros. According to various surveys the region has the cheapest average beer prices too.

Let's start with **Joseph Holt** (0161 834 3285), the brewery of which lies less than a mile north of the city centre. Founded in 1849, it brews a very strong and very cheap bitter of 4% strength as well as a mild and seasonals. The bitter's the star and despite the occasional poor barrel, is outstanding value – one of cheapest undiscounted real ales in the kingdom. A few miles further north is **JW Lees** (0161 643 2487). Located at Middleton Junction, Lees was founded in 1828. They brew a full range of beers, bitter and mild, as well as the lovely Moonraker, at 7%. As for bottled beers the King of the Hill nationally must surely be Lees' Harvest Ale, released every 1 December. At 11.5% it's got the consistency of port but after the initial shock ale connoisseurs will fall deeply in love with it. produced. In Moss Side is **Hydes** (0161 226 1317), founded in 1863, again offering good-value bitters and milds with seasonal options. Meanwhile, seven miles southeast in the suburb town of Stockport, is **Robinson's (0161 612 4061)**, founded in 1833, with a range of beers including the devilishly potent Old Tom at 8.5%. All of the above are family concerns that occupy delightfully quirky old premises that could be the stage sets for Willy Wonka's Chocolate Factory.

Some 20 micro-brewers tantalise the tastebuds of local drinkers as well with an array of imaginative and high-quality brews. Two City Life favourites are: **Marble Beers 9A** (0161 819 2694) and **Phoenix Brewery** (01706 627009). The first of these sits in its own pub close to the city centre and produces a range of beers such as Manchester Bitter (4.2% ABV), the classic Lagonda IPA (5%) and the potent Chocolate Heavy (5.5%). Ginger Marble (4.5%) delivers a real ginger slap. Phoenix Brewery is located north of Manchester in Heywood and produces lovely stuff such as the citrusy Arizona (4.1%) and the maltier yet still hoppy Wobbly Bob (6%).

Given the range in Greater Manchester it's curious that these beers scarcely appear in restaurants and hotels. In fact it's insanity. Bitter, for example, is as good an accompaniment to red meat as red wine. Also, it would be impossible to go into a French restaurant and not be able to drink a bottle of the local wine. Here, despite the exceptional beers produced, the customer is denied the pleasure of something Manchester does exceedingly well. It's incomprehensible for local and visitor alike.

The best real ale festival around takes place in January: the **CAMRA Winter Ales Festival** at New Century Hall, Corporation Street.

Brain juice

Pubs can be very good for the brain. In 1795, the Thinking Club was formed at the Coopers' Arms. At the first meeting there were 300 present, and silence prevailed for one hour. There is no record of what the theme was, or whether the 300 attendees just thought about whatever came to mind. Nor is there any clue as to what came of their collective thinking. Still, it sounds more worthy than a typical pub game from the C19. This was Clout Ear. Ten or more men would throw diverse low value coins into a flat cap. A referee would count how much was in the cap. Then each would take a turn, blindfolded, to guess the correct amount using their touch alone. After a short while, they would make their guess and, if correct, keep the money. If they were wrong, they would be struck over the head a pre-determined number of times with a heavy metal beer tray. Apparently this was thought amusing: at least it was more active than watching the football on Sky TV.

Local specialities

In Bury, a 20-minute tram ride north of the city, it's been going on commercially since at least 1818. You would kill the pig, collect the blood in a bucket and then roll your sleeve to the shoulder, stick your arm in to the elbow and stir. Pieces of fat were added and herbs for flavouring and eventually you had **black pudding**. Eaten fresh unaccompanied or with mustard, it is delicious. Also keep an eye out for the World Championship Black Pudding Throwing competition in Ramsbottom every September.

Alongside black pudding, Lancastrians, especially in the former cotton producing districts around Manchester, would eat **cow heel pie**: steak and heel cooked together in gravy under a pastry topping or as a stew. Also popular was **rag pudding** or **beef roll**: minced steak, ham, breadcrumbs, anchovy sauce, flavourings, egg and milk bound inside a muslin cloth and boiled or steamed. You've probably heard of **Lancashire hotpot**: trimmed lamb chops, potatoes, onions and mushrooms, in layers, with trimmed lambs' kidneys as an optional extra. Not for the squeamish is **tripe**: the stomach lining of a cow, best eaten cold with plenty of vinegar. A more delicate dish was **emerald eggs**: fine-chopped parsley placed in the buttered cups of the egg poacher and the eggs turned out with the parsley on top. The inhabitants of our neighbour city, Liverpool, are even nicknamed after their local meat and veg stew: **scouse**. Several areas of Lancashire retain traditional dishes, with their colourful names intact thus: **slappy** – pie on a barmcake, **babbies yed** – meat pudding (pie), **slavvery duck** – faggot, **scraps** – fish batter and chips left in cooking fat/oil, **pea wet** – juice from peas, as in 'chips and pea wet.'

Many dishes are seasonal. Traditionally, Christmas **mince pies** were prepared with minced beef, sweetened with dried fruit, raisins, sultanas and spices. On Bonfire Night, a typical speciality was **black peas**, soaked for 24 hours, boiled up and eaten again with copious quantities of vinegar.

Mushy peas served locally in chip shops are a classic regional speciality.

Untrustworthy Tykes claim that they invented **fish and chips** but the first fish and chip shop in the country opened in 1863 in Mossley, 12 miles east of Manchester. Chips, and in some areas like Wigan even pies, are frequently served in barms or **barmcakes**, which the rest of the country calls bread rolls.

Lots of sweet stuff comes from the region, including **Eccles cakes**, raisins inside sugary buns, together with tasty **Manchester tarts**, a pastry base with jam topped by custard, occasionally sprinkled with coconut. **Goosnargh cakes** are a sweet confection of butter, caraway seeds, flour and loaf sugar that should not be missed. **Bilberry tarts** made from the moorland fruit are wonderful too, but for even greater sweetness a stick of **Blackpool rock** can be sampled. Equally tooth-rotting but far nicer are the boiled sweets such as **Uncle Joe's Mintballs** from Wigan. **Love Hearts**, meanwhile, come from New Mills on the edge of the conurbation.

The lush grass of the meadows encourages the ruminants to produce a creamy milk perfect for the delicious crumbly **Lancashire cheese** and its **Cheshire** brethren.

Local drinks abound too. Aside from ale there is Vimto (the popular herbal drink now gone fizzy), dandelion and burdock, sarsaparilla (from the root of the same name), blackberry vinegar (a medicinal warmer for winter), rhubarb wine and ginger wine. Red Rose Whisky from Wigan is the only English whisky and is as old as the Pennine Hills that supply its water. But beware the most vicious local dish, which comes from the north of Manchester. This is, of course, the Clockwork Orange. You'll find this described in the book of the same name by Mancunian writer Anthony Burgess.

ENTERTAINMENT

Morrissey

Popular music

The entertainment possibilities are huge in Manchester. To keep informed about the changing scene, get hold of the *City Life* supplement in the Friday edition of the *Manchester Evening News.*

Manchester has often been the engine room of British pop. The city's history has been music throughout - C19 German immigrants complained how the locals preferred to sing rather than listen to symphonic music, which is part of the reason why the Hallé Orchestra was created. The fact that Manchester is so cosmopolitan has also helped the music flow: the cotton industry was global and thus people brought their music from all points. Even before the days of mass media and telecommunications, the city was quick to consume the black music coming out of America – first jazz and then the rock'n'roll of the '50s.

This, together with and other factors, helped turn the city into a musical whirlwind that ripped through such clubs as The Twisted Wheel (see page 211): a 1960s cultural touchstone that refused to become mainstream and pointed to the future independent spirit and maverick personality of the city.

Chart success came early. The Beatles and the Merseybeat were renowned but Manchester was buzzing with its own boom time. Bands like The Hollies, Herman's Hermits, Wayne Fontana and the Mindbenders and Freddie and the Dreamers enjoyed international success in the mid to late '60s. For six heady weeks from 10 April to 15 May, these bands nestled in the number one spot in the US Billboard Top 100. The Hollies had the longest chart life of the bands with hits such as 'He Ain't Heavy (He's My Brother)'. The Hollies and Herman's Hermits had hits written by local lad Graham Gouldman such as 'Bus Stop', 'Look Through Any Window' and 'No Milk Today'. In 1969, Gouldman teamed up with Eric Stewart, guitarist with the Mindbenders, and then with fellow Mancunians Kevin Godley and Lol Crème to form 10cc. This pop act, at the height of their powers in the '70s, achieved fame through their clever singles and pioneering sampling techniques. Their hits included million selling single 'I'm Not In Love'. Other big local acts of the period included Roy

ENTERTAINMENT

The Hollies

Harper, Sad Café, Sweet Sensation, Elkie Brooks and Barclay James Harvest.

Punk officially hit the city in July 1976 when the Sex Pistols played two concerts at the Lesser Free Trade Hall (see Rock Tour page 214). On the same bill were premier exponents of Manc-punk The Buzzcocks as well as Manchester noiseniks Slaughter and The Dogs. The Buzzcocks specialized in hacked-up power-pop, as epitomized by classics such as 'Ever Fallen in Love', while other luminaries, such as the Drones, played taut speed-driven punk. The scene thrived in Manchester not least due to the urban decay and angry spirit that generated the punk ethos. Young people found it difficult to get jobs and felt alienated in a run-down city that had lost its way. Oh, and also punk bands were actually allowed to play gigs here, unlike many other cities. Some of this attitude, however, was down to pragmatics as much as posturing, as can be seen in the photographs of Kevin Cummins, who along, with Paul Morley, documented the explosive rise of punk. According to Cummins: "I've got a Frantic Elevators session, with Mick Hucknall [of Simply Red], that's all in silhouette because they were signing on and didn't want to be recognised. That was the moody Manchester look."

Around this time, in 1977, Mark E. Smith formed The Fall. Although spawned by the punk scene, this is a band that defies any attempt at categorisation. Except for the ever-present Smith, who provides wry, hilarious lyrics in his trademark deadpan delivery, the lineup is ever-changing. Perhaps it is the dominance of one personality over an otherwise shifting cast of members that explains why The Fall have proved such an enduring symbol of free thinking. Whatever the explanation, the music is so idiosyncratic that they inspire devotion in many thousands, and complete indifference in many more.

It was the Sex Pistols gigs which inspired, not only a cataclysmic shift in the Manchester music scene but the creation of Factory Music (see page 204). Less of a record label, more of a dominant ideology, their hegemony would have been complete but for failing to sign The Smiths, who opted instead for the London-based Rough Trade. To digress, there's a very funny scene in the movie dedicated to Factory, *24 Hour Party People*, in which Factory boss, Tony Wilson has a vision of God (who happens to look just like Tony Wilson), who says, "It's a pity you didn't sign the Smiths, but you were right about Mick Hucknell. His music's rubbish, and he's a ginger."

Despite the dominance of The Smiths (see pages 208-209) and New Order (see page 204 - Factory Music) for much of the '80s, it wasn't until the decade was drawing to a close that Manchester really stamped its identity on the international music scene. Fuelled by a revolution that had seen the city's youth embrace and nurture the sounds of Chicago's house scene, played by DJs such as Mike Pickering, Graeme Park and John Da Silva at the Haçienda, Manchester exploded into the world's press. A Guy Called Gerald's 'Voodoo Ray' and 808 State's 'Pacific State' provided the club anthems.

Thanks to a combination of the new dance drug ecstasy and an already well developed musical openness, the city was dancing to a new and hybrid beat. House music, for a time, managed to cross the musical divide – guitar bands were going out dancing and clubbers were checking out live music. Out of this magical mish-mash emerged bands like The Stone Roses (see page 205) and Happy Mondays (see page 204 - Factory Music), who pilfered from Britain and America's pop past, sieving the sounds through a backdrop of mutating

Factory

"Factory Records are not actually a company. We are an experiment in human nature."

Spurred on by the Sex Pistols gig, in the summer of 1976, Granada TV presenter Anthony Wilson, and actor Alan Erasmus, started putting on gigs and hosting 'Factory' nights at the Russell Club in Hulme. This eventually led to the creation of Factory Records in the same year. Peter Saville was employed to design the posters and record producer Martin Hannett also came on board. The fifth partner, Rob Gretton, was to become the manager of the label's most successful bands. Early signings included A Certain Ratio (who would stay), and Orchestral Manoeuvres in the Dark (who bolted to Virgin Records shortly afterwards). The first Factory LP, Joy Division's *Unknown Pleasures*, was released in June 1979.

Tragedy hit relatively early when Joy Division singer Ian Curtis committed suicide at his home in Macclesfield in 1980. The rest of the band, Bernard Sumner, Peter Hook, Gillian Gilbert and Stephen Morris, reformed as New Order, changing musical direction, and scoring hits, including 1982's dance anthem 'Blue Monday'. This had a Saville designed sleeve, meticulously copied from a floppy disc that was supposed to have been so expensive to create that the band lost money for every copy sold. It was the biggest selling 12 inch single of all time.

Emboldened by their success, rather than dismayed by their apparent talent for losing money, New Order went on to open the Hacienda club in conjunction with Factory. Initially it was not a success but went on to become the most renowned club in the world. The owners claim they never made any money from it, and in fact probably lost a fortune.

Every item on the Factory catalogue was given a FAC number. So every album and single naturally came under this scheme, but so did the Hacienda (FAC51), Dry Bar, which started off the bar trend (FAC251). Even more esoteric objects came within the cataloguing system. For example a bucket on Styal Mill water wheel is Fac 148.

The band that courted the most controversy on the label was The Happy Mondays. Indelibly associated with 'baggy Madchester' and an alarming appetite for chemical stimulants, Shaun Ryder and his crew typified the 'don't-give-a-shit' attitude of the scene. So much so that the band imploded during the recording of *Yes Please*! The Mondays flew to Barbados, ostensibly to escape the party scene in the city, but ended up blowing their recording budget on crack.

Factory was famous for its non-commercial spirit. Wilson's contract with New Order reputedly consisted of one sentence promising them total artistic freedom and ownership of their music scrawled on a paper napkin in his own blood. But in the end the unprofessional attitudes caused the downfall of the label. New Order moved to London Records, the Hacienda began a series of closures and the Factory offices shut down for good.

The story of the label was captured in Michael Winterbottom's colourful film *24 Hour Party People* in which Steve Coogan played Wilson. Many people, including the Buzzcocks' Howard Devoto, disputed the filmic version of the facts, but nevertheless the chaotic sprit of the times is captured. This year sees a more serious film on Joy Division, *Control*, from their video director Anton Corbijn. Once more this will no doubt underscore the significance of Factory.

Anthony Wilson and Steve Coogan

ENTERTAINMENT

house music – dubbed 'acid house' courtesy of its hypnotic, drugged-up ambience. At that moment everybody wanted to be Mancunian, the Mondays' EP *Madchester: Rave On*, encapsulating the mood perfectly. The relaxed 'baggy' look, flares, bum bags, trainers and so forth, grabbed the musical world's imagination by the throat. Perhaps grabbed it a little too hard as many visitors still expect to see a Manchester full of the baggy stereotype.

Even terminally unhip outfits like Oldham's Inspiral Carpets found themselves in the charts, soon followed by the Northwich-based band The Charlatans. The Charlatans second single 'The Only One I Know' was a top ten smash – 14 years and numerous albums later, including three number ones, they are still riding high. Even perennial Manchester troopers James hit the big time with 'Sit Down', their LPs sending them off to stadia around the world.

After a while the baggy ride petered out and the city might have been at a musical loss if it were not for some brilliant pop tunes in the shape of Take That. Quality pop has always been part of the city's charm. Both Mick Hucknall from Simply Red, and Rochdale chanteuse Lisa Stansfield, have over two decades shown they have staying power if not always critical approval.

Back in Indie-land as Take That started bopping about on stage, Wigan's Verve were starting to come into their own. But it was the retro-Britpop stylings of Oasis, who smashed it globally and defined Manchester, guitars and the nineties for many commentators. The world of bloke had arrived. 'Manchester, mad for it', as Liam Gallagher allegedly and no doubt nasally affirmed.

And of course, throughout the last twenty years or so, Morrissey, freed by his Smiths split, has plugged away as a solo artist. Given his early obsessions with the kitchen sink dramas of Northern England, he has, improbably and hilariously, become a spiritual icon to sections of Latino youth in California. His last two albums *You are the Quarry* and *Ringleader of the Tormentors* have seen him return to the top of the charts and gain firm critical approval. The first of these albums also saw him play Manchester again. Like men in their forties at a school reunion looking back with nostalgia, he seems to have fallen in love with the city once more. As a performer he's scarcely been away since this late blossoming affair. But Mancs approve heartily. In many respects Morrissey is the troubled spirit of the city all summed up in one remarkable, if maverick, man.

Back to the story though. Ultimately the Oasis brand of bloke-rock didn't do the city many favours. For much of the late '90s Manchester was deluged by a sea of mop-topped, monosyllabic Liam-a-likes who inevitably refused to take their coats off indoors no matter how warm it got.

The Stone Roses

When The Stones Roses (Ian Brown, John Squire, Gary 'Mani' Mounfield and Alan 'Reni' Wren), released their eponymous debut album in May 1989, it instantly became a classic- maybe not with the critics, at first, but with the fans, and now it constantly scores highly in those ubiquitous 'best of' charts. It blended Manc arrogance with almost painful vulnerability and tenderness, drawing on religious imagery and the political idealism of the Paris riots; it has a loping groove that underpins melodic chiming guitars. From this pinnacle the only way was down. It took five years to make the disappointing follow-up, the *Second Coming*, the relationship between Brown and Squire dissolved amidst accusations of drug abuse and to cap it all there was a disastrous performance at the Reading Festival. It is singer Ian Brown, all swagger, attitude and eccentricity, who has forged the most successful solo career, although Mani is now a member of Primal Scream.
Key album: *Stone Roses*

Not that everybody slumped into grump. Quirky, mild-mannered Badly Drawn Boy has produced some entertaining whimsy in the intervening years, whilst the full-on sound of the Doves has injected firepower and up-front sensitivity. Bands like Elbow have bubbled under for yonks, delivering interesting tunes and some sparkling wordsmithery. I am Kloot have done likewise, while city-based dance act Mint Royale have kept the nation's feet tapping.

Take That

A manufactured boy band but the love they inspired in thousands of teenage girls was all too real. Childline set up an emergency hotline the day in February 1996 that Take That split. Constructed by pop-Svengali Nigel Martin Smith, they consisted of Gary Barlow (dependable, take home to mum type), Mark Owen (elfin cutie pie), Robbie Williams (wisecracking cheeky chappy), Howard Donald (err, dancer) and Jason Orange (ditto). 'The That', as they were affectionately known, set the blueprint in this country, for the boy-band style (matching clothes and dance routines) and are to blame for the imitators that followed, but with a bunch of cracking pop songs under their coordinated belts they are easily forgiven. Robbie went on to do his own, often naked, thing, poking fun at the other members of the band. In 2006 he went into rehab (again), the others reformed and went to number one with, 'Patience' and sold out concert venues across the land. Everything changes you could say. Key album: *Everything Changes*

In 2007 though the music scene in Manchester isn't held together by an overall sound or style. Instead it's as fractured as a the pattern in a kaleidoscope. In one corner there are the acoustic leanings of the nu-folksters such as Isobel Heyworth, Sam Hammond and Liam Frost. Other names include The Decemberists, Cherry Ghost, and The Library Trust. Try looking for the Malastruganca compilation album for a list of even more obscure names.

In terms of production, there are, at the last count, more than 20 different record labels in the city area. These cover all musical genres and types, from the vaudeville of Mr. Scruff to the drop-out slacker pop of Autokat on Akoustik Anarkhy. Twisted Nerve run by Andy Votel, have been music press darlings. Aim's Andy Turner has set up new North West beats and bits imprint Atic. Other labels worth mentioning include Faith & Hope, Fat City Records, Sub Tub Players, Pleasure, Paper Recordings, Skinny Dog and Valentine Records.

The scene is about more than bands and records these days. Club nights regularly have live bands playing and artistic 'spaces' such as Islington Mill, where like-minded folk can get together, have become a central focus. Manchester acts as a locus for live music events. Music industry types descend on the city for the In The City convention, beeps and blips get their turn in the sun with Futuresonic, while this year's big event is the return of the legendary Deeply Vale festival, described by Q as 'the North West's Glastonbury'.

So what holds such a disparate troupe of folk together? The revolutionary spirit that has so informed the city's politics is also its cultural engine. None of the traditional barriers between the arts trap Manchester's artists- they freely experiment and question.

All this talk of the snap and crack, the energy of Manchester culture, brings us to a quote from the 19th century philosopher Alexis de Tocqueville. He saw fit to dub Manchester 'the new Hades' and irreverent Mancs would not disagree- there is enough creative fire going around, and as everybody knows, Manchester, just like the Devil, has all the best tunes.

Gig venues

Mentioned here are the more established venues in Manchester. It would take a massive amount of space to mention all the places where live bands perform.

Manchester Academy (Oxford Road, University. 0161 275 2930 *www.manchesteracademy.net*) – Academy 1 (Academy) holds national and international touring acts, Academy 2 (Main Debating Hall) up-and-coming acts, and Academy 3 (Hop and Grape) gives space to young locals and more eclectic types.

Apollo (Ardwick Green. 0870 4018000) – Tours from big name bands, as well as the occasional comedy gig. The veteran heart of Manchester music for many locals and the venue in which they first saw a major act.

Bierkeller 9D (Piccadilly, City. 0161 236 1807 *www.bierkeller.co.uk*) – Host to Club NME and Blowout nights featuring touring and local bands.

Castle (38 Union Street, Oldham. 01706 882 759 *www.castlelive.com*) – Essential Oldham hangout for up 'n' coming rock/pop acts and tribute bands.

Life Café 4E (Peter Street, City. 0161 833 3000) – Live rock and indie acts in the downstairs Late Room.

Lowry Centre (Salford Quays. 0870 787 5780 *www.lowry.com*) Provides a platform for more mature acts.

MEN Arena 6A (Victoria Station, Hunts Bank, City. 0161 950 5000 *www.men-arena.com*) – For international names the place to play. The near 20,000-capacity venue regularly allows the world's biggest artists to put on the most extravagant of shows. You're bound to have a good night should you be near the front, but if you're sitting at the back, two-tiers up, you're going to need binoculars to see Kylie shake her posterior.

Night & Day Café 9C (Oldham Street, City. 0161 236 4597 *www.nightnday.org*) – Emphasis on supercool indie, folk and rock attract differing crowds.

Retro Bar 9G (Sackville Street, City. 0161 274 4892 *www.retrobarmanchester.com*) – Off the beaten track student hangout that has grown in the last year or so into an essential hub for Manchester's starlet garage/punk acts.

Roadhouse 9D (Newton Street, City. 0161 237 9789 *www.theroadhouselive.co.uk*) – Live rock and indie bands usually keep the place packed out.

Star & Garter 10F (Fairfield Street, City. 0161 273 6726 *www.starandgarter.co.uk*) – Small indie and local bands, also club nights including the legendary Smile.

Oasis

After the post Madchester burnout a likely looking re-ignition came in the form of Oasis. Originally known as the Rain, the swank and the swagger, as well as the tunes, ensured worldwide success. In selling figures at least, they eclipsed their heroes, who included Johnny Marr of The Smiths and Ian Brown of The Stone Roses. Oasis first played live in August of 1991 at the Boardwalk without Noel Gallagher who was a roadie for the Inspiral Carpets at the time. A few months later Noel was in charge, the principal songwriter and more reflective voice of the group, at least in comparison to the hotheaded Liam.The brothers' feuds, with outsiders and with each other, became legendary, and after the blistering first album, *Definitely Maybe*, they were constantly in the media stumbling out of the Met Bar or wishing members of Blur would 'die of AIDS'. Oops. The quality that set Oasis apart in those fey indie times was the braggadocio and their blustering, muscular brand of rock. After an excellent follow-up album, *What's the Story, Morning Glory*, musically the inspiration dried up, although the group remain consistent stadium rockers. Key album: *Definitely Maybe*

ENTERTAINMENT

The Smiths Room at Salford Lads Club

The Smiths

Of all the Manchester bands the Smiths remain the most seductive. The voice and words of Morrissey, the guitars of Marr and that sturdy rhythm section combined over five brief years (1982-87) to such good effect that people still can't get the music out of their heads. Whilst 10cc, the Buzzcocks, New Order, the Stone Roses and many other Manchester bands have been important, even great, the Smiths were special: a team which delivered a sound rich with yearning and wit. And despite the overwhelming presence of Morrissey it was a team.

As Brett Anderson of Suede once said, "Morrissey turned the pages of his diary into art and that is the requirement of great music: to speak from the heart. And while Morrissey was a very skilful lyricist, he wasn't really anything without Johnny Marr. Nobody played guitar like that before and nobody has played like that since."

As for the beginning, Smiths fans can look away now- these facts are probably engraved on their hearts and minds. Johnny Marr called round on Stephen Patrick Morrissey at his home in Kings Road, Stretford, in the spring of 1982. Then the pair recruited local boys Andy Rourke, as bass player and Mike Joyce, as drummer. The name the Smiths was chosen to stand in plain counterpoint to the glamorous New Romantic names popular at the time such as Depeche Mode.

The Smith's rejected a deal with Manchester's Factory label in favour of London's Rough Trade label. The first single, 'Hand in Glove,' was not a chart success, reaching number 123. However, critics claimed it was the finest love song of the year. By this time, the media were already well aware of the Smiths. This was largely due to Morrissey's cantankerous, eccentric persona, enhanced by wearing a hearing aid and stuffing flowers down the back of his trousers. In total four classic albums and numerous compilations were produced in the brief period between 1984 and 1987.

The albums were *The Smiths, Meat is Murder, The Queen is Dead* and *Strangeways Here We Come.*

Another important strain in the Smith's songbook was the glowering, gloomy city of Manchester itself, which in the eighties was going through its toughest years of modern times. From 'Reel around the Fountain' to 'I won't share you', the city's grey and powerful presence is woven into the thread of Morrissey's lyrics.

By 1987 band relationships were becoming strained, with Morrissey allegedly unhappy at the amount of time Marr spent working on side projects, and Marr resenting Morrissey's obsession with covering 1960s pop artists. Marr said, "'Work Is a Four Letter Word' I hated. That was the last straw, really. I didn't form a group to perform Cilla Black songs."

The split went it came was a bitter - in 1996 a £1m royalties claim was brought by drummer Mike Joyce against Morrissey and Johnny Marr, after payments had been stopped to the former band members.

The constituent parts went on to pursue their own various projects, while occasionally sniping at each other in the press. Recently, Morrissey revealed that the group had been offered £5 million to play the Coachella festival. In a typically candid

"I would rather eat my own testicles than reform The Smiths, and that's saying something for a vegetarian."

interview Morrissey said: "I would rather eat my own testicles than reform The Smiths, and that's saying something for a vegetarian."

An odd fate has befallen this most individual of bands: their gradual inclusion into the mainstream. The perennial outsiders are now cited by pretty much every young vaguely indie band as an inspiration. Worse, who would want to be foisted with the responsibility of spawning Emo, lyrically at least? Even the leader of the Conservative Party, David Cameron, carries Smiths' songs on his iPod. Of course that such an anti-Establishment band has been adopted by the Establishment is amusing. It might even appeal to Morrissey's sense of humour.

➤ To this day, the pulling power of the band remains strong. Fans come from all over the world to visit the sites associated with the band or just to be in the city from which their heroes hail. The first port of call should be **Salford Lads Club** (0161 872 3767). This building, fascinating in itself, provided the backdrop for the inner sleeve of *The Queen Is Dead*. There's a small but sweet museum devoted to the Smiths inside, see picture previous page. Call ahead to make sure the place is open. There are occasional, usually monthly, Smiths and Morrissey nights at the **Star and Garter**.

For those who require a more comprehensive look than our tour from page 214 can offer, purchase *Morrissey's Manchester - the Essential Smiths Tour* by Phill Gatenby. Best of all hire a taxi and get the driver to play 'The Boy with a Thorn in his Side' or 'Headmaster Ritual', full-whack, as you power over the Mancunian Way or weave through the buses on Oxford Road. That way you can make a road movie of Manchester, with the Smiths as soundtrack.

Clubbing

Manchester's clubbing opportunities are legion and ever-changing. We can't do justice to them all here, so a representative sample will have to suffice. Needless to say, you will find something here to your taste, but the fun is in the finding out. A directory with contact details follows this breakdown - also check out the gig venues on page 207.

Indie

Blowout- what other club could you visit and hear Bloc Party, Kaiser Chiefs, Tom Vek, Nine Black Alps, The Magic Numbers, Clor and The Longcut? What? Any student disco? Okay, well let us re-phrase that: where else could you see them live? Along with the next wave of top talent? Blowout's (www.blowout.org.uk) booking policy is almost unrivalled as we go to press. Although if its quality stage sets you're after - taking you well into those small hours - also worth checking is High Voltage at the Music Box. For up-to-date indie try Fight Club and Up the Racket both at Retro Bar. Don't forget 42 Street or 5th Avenue (as if you could) for guaranteed indie shufflings to Manchester classics. Old hands might remember The Venue, which has made a reappearance on Jacksons Row. The Star and Garter is home to both the classic Smile, the shinier and more glamorous Keys, Money, Lipstick and a Smiths night which regularly gets packed out.

Rock

Occasional rock night at Charlie's, Spandecks (Fridays www.myspace.com/spandecksrocks) calls itself 'a mucky hair metal night for the those who have a passion for spandex, hairspray and revolving drum kits.' Or just a hell of a party. Rock-types will also find a welcome home at Jilly's any night of the week (try the all-nighters on Fridays to see some interesting sights at 6am) or try the Ritz on a Monday and Satan's Hollow on a Tuesday. In what now seems an entirely obvious move, The Ruby Lounge, combines metal music and stripping on a Saturday night in the tastefully named Caged Asylum.

Hip-Hop/ D'n'B

Check out the drum 'n' bass stylings from Ape. Originally a weekly event it now puts on occasional shindigs. So far events featuring Roni Size and Rahzel have been

very popular, check www.apemanchester.com for the next event. Norvun Devolution (www.norvundevolution.com) at the Roadhouse is promoting itself as 'a collective consisting of musicians, DJs, visual artists, turntabalists and MCs.'

House

The infamous Tribal Sessions is back at Sankeys, providing a steady diet of everything from tribal house to breaks. You may also have heard of Bugged Out, the legendary Manc night that's been across the country and back (www.buggedout.net). An oldie is Venus at Club V (Saturdays) and Twisted Elegance ramps up the glamour at Ampersand. For something on the harder side try Filth at the Music Box (Wednesdays) or the deeper Stylus, (monthly Fridays at The Attic)

Breaks and Bleeps

Tangled launched in 1993, but this stalwart (actually Manchester's longest-running club night) remains as relevant as it did then. Its move from the Phoenix to the similarly-sized Club Academy currently ensures that progressive/tech house and trance are as well represented as nu-skool breaks. Regular appearances from the likes of James Holden, Hybrid and Rennie Pilgrem complement an excellent team of residents. If you like the sound of this, try giving Kindergarten (Attic) and Fuse (Roadhouse) a go too.

Soul 'n' Funk

Eyes Down shares a similar musical pedigree with Electric Chair (as well as a resident DJ in Kelvin Brown). This ambitious yet intimate night down in the Roadhouse (first Friday of every month) is a contemporary soul music lover's wet dream. Journeying the sublime sounds consistently coming out of Detroit in addition to various reggae, house and jazz-flavoured diversions, it has also welcomed reclusive innovator Moodymann. Twice. The same venue also plays host to the more hip-hop biased Fat City affiliate, Friends & Family, while Roots Before Branches (Dry Bar) has been known to plough a similar groove. More mainstream is Sub-space's Superfunk (Saturdays) Funkedemia (One Central Street). Nostalgia buffs can head to The Twisted Wheel at Legends (see boxout this page) and experience some of the original chalk'n'sweat atmosphere.

Roots/Reggae

Blood and Fire is at the Mint Club every Sunday, while there is usually a reggae night every Thursday at Big Hands, except the last Thursday of the month. Luckily that's exactly when Hot Milk is at the Attic so you can still get your fix. Check out the Blood and Fire website to keep up with Manchester's sometime sluggish reggae scene, perhaps a new night will pop up to inject some more energy soon (www.bloodandfire.co.uk).

Eclectic

Electric Chair has an intoxicating reputation distilled from ten years of riotous partying. The Unabombers' flagship offering, for many, represents the late night sound of the city. Fusing house, disco, broken beat, emotive techno and neo-soul, it rapidly outgrew its original home at the Roadhouse to find the larger, equally glitz-less subterranean setting of the Music Box where it resides today. High-calibre guests including Laurent Garnier, Jazzanova, Derrick May and DJ Spinna have ensured that each month's execution is a sell-out. Still, if you don't beat this particular queue, do remember those masterminds over at the Chair's headquarters also devised Nish

Twisted Elegance

Twisted Wheel The original Manchester clubbing experience

The origins of Northern Soul are well documented in several good books, try *The In Crowd* (by Mike Ritson and Stuart Russell). These tell tales of lads in wide strides and lasses in swirling skirts and a strange white substance (the chalk they used on the floors that is) dancing the night away to obscure American Soul classics in the '60s and '70s. Leading American artists played live at the club too and the Wheel also pioneered all-nighters. Memories are fond. 'Manchester wasn't the gentrified place it is today. A trip to the Wheel meant dodging winos, pimps, nutters, hookers, muggers, residual football hooligans, Manchester Drug Squad and other assorted low life just to get to the front door. One foot inside though and you were enveloped by this sound and atmosphere like no other. It made your hair stand on end and your elbows burst. You didn't need to take amphetamines to get high but we did anyway. We danced through the night on concrete floors with condensation running down the walls and wanted to be nowhere else in the world.' Along with the Wigan Casino, The Twisted Wheel, was the most important location in this sometimes obsessive scene. The club first opened in Brazennose Street, off Albert Square, in 1963, moving 18 months later to Whitworth Street. In 1971 it closed but in 2002 was revived on the last Friday of every month at Whitworth Street, www.twistedwheel.net

Nash Nosh (Mint Lounge), Harter Street Lounge (Charlie's) and younger, sexually liberated step-sibling Homoelectric (various venues). Keep It Unreal is the home of Mr. Scruff, a masterchef serving up a recipe prepared over five hours consisting solely of him and his records - available from the Music Box on the first Saturday of every month and proving to be rather delicious when served piping hot. Glamorous types could try Romp, a sexy mix of electro, hip-hop and eighties hits (Thursdays, One Central Street). Another good bet for snappy dressers is Clique (www.clubclique.co.uk), shiny pop music for cute club kids in the basement of Joshua Brooks, Clique appears on the last Friday of the month and regularly sells out. Expect to hear the likes of New Order, Le Tigre, The Gossip and Hot Chip. As the tagline says its digital dance-pop for your head, heart and hips. Good news for those who like their indie mixed with a techno/electroish vibe (of course, darling, of course) the wonderful Tramp! is back. It was meant to be lurking at the Bierkeller but since that establishment's sad closure it is currently homeless. Check the website (www.trampclub.com) to find out which dark corner of Manchester's club scene it gravitates to next. Finally a new night that might be worth checking out is One Central's Guilty Pleasures, (we are sure you've heard of the concept, so bad its good etc..) every Friday from March.

The Hacienda The most famous Manchester Clubbing Experience

Fac 51 Haçienda (also known as simply The Haçienda, or the Haç) was feted by many as single-handedly reviving the club scene in the whole country- never mind Manchester. Working to a perfunctory brief; 'big bar, small bar, food, stage, dance-floor, balcony, and a cocktail bar in the basement', Ben Kelly was given unlimited freedom to convert a former yachting showroom into a wonder of industrial-inspired design (see picture page 46). Jointly owned by the Factory label and New Order, the club was run along such amateurish lines that it consistently lost money. At first the club was half empty, but started to find its groove as a live space as well as a club. This was the first UK place to host Madonna. Ground-breaking nights such Nude, Hot and (later on) Flesh began pulling the punters in and with the advent of ecstasy and 'the Summer of Love' popularity spiralled out of control and middle market, middle minded American magazine *Newsweek* put the Hacienda phenomena on its front cover. But the good vibes couldn't last forever, and trouble with gangs and drugs lead to the licence being revoked on more than one occasion.

The Whitworth Street West site has recently been rebuilt as apartments but has kept its iconic name. When the original showroom was pulled down, bricks were auctioned off at £5 a pop. Bassist Peter Hook from New Order is currently writing about the highs and lows (of which there must be many) of owning one of the world's first superclubs.

Student

Ah yes finally we get to the student nights. For those just come to the city to expand your minds academically, here's a chance to undo all the good work with cheap drinks and childish behaviour. Try Vodka Island (Tiger Tiger) or Club Tropicana (sadly drinks aren't free, but as close as they could get) for cheap thrills, then there's the 70's wormhole that is Lovetrain at The Ritz or you could try the Fallowfield stretch of bars for like-minded souls.

Club directory

42nd Street 5E (Bootle Street, City. 0161 831 7108. www.42ndstreetnightclub.com) – A classic Manchester indie night. **5th Avenue 6E** (121 Princess Street, City. 0161 236 2754. www.5thavenuemanchester.com) – Plays indie and student anthems. Opens Mon, Thu-Sat. **Ampersand 4E** (Longworth Street, City. 0161 832 3038) – If there's a place to wear sunglasses after dark in Manchester, it's probably here. **The Attic 7G** (50 New Wakefield Street, City. 01612366071) – A bit rough around the edges, but good for techno/electro nights. **Bed 8F** (50 Sackville Street, City. 0161 236 8300) – Strangely enough, probably not the best place for 40 winks. **Big Hands** (Oxford Road, University. 0161 272 7779) – The little bar with the big rep. It's where the Academy bands go post-gig. **Birdcage 7B**

Mint Lounge

(Withy Grove, opp Printworks. 0161 832 1700) – Burlesque nights are the big draw. **Brickhouse 5G** (66 Whitworth Street West, City. 0161 236 4418) – Reliable spot for indie shambling. **Centro 9B** (Tib Street, City. 0161 8352863. www.centrobar.co.uk) – Good music. Better beer. An essential bolthole from modern life. **Charlie's 7F** (1 Harter Street, City. 0161 237 9898) – Mad little dive where you could end up having a dismal time of one of the best nights of your life. **Club V 5D** (111a Deansgate, City. 0161 834 9975) – Make it glam. **Cord 9B** (Dorsey Street, off Tib Street, City. 0161 8329494 www.cordbar.com) – Dig out those rare, vintage trainers and get down with the Oldham Street Muso-Mafia. **Fab Café 7F** (111 Portland Street, City. 0161 236 2019) – Nights of retro and funk, theme songs and kitsch. A true one-off. **Jabez Clegg** (2 Portsmouth St, University. 0161 272 8612)– Next to the Uni so naturally popular with students. Live bands. **Joshua Brooks 8F** (106 Princess St, City. 0161 273 7336) – A club that has recently got its act together with some good nights. **King's Arms** (Bloom Street, Salford. 0161 832 3605) – Home to Rain Or Shine and a great boozer to boot. **Legends 9F** (Whitworth Street, City. 0161 2365400) – Whether you get the night you were expecting or not, an evening here will certainly live long in the memory. **Matt and Phred's Jazz Club 9C** (Oldham Street, City. 0161 831 7002. www.mattandphreds.com) – Manchester's best jazz club. **Mint Lounge 9C** (Oldham Street, City. 0161 228 1495. www.mintlounge.co.uk) – Quirky, eccentric and interesting. **Music Box 6F** (Rockworld/ Jilly's complex, 65 Oxford Road, City. 0161 236 9971. www.themusicbox.info) – Impeccable reputation. Holds monthly club nights including Electric Chair and Keep It Unreal. **One Central Street 5E** (Central Street, City. 0161 2119000. www.onecentralstreet.co.uk) – Cool, but never cold. A class set-up with impressive DJs. **Po Na Na Souk Bar 7G** (42 Charles Street, City. 0161 272 6044) – A chilled, funky club, in fact so laid back it's almost horizontal. **Ritz 6G** (Whitworth Street West. 0161 236 4355. ritznightclub.co.uk) – Manchester institution where at least one weird thing is bound to happen every night. **Roadhouse 9D** (8 Newton Street, City. 0161 237 9789. www.theroadhouselive.co.uk) – Small, intimate live band venue. Also with many excellent club nights. **Rockworld 6F** (Oxford Road, City. 0161 236 9971. www.jillys.co.uk) – Playing classic rock, '80s, indie, dance and goth. The city's second oldest club. **Sankeys** (Beehive Mill, Jersey Street, Northern Quarter. 0161 661 9668. www.tribalgathering.co.uk) – Regular top three UK club contender and home to the awesome Tribal Sessions. **South 5D** (4a King Street, City. 0161 831 7756) – The Rock and Roll Bar on Fridays plays Hammond organ kitsch, '60s guitar and northern soul. On Saturdays, ex-Inspiral Carpet Clint Boon plays pop at his Disco Rescue. **Star and Garter** (18-20 Fairfield Street, City. 0161 273 6726. www.starandgarter.co.uk) – Also a live venue for new bands. **Tiger Lounge 6E** (Cooper Street, City. 0161 236 6007) – Kitschy 60's themed place that is fun or glum depending to taste.

Rock tour

Follow the pedestrian symbol for the the walking part of this tour and the vehicle symbol for the parts that require bus, taxi or car. The tour does not pretend to cover all the sites associated with pop music in the city but provides an interesting, varied, even attractive way around some of them.

START the tour at the Town Hall main entrance. Proceed to Lloyd Street in the left corner of Albert Square. Down the street, under the modern building opposite Boutique, was Manchester's equivalent of the Cavern Club – the **Oasis Club**. Opened in 1961 as a jazz venue, it soon started to feature 'beat' music. In February 1962, The Beatles played their second gig there, to an unconvinced Manchester audience. The following night, local band The Hollies got a rousing reception. On the Sunday Rolf Harris and the Kangaroos played. It was said that the Oasis had the second largest consumption of Coke in the North West. That's Coca-Cola, of course – like most live music clubs of the time, the Oasis had no alcohol licence. Also gone is the nearby **Twisted Wheel Club**, which pioneered the first all-nighters – teenagers and youths would bring a blanket and lie down in a corner when they got tired. However the second site of the Twisted Wheel has a revival night on the last Friday of the month - see the Clubbing section above.

From the Oasis, take Southmill Street to Peter Street. The grand building opposite was formerly the **Free Trade Hall**, it's now a hotel. In 1966, Bob Dylan was booed and called 'Judas' by the folk audience for returning for the second half of his set with rock and roll music. In July 1976, The Sex Pistols appeared twice in the smaller room here. In the building dedicated to Mancunian single mindedness, The Pistols inspired the locals to set up their own record labels. The Buzzcocks were the first, producing the *Spiral Scratch* EP.

Behind the Free Trade Hall is the great arch of **G-Mex**. It was here, in 1986, that the Festival of the Tenth Summer was held – ten years on from the concert above. This legendary event in the city was headlined by New Order and The Smiths. G-Mex was formerly Central Station and it was in the station buffet where Peggy Gallagher – mother of the Oasis brothers – first worked in Manchester.

Now follow Lower Mosley Street down to the junction with Whitworth Street.

Haçienda then

Haçienda as apartments

Elbow play the Ritz

The apartment block on the left corner here was **the Haçienda.** This iconic building has now been demolished for apartments. The Haçienda, for a time, was the world's most famous club – it even appeared on the cover of staid American magazine Newsweek. It was the original of the new generation of superclubs and defined an era that created modern dance music – albeit fuelled by ecstasy. The Haçienda was opened in 1982 by Factory Records and New Order. It closed in 1997, a victim of poor administration more than the well-publicised gang problems. Madonna played an early gig here, as did a whole roll call of British music. One of the Haçienda legends relates how the Happy Mondays kidnapped '60s star, Donovan, from a small club 30 miles away in Colne and brought him to the Haçienda. Kidnapping must rank as one of the most bizarre courtship rituals, because later Shaun Ryder would move in with Oriole, Donovan's daughter, and even produce a child.

From here you can make the short detour left to the **Ritz**, Whitworth Street West. This was a Jimmy Savile club from the 1950s, and is still a club today – literally the oldest swinger in town. The Smiths played their first concert here in October 1982. The club also featured in one of Morrissey's favourite movies, local girl Shelagh Delaney's *Taste of Honey*.

Return to the Haçienda but cross, left, under the railway arches to Little Peter Street and turn right. On the right, midway down, is the tall brick building with the high gables that was once the **Boardwalk**. This provided rehearsal space in the late 1970s for, amongst others, Joy Division and the Frantic Elevators – the punk first band of Mick Hucknall. Late in 1986 it became one of the city's brightest live venues – as much a part of the Madchester phenomena as the Haçienda. Oasis played their first live performance here in August 1991 without the elder Gallagher. Brother Noel was in the sparse audience having just been released from role of roadie with the Inspiral Carpets. Jealous at youngster Liam beating him into a band, Noel informed the group that he would take control after, the story goes, impressing them with 'Live Forever'.

At the junction with Deansgate, turn right to the big bike sculpture. Cross over to Castle Street and follow this to **Barça** bar. Barça, attractively situated on the canal side, was formerly part owned by Mick Hucknall of Simply Red. Hucknall's sweet voice is one of the greatest successes of Manchester's recent musical history – he has achieved record sales of over 40 million. He is simply red – ginger hair, fan of Manchester United and member of the Labour Party.

Cross over the white sickle bridge and walk towards the Key103 radio studios in **Castle Quay**. Over the studios are the big penthouses. Jason Orange of Take That lived in one of these during the mid-'90s and grew accustomed to having long queues of girls waiting for a glimpse of him.

To continue the walking tour, follow the canal to the old church with the tower and then go straight over Deansgate on to Whitworth Street West, past the Ritz back to Oxford Road, and rejoin the walking tour on page 218.

Behind Castle Quay is the large road junction at the end of the Mancunian Way. You can make a detour right here almost a mile along Regent Road before turning left on Goodiers Drive to Coronation Street and **Salford Lads Club** (0161 872 3767). This building provided the backdrop for the inner sleeve of The Smiths' *The Queen is Dead*. There's a small museum devoted to the band here - call ahead for access.

The main tour route goes second left at this junction down Chorlton Road. Follow this to Royce Road and turn left. The former church on the left was Morrissey's very early childhood church, **St Wilfrid's**, and he attended the neighbouring primary school. Royce Road veers to the right and becomes Chichester Road.

Continue down to Stretford Road and turn right. Stop at the new **Hulme Park**. This very multicultural area of the city known as Hulme was once one of the most blighted districts, a concrete hell complete with four huge crescents of flats. These rundown horror stories became cheap accommodation for up-and-coming bands. Ian Brown and John Squire shared a flat here as English Rose – named in tribute to The Jam song – and it was from Robert Adam Crescent that A Guy Called Gerald recorded 1988 club anthem 'Voodoo Ray'. Some people liked the crescents and built their own not far away called Homes for Change. A group living here, called 'geomantics', have declared the paved area of the park the world's first UFO landing pad – in honour of the ley lines they say cross here. We await our visitors.

Continue down Stretford Road and turn left down Chorlton Road (on the way you pass Ayres Road, where the legendary Horners scooter shop used to be located, and where Liam Gallagher bought his first machine). At Brooks Bar take the road to the right of The Whalley pub, Upper Chorlton Road, and, after the Tesco, turn right down Kings Road. Continue down to **384 Kings Road**, Morrissey's former house. It was here in 1982 that Johnny Marr called on the quiffed singer. Morrissey already had lyrics, so when Marr came back the next day with his guitar, they could start writing.

Continue down Kings Road to the junction with Edge Lane and turn left. After half a mile, turn left on Wilbraham Road and a little later left again on to Barlow Moor Road. A little way up you'll find on the left the **Co-op Funeral Directors**. This was formerly the Gaumont cinema and in the 1950s saw the first live performance of the Brothers Gibb – the Bee Gees. On Saturdays, children were allowed to mime to records of their choice. One of the brothers tripped on the stairs and broke the single he was carrying. They sang instead, their voices tutored by father and bandleader Hugh Gibb. An instant success, they became a feature around south Manchester cinemas. It won't surprise you to learn that the group

Keppel Road

Southern Cemetery

didn't record 'Stayin' Alive' in the Co-op though. The boys attended Oswald Road Primary School around the corner.

Turn right at Brantingham Road then sharp right on **Keppel Road**. At number 51, Barry and the twins lived for several years. Unfortunately Barry was anything but a good little boy, and in his very early teens was in trouble for burning down advertising hoardings and empty houses. Rather than risk their first born being placed in a youth detention centre, the family emigrated to Australia. Tragedy! Barry has now purchased his old house but for what purpose we have yet to discover.

Continue down Keppel Road, take the next right and then turn left on Barlow Moor Road. Follow this to **Southern Cemetery**. The gates to this huge necropolis were featured in the mis-spelt Smiths song 'Cemetry Gates'. It pleased Morrissey and zany Manchester performer Linder Sterling to take melancholic strolls together through the tombs.

Cross over Princess Parkway, keeping on Barlow Moor Road, past **The Beeches** – a dead-end street on which Shaun Ryder of Happy Mondays/Black Grape fame lived for a short time. Turn left on **Palatine Road** to number 86, a large detached house now split into flats. From 1979 until 1990, the highly influential but chaotically run Factory Records worked out of here. Return to Barlow Moor Road and continue east to Didsbury. Cross over Wilmslow Road to School Lane. After half a mile, turn left up Parrs Wood Road. The school to the right, at the junction, is **Burnage High School** – this was the school the Gallagher brothers attended. Liam got into trouble for fighting here but was popular with the girls for his charming cockiness.

Continue down Parrs Road to Fog Lane and turn right. This area is Burnage. Just before the railway bridge is a tiny record shop. According to Paul Gallagher in the book *Brothers*, 'we were lucky to have **Mr Sifter**'s record shop. Sifter's was our musical oasis in Burnage. Noel and I used to love going through the racks of old vinyl albums, seven-inch singles and picture discs'.

Cross over the traffic lights on Kingsway to Burnage Lane and turn left. The traffic lights were featured in the song 'Shakermaker' by Oasis. A short way along Burnage Lane, on the right, is Cranwell Drive. In a house here the Gallaghers spent their adolescent years. Follow Burnage Lane past **St Bernard's Primary School and Church** – which Noel and Liam both attended.

At Grangethorpe Drive, turn left to Kingsway. Turn right on Kingsway. At the first roundabout, take immediate left and then sharp right up Birchfields Road. Turn left at Dickenson Road. On the right near the junction with Wilmslow Road are some gable ends of 1970s houses. One holds a Blue Plaque. **The Wesleyan Chapel** previously here was converted into

BBC studios in the 1950s. Britain's pop music show, axed in 2006 – *Top of the Pops* – started here on New Year's Day 1964, presented by Jimmy Saville. Local band The Hollies sang 'Stay' and the Rolling Stones performed 'I Wanna Be Your Man'.

At Wilmslow Road, turn right through Rusholme and the Asian restaurants. One of the last restaurants on the right is the **Sangam** where Take That recorded part of their video for their song 'Everything Changes'. Staff claim that fans have eaten more than 2,000 curries there.

Further down, after the hospital, is the University and on the right the **Holy Name** church that features in the Smiths song 'Vicar in a Tutu'. Many bands or musicians met or have been associated with the Universities. Thus it was here that The Chemical Brothers came together. Continue past the BBC studios to The Palace Theatre.

Here the walking tour can be picked up again. On the left is the old gents converted into a bar called **the Temple** which has an excellent jukebox full of Manchester tunes. Opposite, across Oxford Street, is the **Music Box** and **Rockworld** (formerly Rafters), where Warsaw played their second gig in 1977. They returned as Joy Division the next year and were spotted by Anthony Wilson and signed to Factory.

Continue up Oxford Street to the new **Circus** office development. The Plaza, formerly sited here, used to be another of Jimmy Savile's early clubs – on one early '60s night, he pulled in the punters by offering

a free polio jab with each ticket. Turn right in front of the Central Library, follow the arcade of the Town Hall Extension and then turn left down Lloyd Street to Albert Square and the start of the walk. If you wish, follow Mosley Street to Piccadilly Gardens. The last statue on the right, on Piccadilly itself, is the **Duke of Wellington**. This provided the backdrop for the Buzzcocks' *Spiral Scratch* EP.

You should also make a trip up **Oldham Street**. This area now bears the name the Northern Quarter. It is the true spiritual heart of Manchester's music scene and there are record shops on every side. It's a good place to end the tour.

On the pavement close by **Dry Bar** is Tim Rushton's 'Sound Bites' (pictured below) commemorating the city's musical achievement. Dry Bar (pictured page 46) was originally owned by Factory and New Order and when it opened in 1989, started a revolution in bar style with its hard, utilitarian design. **Eastern Bloc Records** close by was the home during the Madchester years of 808 State.

Jazz

The traditional Manchester jazz venues are Band on the Wall and its near neighbour **Matt & Phred's Jazz Club**, but **BOTW** is closed for renovation until 2007. If Manchester remains better supplied with nightclubs than jazz haunts, it means that the musicians who do survive are dedicated and talented.

Once a year, in June, Manchester Jazz Festival gives a platform to the brightest Manchester musicians. Players like John Ellis, Munch Manship and Mike Walker routinely make nonsense of the distinction between world and local talent. It would be hard to find a comparative scene anywhere in the UK of such turbulence and vitality. The 2006 festival runs from 22–29 July, check www.manchesterjazz.com Also look out for the Wigan Jazz Festival in July, which some say is as good as that in Montreux.Some Jazz venues include: **Blue Cat Café** (Shaw Road, Heaton Moor. 0161 432 2117) **The Bridgewater Hall 5F** (Great Bridgewater Street, City. 0161 907 9000. www.bridgewater-hall.co.uk) **Didsbury Cricket Club** (Wilmslow Road, East Didsbury. 0161 445 5347. www.didsburycricketclub.org.uk) **Green Room 6G** (Whitworth Street West, City. 0161 615 0500) **Matt and Phred's Jazz Club 9C** (Oldham Street, City. 0161 831 7003) **Rhythm Station** (Nawhallhey Road, Rawtenstall. 01706 214039) **The Royal Northern College of Music** (Oxford Road, University. 0161 907 5278. www.rncm.ac.uk)

Folk

If you're looking for traditional, finger-in-the-ear, Arran jumper folk music like Ewan MacColl used to make then you might have a hard time. (Incidentially, MacColl was the father of late singer Kirsty MacColl, and he was the songwriter of 'Dirty Old Town' and 'The First Time Ever I Saw Your Face', covered famously by Roberta Flack.) But there has been a resurgence in well-attended singers' clubs (some of which put on booked artists once a month or so).

Try arts centres and bars such as **Bury Met** (0161 761 2216), **Blue Cat Café** (0161 432 2117), **Manchester University Students' Union** (0161 275 2930), **Burnley Mechanics** (01282 664400), the **Witchwood** (0161 344 0321) in Ashton-under-Lyne and the **Citadel** (01744 735436) in St Helens. There are Irish sessions at city centre pubs like the **Jolly Angler, Peveril of the Peak 6G** and the **Salutation**, as well as the **Ducie** in Hulme. A traditional British pub sing-a-long takes place every Wednesday at the **Hare and Hounds 8B** pub on Shude Hill. Check out the **Instituto Cervantes 3F** (Deansgate, City. 0161 661 4200) for a programme of Spanish events including folk music..

Manchester Jazz Festival

ENTERTAINMENT

Folk train

A real curiosity takes place on the second Saturday of the month: the **Hathersage Rambler Folk Train** which departs Piccadilly at 11.46am, calling at all stations to Hathersage, where musicians and audience adjourn to the Little John Hotel for refreshment before returning to Manchester on the 2.32pm. No booking – just turn up and buy an ordinary rail ticket. And there's no charge for the entertainment. The scenery is wonderful and the company eclectic. This service has been joined by a similar service to Glossop, which, at present, runs on the fourth Thursday of the month at 6.39pm from Piccadilly Station. For further details, visit www.hvhptp.org.uk/folktran.htm#manc

Classical music

The city is home to four professional orchestras – **the Hallé, BBC Philharmonic, Manchester Camerata** and **Northern Chamber Orchestra** – and a vast number of other music-making organisations. **Chetham's School of Music** and the **Royal Northern College of Music** are internationally recognised centres of excellence here, and the **University of Manchester** has a faculty and programme of international distinction.

If you are in the city centre, check out the programmes at the **Bridgewater Hall, Chetham's, St Ann's Church** and the **Cathedral**: there is a myriad of lunchtime performances as well as evening concerts. The Hallé, BBC Philharmonic and Camerata perform their own series at the Bridgewater Hall (and the BBC Philharmonic also play in their own studio at the BBC; while the Camerata have a special link with the Royal Northern College and give a series there). Visiting international soloists and orchestras come to the Bridgewater Hall, and chamber music is to be found in almost every venue, including the **University of Salford's Peel Hall**.

Touring opera comes to the Palace and Opera House theatres regularly, while the Royal Northern College of Music presents its own high-quality productions. The other main focus for opera is the **Lowry** arts centre in Salford: Opera North are in residence three times a year, and other companies visit. Looking further afield, the Cheshire countryside has its own Glyndebourne in the form of **Clonter Opera** (01260 224514 www.clonteropera.com) – a theatre on a farm, where the best of young singers come to study and perform, and the public accommodation is sufficient for every member of the audience to dine indoors (something Glyndebourne itself cannot offer to all). Buxton's lovely Edwardian Opera House is a gem not be missed, and home to both the annual Buxton Festival, with its in-house productions every year plus visiting productions, and the popular International Gilbert and Sullivan Festival.

Organ music enthusiasts should not miss a visit to the Bridgewater Hall, the splendid Victorian great hall in the Town Hall (which possesses a 19th century Cavaillé-Coll), the Cathedral, St Ann's, and the Royal Northern College concert hall.

Manchester hosts several two or three-yearly international festivals: the Glories of the Keyboard Festival is held at the Bridgewater Hall; the International Cello Festival, International Violin Competition and a whole set of other festivals for wind, brass and individual instruments at the RNCM. If you want to join an orchestra yourself, you might think about the amateur Gorton Philharmonic Orchestra – it's even older than the Hallé.

The area's grand houses and stately homes promote concerts over the summer, including Tatton Park in Knutsford, Arley Hall near Northwich and Gawsworth Hall near Congleton.

The Hallé Orchestra **0161 237 7000**
www.halle.co.uk. The Hallé Orchestra, now based at the Bridgewater Hall, is the oldest professional orchestra in Britain still performing. It was created in 1858 and proved so successful that Charles Hallé, the German piano virtuoso and conductor who had already put his roots down in Manchester, decided to continue with an annual winter concert series of his own in the Free Trade Hall (now the Radisson Edwardian Hotel). That began on 30 January, 1858, and has continued ever since – from 1996 in the Bridgewater Hall.

Hallé was keenly supported in his move to the city (in 1848) by the large German expatriate business and professional community of Victorian Manchester, but he rapidly acquired a following among all sectors of the city's population. When he died in 1895, 40,000 people lined the route of his funeral cortege.

There have only been eight permanent conductors of the Hallé Orchestra since then: they include Hans Richter, enticed away from the Vienna Conservatory, Sir Hamilton Harty, and Sir John Barbirolli, who rebuilt the orchestra from scratch in three weeks in wartime 1943 and continued at th helm until his death in 1970. Mark Elder is the present music director and credited for taking the orchestra again to heights of excellence equal to any in its past. Recordings issued on the orchestra's own label in recent years have built its reputation throughout the world. Most major conductors of international status visit the Hallé from time to time or have been associated with it in the past.

In the winter season from September through to May the Hallé presents a series of Thursday concerts in an unbroken tradition going back to 1861, plus a monthly 'Opus One' series, with each concert given three times over and drawing an aggregate audience exceeding that of many pop events, the 'Halle Collection' of special weekend presentations, and a large number of Pops, family concerts, children's events and others designed to introduce newcomers to classical music. It also tours the north of England, appears in the BBC Proms in London, and makes frequent overseas visits. The celebrated Hallé Choir has a history almost as long as the orchestra, and the Hallé also runs its own Youth Orchestra and Youth Choir.

The BBC Philharmonic **0161 244 4001** *www.bbc.co.uk/ orchestras/philharmonic.* THE BBC Philharmonic was formed in 1934, initially as a broadcast variant on the Hallé's membership at a time when the latter did not offer full-time employment to its musicians, but became fully self-contained, with its own full-time membership, in 1942 (the Hallé followed suit just afterwards, when Barbirolli arrived). Originally the BBC Northern Orchestra, then BBC Northern Symphony Orchestra, it is now a true heavyweight on the international stage. It performs regularly in the Bridgewater Hall as well as recording and playing live for radio in the BBC's own studio concert hall. The current principal conductor is the Italian Gianandrea Noseda, and the orchestra also boasts Yan Pascal Tortelier, Vassily Sinaisky, James MacMillan and Sir Edward Downes on its list of regular conductors. Its lauded education and community department takes its work all over the country, and the orchestra even has a special relationship with *Blue Peter*, the children's TV programme, as well as recording for the Chandos label and playing a major role in the BBC Proms in London.

Manchester Camerata **0161 226 8696** *www.manchestercamerata.com.* Founded in 1972, Manchester Camerata is one of Britain's leading chamber orchestras, with its principal conductor Douglas Boyd and principal guest conductor Nicholas Kraemer. Its flagship concert series is the Bridgewater Hall, it has a special relationship with the RNCM, performing and teaching there, and it performs at festivals and concerts throughout the country and abroad. It also has an extensive educational programme, and has begun making acclaimed recordings.

Northern Chamber Orchestra **0161 247 2220** *www.ncorch.co.uk.* The Northern Chamber Orchestra is now in its 40th season, and performs mainly in smaller venues outside Manchester city centre, in Lancashire, Cheshire and further afield, but is based at Manchester Metropolitan University in Wilmslow Road. It has an impressive series of recordings to its credit.

Principal venues

Bridgewater Hall **5F** (Lower Mosley Street, City. 0161 907 9000. www.bridgewater-hall.co.uk) **Chetham's School of Music** **6A** (Long Millgate, City. 0161 839 9644. www.chethams.com) **Gorton Philharmonic Orchestra** (0161 438 1699. http://myweb.tiscali.co.uk/gortonphil) **The Lowry** (Pier 8, Salford Quays. 0161 876 2000. www.thelowry.com) **Manchester University Department of Music** (Denmark Road, University. 0161 275 4982. www.art.man.ac.uk/MUSIC/home.htm) **Royal Northern College of Music** (Oxford Road, University. 0161 907 5278.www.rncm.ac.uk)

Information on amateur musical societies is available in the NFMS Handbook, published by the National Federation of Music Societies. For North West contacts, log on to *http://mmnwsec.users.btopenworld.com*

ENTERTAINMENT

Theatre

Manchester's formal theatre didn't officially start until the C18, and even then there was some opposition. In 1775, a London debate regarding the opening of a theatre in the town was reported locally in the following terms: 'The Bishop of London opposed the bill for a theatre on the grounds that Manchester was a manufacturing town, and nothing could be more destructive of the political welfare of the place.' In contrast, the Earl of Carlisle happily supported it. Why? Because Manchester had now become a seat of Methodism. 'I know not of any way so effectual to eradicate that dark, odious, and ridiculous enthusiasm,' he said, 'as by giving to the people cheerful, rational amusement, which may operate against their methodistical melancholy.'

The town took this amusement to heart, Methodists or not. A hundred years later and Manchester was way ahead of any other city in the country for its number of theatres and music halls (with the exception of the capital). A key figure in this artistic renaissance was that of Annie Horniman, daughter of a prosperous Victorian tea merchant family, who used her not inconsiderable wealth to subsidise various repertory theatres. One of those was the **Gaiety** on the corner of Peter Street and Mount Street, which she bought and refurbished in 1908: the Library Theatre Company is a direct descendant. Miss Horniman's pioneering efforts in support of the repertory tradition is today honoured by a commemorative plaque in the entrance of Television House, site of the original Gaiety.

Principal theatre venues

Bolton Octagon Theatre Howell Croft South, Bolton. **01204 520661.** *www.octagonbolton.co.uk.* The Octagon has established itself as one of the North West's most exciting production houses, with an impeccable reputation for quality drama The theatre also hosts touring theatre productions and regular Saturday children's theatre shows. The Octagon Education Department runs a popular weekly youth group, activ8, where budding thesps can flex their acting muscles. 2007-08 sees the Octagon's 40th anniversary celebrations.

Bury Met Market Street, Bury. **0161 761 2216.** *www.themet.biz.* This performing arts organisation based in an impressive Victorian building stages everything from comedy nights and gigs to children's, amateur and small-scale touring theatre productions. The Met run regular singing, dancing and acting workshops (call 0161 761 7107 for details). The Met is also one of the only venues to host drama workshops specifically for disabled children.

Buxton Opera House Water Street, Buxton. **01298 72190.** *www.buxton-opera.co.uk.* This old theatre in the beautiful Derbyshire town was recently refurbished. It hosts touring drama productions as well as opera, ballet and occasional live gigs. The Opera House has recently taken over the management of the 100-seat Pauper's Pit, situated in the Old Hall Hotel across the road, where you can catch some interesting fringe theatre.

Contact Theatre Devas Street, off Oxford Road, University. **0161 274 0600.** *www.contact-theatre.org.* This is a flamboyant Gaudi-like castle with steel turrets, spears as supporting struts, and an entrance like the curtain over a proscenium arch. Contact prides itself on being the only building-based theatre in Britain to create work specifically for young people – though there's enough broad appeal to attract audiences of all ages (provided they're open minded). Aside from hosting cutting-edge touring shows and creating their own in-house work, Contact also hosts regular dance, acting and MC-ing workshops. And once a month there's Flip The Script, a playwrighting slam where new writers get to see an extract from their masterpiece performed by professional actors in a live environment. The audience favourite returns the following month.

Green Room 6G **54/56 Whitworth Street West, City. 0161 615 0500.** *www.greenroomarts.org.* Situated underneath a railway arch, this is Manchester's premier experimental performance space. It has an enviable reputation for attracting all kinds of weird and wonderful, sometimes infuriating, international work. There are various one-off nights in the bar, as well as club nights and off-the-wall theatre 'happenings'. The Funday Sunday offers creative play sessions for youngsters, usually followed by a theatre performance. Speakeasy is a popular open mic night, where fledgling performers – including poets, MCs and stand-ups – get the chance to show what they're made of. Artistically speaking, of course.

Instituto Cervantes 3F **326-330 Deansgate, City centre. 0161 661 4200.** The Spanish Cultural Agency promoting events ranging from cinema to classical music and the visual arts. Usually very cheap or free.

Library Theatre 6E **St Peter's Square, City. 0161 236 7110.** *www.librarytheatre.com.* Located in the basement of one of the city's most beautiful buildings, the Library enjoys an outstanding reputation, staging everything from classical and modern drama to comedies and seasonal children's shows. Artistic director Chris Honer believes it's "the play that matters – and the play should be done with coherence and passion".

Lowry **Pier 8, Salford Quays. 0161 876 2000.** *www.thelowry.com).* Often dubbed Salford's Guggenheim, the Lowry is a receiving house of the first order, with two stages, the Lyric and Quays. The Lyric has the largest stage in the provinces and a full orchestra pit. The Lowry has established itself as a major cultural force, hosting classic and modern touring productions. The addition of the Studio has given it a space in which to put on more intimate, experimental work. The outreach team run all manner of dance and drama courses, for children and adults. There are also regular summer schools. For a full description of the building, see page 105.

Oldham Coliseum **Fairbottom Street, Oldham. 0161 624 2829.** *www.coliseum.org.uk.* One of the oldest theatres in the region, the Coliseum can lay claim to helping start the careers of Stan Laurel and Charlie Chaplin – both performed there in the early days of variety. More recently, Minnie Driver and Ralph Fiennes both earned their Equity stripes on the Coliseum stage. The theatre favours a staunchly populist approach to programming, staging a mix of comedies, dramas and pantomimes: the latter so popular that tickets go on sale a full year in advance.

Opera House 3E **Quay Street, City centre 0161 242 2503.** *www.ticketmaster.co.uk.* Drop-off point for glossy West End musicals and comedies, with weekly visits that appeal to coach parties. The Opera House has a slightly faded, but still glamorous, period interior. On opening night you can usually catch a soap star or two mingling in the Circle Bar.

Palace Theatre 6G **Oxford Street, City centre. 0161 228 6255.** *www.ticketmaster.co.uk.* Sister venue to the Opera House, the Palace also hosts big-budget musicals and comedies,

Manchester Opera House

though there's the occasional visit from more highbrow companies like the English National Ballet. The annual panto is the biggest in the North, and usually has a TV star or two in the title role.

Royal Exchange Theatre 5C St Ann's Square, City. 0161 833 9833. *www.royalexchange.co.uk*. Mingling traditional productions with the radical and the extreme, this theatre and its superb company is always worth dropping in on. Its space module performance space sits inside the former headquarters of the cotton industry: look up and around and you'll eventually locate the final stock prices hanging from the ceiling - for a fuller history of the building see pages 70-73. Some of Britain's best and most famous actors have played at the Exchange: Pete Postlethwaite, Helen Mirren, Clive Owen, Amanda Donohoe, Albert Finney, David Threlfall and so on. Refurbished after the Manchester bomb, the Exchange now has an excellent Studio Space, which hosts challenging in-house productions, as well as edgy and experimental touring work.

Waterside Arts Centre Waterside Plaza, Sale. 0161 912 5899. *www.watersideartscentre.co.uk*. An impressive new visual and performing arts centre situated by the side of the Bridgewater Canal. The Waterside offers a broad mix of music, comedy and drama, as well as exhibitions and participatory events.

Royal Exchange Theatre

Comedy

Manchester and Lancashire humour is dry as dust, laced with irony bordering on sarcasm and tinged with madness. The city has a tradition of merry-making that stretches back centuries. The traditional wakes week festivals were a particularly colourful time, with lots of slapstick. Two of the more famous Manchester comedians from the first 70 years of C20 were Will Hay and Jimmy Jewel. Another was the scandalous Frank Randle, notorious for his blue material and bad behaviour. He was banned from various Manchester venues including the Opera House. For revenge, he hired a light aircraft and bombarded the city with toilet rolls. More recently the comic genius of Les Dawson has lit up stage and screen. Some gems of his include: "There is no such thing as unemployment in Manchester, just an ugly rumour by a lot of out of work people" and "we lived so far from the Town Hall, the rent collector was Norwegian". Once on stage in London, Dawson held up a piece of paper, squinted at it, and then asked if the audience could sing 'Happy Birthday' for Gladys who he'd just learned was 111. He played the accompaniment on his piano in his characteristically out of tune fashion until he suddenly broke off. "Sorry," he said with doleful countenance, "I've read the note again. It doesn't say she's 111, it says she's ill." In the same Lancashire tradition of storytelling touched with the surreal, Victoria Wood and Mike Harding have entertained audiences for many years. The other major act from the old school in Manchester has been, oh dear, Bernard Manning.

In the '70s, The Young Ones met at Manchester University. Or rather their alter egos did, in the form of fellow students Rik Mayall, Ade Edmondson and Ben Elton who would write and star in the riotous TV comedy of the '80s.

Then came Steve Coogan and John Thomson. Coogan has proved one of the great comic originals with characters such as Alan Partridge. Both he and Thomson have moved from stand-up to the screen

Frog and Bucket

Ape and Apple

– Thomson most notably with Manchester-based Cold Feet. More recently Caroline Aherne, Johnny Vegas and Peter Kay have created huge reputations for themselves both on stage and screen. Bolton's Peter Kay, in particular, following his TV show *Phoenix Nights*, has prospered becoming the biggest box office hit in comedy. So where do you go to see the TV faces of tomorrow on a regular basis? In the city centre, the Frog and Bucket was, for some years, the city's only full-time comedy venue. The Barrel of Laughs nights on Friday and Saturday still play host to a mix of local and touring acts.

After more than 20 years of deliberation, Comedy Store owner Don Ward finally opened the doors of his only other club outside London in September 2000 on Deansgate Locks. The club's opening boosted an already vibrant scene and it quickly established itself as a key player nationally, not only in the North, especially with its co-ordination of the Manchester Comedy Festival in autumn every year. They were joined soon after by other big players Jongleurs and more recently Opus in the Printworks. Though Jongleurs closed in 2006 they are expected to re open in an another venue in 2007.

Elsewhere smaller comedy nights seem to pop up every week yet often fail the next. Toby Hadoke's Malarkey's night, at Bar XS in Fallowfield, is a rare example of nights that have succeeded. A renewed interest in the suburbs also seems underway, with venues such as Mirth on Monday at Chorlton's Iguana Bar establishing themselves on the circuit and showing ambition to grab a slice of the scene.

Comedy venues

Ape and Apple 5D (John Dalton Street, City. 0161 839 9624) **Apollo** (Stockport Road, Ardwick Green. 0161 242 2560) **Bridgewater Hall 5F** (Lower Mosley Street, City. 0161 907 9000) **Bolton Octagon** (Howell Croft South, Bolton. 01204 520661) **Bury Met Arts Centre** (Market Street, Bury. 0161 761 2216) **Comedy Store 5G** (Deansgate Locks, Whitworth Street West, City. 08705 932932) **Contact Theatre** (Devas Street, off Oxford Road, University. 0161 274 3434) **Dancehouse** (Oxford Road, City. 0161 237 9753) **Frog & Bucket 9B** (Oldham Street, City. 0161 236 9805) **Green Room 6G** (Whitworth Street West, City. 0161 615 0500) **Iguana Bar** (Manchester Road, Chorlton. 0161 881 9805) **Lowry** (Pier 8, Salford Quays. 0161 876 2000) **MEN Arena 6A** (Victoria Station, Hunts Bank, City. 0870 190 8000) **Opera House 3E** (Quay Street, City. 0161 242 2525) **Opus 7B** (Printworks, Withy Grove, City Centre. 0161 834 2414) **Palace Theatre 7G** (Oxford Street, City. 0161 228 6255) **Tameside Hippodrome** (Oldham Road, Ashton-under-Lyne. 0161 236 6071) **Waterside Arts Centre** (Waterside Plaza, Sale. 0161 912 5616) **XSMalarkey** (Bar XS, Wilmslow Road, Fallowfield. 0161 257 2403).

Cinema and TV

The most luxurious cinema in Manchester has to be Odeon Manchester, a 20-screen, 40,000sq ft family entertainment centre, also home to the largest IMAX cinema in the UK. Here you have the option to upgrade into the Gallery with its leather seating and private bar. All the multiplexes run weekend lates, starting between 11pm and midnight. Films during the day tend to start from 11.30am, with last showings around 9.30pm or later, although many suburban cinemas show films in the evening only. Cheaper seats can often be found before 4pm or on Mondays. Nearly all the cinemas in Greater Manchester run weekend matinees, usually aimed at children. Most preview new films on Thursday evenings and several of the larger multiplexes show niche market films and/or re-issues regularly.

Coronation Street

The most enduring Mancunian TV landmark has undoubtedly been Coronation Street – produced by Granada TV. This has been a British institution almost from its inception in 1960 and is now the longest running soap opera in world television history. You can tune into this homely tale of the day to day life of Northern folk on four nights a week from 7.30pm. Careful, though: after giggling at the first two episodes you might get hooked. Up to a third of the UK's 58m population tune in to the crisis episodes. The Street is popular in other countries – when the New Zealand government tried to move the scheduling of the programme some years ago, the resulting protest nearly brought it down. If you want a sneaky look at the set, take a trip down to the free Museum of Science and Industry, buzz up to the second floor Xperiment! and look out of the window. The set is directly below you.

Cornerhouse, a cinema-cum-art-gallery opened in 1985, is the place to go for an excellent selection of current and re-issued art house films. This is also the place to see the more specialised British films, and foreign language movies. There are regular talks with visiting film directors and educational courses too. As the major art house cinema, it stages a number of major films festivals every year, with the !Viva! Spanish Film Festival and Mavericks in Manchester: Festival of Americian Independent Film being particularly popular.

Manchester is also home to the Manchester and Salford Film Society, perhaps the world's oldest film society, whilst Kino, which presents screening in pubs, cafes and other out of the way venues, is the area's major avant-garde film club. It features the best of underground and new cinema through annual events like the Kino Festival of New Irish Cinema and the Kino Short Film Festival.

The city hosts a large UK independent TV company, Granada TV, which produces Coronation Street - see panel. It has the largest regional centre for the BBC in England too, with plans for many departments to head north from London in 2010.

Manchester has been in the movies on many occasions, often disguising its eclectic urban scenery as somewhere else. The city and its satellites have been, amongst others, St Petersburg, Moscow, Hong Kong, New York, London and Shanghai. Many dramas

***Hell is a City* being filmed in 1959**

on TV and film have used the Town Hall as a body double for any large civic Gothic building. Movies filmed or part filmed in the area include Tony Richardson's *A Taste of Honey*, David Lean's *Hobson's Choice*, Val Guest's *Hell is a City*, Albert Finney's *Charlie Bubbles*, Warren Beatty's *Reds*, Stephen Spielberg's *Empire of the Sun*, John Schlesinger's *Yanks*, Louis Malle's *Damage*, Jim Sheridan's *In the Name of the Father* and Damien O'Donnell's *East is East*. More recently, the city was host to the *Alfie* remake starring Jude Law.

TV dramas have included (deep breath) *Sherlock Holmes, Cracker, Prime Suspect, Brideshead Revisited, Moll Flanders, First Amongst Equals, Gold, Painted Lady, Cold Feet, Queer as Folk, Pride and Prejudice, The Royle Family, City Central, Cops, Clocking Off, Bob and Rose, Linda Green, Cutting It, Second Coming, State of Play* and *Shamelees*. Unsurprisingly the city has had its own Film Office since 1995. Other shows filmed in Manchester have included *A Question of Sport, Stars in Your Eyes* and *You've Been Framed*.

Manchester also plays host to several TV production companies, the most celebrated of which is Nicola Schindler's Red Productions, responsible for several of the above dramas, such as *Queer as Folk*. Red was a pioneer of what could almost be classed as a new realism in drama, an echo perhaps of *A Taste of Honey* which was penned by local writer Shelagh Delaney. These new dramas depict tough, working-class life relieved by rough humour. Notable exponents are the locally based Russell T Davies and Debbie Horsfield. Another local writer who has achieved national fame is Paul Abbott with his brutal but hilarious sitcom about council estate life, *Shameless* (he also wrote *State of Play*).

Salfordian actor Christopher Eccleston in 2005 reinforced his reputation with his role as The Doctor in the BBC's *Doctor Who* (the main scriptwriter of which was Russell T Davies), before deciding to quit after a single series, worried that he might be typecast. But the biggest Manchester-based hit of recent years has been *Life on Mars*, with John Simms and Philip Glenister combining perfectly in a rollicking and nostalgic 1970s cop show.

Casinos and lap dancing

For those who've over-dosed on all the culture Manchester has to offer and are looking for something a little more lowbrow there are plenty more options. The big news is that the new super casino is coming this way. It will be situated in Eastlands, near the Manchester City ground (giving rise to some terrible jokes about crap games). Until this slice of Vegas arrives on our doorstep there is the newly opened and very good-looking, Casino 235 **7E** (Great Northern Warehouse, Watson Street. 0161 828 0300.) which also has a couple of restaurants. Another gambling option is the Grosvenor casinos **7G** and **7E** (Whitworth Street and 35-39 George Street. 0161 236 7121). For those who like their thrills a little more visual, so to speak, there are 'gentlemen's clubs' such as Boutique **5E** (18-22 Lloyd Street 0161 832 8005), Ruby Lounge **7C** (28-34 High Street) and Long Legs **7E** (46, George St 0161 237 3977). We neither condone nor condemn this entertainment but remind revellers everywhere to enjoy Manchester's earthly delights with moderation and decorum. If you feel driven by demons to attempt karaoke, a good place is the Orchid Lounge Bar **7E** (Portland Street, City centre. 0161 236 4773), where you can worry the vocal cords in either English or Cantonese.

Some Greater Manchester cinemas

AMC Cinemas 4F (Great Northern, Deansgate, City. 08707 555657)
Cornerhouse 7G (Oxford Street, City. 0161 200 1500. www.conerhouse.org)
Odeon Manchester 7B (Printworks, Withy Grove, City. 08700 102030. http://thefilmworks.co.uk) **The Plaza** (Mersey Square, stockport. 0161 477 7779. www.stockportplaza.co.uk) is a splendid Art Deco building from the 1930s. It provides classic movie nights, live stage shows, musicals, stand-up comedy and dance performances. There's even an organ. Positioned on a lift, the instrument rises out of the floor and can be played before shows, during silent movies, variety acts and musical interludes between films..

ENTERTAINMENT

Literature

Considering Manchester's heritage, it comes as no surprise to learn that the city's literary history was shaped by themes of class and social justice in works often as trail-blazing as the industry which provoked them.

In 1844 Friedrich Engels was inspired to write his seminal work *The Condition of the Working Class in England* following a visit to Manchester. The same division between rich and poor went onto inspire enduring works of Victorian fiction, most famously those of Elizabeth Gaskell (see page 21), but also that of Mrs G Linnaeus Banks whose 1876 novel *The Manchester Man* laments the loss of the pre-industrial age.

If industry altered the landscape, half a century later it was the decline of this industry which was to give rise to another controversial work, Walter Greenwood's 1933 social-realist novel *Love on the Dole,* which described the bleak lives of a poor brother and sister in Salford. This setting was revisited, in Shelagh Delaney's 1959 'kitchen-sink drama', *A Taste of Honey.*

By the second half of the C20, it was the turn of Manchester's most famous literary son, Anthony Burgess, to turn an impoverished background into a catalyst for great literature. Author of over 30 novels including *A Clockwork Orange,* Burgess's historical novel, *Any Old Iron,* is set partly in the city and the first of his two-volume autobiography, *Little Wilson and Big God,* is all about growing up here. In 2004 a study centre and archive, the International Anthony Burgess Foundation, was established in Withington.

In 1821 Thomas de Quincey recollected his Manchester childhood in the chronicle of ecstasy and torment, *Confessions of an English Opium Eater.* Since then, numerous Manchester writers have drawn on their beginnings, from Andrea Ashworth's harrowing memoir of poverty and violence, *Once in a House on Fire* to Carol Birch's East Manchester epic, *Turn Again Home* and Joe Pemberton's tale of 1960s Moss Side, *Forever and Ever Amen,* to Howard Jacobson's *The Mighty Waltzer,* a humorous account of a Jewish child in '50s Manchester.

Manchester's contemporary fiction scene could be said to be dominated by crime, with a trio of female writers finding success in evoking the shadier side of the city: Mandasue Heller, Val McDermid and Cath Staincliffe. Manchester's contemporary children's writers include Melvin Burgess, author of teenage shock-lit *Junk, Lady* and *Doing It,* and Adele Geras, who has written over 80 children's books and whose bestselling novel for adults, *Facing the Light,* has seen her leading an Aga-saga revival.

Alan Garner's *Weirdstone of Brisingamen* and *Elidor* are children's adventures set in the area from the 1960s. Two children's classics from even earlier are *101 Dalmatians* and *The Secret Garden,* which were penned by Manchester writers Dodie Smith and Frances Hodgson Burnett, respectively.

Manchester poets include the Salford-born David Constantine and Sophie Hannah, Adele Geras's daughter. Then there's punk poet John Cooper Clarke, Lemn Sissay and his clever wordplay and award winning poets and adopted Mancunians Jackie Kay and Carol Ann Duffy. Manchester is also home to the poetry publisher Carcanet Press and a branch of The Poetry School.

Manchester Literary Festival takes place in October and brings together national and international talent with the best home-grown writers. Manchester is also home to two highly-regarded Creative Writing schools; those of MMU and Manchester University. British novelist Martin Amis is joing the staff of the lattter in their Centre for New Writing, in September 2007.

Some venues and organisations

International Anthony Burgess Foundation (Tatton Grove, Withington. 0161 434 1748. www.anthonyburgess.org) **Commonword 5E** (Friends Meeting House, Mount Street, City. 0161 832 3777) Non profit writing and publishing organisation. **Manchester Poets** (0161 429 6385) **Poetry School** (Manchester. www.poetryschool.com, linda@poetryschool.com) **www.literaturenorthwest.co.uk** – updates on the region's indie presses and literature events.

Ryan Giggs of Manchester United shows off his skills for the next generation

Sport

Manchester has long been obsessed by sport, which means there is lots of sport to watch and do in and around the city. This section gives you an idea of just how much.

If London is the nation's political capital, then Manchester can lay a strong claim to being England's sporting stronghold. The jewel in the crown is the world famous football club Manchester United, but Manchester City, Bolton and Wigan complete an impressive representation in top-flight football. Sale Sharks and Lancashire are right at the top of their respective sports of rugby union and cricket, while Salford and Wigan compete in rugby league's Super League. If you add boxer Ricky Hatton into the mix, then you're left with an impressive sporting landscape. Such excellence on the professional field inevitably feeds down to grass roots level where there is lots of activity across a wide range of sports.

The city has also been important in the development of sport. For instance it was at the Royal Hotel in 1888 that the world's first professional football league was formed. The city has also played an important role in sports such as cycling, skating, horse racing, dog racing and cricket. Mancunian William Marsden played a crucial part in this with his campaigns for a half-day holiday for workers on Saturdays. This was achieved by 1843 and with their newly released spare time the working class embraced leisure activities with a passion. At the same time an increasingly mannered middle-class hit on the idea of codifying sports in order to prevent the drunken chaos of earlier sporting activity. The result was that the formally organised sport we recognise today was developed in Britain well before other countries. This could easily be exported which is why much of the world plays football, cricket, rugby, golf and so on.

2007/8 also sees the centenary of the Professional Footballers Association - the footballer's union - based in Manchester. It is only appropriate that it is based here. It was a successful strike by the whole Manchester United team in 1909 which emphasised the need for such a organisation.

Ice Wall at North Face in the city centre

Football

If you want to see a local match, please remember, fixtures are sometimes altered or made all-ticket at short notice and membership may be required. Full listings can be found on the Manchester Evening News website, www.manchestereveningnews.co.uk.

Getting tickets for Premier League matches is difficult at United. If you're from abroad then you might try in your own country of origin, otherwise unless you know a season ticket holder who isn't going then you only have the steep prices of the touts to fall back on. Tickets for some European, FA Cup and Carling Cup matches go on open sale, check the website or call ahead for details.

Tickets for most Manchester City matches can be bought on the day from the ticket office at the ground – the stadium will usually have around 40,000 rather than the 48,000 capacity – ring ahead to check. Tickets for games against United are usually sold out, so if you want to go book ahead very early.

If you can't get to United or City then football fans staying in the city region should seriously consider the short hop to Bolton Wanderers or Wigan Athletic, the region's other Premiership teams. Both are easy to get to on the train from Manchester. However, don't despair if you can't get to a Premier League match. Oldham Athletic (who play at Boundary Park), Bury (Gigg Lane), Rochdale (Spotland), Stockport County (Edgeley Park) and Macclesfield Town (Moss Rose) all play in the Coca-Cola League and are within easy reach of the city. A new addition to the region's footballing scene is rebel club FC United, which was formed by disillusioned Manchester United fans after the takeover of the illustrious Old Trafford club. FC United clinched promotion in their first season, regularly attracting crowds in excess of 3,000, and contested the North West Counties Division One in the 2006/2007 season. They play at Gigg Lane. The good thing about the smaller clubs is that they take you to the heart of grass roots football where you can get misty-eyed about the old days before commercialisation dominated the sport. Most of the lower league clubs have very reasonable ticket prices and great deals for families. The football season runs from August to May.

The bronze statue of **Sir Matt Busby** watches over fans as they enter Old Trafford – the man who made Manchester United a world famous name >

Manchester United

Sir Matt Busby Way, Old Trafford 0870 4421994 *www.manutd.com* ***Tickets from £23 adults, £11.50 children, but see football introduction above.***

To say Manchester United is a globally famous football club doesn't do anymore. You have to talk in superlatives. It has the biggest national membership of any sporting institution in the world, over 140,000, it has the largest number of overseas fan clubs with the largest number of members in these fan clubs. Despite the controversial takeover of the club by American business tycoon Malcolm Glazer in 2005, United are still the most profitable club in world football.

But why? As is the way with the world the germ of the popularity and success lies in tragedy. When several Busby Babes (see panel next page) died so cruelly in the Munich disaster, they acquired the sort of fame that only the deaths of the young attract. Thus United gained a similar glamour as Marilyn Monroe and James Dean would in later years. Then of course there is the playing style – traditionally 100mph football allied to skill and verve. These days, stars from home and abroad such as Wayne Rooney and Cristiano Ronaldo are major draws. The history and the style, allied to success on the field (especially in the nineties as European football gained global appeal), accounts for the appeal.

To cater for demand Old Trafford's capacity has been extended to just over 76,000 making it easily the biggest club ground in the UK.

Museum and Tour

Open: 9am-5pm - closes 30 mins before kick-off on match days. Tours every day 9.40am-4.30pm except match days. Always book ahead to avoid disappointment. ***Museum only: adults £6,*** *children £4.25, family £17.50. Museum and tour: adults £9.50, children £6.50, family £27.*

The purpose-built museum has it all including a movingly told Munich disaster exhibition and a heady celebration of the Treble triumph in 1999. There's state-of-the-art technology, including a call-up system that allows kids and grown-ups to replay favourite goals, commentate on a match and test their United knowledge – you can even test the power of your foot by whacking a ball into a net. The museum is fine in its own right but the tour gives the real value. You visit the changing rooms and the players' lounge but for many, the highlight is walking down the tunnel to the pitch side to get a player's eye view of the stands. *Toilets, parking, food and drink, shop, schools and group visits, pram and disabled access.*

Honours

League & Premiership championship: **winners 1908, 1911, 1952, 1956, 1957, 1965, 1967, 1993, 1994, 1996, 1997, 1999, 2000, 2001, 2003**
FA Cup: **winners 1909, 1948, 1963, 1977, 1983, 1985, 1990, 1994, 1996, 1999, 2004**
League Cup: **winners 1992, 2006**
European Competitions: **European Cup winners 1968, 1999, Cup Winners' Cup winners 1991, European Super Cup winners 1991**

Party like it's 1999

This was a defining year for the club. Two new arrivals would help the campaign, Jaap Stam from PSV Eindhoven and Dwight Yorke from Aston Villa. A dramatic season from start to finish included United scoring twice at the end of the game to beat Liverpool 2-1 in the fifth round of the FA Cup: an epic European Cup quarter final victory home and away against Inter Milan: a simply breathtaking FA Cup semi-final replay against Arsenal crowned by Ryan Giggs, who ran and weaved and then whacked the ball into the net: a European Cup semi-final against Juventus when United came from two goals down to win 3-2: followed by a last game defeat of Tottenham to win the Premiership and a shrugging aside of Newcastle to collect the

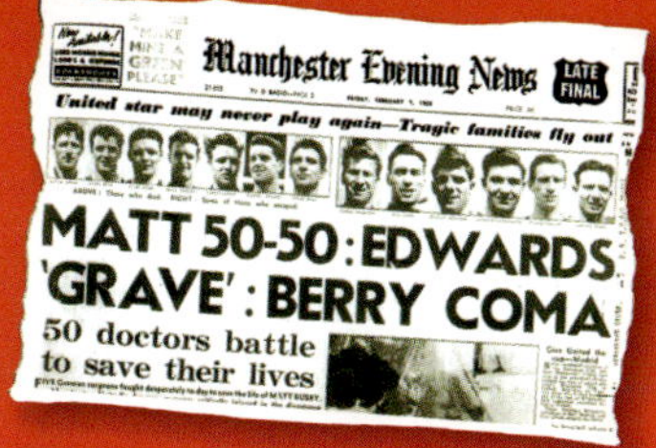
Manchester Evening News LATE FINAL

United star may never play again—Tragic families fly out

MATT 50-50: EDWARDS 'GRAVE': BERRY COMA

50 doctors battle to save their lives

Busby Babes and the Munich Disaster

In 1951 two young players turned out for United against Liverpool, Roger Byrne and Jackie Blanchflower. The Manchester Evening News ran the headline 'United's Babes, Cool, Confident' and the term Busby Babes was born. More youngsters joined the first team in 1953 including Duncan Edwards, who debuted at age 16. After winning the First Division title for a second time the Babes, against the advice of the Football League, became the first English team to enter the European Cup. The first ties proved comfortable. But against Athletico Bilbao in the quarter-finals United lost 53 away. The return was at Manchester City's Maine Road ground - City had floodlights and United didn't - in front of 70,000 fans. One journalist described the event as the greatest match with the greatest crowd and the greatest centre forward he had ever seen. United won 3-0 with Tommy Taylor outstanding. United were on win bonuses of £3, the Bilbao players would have received win bonuses of £200 each. The European Cup dream ended against the mighty Real Madrid in the semi-finals but at least United won the league title again. In 1958 United played well in Europe once more and reached the semi-final of the European Cup with a win over two legs against Red Star Belgrade. Then disaster struck.

On 6 February 1958, the BEA plane carrying the team back from the Red Star Belgrade game stopped for refuelling in Munich. In an attempt to take off again, the aircraft slewed over the end of the runway and crashed into a house, a tree and a cabin. In all the final death toll would be 23 including nine players: Roger Byrne, Tommy Taylor and Duncan Edwards amongst them. The other victims included some of the most prominent sports writers of their time, such as Frank Swift and Eric Thompson, and several club officials. The whole country, and many around the world, mourned the loss of this elegant young team.

SPORT

United timeline

1878 Newton Heath Lancashire and Yorkshire Railway Football and Cricket Club founded.
1892 Promoted to the First Division of the football league.
1902 The name Manchester United adopted.
1908 United are crowned First Division champions for the first time, they also win the Charity Shield.
1909 The team beats Bristol City 1-0 to win the FA Cup.United strike.
1910 The club move to Old Trafford.
1911 First Division title won again.
1922 United relegated.
1926 United promoted back to the First Division
1931 The club is relegated again and for the first match of the following season attract only 3,507 fans to Old Trafford.
1936 United promoted to the First Division.
1937 Relegation once more.
1938 Promoted back up again.
1941 Old Trafford bombed during a Nazi attack on Trafford Park.
1945 Company Sergeant Major Matthew Busby becomes manager.
1948 United set the record (still existing) for the highest ever English league attendance of 83,260 against Arsenal in 1948, the match was played at Manchester City's Maine Road stadium because of the bomb damage at Old Trafford.
1948 United win the FA Cup against Blackpool.
1951 Age of 'Busby Babes' begins and the First Division title is won.
1952 Title won again, Charity Shield won.
1956 United win the First Division title, enter the European Cup and reach the semi-finals.
1958 The Munich Disaster (see previous page)
1963 With the famous team of Bobby Charlton, Denis Law and George Best now united the team win the FA Cup 3-1 against Leicester.
1965 First Division won.
1967 First Division won again.
1968 The European Cup won 4-1, at Wembley, against Benfica. United become the first English team to win the trophy.
1969 Matt Busby steps down.
1973 George Best leaves the club.
1974 United relegated to the Second Division, helped on their way by a Denis Law backheel playing for Manchester City.
1975 United promoted back to the First Division with Tommy Docherty in charge.
1976 United lose FA Cup final to Southampton.
1977 United beat Liverpool 2-1 in the FA Cup final.
1979 The famous three minute FA Cup final- United lose 3-2 to Arsenal in the last minute after scoring twice to equalise in the 86th and 88th minutes.
1981 Ron Atkinson is appointed manager.
1983 Bryan Robson becomes the most expensive British player (£1.5m). United beat Brighton, after a reply, in the FA Cup final. Earlier in the season they had lost to Liverpool in the League Cup final.
1985 United beat Everton 1-0 in the FA Cup final.
1986 Alex Ferguson becomes manager.
1990 FA Cup final triumph against Crystal Palace in a reply saves Ferguson's job.
1991 United win the Cup Winner's Cup against Barcelona, 2-1.
1992 Nottingham Forest defeated in the League Cup Final. Peter Schmeichel, the best goalkeeper in United's history, arrives.
1993 After 26 years United win the title – the inaugural Premiership title, galvanised by the arrival of Frenchman Eric Cantona for whom the word maverick seemed to have been invented.
1994 United win the double – Premiership and FA Cup - beating Chelsea in the final 4-0. Sir Matt Busby dies.
1996 The year of 'the Fergie Fledglings' and another double, this time beating arch-rivals Liverpool 1-0. This was the famous team of kids, as Ferguson's youth policy blossomed with the arrival in the regular first team of Gary and Phil Neville, David Beckham, Paul Scholes and Nicky Butt to join the already established Ryan Giggs.
1997 The Premiership won again, Cantona

▲ **Manchester United** the Busby Babes

leaves.
1999. The team win the treble, Premiership, FA Cup final, European Cup in the most dramatic season of the club's long history.
2000 United win the World Club Trophy in Japan and retain the Premiership.
2001 With a third title in a row the club land a treble of titles.
2002 Rio Ferdinand becomes the most expensive British player at £30m when he signs for United.
2003 United grab the Premiership crown once more as Arsenal collapse in the final weeks of the season.
2004 United beat Millwall 4-0 in the FA Cup. Supporters demonstrate fan power by protesting against proposed takeover by American businessman Malcolm Glazer.
2005 A disappointing season, apart from the signing of exciting young England forward, Wayne Rooney, ends with losing the FA Cup Final to Arsenal. United legend George Best dies in hospital, aged 59, after multiple organ failure. The charismatic winger, one of the most naturally gifted footballers the world has seen, fought a long battle with alcoholism and finally died on November 25. The American Glazer family take over. From a club which was happily solvent United become a club £790m in debt. Many fans throw away their season tickets and set up FC United.
2006 United win the League Cup, thrashing Wigan 4-0 in the final. The Reds sign Michael Carrick from Tottenham for £18m in a bid to solve their midfield troubles. The deal underwhelmed many fans at the time, but it proved to be another astute signing by Ferguson.
2007 Spurred on by the brilliance of Rooney, Paul Scholes and Ronaldo United head the Premier League table at the start of 2007 playing fast, exciting football.

Wayne Rooney ➤

▲ **Manchester United's** Treble parade on the open top bus, Deansgate, 1999

could beat Bayern Munich in Barcelona, they could win an unprecedented Treble. Munich scored in the first half and completely dominated the match but United had scored in every European match since the league stages. In the final minute David Beckham sprinted to take a corner. He had just seen the European Cup being decked with Munich's colours. His corner floated in, bobbled around with Munich's defence distracted by the presence of the huge United keeper Peter Schmeichel. It went out to the wing and came back to the centre where it was mis-kicked by Giggs and shinned into the net by Sheringham. A minute later, in time added on at the end of the game, Ole Gunnar Solskjaer chased a lost cause and won another corner. Beckham's cross was flicked on by Sheringham and poked into the roof of the net by Solskjaer. It was effectively the last kick of the match. The treble had been won with the most dramatic turnaround in a major footballing final. The red half of the city went wild again, with parties in the streets and dancing in the fountains. When United returned to the city they were greeted by half a million supporters lining the route of their cavalcade.

SPORT

City timeline

1880 Manchester City enter the world as a church club, St Mark's of West Gorton, subsequently they become Gorton playing at the charmingly named Pink Bank Lane.
1887 The name Ardwick FC is adopted.
1892 Ardwick enter Division Two.
1893 The club goes bankrupt but re-emerges as Manchester City.
1899 City promoted to Division One.
1904 The club wins the FA Cup 1-0 against Bolton.
1905 Billy Meredith, who would also play for United, is suspended for allegedly attempting to bribe an Aston Villa player. Eventually 17 players and two directors suspended from club activity for seven months.
1923 The club moves to Maine Road, Moss Side.
1926 City meet Bolton again in the FA Cup final but lose 1-0 and are also relegated.
1929 City promoted to the First Division.
1933 City lose again in FA Cup final to Everton, 3-0. Against Everton the players had worn numbered shirts for the first time in a final, oddly from 1-22 across both teams.
1934 City reach FA Cup final again and this time beat Portsmouth 2-1.
1937 Under Wilf Wild the club wins its first Division One championship.
1938 City relegated - after scoring more goals than other team including the Champions Arsenal, an exciting season for those who love goals.
1947 Promoted to the First Division again.
1955 City lose the FA Cup final to Newcastle United 3-1.
1956 City win FA Cup final against Birmingham City 3-1 with City's German goalkeeper and an ex-prisoner of war, Bert Trautmann, playing the last 15 minutes with a broken neck.
1968 Another First Division championship arrives in what is considered the Golden Age of Manchester City with players in the next few seasons including Mike Doyle, Colin Bell, Francis Lee, Tony Book and Tony Coleman.
1969 City win the FA Cup final against Leicester 1-0.
1970 A European Cup Winners Cup arrives at Maine Road in 1970 courtesy of a 2-1 victory against Gornik Zabrize of Poland.
1976 The last major honour of the club is collected in the League Cup final when City beat Newcastle United 2-1.
1981 City defeated by Tottenham Hotspur in a replayed FA Cup final.
1983 Relegated to Division Two.
1985 Return to Division One.
1987 Back down again.
1989 Up again.
1996 Down again. The season includes the shortest appointment in City's team management history when Steve Coppell, appointed in October, quits after 32 days citing health problems.
1998 The unthinkable happens and City slip into the third tier of English football for the first time in their history - as neighbours United secure the Premiership title yet again. On the first day of the new season in the Second Division, City's home attendance was equal to that of all the other clubs playing in the same division that day, a token of how far they had fallen.
1999 With Joe Royle at the helm City win an incredible play-off at Wembley against Gillingham – coming back from two goals down in the dying minutes - to climb back to the First Division.
2000 After another tense final game of the season City are promoted back into the Premier League.
2001 Relegation once more.
2002 With Kevin Keegan taking charge, City are promoted again.
2003 City take leave of Maine Road and move back towards their roots in east Manchester as they take possession of the 48,000 City of Manchester Stadium, the former home of the Commonwealth Games.
2005 Stuart Pearce takes over as temporary manager from a weary Keegan.
2006 With Pearce installed as City's permanent manager, the Blues started the season brightly. However, after an FA Cup quarter-final exit against West Ham their season fizzles out to leave fans with that familiar feeling of frustration. The arrival of Micah Richards as a first team player gives some cause for hope.
2007 City's trademark inconsistency dogged them again as they swung between dreams of Europe and the threat of relegation. In January Pearce was appointed temporary boss of England's Under 21 side, angering many fans who thought his focus should be fully on the Blues.

Manchester City Football Club

City of Manchester Stadium (see picture page 246), Eastlands, Manchester 0870 0621894 *www.mcfc.co.uk*

Tickets from £21 adults, £11 children, see football introduction above.

If you studied a graph of the development of Manchester City it would resemble a particularly alarming medical chart - peaks of rude health interspersed with troughs so deep you could get lost in them. Indeed the wearisome epithet of 'long-suffering' could almost be adopted as the club slogan. However it should be remembered that for much of the two Manchester clubs' existence, City were the equal of United in prestige, certainly until the late 1970s.

The fans are rightly famous for their humour. Every season has a new chant but the most bizarre in the long story of the English game is City's existentialist chant when the team is either performing very well or very badly of, 'We're not really here.'

The Manchester City Experience

Adults £8.75, children £4.75 - price includes City Experience and Stadium Tour.

All visits must be pre-booked.

Award-winning museum and tour dedicated to the ups and downs of the club. There's a broad selection of memorabilia and exhibitions tracing the history of City from its humble origins to its present Premiership rollercoasting. Key players and individuals are described. You can commentate on City goals and relive favourite moments on the video jukebox. As with the United museum and tour, the best part of all is the behind-the-scenes walk of the beautiful City of Manchester Stadium, including the players' tunnel, dug-outs and one of the executive lounges.

Toilets, parking, food and drink, shop, schools and group visits, pram and disabled access.

Honours

Division One Champions: 1937, 1968
FA Cup: winners 1904, 1934, 1956, 1969
Football League Cup: winners 1970, 1976
European Competition: European Cup Winners' Cup winners 1970

Blue Moon

You can say many things about Manchester City, but you cannot accuse the club of being dull. Ever since its inception in Gorton in 1880, the Blues have put their followers through a host of highs and lows. A perfect example of the club's mercurial spirit is the two seasons spanning 1936-1938. In the first of those campaigns, City won the First Division for the first time in their history. A year later they were relegated, despite scoring more goals than anyone else in the top flight. The Blues were then involved in one of the most memorable FA Cup finals of all time in 1956. They beat Birmingham 3-1 in the final, but the game was remarkable because City's goalkeeper Bert Trautmann played on after breaking his neck. The club's golden era came in the late 60s when the likes of Mike Summerbee and Colin Bell were in full flight, but latterly the club has fallen under the shadow of Manchester United. With no trophies to speak of in the last three decades, Blues fans have had to turn to alternative methods to attract attention. In the late eighties the club started a craze which culminated in thousands of inflatable bananas being brought along to games by City fans – a bizarre and hilarious sight that reflected the heart and spirit of the club.

Other Greater Manchester Clubs

Premiership: Bolton Wanderers *(Reebok Stadium, Burnden Way, Lostock, Bolton. 01204 673673. www.bwfc.co.uk)*. Bolton has a museum and tour and is another Premiership option in Greater Manchester. Under manager Sam Allardyce the club has become a respected and admired team in the Premiership punching well above its weight. ***Tickets from £21 adults, £10 children.***

Wigan Athletic *(JJB Stadium, Wigan. 01942-774000. www.wiganlatics.co.uk)*. Wigan were the surprise package of the 2005/2006 season under the guidance of manager Paul Jewell, but have struggled in their second season of top-flight football. Wigan is primarily a rugby area, however, so just to be in the Premiership has been an achievement for them. The good news is that tickets are very easy to get hold. ***Tickets from £15 adults, £10 children.***

League One: Oldham Athletic *(Boundary Park, Sheepfoot Lane, Oldham. 0161- 624 4972. www.oldhamathletic.co.uk)*. ***Tickets from £14 adults, £3 children.***

League Two: Stockport County *(Edgeley Park, Hardcastle Road, Edgeley, Stockport. 0161-286 8888. www.stockportcounty.com)*. ***Tickets from £16 adults, £5 children.***

Bury *(Gigg Lane, Bury. 0161-764 4881. www.buryfc.co.uk)*. ***Tickets from £14 adults, £7 children.*** **Rochdale** *(Spotland, Wilbutts Lane, Rochdale. 01706 644648. www.rochdaleafc.co.uk)*. ***Tickets from £11 adults, £3 children, but under sevens can get in free to the Family Stand.*** **FC United** *(Gigg Lane, Bury, 0870 626 0295. www.fc-utd.co.uk)*. Ok, it's way down the league pyramid but this rebel club has a singular history which seems part of the radical Manchester tradition. And it has also captured a large and enthusiastic following who sing their hearts out every game.

Five-aside football

Have a match yourself at **JJB Soccer Dome** *(Trafford Way, Trafford Park. 0161 772 7400 www.jjbsoccerdome.co.uk)*. Splendid, mostly indoor, artificial pitches. ***Saturdays, £38 indoor, £30 outdoor. Week and Sundays (before 5.00pm) £38 inside, £30 outdoor; (after 5.00pm) £52 indoor, £42 outdoor.*** **Power League** *(Union Street, Ardwick. 0161 272 7227. www.powerleague.co.uk)*. The closest pitches to the city centre. ***Outdoor floodlit pitches, Mon-Thu £24.50 per hour before 4pm, £49.50 per hour after 4pm; Fri-Sun £27 per hour.*** There's also the new **Soccer Zone Arena** *(Roman Road, Hollinwood, Oldham, OL8 3PT 01617646768, www.soccerzoneuk.com)*. ***£35 at peak times (7pm-10pm) and £27 off peak.***

Cricket

Cricket has been to the English what bullfighting is to the Spanish - without so much blood. It is a sport the joys of which are an unfathomable mystery to the citizenry of non-playing nations.

The most important matches are the internationals, or 'Tests', that can, theoretically, last from 10.30am until 5.30pm over five days and still finish in a draw. The season runs from April to September. For cricket novices the one-day games are recommended especially the dramatic day/night matches and the Twenty20 games that last less than three hours. Tickets for **Lancashire Cricket Club** are always available.

Cricket also has an arcane language

< **Bolton Wanderers'** Kevin Nolan (right) celebrates a goal, with team mates Andranik Teymourian (top) and Nicolas Anelka (left), during a Barclays Premiership match at the Reebok Stadium, Bolton

Lancashire timeline

1816 Lancashire Cricket Club enters the world named 'Aurora', in Salford.
1832 The team changes its name to Manchester Cricket Club and moves to Hulme.
1846 Manchester (with 18 players) take on an All England XI and lose.
1847 The All England XI visit again and on the point of defeat abandon the match – see 'Not Cricket' next page.
1857 Manchester moves to Old Trafford.
1864 Lancashire Cricket Club founded. Old Trafford becomes their home.
1878 Australia play Lancashire.
1880 The Lancashire and Manchester Clubs formally merge.
1881 The team wins first undisputed championship.
1895 A.C.Maclaren makes 424 against Somerset – still Lancashire's highest ever score.
1898 Victor Trumper playing for Australia against England scores a century before lunch at Old Trafford.
1926-1930 Lancashire win four out of five Championships.
1950-1968 Brian Statham becomes a Lancashire hero taking a county record, of 1816 wickets - plus 252 Test wickets.
1956 The 'Laker Match' - England bowler Jim Laker takes 19 Australian wickets in a single test match.
1971 The Gillette Cup semi-final in 1971 has an incredible finish with David Hughes hitting 24 in the final over to win the match for Lancashire. The early seventies were a period of one day glory for Lancashire led by West Indian captain, Clive Lloyd.
1990 Lancashire becomes the first club to win both one-day trophies in a single year.
1998 Another double is achieved when Lancashire win the AXA League and the Natwest Trophy
1999 Lancashire crowned day/night league champions. A haul of eight tournament wins in the 1990's made them the side of the decade. The county also had the privilege of supplying the national team with its captain, Michael Atherton - he has captained England in more Test matches than any other skipper.
2005 One of the great Test draws of all time is played out in the Ashes with Australia. The latter are left with one wicket standing with the final delivery of the fifth day. Lancashire and England player Andrew Flintoff (pictured against another team) plays a lead role.
2006 Lancashire put up a valiant battle for the County Championship but a combination of inclement weather and Sussex skill conspired against them. Sussex also beat Lancs in the C&G Trophy final to rub salt into the wounds. The challenge remains for the club to seize the County Championship which they haven't won outright since the 1930s.

composed of curious words and phrases such as googlies, silly mid-offs and second slip. Only people with a serious amount of spare time should attempt to learn these. Truly though, there is no better way to lounge through a sunny afternoon than watching cricket whilst sipping a pint or two of ale. Old Trafford is the local headquarters of course, but it is equally satisfying to travel down to Didsbury to take in an amateur match. Particularly idyllic grounds include those at Greenfield, in Saddleworth, and Alderley Edge in Cheshire.

Lancashire County Cricket Club

Talbot Road, Old Trafford, Manchester 0161-282 4000 *www.lccc.co.uk* ***Tickets from £10 adults, £5 children and are always available.***

Lancashire play most of their home games at Old Trafford and others at Liverpool, Southport, Lytham St Annes, and Blackpool. England all-rounder Andrew Flintoff plays for the club, and although he is on international duty for most of the season, he does turn out for the Red Rose county. He is becoming a true great of the game, and any cricket fan should jump at the chance to see him play. Named Wisden world cricketer of the year for 2005, barely anyone can hit a ball as hard or far as Flintoff. The Old Trafford Stadium has completed a five-year development plan, which has seen the frontage of the pavilion modernised, and the finest indoor cricket school in the country built. There is now also The Lodge, a mid-range hotel with balconies overlooking the pitch. Finally there is a small but well-appointed museum. Over the next few years there will be a much more dramatic redevelopment involving a large scale reconstruction of the ground.

Alderley Edge cricket ground

Honours

County Champions: 1881, 1897, 1904, 1926, 1927, 1928, 1930, 1934 Joint Champions: 1879, 1882, 1889, 1950 Nat West/Gillette Cup: 1970, 1971, 1972, 1975, 1990, 1996, 1998 Benson & Hedges Cup Winners: 1984, 1990, 1995, 1996 National League Champions: 1969, 1970, 1989, 1998, 1999 County Championship Division 2: champions 2005 Refuge Cup Winners: 1988

Other cricket clubs

There are a host of smaller cricket clubs in the area to enjoy, indeed the North West leagues especially around South East Lancashire and Manchester, are perhaps the strongest in the country. For details, both of grounds and if you want to join a team, then contact the **Lancashire Cricket Board, 0161 282 4029** *www.lancashirecricket.co.uk*

Not cricket

There could be skulduggery in the gentleman's game in the C19. In 1847 an England XI travelled north to play the Manchester club. With defeat imminent the visitors decided the game should end as they said they had to travel on to Birmingham for the next match that night. Later a member of the team would admit that they had spent the night watching Jenny Lind, the 'Swedish Nightingale' on stage in Manchester. Almost £40,000 in bets had to be declared null and void.

Rugby League

In 1895, the Northern Union split away from the Rugby Union over the question of 'broken time' payments (or professionalism), and Rugby League was born. Over the years, it developed unique laws (notably 13-a-side) to make it a more spectator-friendly game, and today Greater Manchester supports several professional clubs (with other clubs in Cheshire, Merseyside and West Yorkshire

Salford Reds' Malcolm Alker

Sale Sharks' Sebastien Chabel

- no more than an hour's drive away). The biggest Greater Manchester club is **Wigan Warriors RLFC** *(JJB Stadium, Robin Park, Newtown, Wigan. 01942 774000. www.wiganrl.com).* – one of the big four nationally with St Helens, Leeds and Bradford Bulls, despite some troubled seasons recently. ***Tickets from £14 adults, £10 children.*** The nearest Super League club to the city centre is a mere 3 miles (5km) away, **Salford Reds** *(The Willows, Willows Road, Salford. 0161-737 6363. www.reds.co.uk).* ***Tickets from £16-£20 adults, £10 children.*** Other local clubs include **Leigh Centurions** *(0161 628 3677 www.leighrl.co.uk),* **Oldham Roughyeds** *(0161 628 3677 www.roughyeds.co.uk),* **Rochdale Hornets** *(1706 648004. www.rochdalehorents.com).* **Swinton Lions** *(0161 794 6150 www.sprufc.com).* If you think that you're tough and competitive to play Rugby League yourself then contact the above clubs directly for their own training programmes or check out *www.therfl.co.uk* for details of your nearest club.

Rugby Union

Lancashire's RU county sides have traditionally been among the most powerful in the land, although the tug of wealthy southern clubs has bled them of some of their better players. In Greater Manchester, there is just one senior club in the top flight, but it is certainly making an impact. **Sale Sharks** *(Edgeley Park, Edgeley, Stockport. 0161 286 8888. www.salesharks.com),* ***adults from £19, children £9.*** The team, captained by England international Jason Robinson, won the Guinness Premiership title in 2006 under the guidance of Frenchman Philippe Saint Andre. The club has blended the best of the local talent with a host of overseas stars to create a formidable side. Unfortunately, the Sharks' 2006/2007 campaign has been badly disrupted by injury, but with Saint-Andre and key player Charlie Hodgson committed to the club, the future looks bright for Sale. **Other teams include,** Sedgley Park, Manchester, Macclesfield and Orrell who all play in the National Leagues, although the latter are in danger of dropping out after a disastrous 2006/2007 campaign. If you want to play Rugby Union yourself contact the above clubs directly for their own training programmes or check out www.rugbyunion.com for details of your nearest club.

Other sports to do or watch

Athletics

Manchester possesses two of the country's leading clubs, Sale and Trafford. **Sale Athletic Club** *(Dane Road, Sale. 0161 220 3859).* **Trafford Athletic Club** *(Longford Park, Ryebank Road, Stretford. 0161 881 4488).* See also Sport City entry below.

Jogging along

The Great Manchester Run is one of the most prestigious 10K runs in the world and usually takes place each year in May. The 2007 event will see 27,000 competitors run the course that loops around the city centre and Manchester United's Old Trafford stadium. Distance running great Haile Gebrselassie holds the men's record after he completed the course in a staggering time of 27m 25s in 2005. The usual fun-runners trundle along in the wake of the elite athletes, and with bands and fans lining the streets it's a festive occasion.

Basketball

To watch basketball try **Manchester Magic** *(Amaechi Basketball Centre, Whalley Range High School, Wilbraham Road, Whalley Range. 0161 881 0090 www.gmybasketball.co.uk).* John Amaechi, a pupil at Stockport Grammar School in the 1980s, was the first ever Englishman to play in America's NBA, the elite league in world basketball. The Magic's Season runs from September to April. Also try this number if you want a game or contacts for local teams.

SPORT

Boxing

Manchester has a strong boxing tradition and, in Ricky Hatton, one of the best pound-for-pound fighters in the world. At the time of writing his record is 42 fights and 42 wins, 30 by way of KO. His engaging personality and love of Manchester City have won him an army of fans who follow him the world over, and he still trains in Denton, East Manchester. Even though his job is one of the most physically demanding in the world Hatton likes nothing more than a pint of Guinness and a takeaway after a bout – a lifestyle that has attracted criticism from other fighters. For those wishing to have a bash themselves, the **Amateur Boxing Association of England** is a good place to start *(http://www.abae.co.uk/).*

Chess

A huge amount of chess is played to a very high level within the Greater Manchester Area. International grandmasters and former World Championship challenger Nigel Short, is from Bolton. For further details of local clubs, contact the **Manchester & District Chess Association** on **01204 852036.**

Climbing walls

Fit City Broughton *(Camp Street, Salford. 0161 792 2375 www.salford.gov.uk/fitcity-bp.htm).* Legendary bouldering wall for £4 a session. **Manchester Climbing Centre** *(St Benedict's Church, Bennett Street, Ardwick. 0161 230 7006 www.manchesterclimbingcentre.com).* The new big boy of the Manchester climbing scene in an historic church with an impressive array of climbing surfaces – the closest wall to the city centre. ***Experienced climbers can go on from £5, but if you need instruction an hour will cost £25.*** **Rope Race** *(Rope Race, Goyt Mill, Upper Hibbert Lane, Marple. 0161 426 0226).* ***Tall climbing and bouldering walls for adults from £6.50 and children (£4.50-£5.50) with routes reset regularly.*** **North Face** *(4D 130 Deansgate, City),* the city centre store, has an ice wall, and experienced climbers can turn up and have a bash for £20. *Ring 0161 837 6140 or visit ww.vertical-chill.com.*

Ricky Hatton of England before his junior welterweight title fight against Juan Urango of Colombia in Las Vegas, 2007 ›

The XVII Commonwealth Games 2002

THE Manchester Commonwealth Games attracted 1m visitors to Manchester, were watched by 1bn global viewers and had the highest seat-occupancy figures of any multi-sport event. There were 4000 athletes competing for 900 medals with 15,000 volunteers helping out in the organisation. The physical legacy includes Sports City with the City of Manchester Stadium, the National Squash Centre, the Indoor Tennis Centre and the National Cycling Centre as well as Manchester Aquatic Centre, the Regional Bowls Centre at Heaton Park, the Regional Hockey Centre at Belle Vue and from the previous Olympic bids, the Manchester Evening News Arena. In short the Games were an overwhelming success. In 2006 the Times wrote, 'Manchester was an unqualified triumph and restored Britain's prestige. Out of Manchester sprung the (successful) London 2012 bid.'

Cycling

The National Cycling Centre *(Manchester Velodrome, Stuart Street, Manchester 0161 223 2244 www.manchestervelodrome.com).* This is a superb venue with a record-breaking track. There's a year round programme of races, plus other events. ***The general public can try out their bike skills with the regular taster and sampling sessions - £8 adults, £6 children.*** For those after a taste of the outdoors, the **ABC Centreville** club runs cyclo-cross, time-trialling and road-racing activities for a range of ages *(http://www.centreville.org.uk/).*

Dog/Horse Racing

There is only one dog track in the area and a visit with friends is tremendous fun. **Belle Vue** *(Kirkmanshulme Lane, Gorton, Manchester. 0161 223 8000 www.bellevuestadium.co.uk).* On Tue and Thu meetings start at 7.25pm, while on Fri and Sat they are slightly earlier at 7.20pm. Doors open 6pm. As for Horse Racing, the closest races take place just west of Wigan, **Haydock Park** *(Newton-le-Willows, 01942 725963. www.haydock-park.co.uk).* ***Tickets from £5 adults, free for children.*** Forty miles south west of Manchester is **Chester** Races with its Lady's Day in April. **Aintree**, in Liverpool, meanwhile, hosts the most famous race on the planet, the Grand National also in April – Aintree has a museum too.

Golf

There are around 80 courses in Greater Manchester (only eight of which are public, and two of those are nine-holes). A lot of high class golf tournaments take place on links courses on the Lancashire Coast, including periodically The Open, at the Royal Liverpool Course (as is the case in 2006), Royal Birkdale and Royal Lytham St Annes. For any golf fanatics it's worth taking a trip to one of these three gems. Once you've had a taste of true links golf and battled the elements, those parkland courses will seem a doddle by comparison. If you can't make the trip, there are large numbers of golf courses spread throughout Greater Manchester. **Wilmslow** and **Stockport** are fine courses, while the back nine at **Mottram Hall** is a delightful stretch of holes. Most courses are private but there are public courses of high quality. The closest to the city centre and the most accessible, via Metrolink tram, is that at **Heaton Park** and a fine track it is too. Greens fees vary so call ahead. **Heaton Park Golf Centre** *(Middleton Road, Prestwich, Manchester, 0161*

Early Sports

Sport before the middle part of the C19 was a very different animal from the chained beast we have today. It usually comprised wild unregulated behaviour with prolific gambling and vast alcoholic consumption. Not only were the spectators drunk but the players were too: officials weren't drunk because there weren't any.

Some popular sports - if it could be called sport - are notorious today such as cock fighting, dog fighting, and bull baiting. Far more interesting are the activities frequently associated with Wakes Week: the annual celebration marking the saint's day for whom the local church was dedicated. The Wakes were a northern England speciality. In Didsbury there is record from 1825 of 'ass-races for purses of gold, prison-bar playing, grinning through collars for ale, treacle loaf eating, smoking matches, apple-dumpling eating, wheelbarrow racing'.

Other madcap competitions in the area included shinning up a greased pole to retrieve a leg of mutton and chasing a greased pig.

One man, north of the city, for a bet 'ate three pounds of porridge, one quart of water, one quart of milk, one pint of milk, one quart of small drink, two oat cakes; next nine pounds of cowhead without bone, four quarts of water, one quart of ale and three oat cakes... After this he said he would like a dozen penny pies of which he ate seven ' - not exactly sport but extraordinary anyway.

Bear-baiting with barrows and bladders, at Hyde's Cross, Manchester, in 1749

(Middleton Road, Prestwich, Manchester, 0161 654 9899), **Altrincham Golf Course** *(0161 928 0761)*, **Bolton Golf Club** *(01204 843278)*, **Bury Golf Club** *(0161 766 2213)*, **Didsbury Golf Course** *(0161 998 2811)*, **Mottram Hall** *(01625 828135)*, **Oldham Golf Club** *(0161 624 4986)*, **Rochdale Golf Club** *(01706 46024)*, **Sale Golf Club** *(0161 973 1730)*, **Stockport Golf Club** *(0161 427 2001)*, **Wigan Golf Club** *(01257 421360)*, **Wilmslow Golf Club** *(01565 873 620)*. A good driving range is at **Playgolf Manchester** *(Old Park Lane, Trafford Park. 0161 749 7000 www.playgolfworld.com)*. ***Adult/children sessions are £2.50-£13*** depending on the number of golf balls hit.

Gyms

There are plenty of gyms to choose from in the city centre for all the fitness freaks out there, and most charge about £10 for a daily pass. **GL-14** *(0161 228 6789) Canada House, 3 Chepstow Street*, **Bannatynes Health Club** *(0161 236 6864) Regency House, 36-38 Whitworth Street*, **David Lloyd** *(0161 749 2000) Barton Embankment, Trafford Keys, Trafford Park*, **Virgin Active** *(0161 831 0600) 225 Deansgate.*

Hockey

Belle Vue Leisure Centre *(Kirkmanshulme Lane, Longsight. 0161 953 2470)* East of the city centre, this facility boasts 2 water-based hockey pitches, 8 badminton courts and a cricket academy. It is the Regional Performance Centre for hockey. The England senior and junior hockey squads use Belle Vue as their training base as the hockey pitches, used in the Commonwealth Games, are of international standard.

Ice Hockey

Manchester Phoenix *(Altrincham Ice Dome, Altrincham 0161 301 6848 www.manchesterphoenix.co.uk)* Excellent family evening out. ***Tickets £12 adults, £5 for children.*** Season runs from August to April.

Lacrosse

English Lacrosse Association **4D** *(Wood Street. 0161 834 4582. www.englishlacrosse.co.uk)*. The Manchester region is the British centre for this tough and demanding team sport imported from Native American communities.

Artist's impression of Chill Factore

Manchester Tennis and Racquets Club

Founded in 1874 and housed in the current premises since 1886, this club is one of only 22 in the country. There is a racquets court (the fastest racquet game in the world and the forerunner of squash), a squash court, an original skittles alley, and the central feature itself, the real tennis court. Real tennis was famously played by Henry VIII but eventually gave way to the simpler and more flexible lawn tennis. It remains one of the best games for fitness, a combination of tennis, squash and badminton with its own distinct racquet. A professional can be hired to help you get started. If you catch the real tennis bug you'll join a select breed as the game is only played by 2500 people worldwide. That many eh? *33 Blackfriars Road. 0161 834 0616.*

Motorsports, Speedway and Karting

There are three circuits in the area, the best known is Oulton Park, where all sorts of motor sport takes place. High Edge primarily stages stock car and banger racing, while the Three Sisters stages scooter racing and karting. **High Edge Raceway** *(Dale Head Road, Buxton, 01298 78021).* **Oulton Park** *(Little Budworth, nr Tarporley, Chester. 01829 760301/ 08705 125 250).* **Three Sisters Recreation Centre** *(Bryn Road, Ashton-in-Makerfield, Wigan, 01942 720453).* For speedway try Belle Vue where meetings are held on Friday evenings or Sunday afternoons. The Aces have a strong team at the moment and an enthusiastic following – so now is a great time to go and soak up the atmosphere. **Belle Vue Aces** (*Belle Vue Greyhound Stadium, Hyde Road, Gorton, M12. 0161 223 8000)* For public karting try **Daytona** *(Trafford Park, Manchester. 0161 223 2200 www.daytona.co.uk).*

Skiing

The best place locally is **Ski Rossendale** *(Haslingden Old Road, Rawtenstall. 01706 226 4567. www.ski-rossendale.co.uk).* Just across the northern border of Greater Manchester, this has an excellent artificial surface with nursery, intermediate and main slopes – at 200 metres the latter is one of the longest in the country. There are snow boarding sessions too. If you've never skied before, you have to take a training session of at least four hours. ***Adults £16 for up to 2 hours, £18 over; children £10 for up to 2 hours, £11 over.***

England's biggest indoor ski-slope, **Chill Factore**, is scheduled to open at the end of October 2007, and aims to bring an Alpine flavour to the region. Situated opposite the Trafford Centre, Chill Factore will boast a slope 180m long and 100m wide alongside après ski style restaurants.

Swimming

The Manchester Aquatics Centre, used in the 2002 Commonwealth Games *(Booth Street East, off Oxford Road, 0161 275 9450)*, is the closest public baths to the city centre.

Tennis

Manchester's Northern Lawn Tennis Club *(0161 445 3093)* is the premier club in the region. For the **Regional Tennis Centre** see Sport City below.

Watersports

Closet to the city centre, a tram ride away is **Salford Watersports Centre** *(Salford Quays. 0161 877 7252 www.salford.gov.uk/sports/ watersports)* with wind-surfing, kayaks and so on. For two of many centres try, south of the city, **Sale Water Park** *(0161 912 3410)* and north of the city, **Hollingworth Lake** *(01706 373421)* in Littleborough, near Rochdale.

City of Manchester Stadium and the Sports City complex

SPORT

Sport City

Located 2km east of the city centre, off Ashton Old Road, in East Manchester. The entrance is via Gate 11.

This was developed after the spectacular success of the Commonwealth Games in 2002. Anchored by the handsome structure of the City of Manchester Stadium, Sport City provides one of the most concentrated sporting resources anywhere in Europe and includes the Regional Athletics Arena (plus indoor track), the National Squash Centre and the Manchester Tennis Centre. A few hundred metres away is the National Cycling Centre (see page 243).

The complex is spectacular even for a drive round. Make sure you check out the 10m high sculpture by local artist Colin Spofforth of *the Runner* close to the athletics track and the National Squash Centre. This is big but is dwarfed by Tom Heatherwick's *B of the Bang* on the corner of Alan Turing Way and Ashton New Road.

The National Squash Centre *(0161 220 3800)* has seven squash courts and world-class facilities. The centre is the new home of England Squash, the sport's national governing body. It features an astonishing transparent show court which floats to where it's required for competition on a hovercraft. If you take advantage of this facility, you might find yourself playing next to international and national squash stars training on that very show court. *Open Mon to Fri 7am to 10pm, Sat and Sun 9am to 5pm.* ***From £4.20 adults a court for 45 minutes, £2.10 children.***

The Athletics Arena is a £3.5m, 6,000-seater stadium constructed around the Commonwealth Games warm-up track and training area. The arena is used for domestic and international athletics meetings

The stadium is also the base for the **Sale Harriers** athletics club. *The indoor track is open Mon to Thu from 7pm,* ***£3 non members, £2 members, £1 junior members.*** **Manchester Athletics Club** run a Junior Club too.

Amazing deals can be had for the Squash and Athletics Arena through the community sports sessions *(0161 220 3800).*

The Tennis Centre *(0161 220 3840)* has indoor and outdoor courts. Open Mon to Fri 9am to 10pm, Sat and Sun 9am to 6pm. ***From £12 a court, £8 children, £5 for indoor play between 9am-5pm weekdays.***

Indoor Athletics Arena

SHOPPING

Rags to Bitches

Shopping

Manchester is generous place to shop, giving plenty of opportunities to splash out or bargain pick. Recently both the biggest high-street stores and the most chic fashion houses have moved in. These, together with the city's delightful independent boutiques, give shopaholics a very satisfying experience. In this section we concentrate on independent stores. Full address details of stores in the city centre can be found in the directory at the end of this description of Manchester's Shopping. The Suburban Dreams addresses follow the entries in that section.

The very quick guide for shoppers

Northern Quarter: Funky attitude, vintage clothing boutiques and cool record shops where anything, as long its creative of thought and independent of spirit, goes. Highlights include Pop Boutique, Magma Bookshop, Afflecks Palace, Rags to Bitches, Vinyl Exchange, Big Pink… Oh there's too many to mention. Coffee Break: Oklahoma or Love Saves the Day in Vox Pop record shop.

Market Street: High street honeys galore. Pick up a bargain at Primark or H&M or for something a little cooler try Urban Outfitters. The big music chains lie along here too.

The Manchester Arndale: The newly revamped Arndale boasts a huge Topshop, an even bigger Next and all the usual suspects. The Apple shop and Waterstones are handy for those not interested in mid-priced clothing, whilst the Market now supplies excellent fresh, food and snacks.

Exchange Square and The Triangle: Upmarket chains have found a home here. Most visited have to be Selfridges and Harvey Nichols but there is also a Heals for home shoppers with cash to splash.

St Ann's Square and King Street: Getting even more bijou now, expect to find Hermes, Vivienne Westwood, Armani and bespoke tailors and jewellers.

Deansgate: Home to a long stretch of furniture shops, a comfortably large Waterstones and the department store, House of Fraser.

How To Shop Like A... WAG Princess

There have been a slew of articles recently discussing the north/south divide when it comes to fashion, and Northern Girl has been lumped in with the WAG stereotype (by the way WAG means Wives and Girlfriends of over-paid football players, dear overseas visitor). To be fair Manchester United player Wayne Rooney's chick Coleen McLoughlin started the ball rolling; she

Manchester Craft and Design Centre

A former fish market and crowned with a huge glass roof, the Centre is now home to two floors of studios where designers both work and sell their fares ranging from jewellery, ceramics and textiles to furniture and clothing design. Jewellery is the most popular, with plenty of the subtle brushed sterling silver you might expect, but plenty more eccentric offerings utilizing found objects and industrial materials to interesting effect. Always worth a browse with a good café to sit and mull over your purchases. There are good temporary exhibitions too. (17 Oak Street, Northern Quarter 0161 832 4274 www.craftanddesign.com)

SHOPPING

berated women in the south for not making enough effort, but London girls are getting their own back. Liz Jones sad "it seems even Liverpool cannot compete with Manchester, home of the legendary Chessex girls, whose tans are always baked, smiles always dazzling, foreheads always suspiciously shiny." While Melanie Rickey, fashion editor of Grazia magazine, says us northern girls "seem to be living in a different decade and continent (in the north the year is currently 1984, the location Bel Air). It is INSANE the difference between north and south".

This all seems a tad unfair, kooky vintage girls surely outnumber permatanned trophy wives on the streets of Manchester. But let's look at the evidence. There are scores of luxury goods shops in Manchester; even **Burberry** (www.burberry.com) recently announced it was opening its first store outside London in Manchester in New Cathedral Street. But then who can berate a girl for wanting to dress up? So how would a WAG, or aspiring wagette, shop till she drops? Easy. First you get a really great handbag- how about a Birkin from **Hermes 5D** (King Street) or a Roxanne from **Mulberry 5D** (King Street)? Of course if these two leather specialists don't tickle your fancy you can head over to **Selfridges 5C** (Exchange Square) to pick up a Marc Jacobs Stam Bag or **Harvey Nichols 5C** (Exchange Square) for a Chloe Paddington. Let's stay with these two places for a moment; they are very important in the WAG's psycho-geography. Harvey Nichols is sexy indeed, stocking labels like Alexander McQueen, Gucci and local boy Matthew Williamson and of course has the all important restaurant and bar on the second floor, for a post-shopping pick me up. Selfridges has gone for a more relaxed approach, stocking Chloe, Issa and Juicy Couture (a WAG's favourite relaxation outfit) among others and a champagne bar, naturally.

If you're not too tipsy on Cristal head out to **Vivienne Westwood 6D** (Spring Gardens) for corset-inspired couture and **Agent Provocateur 6D** for sexy undies. Then there is **Armani 5D** (King Street) and **DKNY 6D** (King Street) to peruse, **Tommy Hilfiger 5D** (King Street) to visit for a little

Hermes

something to wear for pilates and **Diesel 5D** (King Street) for jeans. Is the shopping over yet? Not quite, it's time to drop into **Swarovski 6C** (Royal Exchange) for some bling or **Mappin and Webb 5C** (St. Ann's Square) for a rock. Then it's off to get one's nails done- shopping is hard work you know.

How to Shop Like A... Man About Town

It seems like blokes get a bit of a rough deal sometimes- no dropping into Primark and picking up 5 dresses, a pair of shoes and a sparkly scarf (or the male equivalent) all for a tenner. Deprived of gaudy peacock ways they have to concentrate on sensible things like quality and cut. But then they generally wear everything they own and haven't got bags of unworn clothes hidden under the bed whispering shopper's guilt in your ear every time you think of them. Manchester is very well endowed with sporty urban casual type shops. Smartness may take a bit more searching out but it is well worth the effort, as every girl loves a man in a really well cut suit. Think of it as primeval instinct to prowl the urban landscape, hunting and gathering, only with Oxford weaves and double cuffs instead of herds of antelope. Happy shopping boys.

Let's start with smart. **Frank Rostron 6E** (Princess Street), **Thomas Pink 5D**(King Street) and **TM Lewin 5D** (King Street) are the places to go for shirts. Frank Rostron

adidas

adidas Performance Centre
52-56 Market Street, Manchester
TEL: 0161 832 6733 • FAX: 0161 832 6745
www.adidas.com

in particular is a Manchester legend, having been beshirting local celebrities and foreign dignitaries since the 60s (you can often see piles of shirts ready to be sent out to embassies across the world). In a similar bespoke heritage vein, **Edwards of Manchester 5C** (Deansgate) have been providing the finest Goodyear-welted shoes since 1830. **James Personal Tailor & Son 6C** (Cross Street) or **Nicholas Jones 5C** (St. Ann's Arcade) come highly recommend for tailoring, or try **Hugo Boss 5D** (King Street) or **Flannels 5C** (St. Ann's Arcade). For that dapper special something perhaps with an elegant Edwardian cut try **Vivienne Westwood 6D** (Spring Gardens).

For street savvy try the spiritual home of all things casual, **Fred Perry 5C**(Police Street) who these days are doing a nice line in knitwear, or for a different slant on the polo shirt, try **Aspecto 4D** (Bridge Street)which stocks some lovely examples from the American brand Penguin. **Westworld 8C** (Church Street) is a home-grown shop which has some nice items but veers towards studenty. Try **Oi Polloi 9C** (Tib Street) for something a little more unusual.

For that difficult to navigate area in-between smart and casual (no don't say the dreaded hyphenate, with its associations of khakis and taking off your tie) there are fashionably up market places such **Richard Crème 4D** (Bridge Street) which stocks serious labels such as Ann Demeulemeester and Dries van Noten, or the menswear departments of **All Saints 5D** (King Street) and **Reiss 6D** (New Cathedral Street) as well as the big department stores

Now for really important, life and death stuff. Trainers. The Offspring in Selfridges is reliable, or you could try **Ran 5C** (St Ann's Arcade), **Robot Lounge 8B** (4 Hilton Street) and **Hussain the Barbers 9C** (Tib Street), all quality independents staffed by sneaker obsessives.

Oi Polloi

How to Shop Like A ... Vintage Queen

There are two possible approaches to second hand clothing. One is to find scraps of old lace, fifties prom dress and paste jewels all impossibly romantic, haunted as they are by the ghosts of times past, of parties left at dawn, powder compacts and chaste kisses… Or to think 'Oh my God the last person who wore this is probably dead.' The unimaginative can stop reading now as vintage has never been stronger in the city, tapped from a seemingly inexhaustible supply (maybe old people had more clothes, although that seems quite unlikely). Now you could go and root out some gems from charity shops, but the thing about vintage shops is they pick out the good stuff from in amongst the C&A rayon pleated skirts, and make sure all the dead mice have been chucked out of the shoes, and just generally get their hands on better stuff than us mere mortals could ever hope to, so the mark-up on the price tag is worth it. Although if you think you have the eye for a pre-loved bargain, we've also included a couple of hints of where to get started.

The kernel of the juicy vintage fruit that is Manchester has to be the **Northern Quarter**. First of all special mention has to go to **My Goodniss** (Thomas Street) which is changing hands very soon. The site will still be a clothes shop, so watch that space, but **MG** has been a lovely addition to the vintage selection available in the city.

Ok, now dry tears and stop by **Rags to Bitches** (Tib Street - see picture 247), which although it ostensibly caters to both

Palace People

Afflecks Palace is legendary among Mancunians. They tend to feel a mixture of nostalgic fondness and slight irritation at the scowling youths that permanently decorate its exterior. The nostalgia being of course for the period of their lives (usually teenaged) when they hung about there scowling and laying their hands on as much chunky silver jewellery, oversized posters and Barry M Dazzle Dust as their meagre allowances would stretch to. Visit during school hours when it is not quite as cluttered up with angst and hormones (only quite, these kids aren't going to let a little thing like the National Curriculum stop them in their pursuit of body piercings and joss-sticks). The place is an absolute testament to independent spirit and, clichés aside, you can find some real treasures. The second stalls are definitely worth the effort of a good rummage, although you may well get lost amongst the rails of 70's Afghan coats (rumour has it Affleck's has its own search and rescue team). **Afflecks Palace 8C** (52 Church Street. 0161 834 2039. www.afflecks-palace.co.uk)

SHOPPING

sexes, is definitely mostly girl friendly. Extra points must be award for the serious consideration given to cake in the shopping experience (often sadly overlooked) and the rather special events- (see boxout below). Now replete with fondant fancies turn onto Oldham Street and head up to **Oxfam Originals** (11 Smithfield Buildings), the high end version of the charity shop which has some really great things, granted, but can be a bit of a slap in the wallet compared to your usual Oxfam. Offset the spending guilt by thinking of all the good you are doing and carry on over the road to **Pop Boutique** (34-36 Oldham Street), the king (or queen?) of the retro sensibility. So much so that you can get your hands on its reproductions of 70s classic styles (the cord flares spring to mind) without worrying your poor little head about the smells-of-old-person dilemma outlined above. **Retro Rehab** (91 Oldham Street) is a newer addition to the vintage market and categorized by decade. Very handy if you are dying for a Nehru jacket or pillbox hat and need to get your hands on it this instant. Around the corner **American Graffiti** (Hilton Street), which started out life in **Afflecks Palace** (Oldham Street), has some brilliant finds but it's all mixed up with the kind of stuff a student might wear to a Love Train night (see Clubbing in the Entertainment section) so a discerning eye is needed. Concentrating on accessories will pay dividends if you don't have time to sift. Finally special mention goes to **Kitty Nation** (Oldham Street) for its vintage homeware and fabric remnants.

Swap Shop

Rags to Bitches has started holding clothes swap parties (As featured in *Vogue*, no less!). You bring the clothes and they supply the drink. It works by everyone bringing at least 5 items that you're prepared to give away and swapping them for other clothes. New clothes for no money- sounds perfect in theory, though we predict some girly catfights over who gets the Missoni scarf and who ends up with home-knitted tea cosy hat. Email: info@rags-to-bitches.co.uk or call 0161 835 9265 to reserve your place.

How to shop...if you know print's not dead

Pick up a book, rub the spine, open the pages, it's a sensuous experience. Now pick up a Pentium processor. Not the same is it, unless you're slightly touched in the head. Try this array of Mancunian new and old stores for size if you feel like book-worming it old – pre-computer – style around knowledge and emotion. **Borders** (Manchester Fort, Cheetham Hill Road) for events, coffee and quick ordering. **Cornerhouse Bookshop 7G** (Oxford Street) for kitsch cards and specialist magazines, art and film books, plus a rack of small press publications and samizdats. **George Kelsall** (Church Street, Littleborough) is the king of second-hand and antiquarian books in the region. This shop goes on and on forever inside some lovely stone buildings. Every subject and genre is covered but you will have to catch a train – regular services – from Victoria Station. **Magma 8C** (Oldham Street) is a super-slick, finger-on-the-pulse art and design bookshop with magazines and gadgets too. **RIBA Bookshop 7F** (Portland Street) is head office for architectural books and big glossy pictures of buildings, - attached to CUBE gallery. **Stanfords 7D** (Spring Gardens) is full of travel books, maps, globes and travel accessories with full mapping services from the Ordnance Survey. **Waterstone's 5C** (Deansgate) remains a dependable source of reading matter, with a good art room. It's also very good for signing sessions and events.

How to shop...to impress the house guests

It doesn't have to be Habitat, let alone, God forfend, IKEA. There's a good choice of places in which to spend lots of money on interesting designer, ditched or refurbished furniture. Start at **Ferrious 6G** (Whitworth Street West) a Mancunian design centre of excellence with furniture, lighting and rugs from in-house designers but also Artemide and others. **Innerform** (Chorlton Mill) has an impressive 6,000 square feet of contemporary urban furnishings. **Rimo 4F** (Deansgate) does a great line in inspirational rugs and carpets, whilst **Simon Green 4D** (King Street West) provides super-stylish designer furniture in sumptuous materials for living, sleeping, storing and dining. Two

Sweet Charity

For those ready to brave the murky waters of real honest to goodness charity shops, follow us. The city centre (with the exception of Oxfam Originals, where all the hard work has been done for you) is not so great for mining the rich charity seam, so head out to the wealthier suburbs instead. Wilmslow, Alderley Edge, Hale and Altrincham have a large range of charity shops and best of all the WAG-a-likes who live there wouldn't even spit on a second-hand piece of clothing (probably not even on a last season one, but that's a different matter) never mind wearing one, leaving all the more for the rest of us. Check www.redcross.org.uk, www.bhf.org.uk, www.oxfam.org.uk, www.cancerresearchuk.org and local charity St Ann's Hospice www.sah.org.uk to find the locations of their shops. Not exactly charity, but good resources nonetheless, are the fleamarkets at Salford (Market Way, every Sunday and Thursday call 0161 736 7845) and Tommyfield Market (Oldham, Wednesdays and Sundays).

real *City Life* faves are **Den 9C** (Oldham Street) and **In-Situ** (Talbot Mill, Ellesmere Street). The first is a wonderful jumble of modern antiques, together with exceptional hand-made and glam furniture designed and upholstered by one of the partners. You can't get better than this for bespoke. There are also get decorative mosaics available from Mark Kennedy. The second is the king of the hill for architectural salvage in Manchester and its only a ten minute walk from Deansgate station. It's so good it's worth a trip just for a fascinating browse with furniture, fittings and fixtures from old schools, pubs, hospitals, houses and churches.

How to shop...for your ears

Manchester has pedigree when it comes to music and that's reflected in the music you can buy. Many of the shops listed here are in the Northern Quarter as are many of the cooler clothing shops, so why not combine a trip. Music for the soul and clothes for the body. **Eastern Bloc 8C** (Oldham Street) is the north west's original house and electronica experts. Then just up the road is **Fat City 9C** (Oldham Street) the highly respected Hip-Hop specialist covering the latest independent and import releases on 12", LP and CD. The neighbour of Fat City is **Vinyl Exchange 9C** (Oldham Street and 67 Bridge Street), a treasure of vinyl but also cds. You can buy, sell or exchange vinyl and CDs at this nationally famous store. It's also recommended for being a goldmine of promos passed on by local DJ's, journalists and industry insiders. Expect to find rare collectibles and general bargains. Over the road is **Piccadilly Records 8C** (Oldham Street). This the city's largest independent music store. It has huge range and excellent back catalogue, including all essential vinyl reissues. It features Manchester music strongly and carries its own Merchandise and tickets for gigs too. In 2007 it won the NME Music Shop of the Year Award. Higher up on Oldham Street is **Roadkill 9C** (Oldham Street) for all those who are anti-dance: strictly rock, metal, punk and weird stuff. Parallel to Oldham Street on Tib Street is **Beatin' Rhythm 9B** (Tib Street), a different beast again, stocked with over 50,000 45s plus CDs, rare and original releases covering soul, R'n'B, funk, doo-wop, pop and Northern Soul. Nearby is **Vinyl Revival 8C** (Hilton Street) which amongst much else carries a sea of Mancunian memorabilia, vinyl, CDs, posters, t-shirts. If you want to buy instruments the best two places are: **Forsyths 4D** (Deansgate) which has been around since before the dawn of time and looks it, for guitars, keyboards, pianos, brass, strings, woodwind, mouth organs, banjos, scores and sheet music plus details of tuition, instruments for sale and musicians required; and **Johnny Roadhouse** (Oxford Road) which has been around since just after the dawn of time. The latter has guitars, brass and so forth but also the best drum department and the best folk department in the north west. As independent retailers go this can't be bettered.

Suburban Dreams

Chorlton Chorlton is a notoriously relaxed artsy little enclave, so head down the main artery of Beech Road (culturally that is, though luckily not traffic wise) and sample such delights as **Jazz** (106 Beech Road 0161 881 0721) for men's and womenswear in

this suitably laid-back fashion joint with an urban feel. Look out for the knitwear and accessories for pieces you won't find anywhere else. For more sartorial goodness, this time a little more dressy and obscure, try **McQueen** (54 Beech Road, 0161 881 4718) with an interesting and eclectic choice of accessories. Finally on the fashion front there is **Nood** (36 Beech Road 0161 860 0461 www.nood.co.uk, run by Alison King (who designs her own AKA label) stocks Religion, Slush and Get Cutey. Brilliantly, they do a tailoring service, which can range from a few simple adjustments to creating a whole made to measure outfit, which can be an invaluable service for special occasions. For the home there is **Avid** (139 Beech Rd) and **Creative Recycling** (40 Beech Rd 0161-881-4422) that surprisingly enough does art from recycled material. Stand out in more ways than one is shoe boutique **Kiss My Feet** (93 Beech Road 0161 860 4800)

Didsbury In Didsbury proper, try **Fonda** Named after Peter, Henry or Jane? We're betting Jane, although as yet they don't seem to be stocking fur bikinis. (677 Wilmslow Rd. 0161 448 1177). What is on offer are lots of quirky designers you may not have heard of (yet) doing delightfully eccentric things with wool and gossamer chiffon. Gorgeous.

West Didsbury On bohemian Burton Road you will find **Hub** (190, 0161 448 9438) an old fashioned boudoir babes dream, piled high with antiques heaped with fashion rarities. There are plenty of labels, but it's those totally essential petit bateau t-shirts that are the real draw (stripy ones in every colour please). Then it's on to **Steranko** (172 Burton Rd, 0161 448 0108) for a more casual fashion hit, this time for both the boys and the girls such as Diesel, Fornarina or Australian label Mooks. **Thunder Egg** (240 Burton Road 0161 434 4236 there is also a city centre branch) is the ideal place to look for cards and presents, but there are rails of clothes for those looking to do a little self-gifting. Burton Road's rival shopping thoroughfare is Lapwing Lane, home to the delicious **Velvet** (41 Lapwing Lane 0161 448 8001). Girls come here on a Friday afternoon looking for that sure-fire date outfit and they are not often disappointed.

Fonda

Trafford Centre

Compared to the city centre, the Trafford Centre is a homogenous experience- there are no surprises here, just the big name high street stores sat in a gilded faux palace of unbelievable bad taste. Yea, you can avoid the rain here but for the discerning visitor or tourist it's a dispiriting experience. The crowds can get ridiculous too especially at weekends and the Christmas period. Destination shops include the **Selfridges**, **Miss Sixty** and the **Apple** shop. When you are done shopping there is also plenty of food outlets and an Odeon cinema. See www.traffordcentre.co.uk for a list of opening times and full list of the extensive facilities, including crèche and parking.

Markets

Christmas Market Chalet-style stalls look suitably twee while selling all sorts of gift-type items. The real draw is the Gluhwein (spicy hot wine) and bratwurst, which smell festively good. The market will run from 15 November to 19 December 2007 in St Ann's Square and Albert Square and will be open between 10am and 8pm (9pm in Albert Square) each day.

Farmers Market: Your chance to get some premium quality meat cheese or vegetables. Best bet is the pie stall. The market is held twice monthly, on the second and fourth weekend (Friday and Saturday) of each month in Piccadilly Gardens. It is open between 10am and 6pm.

Top five... for shopping online

Kitty Nation: Miss Kitty is the proud owner of an online emporium as well as her Oldham Street shop. Lots of good features, like being able to review products bought online and browse by price as well as category, an added extra for those with a limited budget. The homeware and fabric sections are always worth checking. www.kittynation.com

Topshop: If Topshop has gone rather unmentioned in these pages it is surely because everyone knows what the highstreet giant is all about. But we still love it. Visit www.topshop.com to buy their poptastic new season clothes online.

Rags to Bitches: Rags to Bitches has a wonderfully designed site, complete with Manchester skyline and a plane trailing the sign 'as if by magic'. Cute. The shop section of the site is currently being redesigned but the information is always kept up to date (unlike some other sites we could mention) so check the events section regularly to keep informed. www.rags-to-bitches.co.uk

Agent Provocateur: Oooh sexy! Beautifully illustrated, with arty films (remember Kylie on the bucking bronco or Kate in her waspie?), you can also subscribe to their newsletter Knickers Forever. Perfect for gift buying boyfriends a bit nervous of hanging round lingerie shops, just order online, only try to find out her size first. www.agentprovocateur.com

Oi Polloi: Excellent wish list function that wouldn't go amiss on some other sites. Ostensibly to keep a record for yourself, email it to friends, lovers, business associates if necessary to ensure happy birthdays and Christmases forever more. www.oipolli.com

Fashion Market: The aim of the market is to give budding designers a leg up the retail ladder. Clothes, bags, purses, hats and jewellery will are all on sale with an emphasis on craft and creativity. All labels are independent, giving customers the chance to buy one-off designs at reasonable prices, while supporting fledgling talent. The market is held every Saturday from 10am until 5pm, Tib Street, City.

Flower Market: Hang around at the end of the day to pick up some bargain blooms. Thursday, Friday and Saturday in Piccadilly Gardens between 10am and 6pm

Directory

Fashion

adidas originals 6B (The Triangle, Hanging Ditch. 0161 834 2668) **Afflecks Palace 8C** (52 Church Street. 0161 834 2039. www.afflecks-palace.co.uk) **Agent Provocateur** (81 King Street. 0161 833 3735. www.agentprovocateur.com) **All Saints 5D** (52 King Street. 0161 832 2444) **Aquascutum 6C** (24 St Ann's Square. 0161 834 5617) **Aspecto 4D** (37-35 Bridge Street. 0161 834 4875. 10 King Street. **5D** 0161 832 9727. Trafford Centre. 0161 747 2318. www.aspecto.co.uk) **Diesel 6D** (74 King Street. 0161 839 8868. www.diesel.com) **DKNY 5D** (76-80 King Street. 0161 819 1048. www.dkny.com) **Flannels 5D** (4 St Ann's Place. 0161 832 5536. www.flannelsgroup.com) **Frank Rostron 6E** (39 Princess Street. 0161 237 9253) **H&M 7C** (Arndale Centre. 0161 214 1130. 68-70 Market Street. 0161 836 2800) **Harvey Nichols 5B** (21 New Cathedral Street. 0161 828 8888. www.harveynichols.com) **Hermes 5D** (31 King Street. 0161 834 5331. www.hermes.com) **House of Fraser** (Kendals) **4D** (Deansgate. 0161 832 3414. www.houseoffraser.co.uk) **Hugo Boss 5D** (16-18 King Street. 0161 831 9548. www.hugoboss.com) **James Personal Tailor & Son 6C** (James Binney House, 52 Cross Street 2nd Floor. www.jamespersonaltailor.co.uk) **Jill Black 5C** (2 Barton Arcade, Deansgate. 0161 834 5160) **Manchester Craft & Design Centre 8B** (17 Oak Street. 0161 832 4274. www.craftanddesign.com) **Mao 9C** (Tib Street.

0161 833 0077) **Marks & Spencer 6C** (7 Market Street. 0161 831 7341. www.marksandspencer.com) **Miss Selfridge 6C** (74 Market St, 0161 834 3924. Trafford Centre. 0161 747 3895. www.missselfridge.co.uk) **Mulberry 5D** (62 King Street. 0161 839 3333. www.mulberry.com) **My Goodniss! 8B** (40 Thomas Street) **New Look 7C** (48-49 Arndale Centre. 0161 866 8773. www.newlook.co.uk) **Nicholas Jones Bespoke Tailoring 5C** (10 St Ann's Arcade, 0161 834 4992. www.nicholasjonesbespoke.co.uk **Oasis 7C** (7Arndale Centre. 0161 839 843 060. Market Street. 0161 834 3441 www.oasis-stores.com) **Oi Polloi 8B** (70 Tib Street. 0161 831 7870. www.oipolloi.com **Oxfam Originals 8C** (11 Smithfield. Buildings. Oldham Street. 0161 839 3160) **Pastiche 9C** (7 Old Bank Street. 0161 832 8595) **Pop Boutique 9C** (34-36 Oldham Street. 0161 236 5797. www.pop-boutique.com) **Primark 7D** (106 Market St. 0161 923 4772. www.primark.co.uk. 0161 236 5797) **Rags to Bitches 9C** (60 Tib Street. 0161 835 9265. www.rags-to-bitches.co.uk) **Selfridges 5C** (Exchange Square. 0780 8377 377. www.selfridges.co.uk) **Thomas Pink 5D** 58 King Street. 0161 833 1086. www.thomaspink.co.uk) **T.M. Lewin 5D** (44 King Street. 0161 835 1330. www.tmlewin.co.uk) **Topshop/Topman 7C** (1 Exchange Square. 0161 838 0735. www.topshop.com) **Vicky Martin 6B** (Unit 31, Triangle. 0161 832 8234) **Vivienne Westwood 6D** (47 Spring Gardens, King Street. 0161 835 2121. www.viviennewestwood.com) **Urban Outfitters 7C** (Market Street. 0161 817 6640. **Westworld 8C** (59 Church Street. 0161 839 5252. The Triangle. 0161 839 4242) **Zara 5C** (New Cathedral Street. 0161 831 0940. www.zara.com).

Sport/Outdoors

Barbour 5D (5 St. Anns Passage. 0161 832 7234. www.barbour.com) **Blacks 5C** (200 Deansgate. 0161 833 0349. www.blacks.com) **Cast 8B** (49-51 Thomas Street. 0161 832 5100) **Exit 8C** (41-43 Oldham Street. 0161 839 0437. www.exit.uk.com) **North Face 4D** (188 Deansgate. 0161 834 5707).

Shoes and Accessories

Accessorize 5C (2 Market Street. 0161 833 3651. www.accessorize.co.uk) **Boodle & Dunthorne 5D** (1 King Street. 0161 833 9000. www.boodleanddunthorne.com) **Edwards of Manchester 5C** (61 Deansgate, Barton Arcade. 0161 834 1339. www.edwardsofmanchester.co.uk) **Hussain the Barbers 9C** (56 Tib Street. 0161 834 0721) **Mappin & Webb 5D** (King Street. www.mappin-and-webb.co.uk) **Office 5C** (7 St Ann's Square. 0161 832 7337. www.office.co.uk) **Offspring** (Selfridges) 1 Exchange Square. 0161 838 0700) **Robot Lounge 8B** (4 Hilton Street. 0161 839 1800. www.robot-lounge.com) **Ran 5C** (8 St Ann's Arcade, off St Ann's Square. 0161 832 9650) **Russell and Bromley 5C** (2/3 St. Ann's House.

Top five for...Underwear

Agent Provocateur: Dylan Moran once said that men like lingerie because it makes women look like cakes. If that's true then Agent Provocateur is definitely the Mr. Kipling of the underwear world, lots of icing, not much substance and without a doubt will come all wrapped up with a cherry on top.

Marks and Spencer: At the other end of the spectrum is super sensible Marks, which has actually rather glamorised itself in recent years, with mixed results (some experiments are lovely lacey creations, some are a bit bizarre). This is the mum of underwear, comforting, strong and always there in a crisis.

Oasis: Oasis has rather excelled itself in the lingerie department recently with the Odile range, which is definitely on the fripperies side of things, adorned as it is with bows and crystals. Girly maybe, but a chance to get away from those horrible slogan knickers.

Calvin Klein: The big underwear phenomenon of the 90's has gone quiet recently but is still the place to stock up on those minimalist white cotton pants. It also stocks a few more sexy items too.

Primark: Oh Primark. The saviour of many a girl who has spent the night out gallivanting with their cute cotton knickers for only a pound. Yes some are hideous, but then you find fun boy cut shorts decorated with cupcakes and unicorns so you can't really complain.

0161 834 3131. www.russellandbromley.co.uk) **Scholl 5C** (49 Deansgate. 0161 834 8570. www.schollshoes.co.uk) **Size 6C** (18 Market Street. 0161 839 8086) **Shelleys 7C** (Market Street) **Swarovski** (Exchange St. 0161 819 5445. www.swarovski.com) **Topshop Shoes** (20-22 King St. 0161 832 5404. www.topshop.com).

Health and Beauty

Body Shop (24-26 King Street **5D** 0161 819 2505. Royal Exchange **6C** 0161 832 9148. www.thebodyshop.com) **Boots 6C** (32 Market Street. 0161 832 65 33. St. Ann Street. 0161 839 1798. **5C** www.boots.com) **Penhaligons 5C** (Exchange Street St Ann's Square. 0161 835 1155).

T'La

Top five...Aladdin's Caves

Oklahoma: Taking multi-tasking to the extreme by being a gift shop, café, artspace and record shop all in one, its no surprise this place is a higgledy-piggledy heap of crazy *objets*. Currently we love the pastel colored mini-suitcases (very adorable) and the flamingo statuettes. (74 High Street. City. 0161 834 1136)

T'La: The place to go if you need a quick hello kitty fix or perhaps you can't live another second without the latest Cantonese blockbuster. Among the plastic trinkets is a very nice paper selection. (16 Nicholas Street, City. 0161 236 2333)

Fred Aldous: Unbelievable array of crafty bits and bobs. Spend hours getting mesmerised by the glitter and sequins. Oooh sparkly. (Lever Street, City. 0870 7517302)

House of Haynes: Top fancy dress shop that will bring out the fantasist in you. they make to order too. (1st floor, 32 Oldham Street. City. 0161 237 3775)

Thunder Egg: A whole range of snappy, voguish clothes, cards, gifts and general inspiration. (22 Oldham Street. 0161 235 0606)

Furniture and Salvage

Den 9C (Oldham Street. 0161 226 7854) **Ferrious 6G** (61 Whitworth Street West. 0161 228 6880) **Innerform** (Chorlton Mill, Hulme Street. 0161 238 8558) **In Situ** (Talbot Mill, 44 Ellesmere Street, Hulme. 0161 839 5525) **Rimo 4F** (273 Deansgate. 0161 832 9911) **Simon Green 4D** (43 King Street West. 0161 834 8903).

Books

Cornerhouse Bookshop 7G (70 Oxford Street. 0161 200 1514. www.cornerhouse.org/books) **George Kelsall** (22 Church St, Littleborough. 01706 370 244) **Magma 8C** (24 Oldham Street. 0161 236 8777. www.magmabooks.com) **RIBA Bookshop 7F** (113 Portland Street. 0161 236 7691. www.ribabookshops.com) **Stanfords 7D** (39 Spring Gardens. 0161 831 0250. www.stanfords.co.uk) **Waterstone's 5C** (91 Deansgate. 0161 837 3000. Manchester Arndale. 0161 832 8563. Trafford Centre. 0161 749 8623. www.waterstones.com).

Music

Eastern Bloc 8C (Central Hall, Oldham Street. 0161 228 6432. www.easternblocrecords.co.uk) **Fat City 9C** (20 Oldham Street. 0161 237 1181. www.fatcity.co.uk) **Forsyths 4D** (126 Deansgate, City. 161 834 3281. www.forsyths.co.uk) **Pelicanneck 8B** (74-76 High Street. 0161 834 2569. www.pelicanneck.com) **Piccadilly Records 8C** (G9 Smithfield Building, Oldham Street. 0161 839 8008. www.piccadillyrecords.com) **Roadkill 9C** **Vinyl Exchange 9C** (18 Oldham Street. 0161 228 1122. 67 Bridge Street. 819 5440. www.vinylexchange.co.uk) **Vox-Pop 9C** (53-55 Thomas St. 0161 832 3233. www.voxpopmusic.com).

Hairdressers

Toni and Guy (0161 228 1999) Visit the academy on Queen Street for a cheap haircut **Vidal Sassoon** (0161 827 7140) **Razor's Edge** mini chain (0161 832 7747 for branches) **Hedonist 8C** (Tib Street, City. 0161 833 0800) **Nicky Oliver 8C** (32 Oldham Street, City. 0870 4380644) **Andrew Collinge 6C** (11 Chapel Walks, City. 0161 834 1616).

City trail for kids

This trail across the city centre is a way of discovering some of the secret delights of Manchester. The hour long route goes through a very interesting part of the city which many people miss and offers tantalising glimpses of statues, artworks and curiosities along the way. So take a look at the pointers below and then at the pictures and once you've found the thing they belong to move on to the next. Kids and families will have to sometimes look up, sometimes look down but definitely look harder at the city around them. The first pages show the route and the kids should do this part. The last two pages explain what the things you have found mean.

1 Start in Piccadilly Gardens near the fountains to find this first clue, you might have to look up – who is the man shown in this first clue?

2 Nearby close to a bar called Kro you will find the next clue it might be a bit of a battle – look for a man with a big hook nose. Who is this man?

3 Walk though the Gardens towards the coffee shop Caffé Nero and find a lonely wall standing all on its own. Can you see what the third clue belongs too? Read the sign to find out why it is here.

4 Be a sport and find the fourth clue attached to the Abbey National Bank.

5 Cross over the tramlines and walk up Tib Street between Debenhams and Starbucks. Before the traffic lights find the cracked-up clue number 5. Can you find the name of the artist who did the work?

1

2

3

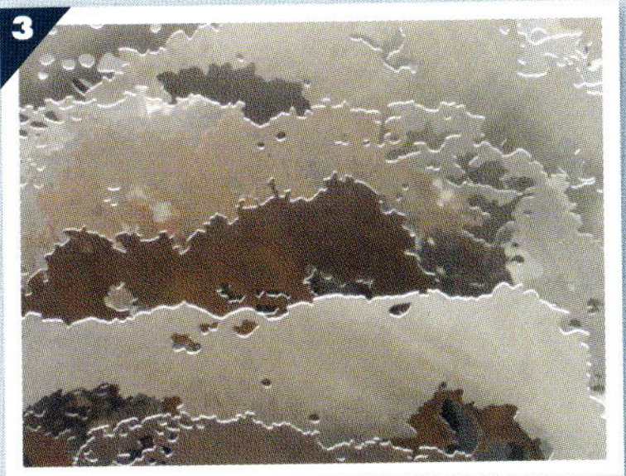

4

5

KIDS

6 Turn right at the traffic lights here onto Church Street and then next left on to Oldham Street and cross over. Follow Oldham Street past Magma shop to Pop Boutique to find clue 6. What do you think it is?

7 Cross back over Oldham Street to the shop called Forbidden Planet and then turn left down Hilton Street before taking the first right up Tib Street. Follow this to Centro Bar and turn left down Dorsey Street. You should be able to see the moo-ver and shaker that is clue 7 from here.

8 Walk under clue 7 and you'll see the old fish market which now houses the Manchester Craft and Design Centre (MCCA). For our route though, take the street on the left of this as you are looking at it – Copperas Street. Look along the wall of the MCCA to find clue 8.

9 Follow Copperas Street to cobbled High Street and turn left with the entertaining sculptures of fishermen on the façade of another old fish market. Where the cobbles end, take a fruity look around for Odd Bar and clue 9.

10 Turn left on to Thomas Street and take the first right down tiny Brick Street. At the first junction with equally tiny Back Turner Street try and spot the colourful little alien that is clue 10.

11 Walk down Brick Street to the junction with Turner Street and turn right. The Buddhist Centre is straight over the road but see if you can handle finding clue 11.

KIDS

12 Continue along Turner Street to High Street, turn left and then right, following the tramlines to the junction with Shudehill. Cross at the lights follow the tramlines down the hill, this becomes Balloon Street, to the junction with Corporation Street. Can you spot clue 12?

13 Nearby you might also find clue 13.

14 Turn left on Corporation Street past the Cooperative Bank and walk to the big Next at Manchester Arndale. Cross over to Exchange Square and onto the curved building - the Triangle Shopping Centre. Near the entrance you might find the next clue. .

15 Follow the wall of the Triangle past the old black and white pubs. Further down the hill, on one of the buildings on your right look for clue 16.

16 Return to the old pubs and turn left along cobbled Cathedral Street. You might spot the golden number 16 clue before the cobbles run out.

17 Continue straight on from New Cathedral Street down Long Millgate and then down by the red brick wall of Chetham's School of Music. On the right is a water feature (it may not be turned on) which forms a stream running into a pool. Somewhere on this water feature find clue 17. Congratulations you've finished.

14

15

12

16

13

17

City trail solutions

These are the solutions and answers to the clues in the trail on pages 260-261.

1) This is St George, England's patron saint, fighting the dragon right on top of the big monument to Queen Victoria (1837-1901), the country's longest reigning monarch. When the statue was put up in 1901 it was called the 'most inept' in the country. Was this fair? Does the Queen look like a 'fat beetle' as one commentator has said?

2) The man with the big nose is the Duke of Wellington and the scene on the panel shows the Battle of Waterloo which the British and their allies won against Napolean and the French. Wellington would later be the Prime Minister. Other panels show him as a politician.

3) This is the Tree of Remembrance put up in 2005 to remember the civilian war dead of Manchester. The sculptor responsible has the fabulous name of Wolfgang Buttress.

4) The world's first professional Football League was founded here in 1888 but neither Manchester City nor Manchester United were big enough to join until later. At the time they were Ardwick FC (City) and – take a deep breath - Newton Heath Lancashire and Yorkshire Railway Football and Cricket Club (United). No wonder they changed the name.

5) You are now in the Northern Quarter of Manchester and here come the penguins. This mosaic refers to a Manchester club night. All the mosaic panels here are by Mark Kennedy and all have Mancunian links although its hard to guess it sometimes. The mosaics are attached to Afflecks Palace which contains four floors of independent boutiques and is great fun to visit although some shops are really just for adults. In the Northern Quarter streets you'll see plenty of interesting artworks such as the Tib Street Horn by David Kemp on the fragment of building opposite the mosaics – can you see a moon and an umbrella?

6) You'll have to look down when you get to Pop Boutique. Manchester has a rich heritage of pop and rock music and these panels in the pavement refer to that. The one on our picture shows part of the Union Jack guitar Noel Gallagher from the band Oasis used to play.

7) Yep it's a cow, or half a cow, by Tracey Cartledge. This one is Moolin Rouge, a dancing cow from the Moulin Rouge in Paris obviously. The cow dates from when Manchester hosted the international art festival called Cowparade in 2003. In the gardens round the corner you'll find another cow, this time Lily by Beverley Fry.

8) On the side of the Craft Centre is Mr Smith's Dream a ceramic work showing stairs disappearing upwards – perhaps Mr Smith is about to go to bed and dream.

This used to be the pet shop area of Manchester and Mr Smith had a pet shop here. It was originally intended that there'd be lots of tiled panels in these streets in which the pets would dream about where they'd come from. The other ones never got finished.

9) High on the gable above Odd bar is a ceramic pineapple by Kate Malone called Queen Pineapple – there's another in Manchester Art Gallery. The pineapple was the symbol for hospitality and luxury – this one certainly looks very smart whatever the weather.

10) This is a tile of a space ship from the early digital game Space Invaders. In 2003 an eccentric gent made a trail of silly Space Invader and Pacman shapes around the city and this is one. Try and spot some others as you walk. Above it is a colourful street sign. In the Northern Quarter north and south street signs have blue writing on a white background and east to west tiles have white writing on a blue background.

11) The door handle is part of Oklahoma café and shop. This crazy little place makes for an ideal place for a break with its shakes, smoothies and cakes. It also has a mad selection of gifts too – although many are just for grown-ups.

12) The clue is on the statue. It's the little boy's face gazing up at Robert Owen. Owen was a pioneer in improving working and living conditions 150 years ago especially for children. Owen first became successful in Manchester before opening New Lanark Mills near Glasgow. He promoted the idea of 'co-operation' where people shared the profits they made.

13) Up on the wall, across the tramlines you'll see the words New York. At one time the Cooperative Movement, which occupies the buildings around here, had branches all over the world. Can you spot other city names?

14) Clue 14 is a mosaic of the coat of arms of Manchester on the Triangle Shopping Centre. There's a boat for this land-locked city because Manchester depended on trade and ships so much. The three lines are for the three rivers in the city centre, the Irwell, the Irk and the Medlock.

15) Clue 15 is a cartouche – which is a carved panel with words – on the side of Mynshull's House. Thomas Mynshull gave his house here to help 'poor, sound and healthy boys of Manchester in honest labour and employment.' Very nice, but hey Mr Mynshull what about the girls?

16) On the side of the Cathedral is the golden (actually gilded, not real gold) Mother and Child sculpture by Charles Wheeler. Not very exciting but it moves us on.

17) The last clue was the easiest thing to find on the whole trail but 18 is one of hardest. It's moulded on the metal of the last part of the water course before it falls into the fountain pool at the bottom of the slope. You're looking for a bee, the animal symbol of Manchester because the city was and is 'a hive of activity.' Well done, pester your mum for a drink and a cake now, you deserve it.

Manchester Pride

Gay and lesbian

In little more than a decade the area of Manchester now celebrated as the city's Gay Village has morphed from a run-down and neglected post-industrial wasteland into one of the city centre's liveliest quarters. There was a time when the only people to be found down this neck of the woods of an evening would be pimps, prostitutes and petty criminals but, during the '90s, that all changed and now the Village is awash with bars, restaurants and clubs. In fact, the Gay Village has proved so successful that virtually every major city is attempting to replicate Manchester's success. The transformation has certainly proved inspiring to creative types and several major television dramas have been filmed in the village. Manchester based Russell T Davies, now famed for his witty revival of *Dr Who*, wrote the controversial series *Queer as Folk* and then returned to the Village with *Bob and Rose*. The long-running drama, *Cold Feet*, frequently filmed in the area too and even the soap *Coronation Street* recently visited the Village when a gay storyline was featured. Tony Warren, the creator of Coronation Street, told the story of the gay life in Manchester during middle part of the twentieth century in his splendid novel, *Behind Closed Doors*. More recently Nicholas Blincoe explored the shady scene of the locale in *Manchester Slingback*. Crime writer Val McDermid and Manchester based novelist Paul Magrs have also given a more contemporary vision of the Gay Village in their books.

The Village really comes into its own each year when the area hosts Manchester Pride. Known by many names over the years (GayFest and Mardi Gras to name but two) this festival has developed from humble origins as a modest consciousness-raising event to one of the biggest celebrations of all things lesbian, gay, bisexual and transgender in the country. Last year's event raised more than £130,000 for local charities and good causes and attracted hundreds of thousands of visitors to the city from all around the world. This summer, Manchester Pride takes place between 17-27 August and promises to be the usual mix of clubbing extravaganzas and partying until obscenely late hours. All of which will be aided by the changes in the licensing laws allowing many of the clubs in the Village to serve alcohol until breakfast time.

Alongside such excess, there is a chance to join in sporting events, to catch a whole range of cultural actvities and join traditional parade through the city centre which brings Manchester to a standstill.

You could also join one of the guided tours which follow the the Lesbian and Gay Heritage Trail (see page 268), a fascinating examination of Manchester's queer history. The route is marked round the city centre with a series of rainbow tiles inlayed into the pavement. You can get a leaflet from the Visitor and Information Centre in St Peter's Square if you want to self-guide yourself around. For details of all these events and information on how to buy tickets visit www.manchesterpride.com.

Recorded gay history in Manchester stretches back two centuries - . However, it wasn't until the '90s that gay people began to become much more visible. The opening of Manto in 1992 signaled a change in direction. This wasn't a shady tucked away little bar but had huge open windows proudly showing it was out and proud. In many ways Manto set the scene for Manchester coming out of the closet. Soon, Canal Street was booming with new bars and clubs appearing everywhere and now, with the recent Civil Partnerships Bill, Manchester is also one of the best cities for gay couples to tie the knot.

Geographically the Village is a relatively small area between Portland Street and Whitworth Street, on both sides of the Rochdale Canal. There are triumphantly old-school bars complete with foul-mouthed drag queen DJs, there are plenty of places for a quiet romantic meal, punters can dance away till dawn to commercial house, mooch about to emo and indie or head to urban nights such as Homiesexual and Club Zindagi. The erratic club night, Homoelectric, remains one of the most acclaimed events in Manchester and takes place every few months at Legends, featuring some the coolest DJs around. Bars such as Taurus, Velvet and AXM bring a sophisticated ambience to Canal Street. Meanwhile, Vanilla and Coyotes attract a loyal crowd of women and host a wide variety of club nights aimed specifically at women and their gay male friends.

There is much more to the Village than sheer hedonism though. The area was one of the first quarters of the city to embrace loft apartment living and a whole array of services have sprung up catering for a gay clientele. There are hairdressers, solicitors, travel agents, a deli, financial advisors and, of course, the obligatory tanning salon and gym. Local charity, the Lesbian and Gay Foundation provides invaluable health and social advice to the whole community. The city is also home to the annual Queer Up North festival; a showcase of innovative performance from around the world which takes place during May at various venues around the city centre. Visit www.queerupnorth.com for up-to-date listings of events. And, in the relative tranquility of Sackville Park, you can visit the Beacon of Hope, the first AIDS memorial in Britain, or take a seat on a bench next to a statue of Alan Turing which commemorates the brilliant gay mathematician who lived for a time in Manchester.

All in all the Village remains one of the most vibrant quarters of Manchester, a place to flirt with the bar-staff and party until you drop or simply enjoy a quiet alfresco drink and watch the narrowboats on the Rochdale Canal tootle by.

Gay to Z

AXM 8F – A stylish bar offering regulars a private membership scheme with VIP benefits. Canal Street 0161 236 6005.

Baa Bar 8F – Mixed bar open late all week. Sackville Street. 0161 247 7997.

Churchills 8E – Old style boozer with a cheap menu and home to sometimes tortuous karaoke sessions. *Open late Mon to Sat.* Chorlton Street. 0161 236 5529.

Clone Zone 8F – Your very own gay supermarket catering for all things of an adult nature. *Open late.* Sackville Street. 0161 236 1398.

Coyote's – Converted warehouse bar popular with a female clientele complete with pool table and late night club events. *Open late Tue-Sun.* Chorlton Street. 0161 236 4007.

Cruz 7F – The grande dame of gay clubbing in Manchester, Cruz pulls in a varied mix of people with a soundtrack of commercial dance, pop and camp classics. The basement is home to specialist men-only nights such as Kink. *Open Mon, Wed, Thu, Fri, Sat & Sun.* 101 Princess Street. 0161 237 1554.

Eden 8F – Relaxed bar offering a good menu and a chance to drink on the venue's very own canal barge, weather permitting. Canal Street. 0161 237 9852.

Essential 8E – Huge and very popular gay club open Friday to Sundays playing commercial dance and pop with regular live PAs. Minshull Street/ Bloom Street. 0161 237 5445.

Falcon – Contemporary men-only bar catering for a younger crowd. *Open every evening until late.* Richmond Street.

Gaia 8F- Sophisticated loft-style bar and restaurant open late Fri/Sat. Sackville Street. 0161 228 1002.

Green Room 6G – Gay friendly bar and theatre, home to many of the Queer Up North shows. Whitworth Street West. 0161 615 0500.

Hollywood Showbar 7F – Brash and bawdy and outrageously camp this bar offers karaoke, a pianist, strippers and cabaret. *Open late Mon to Sat. Bloom Street.* 0161 236 6151.

Legends 9F – Labyrinthine and very masculine club that also hosts the much more mixed night *Homoelectric*. Whitworth Street. 0161 236 5400.

Lesbian and Gay Foundation – Charity providing many health and social services for the gay community. Princess House, Princess Street. 0845 330 3030.

Manto 8F – The innovative bar launched in 1992 now sprawls over three floors with funky lounge area in the loft. Host to *Homiesexual* and to the legendary all night Breakfast Club on Sat. Canal Street. 0161 236 2667.

Napoleons 8F – At over thirty years in age, Napoleons claims to be the oldest gay club in Europe. Popular with the TV/TS crowd on Weds. *Open late all week.* Bloom Street. 0161 236 8800.

New Union 8F – One of the oldest bars in the Village, the New Union still offers old-style cabaret featuring the Showgirls of Manchester on Sundays. *Open late all week. Canal Street.* 0161 228 1492.

Hollywood Showbar

Coyote's

Gay Village

GAY & LESBIAN

New York New York 7F – Mixed bar downstairs, men only upstairs at weekends. *Open late all week.* Bloom Street. 0161 236 6556.

Paddy's Goose 8E – Unassuming little bar popular with trannies and handy for the bus station. Bloom Street. 0161 236 9709.

Poptastic 7F – Recently celebrated their tenth anniversary the Poptastic crew host an indie-trash disco renowned for the invention of the shagtag for those too shy to speak.. *Tues &Sat. Mutz Nutz.* Princess Street. 0161 236 6264.

Queer 8E –Light and airy bar from svengali Nigel Martin Smith. Host to *Essential* war-up events at weekends. Canal Street. *0161 228 1360.*

Rembrandt Hotel 8F – A bar and hotel resolutely popular with a slightly more mature masculine crowd. Sackville Street/ Canal Street. 0161 236 2435.

Sp!r!t 8F – Deceptively spacious lounge bar popular with a younger crowd. Canal Street. 0161 237 9725.

Taurus 9E –Tucked away at the very top of Canal Street, Taurus offers excellent food and friendly service from glamorous host Polly and his staff. Taurus was voted *City Life* Bar of the Year 2003 and now regularly hosts theatre events in the basement lounge. Canal Street. 0161 236 4593.

The Outpost – The sister venue to Legends offering a haven for bears and masculine types. *Open late all week.* Whitworth Street. 0161 236 5400.

Thompsons Arms 8E – Facing the bus station, this bar once hosted demented after-hours club night *Danceteria* but has undergone recent renovation. Upstairs is home to monthly gay Asian night *Zindagi* and other specialist events. Sackville Street. 0161 237 5919.

Tribeca 8F – Contemporary New York style bar that draws a mixed crowd. *Open late at weekends.* Sackville Street. 0161 236 8300.

Vanilla 8F – Billed as the lesbian Mecca of the north, Vanilla offers happy hours, themed nights, a pool table and welcome gay male guests. *Open late all week.* Richmond Street. 0161 288 2727.

Velvet 9E – Recently extended, Vanilla offers a theatrical bar upstairs and a dedicated restaurant in the basement. *Open late at weekends.* Canal Street. 0161 236 9003.

Via 8F – Multi-award winning bar winding round countless levels with separate restaurant area. *Open late all week.* Canal Street. 0161 236 8132.

Villagio – Relaxed and friendly Italian restaurant. Canal Street. 0161 244 5222.

Out in the past
- a trail around Manchester's Lesbian and Gay heritage

During EuroPride 2006 a heritage trail through Manchester's Lesbian and Gay past was created. It follows a route through the twists and turns of 200 years of homosexual history and provides an often painful, often amusing, insight into the years where the right to decide upon your personal relationships wasn't your own. It also illustrates the resolve and courage of so many in finding hidden, or not so hidden, corners in which to express their sexuality.

The trail starts at the New Union pub at the junction of Princess Street and Canal Street, and can be followed via a series of rainbow mosaic panels set into the pavements. In the Northern end of the city the trail passes the site of the Manchester Labour Press. This was one of the most progressive publishers in the country and counted amongst its directors, Edward Carpenter (1844-1926), gay poet and visionary. In 1894 he published here, for private circulation, *Homogenic love, and its place in a free society*, which even at this very early date explained and validated homosexual relationships and scorned current legislation. He wrote, in the book, 'It is difficult, of course for outsiders not personally experienced in such matters to realise the great strain and tension of the nerves under which these persons grow up from boyhood to manhood – or from girl to womanhood – who find their deepest and strongest instincts under the ban of society around them.' A copy of the booklet can be found in John Rylands Library later on the trail.

The best fictional documentation of Manchester's gay community pre-liberalism in the 1960s comes via Tony Warren, the creator of Manchester based soap, *Coronation Street*. His novel *Behind Closed Doors* is a moving coming of age novel set in 50s Manchester and is worth seeking out. This is his description of the now long gone Café Royal. 'Cigarette smoke and chatter and music were drifting up to meet them. Was there anybody here he knew? It was a long narrow room with a curving thirties counter undulating right down the left-hand side. The pianist was tucked away in the corner; he had several glasses of gin, each one accompanied by a little bottle of tonic, lined up on top of the grand piano. Behind the pianist, opposite the counter, was a wall full of alcoves. Peter had to look twice to be sure that he was seeing properly. The alcoves were full of fairly posh-looking couples – men and women. Could he be in the right place? Another quick glance round the whole cocktail bar and he had the ground rules straight. They were a bit like life itself: queer people were standing warily on their feet while normal ones were sitting down.'

ACCOMMODATION

Great John Street Hotel, rooftop hot-tub and terrace

Accommodation

The Manchester hotel scene has come on leaps and bounds in the last decade. From the mundane and the mediocre in the early '90s, the city now has a couple of five-star glamour pusses, its own private boutique mini-chain, bags of four and three-star accommodation plus a proper backpackers hostel. But it's not all rosy. The city still suffers from a lack of good B&Bs close to the city centre and it could do with more central pub accommodation as well. Meanwhile Manchester is just plain rubbish for convenient camp and caravan sites. Despite the splendour of the five stars, this gap in the city's tourism armoury needs to be addressed and the sooner the better.

SIGHTSEEING

A useful one-stop site for accommodation and booking late rooms is http://www.visitmanchester.com/. It also has goof advice for travellers in groups.

Five-star hotels

Lowry Hotel 4C 50 Dearmans Place, Salford, City. **0161 827 4000.** *www.rfhotels.com* or *www.thelowryhotel.com. 165 rooms. £125-£1595 single, £145-£1845 double.* The Lowry delivers five-star opulence with elegant rooms, marble en-suite bathrooms, E'Spa beauty salon and the much-improved River Room restaurant. Packages include the Pyjama Party, which includes a visit from The Lowry Hotel's beauty expert with a selection of cleansing and manicure products. Very close to all the central amenities with a roster of the rich and famous as guests.

Radisson Edwardian 5E Free Trade Hall, Peter Street, City. **0161 835 9929.** *www.radissonedwardian.com. 263 rooms. £105-325 rates vary according to the time of year.* Manchester's latest conversion retains features of this important city building's original charm (see page 55) whilst incorporating new construction and state of the art technological detail. There is OpusOne restaurant too and a spectacular a health spa. Centrally located for all amenities and popular, darling, with celebrity visitors - Manchester United often stay here the night before home games to build team spirit.

The River Bar, The Lowry Hotel

Boutique hotels

Eleven Didsbury Park 11 Didsbury Park, Didsbury. **0161 448 7711.** *www.eclectic-hotel-collection.com. 20 rooms. From £150-260.* No chintz in sight in this converted suburban Victorian villa, just cool design and contemporary style. Guests also get a lovely walled garden to lounge in during summer. Round the corner on the main Wilmslow Road is the 27 bedroomed Didsbury House Hotel (0161 448 2200 www.eclectic-hotel-collection.com), the second in this sophisticated mini-chain, with standard room rates of £150-£260 (check website for last minute deals). Here you can expect more beautifully designed public areas, rooms and gardens, together with a So Spa.

Great John Street Hotel 2E Great John Street, City. **0161 831 3211/0870 2202277.** *www.eclectic-hotel-collection.com. 30 duplex suites. £235 baby grand, £255 boudoir, £335 grand, £450 grandest(some cheaper rates subject to availability).* Part of the same group as the Didsbury hotels above, this former school house bang in the city centre has a cocktail and champagne bar, gym and rooftop garden. There's even a hot tub up on the roof for pure al fresco indulgence. The hotel is next to Granada Television and the Coronation Street set. The design throughout reflects the proprietors' love of the contemporary.

Four-star equivalent

Alias Rossetti 9D 107 Piccadilly, City. **0161 247 7744.** *www.aliashotels.com* or *www.abodehotels.co.uk. 61 Rooms. £110 double, £130 twin/king, £155 large king, £265 penthouse.* The Rossetti is in the process of becoming part of the Abode chain. The hotel itself sits inside a sparkling conversion of an 1899 building. The five suites named after celebs such as Johnny Cash offer comfort and style and the Café Paradiso provides excellent nosh and the basement has the best club nights in a Manchester hotel. Hopefully the new owners will carry on in the same tradition.

Arora International 18-24 Princess Street, City. **0161 2368999** *www.arorainternational.co.uk. 141 rooms. £135-175 check online for deals.* Pleasant hotel especially notable for Obsidian, its attached restaurant and bar. The 50ft illuminated bar backlit in aquamarine serving an extensive list of cocktails makes it one of chicer hotel bars to drink in.

Hilton Manchester Deansgate 4F 303 Deansgate, City. **0161 870 1600.** *www.hilton.co.uk/manchester. Call ahead for room rates.* The Hilton Manchester Deansgate occupies the first 23 floors of Beetham Tower, a striking high-rise steel and glass monolith located on Deansgate - see page 48. Hard to miss. As well as a 20-metre heated indoor pool, the hotel houses three spa rooms offering massage and beauty treatments, a sauna and a gym and if healthy living is not your thing there is Cloud 23, a bar on the 23rd floor with stunning views of the city. It's apparently not just a four star but a four star deluxe.

Malmaison 9E Piccadilly, City. **0161 278 1000.** *www.malmaison.com. 167 rooms. From £150 standard, £170 superior, £210 suite.* A funky alternative convenient for Piccadilly Station. The rooms aren't the biggest but they have a bold design and are filled with clever touches. The brasserie is an added bonus as are the Petit Spa and gym.

Midland 5E Peter Street, City. **0161 236 3333.** *www.quintessential-hotels.co.uk. 312 rooms. Prices on demand.* A total refurbishment in 2006 provided the Midland with a shot of botox. It made a splash on the news that year by hosting many of the politicians for the Labour Party Conference (with accompanying security often found scaling the walls). Despite the attention, it remains the grand old lady of Mancunian hospitality and its public areas still has real atmosphere. The French Restaurant remains a bastion of fine cuisine and old-fashioned, near perfect service. There's a leisure club with swimming too.

Palace Hotel 7G Oxford Road, City. **0161 288 1111.** *www.principal-hotels.com. 257 rooms. Standard rates £165-£185 but prices fluctuate according to season. Call ahead to check.* Grade II listed, the Palace is impressive (see page 62). The building was the old Refuge Assurance headquarters and it shows in the tiled splendour of the main banking hall. There are two bars, a restaurant and a large function room.

Place Apartment Hotel 10E Ducie Street, Piccadilly, City. **0161 778 7500.** *www.theplacehotel.com. 108 apartments. Standard rate £145-226 enquire ahead.* Very impressive loft apartments with new kitchens and stunning bathrooms. Downstairs is the fine-dining restaurant the Cotton House with its upmarket Champagne Bar.

Three-star equivalent

Britannia Hotel 8E Portland Street, Piccadilly, City. **0161 228 2288/0845 838 1020.**

The Radisson Edwardian Hotel

SIGHTSEEING

www.britanniahotels.com. 363 rooms. £105 to £160. Late deals available. Impressive hotel in important Manchester building (see pg 65). Good central location close to main shops, Chinatown and the Gay Village. Try and get one of the rose window rooms near the roofline to add drama to any romance or illicit affair.

Jurys Inn 5G 56 Bridgewater Street, City. **0161 953 8888.** *www.jurysdoyle.com. 265 Rooms. From £79 per room.* Comfy family-sized rooms, pub grub and reasonable prices. It's convenient for the Bridgewater Hall and the Hallé Orchestra as well as one of the city centre's best pubs, the neighbouring Britons Protection.

Castlefield Hotel 2F Liverpool Road, City. **0161 832 7073.** *www.castlefield-hotel.co.uk. 48 rooms. From £60/90 single and £85/105 double.* Convenient comfort stop with lounge bar and restaurant in the historic Castlefield area and opposite the Museum of Science and Technology.

Old Trafford Lodge Lancashire County Cricket Club, Old Trafford . **0161 874 3333** . *www.lccc.co.uk. 68 rooms. From £54 weekend and £64 midweek for a standard room. Prices subject to change, especially on matchdays.* The hotel is built into the cricket ground and several rooms have balconies looking over the pitch. Unusual location that's perfect for the cricket fanatic.

Premier Travel Inns

Portland Street 6F (The Circus, 112-114 Portland Street. 0870 238 3315), **MEN Arena 5B** (North Tower, Victoria Bridge Street. 0870 990 6366), **GMEX 6F** (Bishopsgate, 7-11 Lower Mosley Street. 0870 990 6444). **Deansgate Locks** (Gaythorne, River Street. 0870 990 6504). www.premiertravelinn.com. *Rooms from £55-60 on average.*

Other city centre accommodation

Try the **Ox 3F** (71 Liverpool Road. 0161 839 7740 www.theox.co.uk) with nine rooms at £49.95 each. The en-suite rooms are simple but attend to all the needs of the weekend breaker whilst downstairs the Ox provides exceptional food. The location in the historic Castlefield area is good too. Perhaps also try the **Burton Arms Hotel 9B** (31 Swan Street. 0161 834 3455) with nine rooms from 19.50 single, £39 twin/double, £19.50 per head triple, £50 en-suites (weekend prices). This is an old pub with bags of charm (or a lived-in feel, or perhaps just scruffy - whichever you prefer). **The Rembrandt Hotel 8F** (33 Sackville Street. 0161 236 1311 www.rembrandtmanchester.com), is handy for the village, with some of the rooms being located on Canal Street itself. Other rooms are little more than half-lit cubes with tiny windows facing an alleyway. Prices from £35. Another centrally located hotel, **The Mitre 6B** (3 Cathedral Gates, City. 0161 834 4128) is snuggled up between the Manchester Cathedral and the gleaming new shops of Exchange Square. The interior is charmingly haphazard, with great views of the Manchester wheel from some rooms. Prices start from £52 but check the online booking companies for discounts. Another alternative is the **Staying Cool** apartments located around the city (www.stayingcool.com call 0161 8351074). Apartments are available from £130 per night.

Youth Hostels

There are two alternatives here. **YHA Manchester 1F** (Potato Wharf, City centre. 0161 839 9960 www.yha.org.uk) has144 beds in dormitories from £16 (under 18)–£21 (adults), £49.50 twin rooms (an extra £3 charge for non-members is applicable and prices rise slightly in the summer season-phone ahead for details). It's cheap and cheerful with self-catering kitchen and canal-side restaurant. For backpackers hostels try **Hatters 9C** (50 Newton Street, City centre. 0161 236 9500 www.hattersgroup.com) which has 23 rooms from £15.50-£30. The same group runs **Hilton Chambers 9C** (15 Hilton Street, City, 0161 236 4414) which has more choice in the types of rooms (e.g. single en-suite is available). From #15-60.

B&Bs/guest houses

Manchester Welcome House (34 Highbank Drive, Didsbury. 0161 448 9053)

SIGHTSEEING

has five rooms at £27 single, £50 double. Further afield, 12 miles (18km) or north of the city, is **Swing Cottage** (31 Lake Bank, Hollingworth Lake, Littleborough, Rochdale. 01706 379094), which won Best Guesthouse at the 2005 Manchester Tourism Awards and has four en-suite lake-view bedrooms and an art and craft studio.

Caravanning and camping.

Two good ones several miles outside the city centre are **Capesthorne Hall Caravan Park** (Siddington, Macclesfield, Cheshire. 01625 861221) to the south, with 30 pitches from £16 per two persons, including electricity. In peak season times (Bank and school holidays) prices go up to £20 for 2 people or £25 for a family. North is **Hollingworth Lake Caravan Park** (Round House Farm, Rakewood, Littleborough, Rochdale. 01706 378661/373919) with 40 pitches. £10/12 per night up to four person, electricity included.

Airport hotels

Perhaps the most convenient of the airport hotels that still has some intimacy is **Etrop Grange** (Thorley Lane, Manchester Airport. 0870 609 6123 www.foliohotels.com). This has 64 rooms from £149 standard, £169 executive to suite 199, though many deals and packages are available at good discounts. The grandest hotel at the airport is the **Radisson SAS Hotel** (Chicago Avenue, Manchester Airport. 0161 490 5000 www. radissonsas.com)with 360 rooms from £110-260 though prices vary quite a lot with the season. There are plenty of offers and deals available, including parking facilities for your car while you are on holiday. Located between Terminals One and Two.

Spas

GL-14 6F (Canada House, Chepstow Street, City.0161 228 6789 www.gl14.com). This popular and good-looking independent business offers E'Spa, Dermologica and Jessica treatments in a modern and edgy looking environment with the Moroccan décor alone worth the visit. The gym and swim facilities are first class. Take your time here and book a day or half-day session. We love their hot stone massages, mud treatments and pedicures. Give them three hours and they'll give you your life back. Swimming pool, gym, spin studio, sauna, steam room, treatment rooms. **Lowry Hotel 4C** (Dearmans Place, Chapel Wharf, City. www.thelowryhotel.com 0161 827 4000) This five-star hotel is already four years old and offers E'Spa, Ishi and Carita treatments in impressively restrained surroundings. Think white walls and Zen-like relaxation with gym, relaxation areas, saunas, en-suite treatment rooms. **Sienna Spa-Radisson Edwardian Hotel 5E** (Peter Street, City. www.radissonedwardian.com 0161 835 9929). Sienna Spa is establishing itself as one of the city's premier spas. Using Elemis products, it's open to the public as well as members and hotel guests. The most impressive feature has to be the mood-enhancing lights in the sauna and steam room - hundreds of fairy lights dotted around the ceiling that gradually change colour as you relax. It's like a disco - albeit a slow, damp one. If you've just got an hour, try their Elemis Skin Specific facial (£58) featuring an intensive hydrating and revitalising range of treatments. It smells divine too. Swimming pool with jet stream, Jacuzzi and spa bath, gym, solarium, sauna and steam room, en-suite changing rooms. **Malmaison 9E** (Piccadilly, City.0161 278 1010 www.malmaison.com).Malmaison has a gym and 'petit spa', with a good range of facilities, but no pool. E'Spa products are used in the treatment rooms, and if you're not a member day passes are available so you can make use of the gym. Access to the facilities is included in the price of a treatment. Try their total body holistic treatment offering scalp, face and body rejuvenation. It's perfect for treating dull skin, tension, circulation and stress, takes an hour and a half, but you'll feel on top of the world for days afterwards. Sauna, Jacuzzi, solarium, sun beds and fully equipped gym. **The Hilton Hotel 3F** (303 Deansgate, City. 0161 870 1650) boasts a Living Well Express gym and Heaven Spa (owned by a local entrepreneur) with three treatment rooms, E'spa products and an exciting vibro-massage chair.

EVENTS 2007/08

Festivals and Festivities

Viva! Film Festival
March 15-25, *various venues*
A showcase of films from the Spanish-speaking nations. See ***www.vivafilmfestival.com.***

Manchester International Film Festival
October 26 - November 4, *various venues*
The short film festival Kinofilm has launched this biennial event. The new festival will combine a mix of features, shorts, animation and documentary, and will showcase premieres and new talent. www.kinofilm.org.uk

Queer Up North International Festival
May 7-May 27, *various venues*
Manchester 's international festival of Queer Arts. www.queerupnorth.com

Manchester Jazz Festival
July 21-28, *various venues*
Visit ***www.manchesterjazz.com***.

Manchester Pride
August 17-27
Manchester 's annual festival celebrating lesbian, gay, bisexual and transgender life. The Big Weekend is 62 hours of celebrations from 10pm on Friday 24 August until midnight on Monday 27 August.
www.manchesterpride.com

Manchester Food and Drink Festival
October 5-15, *various venues*
The biggest urban food and drink festival in the UK taking over restaurants, pubs, bars and city squares and streets.
www.foodanddrinkfestival.com

Manchester Literature Festival
October 4-14, *various venues*
This year's festival will feature Freeplay, a series of events where new writing meets new technology. Independents will be a programme of readings showcasing independent publishing, writing and production. ***www.mlfestival.co.uk.***

Manchester Comedy Festival 2007
October 18 - October 30, *various venues*
The best comedy festival in the country after Edinburgh. Check ***www.manchestercomedyfestival.co.uk*** to find out what will tickle you this year.

Black History Month
October, *various venues*
Talk, performances, music, drama and dance taking place throughout October. Visit ***www.actsofachievement.org.uk.***

Manchester's Festive Markets
November 15 - December 19,
various locations
Manchester's ever popular European Christmas Markets complete with twinkling chalets, festive stalls, continental gifts, luxury goods and taste-bud tempting treats from across Europe. ***www.manchester.gov.uk/markets***

Outdoor Theatre and tours

Twelfth Night
Dunham Massey **June 30,** *Bramhall Hall* **July 6,** *Wythenshawe Park* **July 13-18.**
The same company will also perform The Wizard of Oz (dates tbc) and the Merchant of Venice (also tbc). One of a number of outdoor classics at venues across and just outside the city. See ***www.heartbreakproductions.co.uk*** for more details. The 2007 Season at Heaton Park includes Blue Remembered Hills by Dennis Potter July 19-28 and A Midsummer Night's Dream, August 2-18. Visit ***www.feelgoodtheatre.co.uk*** to check details.

Halloween Ghost Walk
Oct 31 - *start point tbc*
Spooky tours of Manchester with ghostly manifestations. Call 07876235638.

Music

Dpercussion 2007
August 4, *Castlefield Arena.*
This year the 'D' stands for decade. 2007 celebrates 10 glorious years of Dpercussion and is set to be the biggest and best yet. To find out more info on featured acts visit *www.dpercussion.com.*

Futuresonic
May 10-12, *various venues*
Describing itself as 'an urban festival of electronic arts and music' this is one for lovers of all things hi-tech. Check *www.futuresonic.com* for more details.

In The City
October 20–22, *various venues*
A weekend for music industry types to get together and decide on next year's big thing, and a chance for the rest of us to catch up-and-comers before they get famous. Check *www.inthecity.co.uk.*

Sport

British Open Athletics Championships 2007
June 15-17, *Sportcity*
Top class disability sport visit *www.disabilitysport.org.uk.*

GB Masters Championships
June 15-17, *Manchester Aquatics Centre*
The best of British swimming visit *www.britishswimming.org.*

BUPA Great Manchester Run
Sunday May 20th, 2007
Britain's biggest and most prestigious 10k returns to the streets of Manchester - a BBC televised event.

North of England Athletics Championships
July 15-17, *Sportcity*
Featuring stars of British Athletics.

Manchester International Men's Trophy Tennis
July 15-22, *The Northern Club, West Didsbury* check *www.lta.org.uk* for more details.

Manchester International Festival

June 28 – July 15, various venues
www.manchesterinternationalfestival.com

The world's first festival dedicated to new work got off to an auspicious start: the opening event, the Gorillaz' live performance at the Opera House received rave reviews and was even nominated for a Grammy. This festival is a slow burner though, that was back in 2005 and the festival proper doesn't start till summer 2007. It should be worth the wait though. Expect events that range from highbrow and arty to populist to just plain mind boggling all with an original theme. So whatever it is, from music to performance art, you can say you saw it here first.

"From the beginning we wanted to reflect the type of city Manchester is. We wanted this festival to have a sense of place. Manchester was the original, modern city, the first city of the new industrial age, thus we wanted to produce a festival that showcased new work. It seemed the entirely appropriate thing to do."

Alex Poots, Festival Director

CITY TRANSPORT

Travelling in and around Manchester

A good new addition to the transport system are the Metroshuttle bus services. These are free and operate on three routes covering all the main city centre areas. They run every ten minutes: Mon-Sat 7am-7pm, Sunday 10am-6pm.

Rail: the city is served by two main rail stations, Manchester Victoria and Manchester Piccadilly, which are supported by other stations around the city centre – Oxford Road, Deansgate and Salford Central.

Metrolink trams: provide a link through the centre of Manchester with on-street stations around the Piccadilly Gardens area and St Peter's Square. The trams also run out to Bury in the north, Altrincham in the south and Salford Quays and Eccles in the west.

Bus: the main bus terminals are at Piccadilly Gardens and Shudehill Transport Interchange - for full information contact GMPTE (details below). A network of night buses operate on Friday and Saturday nights. The buses run from the city centre to most other Greater Manchester town and city centres for a flat rate fare of around £2 depending on the bus company. Check out GMPTE, the local public transport authority in Greater Manchester at www.gmpte.com. Alternatively, you can speak to someone

GMPTE (8am-8pm) 0161 228 7811
Train enquiries: 08457 484950
Metrolink: 0161 205 2000
Information and tickets are also available from GMPTE Travelshops at main bus stations across Greater Manchester.

Metrolink Station at Newton Heath

METRO SHUTTLE ROUTES

Victoria Station
MEN Arena
Victoria
Shudehill
Rochdale Road
Urbis
The Printworks
The Triangle
Corporation St
Withy Grove
Chinese Arts Centre
Thomas Street
Harvey Nichols
Selfridges
M&S
Manchester Arndale
Church St
Oldham Street
St Mary's Gate
Royal Exchange
Boots
Market Street
Deansgate
St Ann's Square
Cross Street
Spring Gardens
Market St
King St
York St
John Dalton St
Piccadilly Gdns
Portico Library
Piccadilly
Albert Square
Town Hall
Charlotte St
Portland St
City Art Gallery
Chinatown
Mount St
Central Library
Princess Street
Central Coach Station
Station Approach
Aytoun St
Piccadilly
Peter St
St Peter's Sq
Oxford Street
Canal Street
Piccadilly Station
Lower Mosley Street
Cube Gallery
Bridgewater Concert Hall
Palace Theatre
Whitworth Street
Universities
Whitworth Street West
Corner House
Oxford Road Station
BBC
Oxford Road
Chester St
Manchester Metropolitan University

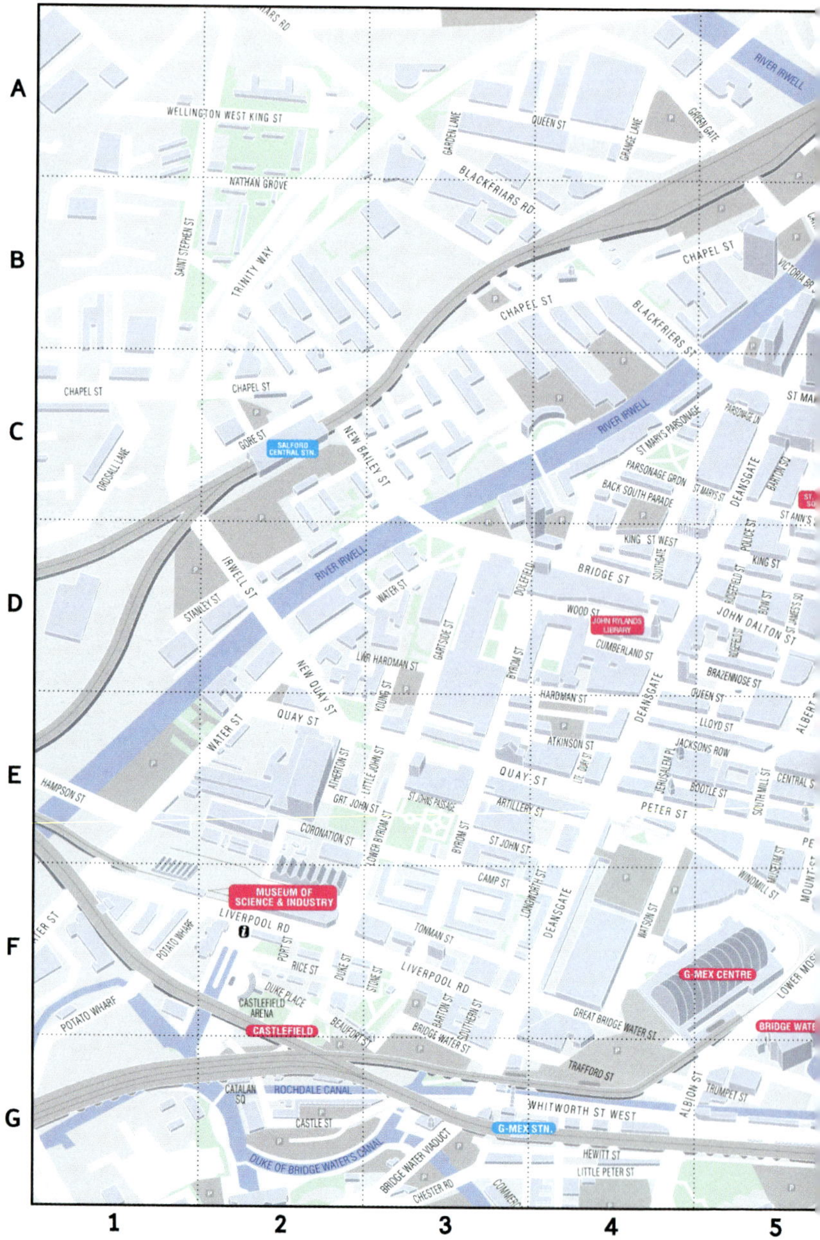
A
B
C
D
E
F
G
1
2
3
4
5
RIVER IRWELL
WELLINGTON WEST KING ST
QUEEN ST
GARDEN LANE
GRANGE LANE
GREEN GATE
NATHAN GROVE
BLACKFRIARS RD
SAINT STEPHEN ST
TRINITY WAY
CHAPEL ST
VICTORIA BR
BLACKFRIARS ST
CHAPEL ST
CHAPEL ST
ST MA
GORE ST
SALFORD CENTRAL STN.
NEW BAILEY ST
ORDSALL LANE
RIVER IRWELL
ST MARYS PARSONAGE
PARSONAGE LN
PARSONAGE GRDN
BACK SOUTH PARADE
ST MARYS ST
DEANSGATE
BARTON SQ
ST ANN'S
KING ST WEST
SOUTHGATE
POLICE ST
KING ST
IRWELL ST
RIVER IRWELL
STANLEY ST
WATER ST
DOLEFIELD
BRIDGE ST
WOOD ST
JOHN RYLANDS LIBRARY
CUMBERLAND ST
JOHN DALTON ST
BOW ST
ST JAMES SQ
GARTSIDE ST
LWR HARDMAN ST
NEW QUAY ST
BYROM ST
BRAZENNOSE ST
YOUNG ST
HARDMAN ST
DEANSGATE
QUEEN ST
QUAY ST
WATER ST
LLOYD ST
ALBERT
ATKINSON ST
JACKSONS ROW
ATHERTON ST
LITTLE JOHN ST
QUAY ST
JERUSALEM PL
BOOTLE ST
SOUTH MILL ST
CENTRAL S
HAMPSON ST
GRT. JOHN ST
ST JOHNS PASSAGE
ARTILLERY ST
PETER ST
CORONATION ST
LOWER BYROM ST
BYROM ST
ST JOHN ST
PE
CAMP ST
LONGWORTH ST
WINDMILL ST
MUSEUM ST
MOUNT ST
MUSEUM OF SCIENCE & INDUSTRY
LIVERPOOL RD
POTATO WHARF
TONMAN ST
DEANSGATE
WATSON ST
PORT ST
RICE ST
DUKE ST
STONE ST
LIVERPOOL RD
G-MEX CENTRE
LOWER MOS
POTATO WHARF
DUKE PLACE
CASTLEFIELD ARENA
BARTON ST
SOUTHERN ST
GREAT BRIDGE WATER ST
CASTLEFIELD
BEAUFORT ST
BRIDGE WATER ST
BRIDGE WATE
TRAFFORD ST
CATALAN SQ
ROCHDALE CANAL
ALBION ST
TRUMPET ST
WHITWORTH ST WEST
CASTLE ST
G-MEX STN.
BRIDGE WATER VIADUCT
HEWITT ST
LITTLE PETER ST
DUKE OF BRIDGE WATER'S CANAL
CHESTER RD

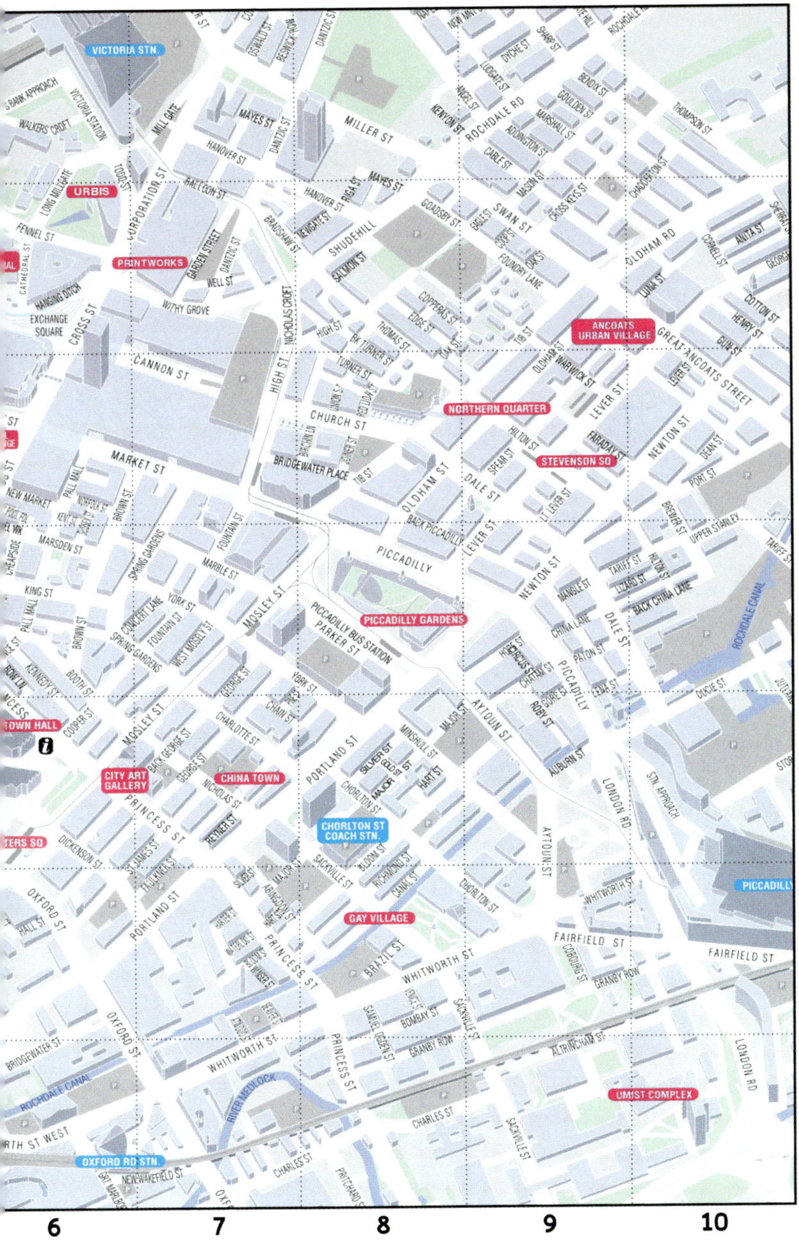

VICTORIA STN.
URBIS
PRINTWORKS
EXCHANGE SQUARE
ANCOATS URBAN VILLAGE
NORTHERN QUARTER
STEVENSON SQ
PICCADILLY GARDENS
TOWN HALL
CITY ART GALLERY
CHINA TOWN
CHORLTON ST COACH STN.
GAY VILLAGE
PICCADILLY
UMIST COMPLEX
OXFORD RD STN.
ROCHDALE CANAL
RIVER MEDLOCK
MILLER ST
ROCHDALE RD
SHUDEHILL
OLDHAM RD
GREAT ANCOATS STREET
CANNON ST
HIGH ST
CHURCH ST
MARKET ST
BRIDGEWATER PLACE
OLDHAM ST
PICCADILLY
MOSLEY ST
PORTLAND ST
PRINCESS ST
OXFORD ST
WHITWORTH ST
LONDON RD
FAIRFIELD ST
AYTOUN ST
NEWTON ST
CORPORATION ST
WITHY GROVE
CROSS ST
KING ST
6
7
8
9
10

To Preston, Blackpool, and the Lake District
To Blackburn
To Burnley
N
0
1
2
Euxton
Chorley
Belmont
Ramsbottom
Egerton
Coppull
Wrightington
Adlington
Walmersley
Tottington
Birtle
Smithills
Astley Bridge
Horwich
Walshaw
Blackrod
Tonge Moor
Heywood
Halliwell
BOLTON
BURY
Standish
Haigh
Breightmet
Shevington
Aspull
Heaton
Lostock
Daubhill
Little Lever
Radcliffe
Whitefield
WIGAN
Westhoughton
Farnworth
Ince
Daisy Hill
Kearsley
Hindley
Platt Bridge
Atherton
Prestwich
Pendlebury
Crumpsall
Walkden
Abram
Tyldesley
Boothstown
Leigh
Swinton
Ashton-in-Makerfield
Worsley
Monton
Pendleton
Leigh Canal
Lowton
Golborne
Haydock
Eccles
SALFORD
MANCH
CITY CE
Trafford Centre
Old Trafford
Newton-le-Willows
Culcheth
Irlam
Urmston
Stretford
Moss Side
Whalley Range
Flixton
Chorlton cum Hardy
Burtonwood
Cadishead
Carrington
Risley
River Mersey
Fearnhead
Partington
TRAFFORD
Sale
Rixton
Sale Moor
Wythenshawe
Broadheath
Northen
Manchester Ship Canal
Timperley
Warrington
Bridgewater Canal
Lymm
Altrincham
River Mersey
Bollington
Bowdon
Stockton Heath
Hale
High Legh
Ashley
Handforth
Manchester Airport
Styal
Mere
Wilmslow
Mobberley
Knutsford
Trent & Mersey Canal
Barnton
Weaverham
Northwich
To Stoke
Cuddington
To Ormskirk
To Liverpool
To Chester and N. Wales
M6
M61
M60
M62
M602
M66
M56
A6
A49
A56
A58
A571
A572
A573
A574
A576
A577
A579
A580
A57
A5082
A6144
A556
A560
A538
A5145
A50
A559
A34
A535
A675
A676
A666
A667
A673
A680

TOURIST INFO ⓘ

City centre
Lloyd Street, St Peters Square
0161 234 3157
www.destinationmanchester.com
Services: Accommodation, coach, theatre and tour bookings plus car hire.

Altrincham/Trafford 0161 912 5931
www.trafford.gov.uk

Ashton/Tameside 0161 343 4343
www.tameside.gov.uk

Bolton 01204 334400
www.visitbolton.com

Bury 0161 253 5111 *www.bury.gov.uk*

Manchester Airport 0161 436 3344

Oldham 0161 627 1024
www.visitoldham.gov.uk

Rochdale 01706 641085
www.visitrochdale.com

Salford Quays 0161 848 8601
www.visitsalford.com

Stockport 0161 474 4444
www.stockport.gov.uk

Wigan 01942 825677
www.wiganmbc.gov.uk

Manchester Transport Museum

PRACTICAL INFORMATION

Police, ambulance & fire services

Telephone 999. The operator will ask if you want police, fire or ambulance. For non-urgent police matters, contact the police switchboard on 0161 872 5050. With health-related matters try – if possible – to make your own way to the Accident and Emergency Department (A&E) of the nearest hospital below or call NHS Direct on 0845 4647. **Manchester Royal Infirmary**, Oxford Road, University (entrance off Grafton Street, 0161 276 1234). **Booth Hall Children's Hospital**, Charleston Road, Blackley (0161 795 7000). **North Manchester General Hospital**, Delauneys Road, Crumpsall (0161 795 4567). **Wythenshawe Hospital**, Southmoor Road, Wythenshawe (0161 998 7070).

Citizens Advice Bureau

Free confidential advice on civil matters, ie debt, benefits etc: 08451 221112.

Visitors with disabilities

Shopmobility in the Arndale Centre (0161 839 5110) provides mobility aids for people wishing to shop in the centre of Manchester (Mon-Sat 9am-6pm, Thu late, Sun 11am-5pm). One of the largest disability and advice lines in the North West is **D.I.A.L Trafford**, John Darby House, 88-92 Talbot Road, Old Trafford (0161 877 8546). They have a sensory impairment centre (environmental aids for people with visual and hearing impairments) and have details of all the other D.I.A.Ls in the area. **Manchester Disabled People's Access Group**, Unit 29 BEBC, Aked Close, Ardwick (0161 273 5033, (Minicom 0161 273 5083 wwww.mdpag.org.uk) also offer help, advice and information.

Bureaux de change

Several **Thomas Cook** bureaux de change are located within the following branches: King Street, Cross Street, Piccadilly, Oxford Street and Market Street, as well as at the airport. Phone 0161 839 0832 for details. **HSBC Bank** on Cross Street (0845 7404404) has a Thomas Cook bureau de change inside. Major **Post Offices** have money-changing facilities, and **Marks & Spencer** offer a money changing facility to tempt overseas visitors. Also try **American Express**, 10-12 St Mary's Gate, 0870 6001060.

Media

Newspapers

Manchester Evening News: free in the city centre and 35p outside the centre (Fridays features the excellent section go section with listings of events, gigs and so on). Local news, gossip, sport, arts, business, features, TV guide etc.

Manchester Evening News Metro: Free weekly tabloid delivered to homes and businesses in South Manchester, with local news, gossip, arts and entertainment.

Metro: Free daily paper available on buses, trams, railways etc.

Others: Most of Manchester's satellite towns have their own papers (eg Bolton Evening News, Oldham Chronicle, which are either daily, bi-weekly or weekly. Most cover local news, sport and business. There are also a variety of free local papers.

Radio

Key 103 (103 FM): chart music for the devoted pop fan.

Galaxy 102 (102 FM): all styles of modern dance and chart music.

Smooth FM (100.4FM): broadcasting soul throughout the North West, with specialist jazz programmes on the evenings and weekends.

BBC Radio Manchester: superb local BBC station for news, lifestyle, comment, documentary, and local sport. Particularly good Saturday morning talk show called Talk of the Town.

Xfm (97.7FM): dedicated rock and roll newcomer.

Internet

The latest news, visitor information and sport from the region is posted on **www.manchesteronline.co.uk** and offers amongst other things, a what's on search facility.

Internet access: Manchester Central Library,

St Peters Square, City (0161 234 1900).
Easy Internet Café, 8-10 Exchange Street, City centre (0161 832 9200).
Interface, inside Debenhams Department Store, 123 Market Street, City centre and at Debenhams, Regents Crescent, Trafford Centre.

Telephones and communications

National Directory Enquiries: 192 (free service from public call box).
International Directory Enquiries: 153 (free service from public call box).
Operator: 100 for services.

Transport

Airport

Serving over 22 million passengers a year, **Manchester** is the largest UK airport outside London. Three terminals, two runways, full facilities, quality airlines and tour operators, and direct destinations covering all five continents go to making Manchester a perfect gateway.
General enquiries: 0161 489 3000.
Flight arrival and departure information: 090 10101000.

Live flight information plus useful information about the airport is found at **www.manchesterairport.co.uk**. The airport has its own rail station located at the heart of the complex. It is connected to the national rail network, with two new spurs from the Manchester to London mainline giving travellers direct access to Manchester city centre, Scotland, Liverpool, Yorkshire, the Midlands and many other towns around the country.

Manchester Airport has a national coach and local bus terminus and taxi ranks, with connections to nearby towns. Many hotels have courtesy buses. It is intended that a Metrolink extension will eventually connect the city centre to the airport, via Chorlton and Wythenshawe. For travellers arriving by car, there are over 20,000 spaces within the long and short stay car parks on site. **Car parks information:** 0161 489 3723.

For hotel reservations on the airport site call 0161 489 2063 or 0161 499 0284.

Rail

General switchboard and timetable enquiries: 08457 484950. A Young Persons Railcard (available for 16-25 years old, and older but full-time students) may be purchased for the year, allowing a third off the usual price. A Senior Persons Railcard offers discounts to people aged 60 and over and there is also a Family Railcard, which offers discounts on most standard fares, provided that the holder is accompanied by a child, who travels for a very low flat fee. The Disabled Persons Railcard gets discounts for a companion as well. Overseas visitors travelling with individual companies will find full details of condition of carriage available on a leaflet from staffed stations. Most stations are non-smoking, but some intercity trains have smoking sections.

National buses

Travelling long distance by coach is cheaper than rail, but invariably takes longer. **National Express** is the only comprehensive nationwide coach service in the UK. In Manchester city centre, it operates out of the Chorlton Street Bus Station. A discount card is available for students of any age and for young people aged 18-25. There is also an Advantage 50 discount card for people over the age of 50. For credit card bookings and timetable enquiries, telephone 08705 808080. You can buy tickets in person at Chorlton Street Bus Station and the Manchester Visitor Information Service above or at designated travel agents. There is a 10% discount for seven days advanced booking.

Taxis

There are two types of legal taxis in Manchester: Hackney Cabs (also known as black cabs) and private hire/mini cabs. Manchester black cabs are licensed by the local council, can be hailed in the streets and can use designated taxi ranks. They carry five persons, and some are suitable for disabled passengers. For more information, telephone **Mantax** on 0161 230 3333 or taxiphone on 0161 236 9974. Mini cabs are four-door saloons, which must be phoned up and booked in advance and are usually cheaper. They cannot use taxi ranks and cannot be hailed in the streets. Warning: any vehicle without licence plates and purporting to be a taxi is not insured and is illegal.

Car rental

Listed below are nationwide car hire companies at Manchester Airport and the city centre – all accepting major credit cards.
Avis: Manchester Airport (0870 1566440) and 1 Ducie Street, City centre (0161 236 6716).
National Car Rental: Manchester Airport (0161 499 3320) and 49 Oldham Road, City centre (0161 834 3020).
Hertz: Manchester Airport (0161 437 8208) and 31 Aytoun Street, City centre (0161 236 2747). Europe Car: Manchester Airport (0161 436 2200).
Budget Rent a Car: Manchester Airport and Unit 1B, Ringway Trading Estate, Wythenshawe (0161 437 0151).

Geography

Manchester lies 35 miles (56km) from the sea, on a flat plain within the armpit of the Pennines. The land rises gently from around 40 metres (130ft) at Manchester Town Hall to over 600 metres (2,000ft) 15 miles (25km) from the city centre on the hilltops. The principal river of Manchester is the River Irwell, which springs from the West Pennines above Bacup and joins the River Mersey at Irlam, eight miles from the city. The Pennine hills form a wall to the north and east of the city. They are largely made of millstone grit forming plateaux frequently terminating in scarp and outcrop. This is a sedimentary rock from the Upper Carboniferous period created under the sea.

The absence of dissolved lime in these rocks ensures that local water stored in reservoirs is 'soft' which, good for bleaching, proved of use in the processes of the early textile industry, as did the fast flowing streams for providing power. In contrast, the Lancashire and Cheshire plains provide a gentle landscape. The plain sits on its north side upon Coal Measures – more than 2,000 metres deep split by seams of coal, particularly abundant around Wigan and Leigh. Under Manchester itself are Triassic sandstones. The original building material of the city was the pinkish red sandstone: you can see this raw in the cuttings of the Castlefield canals in the city centre.

Weather

The average rainfall is 855mm a year. Despite its reputation, Manchester is not the wettest city in Britain. In fact the city is a lowly ninth below other western UK cities such as Swansea (1361mm), Derry, Glasgow, Plymouth and Cardiff. It's a simple fact that the west of the British Isles will always be wetter than the east because of the prevailing Atlantic weather systems. Manchester scarcely experiences snow as it is protected by the Pennines.

Spring: 4.7°C-12°C, rainfall 186mm, sun 425 hours. **Summer:** 11.4°C-21°C, rainfall 223mm, sun 513 hours. **Autumn:** 7°C-13.2°C, rainfall 239mm, sun 281 hours. **Winter:** 1.5°C-6.7°C, rainfall 207mm, sun 160 hours.

'Mancunian Way' by Liam Spencer

Light effects

Manchester, despite its reputation, seldom stays leaden for long, nor is it likely to be flawlessly blue. Frequently the sky is on manoeuvre. Look for endless patterns, scudding clouds charging between the towers of the city centre or wispish cirrus lowering to form mackerel skies over Old Trafford. The sunsets and the dawns here can be spectacular. The buildings help. Stand at Manchester Central (formerly G-MEX) as the sun sinks and the terracotta rear of the Midland hotel fires up like a hot coal. The Quays are another good area for watching sunsets: all that space, water, and light, plus the shinning buildings, invite luminous twilights.

Rainy city

Manchester might not be the wettest city in the UK, but its rainy reputation is set in stone, unlikely to be relieved even if climate change brings the tropics north. A classic joke is, if you see someone in Manchester with a tan, they've gone rusty.

The city's famed dampness has even inspired poets. An anonymous visitor in 1821 wrote:

I arrived in a show'r, in the wet now set off,
Eight days in the place I remain'd;
Seven days seven nights and a quarter, I vow,
By Jove! It incessantly rain'd.
What then? not a day not an hour was I dull:
The Lancashire Lads play'd their parts:
I found every friend of politeness brim full,
And myself in the midst of the Arts.
May Manchester flourish! and if once again
By chance I ere should be brought hither,
I hope that from weeping the clouds refrain,
And grant me a peek at fine weather.

In the second half of the 20th century in 'Watch Your Step - I'm Drenched', Adrian Mitchell imagined revenge:

In Manchester there lives the King of Puddles,
Master of Miniature Muck Lakes,
The Shah of Slosh, Splendifero of Splash,
Prince, Pasha and Pope of Puddledom.
Where? Somewhere. The rain headed ruler
Lies doggo, incognito,
Disguised as an average, accidental mini-pool.
He is scared as any other emperor,
For one night, all his soiled and soggy victims
Might storm his streets, assassination in their minds,
A thousand rolls of blotting paper in their hands, And drink his shadowed, one joke life away.

GEOGRAPHY

INDEX

Heaven and Hell: the blessed and the damned come together on a Manchester street